A HISTORY OF MISSOURI

WILLIAM E. PARRISH

GENERAL EDITOR

A HISTORY OF MISSOURI

VOLUME IV   1875 TO 1919

LAWRENCE O. CHRISTENSEN
AND GARY R. KREMER

UNIVERSITY OF MISSOURI PRESS
COLUMBIA AND LONDON

Copyright © 1997 by
The Curators of the University of Missouri
University of Missouri Press, Columbia, Missouri 65201
Printed and bound in the United States of America
All rights reserved
First paperback edition 2004
5 4 3 2 1   08 07 06 05 04

Library of Congress Cataloging-in-Publication Data
(Revised for vol. 5)

A History of Missouri.
    Vol. 4: prepared by Lawrence O. Christensen and Gary R. Kremer.
    Includes bibliographical references and index.
    Contents: v. 1. 1673 to 1820, by William E. Foley. — v. 2. 1820 to
1860, by Perry McCandless. — v. 3, 1860 to 1875, by W. E. Parrish. — v.
4, 1875-1919. — v. 5, 1919-1953, by R. S. Kirkendall.
    1. Missouri—History. I. Parrish, William Earl, 1931– II. Foley,
William E., 1938– III. McCandless, Perry, 1917– V. Kirkendall, Richard
S., 1928–
F466.H58   977.8   76-155844
ISBN 0-8262-1112-7
ISBN 0-8262-1559-9 (pbk. : alk. paper)

∞™ This paper meets the requirements of the
American National Standard for Permanence of Paper
for Printed Library Materials, Z39.48, 1984.

For Maxine J. Christensen and Lisa D. Kremer
and for Andrew L. and Orvella S. Christensen
and Gertrude A. Kremer
and to the memory of Bernard S. Kremer

CONTENTS

Acknowledgments, IX

I. Return to Localism, 1

II. Railroads as Engines of Economic Growth, 28

III. Social and Cultural Change in Post-Reconstruction Missouri, 53

IV. A Diverse and Sophisticated Economy, 79

V. The Challenges and Opportunities of a Modernizing State, 109

VI. The Reform Impulse and Its Tensions, 135

VII. Joseph Folk, The Missouri Idea, and Progressivism, 161

VIII. Missouri Goes to War, 200

Essay on Sources, 245

Index, 273

ACKNOWLEDGMENTS

We have incurred many debts over the years that we have worked to bring this book to completion. We wish to thank the State Historical Society of Missouri and its Richard S. Brownlee fund for two generous grants that helped make this study possible. The University of Missouri Press contributed a grant and Ed King and Susan Denny helped launch the project. Clair Willcox, acquisitions editor, read the entire manuscript in various stages and gave unerringly good advice. Jane Lago, managing editor, and John Brenner, editor, did their usual fine job on the manuscript. Beverly Jarrett, director of the press, provided needed encouragement and oversaw the process of making a manuscript into a book. Sesquicentennial Series editor William E. Parrish read the entire manuscript and made helpful and much-appreciated suggestions. The authors also benefited from the comments of a second, anonymous, reader.

Gary Kremer received a Creative Development Grant from William Woods University that aided in the completion of this project. The Department of History and Political Science at the University of Missouri–Rolla provided Lawrence Christensen with a sabbatical leave that also greatly aided completion of the work. Chairman of the Department Larry D. Gragg brought his critical eye to some of the chapters and made them better. Fellow department member Donald B. Oster read and gave good advice on chapters as well. James W. Goodrich, director of the State Historical Society of Missouri, read a number of the chapters and once again revealed his able editing skills. Lynn Morrow, Director of the Local Records Program, Missouri State Archives, also read a number of chapters and shared his vast knowledge of Missouri history with the authors. Lynn Wolf Gentzler as associate editor of the *Missouri Historical Review* provided her usual expert advice on improving the material on World War I. We thank the *Review* for allowing us to include the World War I material that appeared earlier in that journal. We also thank the

Midwest Review for allowing us to include material on the Missouri Council of Defense that appeared in that journal and the *Midwest Quarterly* for material on small towns that appeared in that periodical. We also want to acknowledge that without the understanding, encouragement, and support of our wives, this project would not have been completed.

Numerous persons have provided research assistance to us, most especially Christopher K. Hays, who also read much of the manuscript and was especially helpful in the preparation of chapter 6. Others who did research for this project include Patsy Luebbert, Patrick J. Huber, and Pamela M. Miner. In addition, a number of our students have helped to gather valuable information and have provided us with important forums for our ideas. We wish to mention especially Tonya Urban, Jacquelyn Ward, and Cindy Mackey of William Woods University and Erika Nelson, David Burwell, and Faith Bass-Glenn of the University of Missouri–Rolla.

No historical work could be written without the assistance of librarians and archivists. We are especially grateful to the staffs of the following repositories: The State Historical Society of Missouri, The Western Historical Manuscript Collections at the University of Missouri–Columbia and the University of Missouri–Rolla, the Missouri Historical Society in St. Louis and the Missouri State Archives in Jefferson City, the William H. Dulany Alumnae Memorial Library at William Woods University, and the Curtis Laws Wilson Libary at the University of Missouri–Rolla.

While no mistakes should have crept into the book with all of this good help, we take full responsibility for any that may have. Finally, Gary Kremer wishes to express gratitude to his children for the patience and good humor with which they supported his efforts on this book. Randy, Sharon, and Becky have helped in ways that they are probably unaware of. So, too, has grandson Dustin Joseph Kremer.

CHAPTER I

RETURN TO LOCALISM

A few weeks before the 1875 Constitutional Convention was scheduled to meet, the editor of the *Sedalia Weekly Democrat* decided that it was appropriate to offer delegates some advice on how to proceed. "The Convention to remodel the Constitution of the State will soon convene," he wrote, "and there is considerable speculation as to what the Convention will do. We know what it should not do; it should not remain in session one day longer than shall be necessary to complete its labors, nor should it spend one dollar more than is absolutely necessary."

The editor's conservative, even reactionary, comments seem to have been taken to heart by many of the delegates. They spent literally days in the early going of the convention debating whether or not they should spend state money to provide themselves with daily newspapers and arguing over how many clerks and stenographers they should employ at public expense. The 1875 convention, and the constitution it produced, set the tone for political life in Missouri for the remainder of the century. The convention, which gathered for the first time in Jefferson City in May and met for seventy-four days, was dominated by conservative Democrats who had waited a decade to reverse the liberal centralizing provisions of the dreaded Drake Constitution. Sixty-eight delegates gathered for the convention; only eight of them were Republicans. Seventy-five percent of the delegates had been born in the South, with twenty-four percent coming from one Southern state (Kentucky). This was an unusually well-educated group. Of the sixty-two delegates whose educational background is known, nearly two-thirds had attended colleges or universities.

The delegates to the 1875 convention were relatively old, at least by nineteenth-century standards. Sixteen percent were past sixty and another fifty-three percent of the delegates were beyond forty years of age. As historian Floyd Shoemaker has written, "there is little question that so far as governmental institutions and state finance are involved, older men are more inclined towards a conservative attitude than are younger men. . . . If age and mature years nurture conservatism, the Convention of 1875 was a conservative body."

Two-thirds of the delegates to the convention were lawyers, and thirty-five of the sixty-eight had either served under the Confederacy or had strong sympathies with its cause. Senator Waldo P. Johnson of Osceola (St. Clair County) presided over the gathering. His role in the proceedings symbolized the convention's bent: he had been expelled from the United States Senate in 1862 after he joined the Confederacy. Subsequently, he served in the Confederate army as a lieutenant colonel under General Sterling Price. Still later, he was chosen as a senator from Missouri in the Confederate Congress.

For Johnson and every other member of the convention, the Civil War had been a defining event that cast a shadow over their lives for all their remaining days. The doctrine of interposition may have been rejected as a matter of practical politics after Appomattox, for example, but that did not stop the convention from debating for most of a day the issues of secession and nullification. In the end, the language agreed upon declined to declare against the right of revolution. As historian Isidor Loeb has pointed out, "Repeated efforts to amend so as to include declarations against secession and nullification . . . failed by large majorities."

The constitution that Johnson and his cohorts produced was more than a document of governance; it was a statement of philosophy about the relationship between state government and the people it purported to represent. Above all else, the constitution reflected a suspicion toward centralized rule and a proclivity toward localism. This was a direct reaction against the Radical Republican rule of the 1860s and 1870s. The Radicals had expanded the power of the state government and, in the minds of Democrats, had ridden roughshod over the rights and prerogatives of the state's citizens.

The Radicals had, first of all, actually disenfranchised thousands of Missouri citizens with the so-called test oath, which disallowed those persons who could not swear that they had never supported the Confederacy from voting or holding political office. Not surprisingly, in response, then, the new constitution made it more difficult for any standing government to restrict its citizens' rights. On the question of the power of the government to suspend the privilege of the writ of habeas corpus, for example, the 1875 Constitution deleted the phrase "unless when, in cases of rebellion or invasion, the public safety may require it," which had appeared in the state's two previous constitutions. The 1865 Constitution had restricted religious freedom in a way that the 1875 Constitution tried to correct, especially with regard to giving religious bodies more freedom to own property. The 1875 Constitution made it much more difficult to convict a citizen of treason and denied the state government the right to confiscate a traitor's property, which the state could do under the 1865 Constitution.

The new constitution sought to limit governmental power in other ways as well. Indeed, it was not merely specific governmental actions that creators of the new constitution wanted to restrict; it was governmental action generally that these Missourians found so disturbing. Underlying the 1875 constitutional debate was the pervasive sentiment that government, especially state government, could not be trusted to act in the best interests of the citizenry, to protect the citizenry, or to serve the common good.

One way to limit the activities of government was to limit the amount of money the government could receive. The Democrats accused the spendthrift Republicans of running up the state debt to $36 million by the end of the Civil War. Despite postwar recovery efforts and a serious attempt to reduce the state debt, it still stood at roughly $18 million in 1875. By 1875, state property taxes had reached 62.5 cents on $100 valuation and, as historian C. H. McClure has pointed out, "county, city and school taxes were also high." Supporters of the 1875 Constitution wanted to restrict state government's activism by restricting its power to raise money. As McClure writes, the 1875 Constitution fixed "Rigid limits of taxation . . . for every public corporation from State to school district." Taxable wealth had actually declined in Missouri by 1875, to a level of $556,444,456, after reaching an all-time high in 1873. Convention delegates, and Missouri citizens, were still feeling the effects of the 1873 Panic. The taxable wealth of Missourians would not match its 1873 high again until 1882. Hence, the Constitution of 1875, as Frederick N. Judson has written, "introduced for the first time specific limitations upon the rate of taxation." While the constitution allowed the state to get through the lean times by collecting 20 cents on $100, the tax "was to be reduced to fifteen cents on the hundred dollars, whenever the taxable property should amount to nine hundred million dollars," something that did not occur until 1894.

In addition to limiting the power of public entities to tax, the constitution also made a two-thirds vote necessary to legalize any bond. Bonds, particularly railroad bonds, had grown especially burdensome since the end of the Civil War. Indeed, historian David Thelen has pointed out that during the decade after the Civil War, promoters in Missouri persuaded local governmental officials in roughly half of the state's counties to issue bonds totaling approximately $18 million in public aid for more than forty proposed railroads. Often these bonds were approved by local officials who did not seek their constituents' approval, or, worse yet, defied popular votes against the issuance of railroad bonds. Moreover, in many cases the railroads were never built, even though the money had been appropriated and spent. In the minds of most Missourians, they were being taxed beyond their ability to pay by officials who defied their best interests. Something had to be done. The potential seriousness of the situation was revealed in the spring of 1875, just before the constitutional convention met, when a Stone County group calling itself the Sons of Honor threatened to disrupt the county court's proceedings because of their outrage over high taxes.

Although local officials were often blamed for high taxes, the bulk of the blame fell on the shoulders of state legislators who, it was widely felt, passed too much "local and special legislation" aimed at benefiting a limited number of constituents rather than the state as a whole. The 1875 Constitution sought to end this process by prohibiting this kind of legislation from being passed and by expanding the powers of the governor at the expense of the legislature. The new constitution extended the governor's term from two to four years, while requiring legislators to continue to stand for election every two years. The assumption was that a statewide elected governor would be more inclined to favor the interests of the state as a whole than would a locally elected legislator. Also, there was a feeling that legislators would be more likely to toe the line if they knew they had to run for office biennially. For an additional check on ill-advised legislation, the new constitution allowed the governor to veto one or more items that he objected to in an appropriations bill. A legislative override required a two-thirds vote in each house.

4

The new, more restrictive constitution was submitted to a vote of the people of Missouri on August 2, 1875. A surprisingly small number of voters turned out to express an opinion on it one way or the other. In the 1874 gubernatorial election, 261,670 persons cast votes. In the 1876 election, the number rose to 347,274. Yet only 91,205 votes were cast on the 1875 Constitution, the overwhelming majority of them for it. This, in spite of the fact that 222,315 Missourians had voted on whether or not to call a constitutional convention! Carter County, which turned out 173 voters in the 1874 gubernatorial election and 329 in the 1876 election, turned out only 29 in the vote on the constitution, all of whom voted for it. Presumably, few Missourians were troubled by the new constitution and the localism it promoted; indeed, most Missourians may have felt that the constitution made legal what had already become accepted practice.

The political leader entrusted with the responsibility of executing the will of the people as expressed in the new constitution was Charles Henry Hardin of Audrain County. Hardin was elected governor of Missouri in 1874 and took office in January of 1875. Born in Trimble County, Kentucky, in July of 1820, Hardin moved with his family to Old Franklin, Missouri, in Howard County, in the fall of the same year. The family moved to Columbia soon thereafter. Hardin was educated at the University of Indiana and Miami University, graduating from Miami with a law degree in 1841. He returned to Missouri, read law for two years, and was admitted to the Missouri Bar in 1843. Thereafter, he established a law practice in Fulton, the county seat of conservative Callaway County. In 1848 Hardin was elected circuit attorney for the Second Judicial Circuit, which was comprised of the rural Boonslick counties of Audrain, Boone, Callaway, Howard, Randolph, and neighboring Macon County. He was elected to serve in the Missouri House of Representatives in 1852, 1854, and 1858, and was elected to serve in the Missouri Senate in 1860 and again in 1872.

Hardin was obviously deeply troubled by the Civil War and by the secessionist sentiment prevalent in much of the area he represented. He attended the secessionist General Assembly session convened by Governor Claiborne Fox Jackson at Neosho in October of 1861, but he cast the only negative vote on the articles of secession. No doubt Hardin's mere presence at the rump session of the General Assembly antagonized members of the provisional government, and in 1862 he was disenfranchised. He sat out the war on his 550-acre farm in Audrain County and did not even resume the practice of law until war's end. By August 1874, near the end of his second term as a Missouri senator, Hardin found himself being suggested by many Democrats as a compromise, conservative gubernatorial candidate. On August 16, 1874, at the Democratic state convention held in Jefferson City, Hardin was chosen in a close contest over a former Confederate military leader, Francis M. Cockrell. Cockrell, in return, was soon sent to the United States Senate to replace the perennial Democratic foe, Liberal Republican Carl Schurz.

Aware of agrarian unrest and unhappiness, particularly in the wake of the 1873 Panic, the Democrats chose popular agriculturalist Norman J. Colman to run as lieutenant governor, hoping that his agrarian interests and credibility, not to mention his widely read *Rural World,* would dissuade farmers from bolting the party. Colman was born in Otsego, New York, in 1827, into a family of progressive farmers. He moved to Kentucky in 1847 and in 1849 he received a law degree from the University of Louisville Law School. Soon afterward he moved to New Albany, Indiana, where he practiced law and was elected district attorney in 1852. He soon moved again, this time to St. Louis, and within three years he had purchased a farm and taken over the publication of an agricultural periodical called the *Valley Farmer.* Colman later changed the name of this publication to *Colman's Rural World.*

Colman entered Missouri politics in 1854, with his election to the St. Louis Board of Aldermen. In the 1874 election, Colman was critical of third party movements, especially the People's party, which drew strength from disenchanted farmers. He addressed a Grange picnic in Sturgeon in no uncertain terms: "You may get up a third party or forty parties, but you don't create a single more voter by it. The voters are all here. You must put in your best men at the primary meetings and all other conventions, men who will not be sold and delivered and who cannot be bought. . . . If you organize a third party and its success seems to be secured, every renegade and demagogue in the land will rush pell mell into it and you will have a party of office seekers. . . . It will always be denominated as the Grange party, and dissension will arise. . . . And then farewell to our beloved order." Colman stumped the state, urging farmers to support the Democratic party. His stands on issues affecting farmers were ones that they could clearly identify with. Throughout the

1870s, for example, he editorialized in opposition to protective tariffs, arguing that tariffs drove down the prices that farmers received for the goods they produced while raising the prices they paid for goods that they purchased. In the late 1870s, Colman began to strongly support loose money solutions, variously endorsing the free coinage of silver, the printing of paper money, and the abolishment of the national banking system.

Colman's popularity among farmers doubtlessly helped Hardin in the 1874 election. Many would-be Democratic party bolters must have felt like the person who signed his name "Granger" in a letter to the editor of the *Jefferson City People's Tribune:* "Permit me through your columns to give warning to the Grangers of this county, not to have nothing to do with the independent movement clamored for by such journals as the Republican and Globe of St. Louis. . . . The County and State are full of good Democrats now, who are farmers by birth and education. . . . There are farmers in the State worthy of any position on the ticket, and my word for it if we act wisely . . . and enact laws that will do justice to the rich and the poor alike . . . we will soon see the complete success of our most earnest desires." The *Pike County Post* was equally blunt: "We have failed to notice in all that we have seen and heard one satisfactory reasonable objection to the principles of the Democratic party, or one word of just cause or excuse why it should be broken up and a new party organized in its stead."

The strategy of opposition to third parties worked, and Hardin's victory in 1874 closely mirrored the next two gubernatorial elections. Hardin carried 81 of Missouri's 114 counties, with his greatest support coming from those Missourians who like him could trace their ancestry to Kentucky roots. Hardin won nearly every county south of the Missouri River in the southeast quadrant of the state, including the Ozarks counties of Maries, Pulaski, Texas, and Howell. Only heavily German Gasconade, Osage, and Perry Counties in this region voted for Hardin's opponent, William Gentry, a Pettis County farmer who was the People's party candidate and who was also supported by the Republicans. Newspapers supporting Gentry waved the bloody shirt, denouncing Hardin's "support of Claib Jackson" during the Civil War, while assuring their readers that a vote for Gentry was a vote for "a sturdy, sensible old farmer." North of the Missouri River, Hardin carried all of the counties except Adair, Andrew, Atchison, Caldwell, DeKalb,

7

Grundy, Mercer, Putnam, St. Charles, and Warren. All of these counties had large numbers of citizens who either were from or traced their ancestry to northern states, especially Illinois, Indiana, and Ohio. In addition, five of these counties had significant German populations, particularly St. Charles and Warren Counties.

Gentry's strongest support came in the counties south of the Missouri River in the southwest portion of the state, particularly in the Ozarks. Benton, Camden, and Miller Counties formed the northern boundary of Republican strength, which ran south to the Arkansas border, excepting Laclede, Ozark, and Webster Counties. The western border of the Republican region included Cedar, Dade, Lawrence, and Barry Counties, with all of the counties on the western state line south of the Missouri River save one being carried by Hardin. The lone county in this strip carried by Gentry was Jasper, which featured a large population of old-stock Americans from Tennessee and ethnic settlements of Irish, Cornish, Swedish, and German Missourians. Geographer Russel L. Gerlach has pointed out that the settlers of the central and western Ozarks who came from Tennessee were mainly highlanders from eastern Tennessee who tended to be Republicans.

Hardin's term as governor presaged much of what would happen in state government over the next twenty years. Judge John A. Hockaday, Hardin's contemporary, summed up the latter's term in office as follows: "Governor Hardin's administration was emphatically one of retrenchment and reform." No doubt Hardin was interested in cutting back the cost of government, and if he was interested in "reform" at all it was in how to reduce governmental expenditures. In his inaugural address, delivered on January 12, 1875, he told legislators that "the people have wearied of lengthy, annual legislative sessions" and he urged them to be "Prompt, efficient and economical" in their deliberations. Most of all, he urged a reduction in the cost of running government. Grand juries, he said, should be reduced in size from eighteen jurors to twelve. The prison should be leased out, if possible, because that would make it far less expensive for the state to run. And, perhaps most significant, certainly most appealing to the agrarian interests, Hardin expressed a desire to see the railroads regulated in some way and forced to help pay the costs of state government. Hardin summarized his argument as follows: "Although we have some twenty eight hundred miles of railroad with an assessable value, including accompanying property of over fifty millions of dollars, the companies have as yet paid a very inconsiderable tax. It is the purpose of no one to oppress, or place unjust burdens on them; on the contrary there is not a citizen who would not rejoice to see them prosperous and strong. They have been favored by the State and people for twenty odd years, who have assumed and expanded upon them in that time immense sums of money."

Hardin took no real action, however. Perhaps no better example of his style of leadership occurred than when the state faced the devastation of the 1875 grasshopper plague. Thousands of Missouri farmers saw their crops eaten away by insects. State Entomologist C. V. Riley, in a letter of May 18, 1875, urged the governor to at least promote the killing of the grasshoppers by authorizing a bounty for them: "Have you not power to offer a small premium on the part of the State for every bushel of young grasshoppers destroyed? Such a premium would be a powerful incentive to the more destitute of the people in those districts to destroy the pests and thus avert future injury; and at the same time give them the means of earning a living until the danger is past."

Hardin, however, was unwilling to spend any tax money for such a venture, and he responded by proclaiming June 3 "a day of fasting and prayer that Almight[y] God may be invoked to remove from our midst these impending calamities, and to grant instead the blessings of abundance and plenty." No doubt Hardin felt vindicated in his approach when, soon after, the grasshoppers left the state.

The 1876 gubernatorial election was a clear mandate for Democratic rule. Democratic presidential candidate Samuel J. Tilden easily outpolled Republican Rutherford B. Hayes in Missouri in an election that the *Sedalia Weekly Democrat* hoped would "assist to drive the last nail in the coffin of Radical robbery and misrule." A majority of voting Missourians seemed to agree with the editor of the *Glasgow Journal,* who asserted, "Every day that passes seems to develop the fact more strongly that the Democrats are the friends and the Republicans the enemies of economy." Approximately 350,000 Missourians went to the polls and overwhelmingly elected John S. Phelps of Springfield as governor. Phelps polled 199,580 votes to 147,694 for his Republican challenger, former Congressman Gustavus Finklenburg of St. Louis. Republican newspapers, such as the *Kirksville Journal,* continued to try to identify Democrats with the Confederacy and rebellion, alleging that Union Democrats in Missouri had been overtaken by Confederates. The *Trenton*

Republican tried also to capitalize on unsubstantiated news reports that candidate Phelps had taken indecent liberties with a woman on board the steamer *Andy Johnson* while campaigning in northeast Missouri, but even that salacious rumor did not help Finklenburg. Phelps carried eighty-two counties to his opponent's thirty-two.

The new governor, a native of Simsbury, Connecticut, was born on December 14, 1814. He earned a law degree from Trinity College in Hartford, Connecticut, in 1832 and practiced law with his father until 1837. Subsequently he migrated to Springfield, where he was admitted to the bar and later served in the state legislature. In 1844, Phelps was elected to a congressional seat and continued to serve in Congress for the next eighteen years. A strong Unionist, Phelps became a Douglas Democrat in 1860, fought at the battle of Pea Ridge, and served as military governor of Arkansas before poor health forced him to return to civilian life.

Phelps returned to the practice of law in Springfield in 1864, ran for governor and lost in 1868, then ran again and won in 1876. He supported the constitutional restrictions placed on the legislature by the 1875 Constitution. On February 8, 1877, in his inaugural address, Phelps proclaimed his belief that those restrictions would "insure pure and wise legislation." The safeguards of the constitution might "render the enactment of laws more tedious and tardy," but they would ensure that "the responsibility of legislation [would be placed] upon all the members of the Legislature instead of a few."

Phelps identified the constitution's restrictions on spending as one of its greatest strengths. In his elaboration on the need for government to economize, he articulated a philosophy that remained at the heart of state Democratic ideology for as long as the Democrats stayed in power. "We must economize," he urged, "we must reduce the expenditures of our Government. It may be difficult to do so, but it must be done."

A government that failed to economize, Phelps argued, ended up exacting high taxes from its citizens, thereby plundering them. Low taxes promised wealth and prosperity to current and would-be Missourians: "We should endeavor to place taxation at its lowest limit. . . . We invite population. And if to all our sources of wealth and prosperity we can, with truth, say the taxes of the municipal and State governments are low, we offer strong inducements for the enterprising, industrious and intelligent people to make their abode with us. And if the laws we may continue on our statute book, and those which we hereafter enact, shall contain wholesome beneficent and wise provisions, and if our laws shall be faithfully executed and impartially administered, with light taxation and economy practiced in every branch of the public service, we may expect to see the wealth and population of our State rapidly increase."

Phelps's victory in the 1876 election was only one part of the Democratic party's overall success. The Democrats' entire ticket was elected, including all nine U.S. congressmen from Missouri, and the party maintained control of both houses of the General Assembly. Notwithstanding this seemingly total victory, Democratic leaders were worried by discontent within and outside their party. The "Confederate faction" had wanted George Graham Vest, a former Confederate congressman, to head the Democratic ticket in the state instead of Phelps, and they blamed their fellow Democrats for waving the "bloody shirt" in the fight over the party's nomination. Moreover, the Greenback party held a statewide convention in Jefferson City in September 1876, and although J. P. Alexander, the Greenback candidate for governor, received fewer than three thousand votes (less than 1 percent) in the 1876 election, the specter of a widely popular third party frightened the Democrats. Alexander, a native of Kentucky who migrated to Missouri in 1850, received votes from 66 of Missouri's 114 counties. His greatest success came in Lawrence County, which had a long tradition of hostility toward and suspicion of both state and federal government. Alexander garnered 11 percent of the Lawrence County vote.

Alexander's failure to attract more voters statewide was no doubt attributable in part to efforts by newspaper editors to encourage Missourians to remain true to the two-party system. The comments by the editor of the *Kirksville Journal* were typical. He warned his fellow Republicans to avoid the Greenback ticket, which he called a "Democratic side show." He urged Republicans to see that the Democrats' "aim is to draw off enough Republican votes to elect the Democrat ticket" and he rightly predicted that "There is not the ghost of a chance for the Greenback ticket to be elected." He pleaded with Republicans not to "throw away" their votes by voting for a Greenbacker. Democrats likewise urged their party members to remain true to the Democratic cause. The *Boonville Weekly Advertiser* warned Democrats that a vote for a third-party candidate would "aid in continuing the Republican party in power." The editor of the *Knox County Democrat* put the matter succinctly when he urged Democrats in his county to vote "Straight goods this time."

Still, as the events of 1877 in particular were to make clear, many of the state's residents were finding themselves increasingly disenchanted with parties and politicians who seemed unable or unwilling to "fix" the problems that beset them. Farmers, who of course continued to make up the majority of the state's population, were perplexed and angered by the deepening farm depression. They were hurt by the tight money policies of the Hayes administration. They blamed the railroads for price fixing and gouging. They blamed unspecified "middlemen" for paying too little for raw produce and charging too much for finished products. They blamed everyone but themselves, failing to see that their own overproduction and their concentration on one or two cash crops placed them more and more at the mercy of forces over which they had little or no control. Sometimes their frustration spilled over into violence, as in St. Clair County in 1877 when a band of armed vigilantes entered the county courthouse in Osceola and stole all of the official tax records from frightened officials. The vigilantes warned the county judges that they faced lynching if they did not resign immediately. The officials heeded the warning and resigned their positions. Meanwhile, the vigilantes destroyed the tax records so that there would be no basis upon which taxes could be collected.

Perhaps the most frightening event of 1877, however, was a labor strike that culminated in a work stoppage in St. Louis and other parts of the state, most notably in Sedalia, Hannibal, and St. Joseph. Indeed, the strike had actually begun in eastern cities among railroad workers whose salaries had been cut by company owners reacting to the economic crisis created by the 1873 Panic. By late July 1877 the strike had reached St. Louis, where, as historian Robert V. Bruce has pointed out, the Marxist Workingmen's party became the "directing force of the strike." On July 23, 1877, strike agitator Henry F. Allen, a member of the strike committee and a St. Louis sign painter who had a well-established reputation as a supporter of "Co-operative associations" over "competitive commerce," told a crowd of perhaps five thousand, "We workingmen can present such a force that even the government itself must and will comply with our demands."

The strike spread beyond railroad workers to coopers, boatmen, coal stackers, even *Post-Dispatch* newsboys. On the night of July 24, Allen called for "a general strike of all branches of industry for eight hours for a day's work . . . and the nonemployment of children under fourteen years of age," a provision that must have left the newsboys feeling ambivalent about their participation. Within two days, the strikers had brought the economy of St. Louis to a standstill, among other things closing at least sixty factories. The threat of violence was everywhere. Order was not restored until city, state, and federal authorities combined to send a massive armed force into the city. During the spring of the next year, wealthy St. Louis businessmen held the first of their "Veiled Prophet" parades, which were designed as a show of force against lower- and working-class St. Louisans who might question their authority. Whatever unity had appeared to exist among St. Louis's laborers for a brief few days in 1877 could not be sustained either by the Workingmen's party or by efforts at organizing workers, either formally or informally.

The frustrations that led to the 1877 strike and the increased unhappiness of farmers and laborers resulted in at least some opposition to the traditional parties in the 1878 off-year election. Nicholas Ford, a St. Joseph merchant who had previously served in the General Assembly as an Independent, was elected to the forty-sixth Congress in 1878 as a Greenbacker. Ford, a native of Ireland, had come to St. Joseph in 1859. Likewise in that off-year election, two senators, both agrarians, were elected to the Missouri General Assembly on the Greenback ticket. Ahira Manning, an Ohio-born farmer from Gentry County, was elected to represent the Second District, which consisted of Buchanan, Dekalb, Gentry, and Worth Counties. All of these counties except DeKalb had been carried by Phelps in 1876. Manning had been a Democrat until the 1878 election. Likewise, Henry F. Caldwell, a Greenbacker, was elected from the Eighth District, which consisted of Adair, Macon, and Schuyler Counties. Of these three counties, only Adair had voted Republican in the 1876 gubernatorial election. Caldwell, too, was a farmer who had been a Democrat until the 1878 election. Four state representatives, Ezra Hurst of Atchison County, Ephraim Davis of Laclede County, John W. Donover of Livingston County, and Matthew H. Ritchey of Newton County, were also elected on the Greenback ticket. Ritchey's apostasy was most troubling to the Democrats. A Democrat until 1876, he had previously served two terms in the house and one in the state senate.

Greenbackers made additional gains in Congress in 1880, when four of their candidates were elected: Ira S. Haseltine of the Sixth District,

Theron M. Rice of the Seventh District, Nicholas Ford of the Ninth District, and Joseph H. Burrows of the Tenth District. Haseltine was a native of Vermont who moved to Missouri in 1870 and became a leading orchardist in Greene County on a farm just west of Springfield. Rice was an Ohio native who practiced law in his native state before moving to California, Missouri, in 1858. After serving as an officer in the Union army during the Civil War, he moved to Tipton, where he practiced law and later served as a circuit judge. Burrows was born in England in 1840, and migrated first to Illinois and then to Iowa before coming to Missouri in 1862. He ran a store in Cainsville (Harrison County) before buying a farm in Mercer County in 1865. An ordained Baptist minister, Burrows was also very active in the West Fork Baptist Association.

The man looked to by Democratic party leaders to carry the banner in 1880 was Thomas T. Crittenden, a native of Shelby County, Kentucky. Educated at Centre College in Danville, Kentucky, Crittenden studied law in Frankfort in his uncle's office before moving to Lexington, Missouri, in Lafayette County, in 1857 to set up his own practice. A strong Unionist, Crittenden served in the army during the Civil War and rose to the rank of colonel. He moved to Warrensburg after the war. Interestingly, in 1867 he formed a law partnership with Francis M. Cockrell, the future Missouri senator who had been a brigadier general in the Confederate army.

Crittenden was elected to the United States Congress in 1872, but he was defeated in 1874 by John F. Philips, a Sedalia lawyer and former Union soldier who became the law partner of prominent attorney George Graham Vest, a former legislator in the Confederate Congress. Crittenden was reelected in 1876 and was then elected governor in 1880 in an election in which the Greenback candidate for the office, Luman A. Brown, polled more than 36,000 votes, or nearly 9 percent of the almost 398,000 votes cast. Indeed, Brown carried two counties in 1880: St. Clair and Douglas. Crittenden defeated his Republican opponent, David P. Dyer, by a vote of 207,670 to 153,636, carrying eighty-five counties to Dyer's twenty-eight. Once again, Republicans waved the bloody shirt, attacking Democrats "for their abject servile submission to the dictates of the confederate wing of their party." Republicans also criticized the Democrats for failing to support industry more in the state. No doubt Brown's Greenback candidacy hurt Dyer. The *Trenton Republican,* for example, pointed out that "The Democrats carried Nodaway county by 183. There were 939 Greenback votes cast." The lesson was obvious: "When Greenback Republicans get over their foolishness the Republicans will carry that county." Still, even a combined Republican-Greenback vote for Dyer would have fallen far short of Crittenden's total for the entire state.

Crittenden, like the Democratic governors who preceded and succeeded him, advocated a classical Jeffersonian view of state government. In his inaugural address he summarized that position and the role of the Democratic party in achieving it: "The Democracy stands for the foundation principles of the Constitution; for local self-government, as opposed to centralization; for the restriction and diminution of the powers and the interference of government, and for the elevation and the untrammeled independence of the individual citizens; for equal rights, as opposed to privilege and monopoly; for the Republic as opposed to the Empire."

Crittenden's administration was a time of relative prosperity for Missourians, who were finally recovering from the 1873 Panic, despite a disastrous drought in 1881 that sent agricultural profits reeling. For Crittenden, the key to prosperity and stability was the continued expansion of business opportunities and a continued influx of people into the state, which had risen to become the fifth most populous state in the Union. Indeed, Crittenden, in his inaugural address, called Missouri "the very key of the arch of the union." At the heart of his vision of the state's prosperity was a low-tax, minimal-intervention government: "A reduction of the rate of taxation in the counties and State, can be attained by wise and equitable revenue laws, and the natural consequences of such a reduction would be an increase of population and wealth, and those factors, in turn, would cause still further reductions in course of time, by the introduction of more wealth and still greater population. High taxes provoke discontent and invasions of the law, and should not exist one moment beyond their imperative necessity."

Despite Crittenden's view of government, there were two issues that prompted him to exercise greater executive power than he normally would have endorsed. One issue had to do with the Hannibal and St. Joseph Railroad and presaged a growing sentiment in favor of government regulation of the railroads, an attitude that an ever larger number of Missourians were comfortable with. The Hannibal–St. Joseph Railroad had been built before the Civil War with $3 million worth of state bonds. Although an 1865 statute called for the railroad to repay the loan, plus interest, no money exchanged hands until 1881, when the railroad paid $3,090,000 and asserted that it had paid its full indebtedness. Angered that the railroad refused to pay more interest, Crittenden refused to release the lien on the railroad's property and ordered the railroad to be advertised for sale. Stopped from selling the railroad by a court order, Crittenden pursued the case all the way to the United States Supreme Court, which ruled that the Hannibal–St. Joseph Railroad still owed the State of Missouri more than half a million dollars.

Another issue that plagued the Crittenden administration was the James gang. Republicans had made a campaign issue in 1876 and 1880 of Democratic governors' inability to capture and prosecute members of the gang. In addition, the governor was distressed by the "unenviable reputation, at home and abroad," that he thought outlaws such as Frank and Jesse James had saddled Missouri with. Crittenden feared that the presence of widespread brigandry, and the state's image of powerlessness in its face, thwarted businessmen from moving their operations to the state. Likewise, he reasoned, new citizens generally would be less inclined to move to a state known for its lawlessness. Accordingly, on July 28, 1881, Crittenden issued a proclamation that said, in part: "for the arrest and delivery of said Frank James and Jesse W. James . . . I hereby offer a reward of Five Thousand Dollars ($5,000.00), and for the conviction of either of the parties last aforesaid . . . I hereby offer a further reward of Five Thousand Dollars ($5,000.00)." Less than a year later, Jesse James was shot to death in St. Joseph by members of his gang; six months after Jesse's death, his brother Frank surrendered to the governor in Jefferson City. Subsequently, Frank James was tried for the murder of a railroad employee but was acquitted by a jury after the eloquent appeal of his attorney, noted Missouri trial lawyer Charles Philip Johnson.

Crittenden was succeeded in office by John Sappington Marmaduke, the man he had defeated for the Democratic nomination in 1880. Marmaduke was born on his father's farm in Saline County in 1833. His father was Miles Meredith Marmaduke, eighth governor of Missouri. The younger Marmaduke was educated in a rural Saline County school and then went to Chapel Hill Academy in Lafayette County and to Yale University. He was appointed to the United States Military Academy at West Point by Congressman and future Governor John S. Phelps.

Marmaduke graduated from West Point in 1857 and served in the Mormon War in Utah under Colonel Albert Sydney Johnston.

The Civil War was a dramatic event for the young army officer. Nurtured in the tradition of Southern culture and slavery, Marmaduke nonetheless had been raised in a household of strong Benton-Union Democrats. Marmaduke family tradition says that the troubled son sought the aging father's advice and was told that the Confederacy would not and could not triumph and that supporting it could be potentially disastrous. The son nevertheless joined the Missouri State Guard and was commissioned a colonel by his uncle, Governor Claiborne Fox Jackson. After a defeat in battle at Boonville he resigned his state commission and volunteered for service in the Confederate army, and ended up serving his old mentor, Johnston. Subsequently wounded at the Battle of Shiloh, Marmaduke was promoted to the rank of brigadier general. He joined General Sterling Price's forces for a final sweep through Missouri in 1864 and was captured and taken prisoner for the remainder of the war. After the war, Marmaduke traveled in Europe for six months before going into business. In 1875 he entered the world of public service again, as Missouri's railroad commissioner, a position he held until 1880.

A proliferation of political parties in the 1884 election gave evidence to the growing dissatisfaction with the political status quo. Many Greenbackers joined with Republicans again to form what was called the Fusion ticket, headed by gubernatorial candidate Nicholas Ford. Prohibitionists ran their own slate of candidates, and the memory of the Civil War, now nearly a generation gone by, continued to affect Democratic deliberations. C. M. Hubbard, editor of the *St. Joseph Herald,* summed up one perspective on the 1884 gubernatorial race: "Ever since the Democrats have been in power in the State there has been a division of offices by common consent between what is known as the Union element and the Confederate element. The Union will constitute the better element in the party; they are the liberal, enterprising and progressive people. The Confederate wing comprises the mossbacks and fossilized bourbons. The Governorship has been given to the Union wing and Vest and Cockrell, both in the Confederate service, sent to the Senate. Next year [General Joseph O.] Shelby proposes that the Confederates shall also have the Governorship, and is therefore committed to Gen. Marmaduke."

17

Hubbard's hostility toward Marmaduke and the other former Confederates who dominated the 1884 statewide ticket may not have reflected the attitude of all Missourians, but his stance was certainly shared by many. The combined vote of the candidates opposing Marmaduke was less than eleven thousand votes fewer than the former Confederate general received. And whereas Marmaduke's predecessor, Crittenden, had carried eighty-five counties and the city of St. Louis, Marmaduke carried only sixty-five counties and he lost the city of St. Louis. Ford carried fifty counties, no doubt helped in several of them by a strong showing by the Prohibitionist candidate John A. Brooks.

Clearly the opposition to the Democratic party in Missouri was strong and growing. Republicans were increasing the intensity of their call for more government support of business, particularly by means of the passage of a tariff, "the only live issue that exists between the different parties," according to the *Buffalo Reflex*. The *Trenton Republican* assured its readers that "A Republican victory in Missouri would fully enhance the value of property [a] full fifty million dollars the day after the announcement was made." And farmers especially wanted more government control of the railroads and less collusion between legislators and lobbyists. As the *Reflex* argued: "It has become so common in Missouri that we hardly pay any attention to public officials being connected with railroad monopolies." Although historian David March has written that "the state contest [in 1884], like the national campaign between the Democrat Grover Cleveland, and his Republican opponent James G. Blaine, was one of personalities, not issues," a large number of Missourians would no doubt have disagreed.

Marmaduke's role as a railroad commissioner gave him firsthand experience with the growing problems associated with the railroads. Two particular problems, the strikes of 1886–1887 and the controversy over unfair rates charged by the railroads, dominated the Marmaduke administration's relations with the railway companies. Both problems caused Marmaduke to advocate action that seemed to contradict the governmental role he endorsed in his inaugural address on January 12, 1885: "My own opinion is, that people are best governed who have few laws, only those absolutely necessary, plainly expressed and vigorously enforced."

On March 9, 1885, workers on the Missouri Pacific Railway went on strike to protest repeated wage reductions in the face of the company's reports of "a large earning for the road." Fearful of violence and the loss of life and property, Marmaduke orchestrated a gathering of Kansas and Missouri state officials with Mo Pac and Knights of Labor leaders. The result was an agreement to restore wages to the level they had been prior to September 1, 1884, allow for time-and-a-half pay for overtime, and guarantee that wages would not be lowered or personnel terminated without a thirty-day notice.

One year later problems emerged again, this time on the Texas and Pacific line, when an employee was dismissed without the thirty-day notice. By this time, most of the railroad workers had been organized by the Knights of Labor, who ordered a strike on March 6, 1886. Over the next two weeks protest meetings were held in numerous Missouri railroad towns, until the anger of railroad workers turned to destruction of railroad property. Freight traffic ground almost to a halt, and on March 19, 1886, Governor Marmaduke tried to work the same magic he had performed the previous year by calling together Kansas and Missouri officials along with representatives of the railroad and the strikers. This time the ploy did not work. Later in the month a disturbance at Pacific, Missouri, in Franklin County, prompted Marmaduke to send soldiers from the adjutant general's office to restore order. By May the strike had ended, but not before a need for action had been impressed upon Marmaduke. No doubt he agreed with the *State Times,* which called for new regulatory legislation, asserting, "The pretended contract and regulation of railroads in Missouri is a failure, an expensive sham."

On January 7, 1887, in his first biennial message to the General Assembly, Marmaduke summed up the situation as follows:

> That class of common carriers known as railroad companies has become so numerous and their services to the people so necessary, that we cannot dispense with them. Indeed, we cannot allow the operations of their trains to cease, either by the voluntary action of their managers or by the opposition offered by others, for even a few days, because it puts to such great inconvenience and loss the public, in whose interest and for whose benefit their peculiar organization and construction was authorized. . . . It is not right that when a few employees—either officers or laborers, or both—get to quarrelling among themselves, they shall put a stop to a public service until they settle their petty strifes, in which the public have no concern, and which quarrels are in no important particular different from the altercations arising between any other citizens of the State. They should be made to settle these strifes among themselves without involving the business arrangements

of the people. That they should resort to practices which actually endanger the peace of the State and the safety of the lives and property of her citizens is not to be tolerated at all.

Marmaduke was encouraging the legislature to exercise its power by taking a stronger stand in regulating the railroads. Although the legislature failed to take prompt action and adjourned without a regulatory bill, Marmaduke quickly called the lawmakers into special session. On March 25, 1887, he issued a proclamation calling the General Assembly back on May 11, "To provide the legislative enactments necessary or expedient to enforce and execute those laws and principles with reference to railroads and railroad companies which the people themselves have enacted and declared in their constitution." One week after legislators returned to Jefferson City, Marmaduke wrote them a letter in which he again urged them to take action, expressing regret that twelve years of inaction had passed since the adoption of the 1875 Constitution.

The legislature met for nearly two months. By the time it adjourned in early July, several measures had been passed restricting the rates that railroads could charge, eliminating short-haul versus long-haul rate discrimination, and curtailing formation of monopolies to drive out competition. It was the kind of action that warmed the hearts of farmers especially, who interpreted the legislation as a symbolic stand in support of their position. Missourians may have harbored distrust of legislators, but their distrust of the railroads was even greater. Unfortunately, Governor Marmaduke had only a short time to enjoy his new-found popularity. He contracted pneumonia later in the year and died in the governor's mansion on December 28, 1887.

Marmaduke was succeeded by Albert P. Morehouse, who had been elected in 1884 as lieutenant governor on the Democratic ticket. Born in Ohio in 1835, Morehouse moved with his family to Nodaway County in 1856. Morehouse worked as a teacher while reading law, and in 1860 he was admitted to the bar. He began practicing law soon after in Iowa. He returned to Missouri during the Civil War and served for a short time in the enrolled militia.

After the war Morehouse settled in Maryville and established a newspaper known as the *Nodaway Democrat,* largely as a vehicle for opposing the Radical Republicans. He quickly became a Democratic leader, and was elected to the General Assembly in 1877–1878 and again in 1883–1884. Morehouse, by his own admission, had as his major goal the continuation of the strict governmental economy practiced by his predecessor.

Perhaps one of the most significant trends during Morehouse's administration was the tremendous growth in power of the Prohibitionists. The *State Times* argued as early as 1886 that the Prohibitionists were to blame for the Democratic party being "worse divided by local feuds and partisan strife than ever before." According to the *Times,* "Party affiliation will hold [Prohibitionists] no longer. . . . [T]he [D]emocratic party is in more danger now than in the last sixteen years." A "local option law" had been passed in 1887 under Marmaduke, who had advocated high license fees for dramshop operators as a way of decreasing alcohol consumption. In his January 3, 1889, "Biennial Message" to the legislature, Governor Morehouse reported that fifty counties had voted to prohibit the sale of intoxicating liquor within their boundaries. Although Morehouse felt that it would not be wise to pass a statewide prohibition law, he left no doubt in the minds of his listeners about his feelings toward temperance when he said: "I firmly believe the influence of the dramshop is demoralizing to the community in which it is located, and should be reduced to the lowest possible limit."

The unsettled condition of Missouri politics was manifested very clearly in the 1888 election. The Democratic candidate for governor was David R. Francis, described by historian Floyd Shoemaker as "Typical of a new type of leader in the Democratic party." Shoemaker's point was that Francis represented the second generation of post–Civil War political leaders, who were too young to have attained political maturity at the time of the great conflict.

Francis was born in 1850 in Richmond, Kentucky, but moved to St. Louis in 1866 to attend Washington University. After graduating, Francis went to work as a clerk in a city grain commission house. He worked his way up to become vice president and then president of Merchant's Exchange in St. Louis, and was elected mayor of St. Louis in 1885. His popularity as mayor led many Democrats to believe that he would be an extremely strong gubernatorial candidate. On the contrary, Francis actually received a minority of the votes cast, polling a total of 255,764 out of 518,122 cast (49.9 percent). E. E. Kimball, the Republican, received 242,531 votes (46.8 percent), while Ahira Manning, the Union Labor party candidate, received 15,438 (3 percent) and Frank M. Lowe, the Prohibitionist, polled 4,389 votes (less than 1 percent).

One of Francis's biggest problems in the election, in fact, was his urban background and his association with the Union Merchant's Exchange. In the 1860s, the Merchant's Exchange had been given statutory authority to inspect and rate grain. Charges of fraud resulting in farmers being cheated surfaced in the 1880s, and Francis's opponent for the Democratic nomination, Governor Morehouse, charged that the Exchange and, by extension, Francis, were to blame. The *Buffalo Reflex*, which had supported the Democratic ticket in 1884, supported the Republicans and Kimball in 1888 and railed against Francis, calling him corrupt and "the leading grain gambler of the state." The *Reflex* added that how any Missouri farmer could support him was "one of the indescribable mysteries of the day." Francis ran more poorly than expected in rural areas, carrying 68 of the state's 114 counties, but he also ran much more poorly in St. Louis than anyone expected.

The strength of Prohibitionists and Union Laborites was particularly disturbing to Democrats, who assumed rightly that the supporters of these two parties were refugees from their party. The Union Laborites showed particular strength in St. Louis. Although the Democratic candidate for president, Grover Cleveland, carried the City of St. Louis handily, Kimball decisively defeated Francis in the gubernatorial race there. Moreover, eleven of the fourteen state house delegates from St. Louis were Union-Laborites. Traditional laborers were heavily represented: Frederick Swaine was a millwright and carpenter; John B. Dempsey, a carpenter and longtime Knights of Labor activist; Francis S. Rotterman, a vice president of the Boot and Shoe Cutters' Association of St. Louis; Adolph Medara, a St. Louis cigar-maker and union activist; George A. Hoose, a printer and delegate to the Union Labor Party convention in Cincinnati; William J. Nolan, a railroad worker; Thomas Holland, a horse-collar maker; John J. Curley, a mechanic; Philip F. Coghlan, a printer; and John F. Humann, a clerk.

The petitions endorsed by the Union Labor party in its 1888 platform arose from working-class issues and were informed by the writings of single-tax advocate Henry George: a "natural inalienable right to sufficient land for self support," a "graduated land tax," public ownership of the means of communication and transportation, a plentiful money supply, and a number of pro-labor positions, including the abolishment of "the letting of convict labor to contractors." This last issue was one that particularly grated on St. Louis workers. Governor Marmaduke, as well as governors who preceded and succeeded him, had endorsed the contracting out of convicts to private entrepreneurs who ran manufacturing establishments inside the prison walls. The use of prison labor for the production of goods to be sold on the open market undercut the efforts of "free" laborers who were producing similar goods at a much higher cost. Governmental endorsement of this arrangement caused many urban laborers to feel as though a truly radical solution to the problem was needed: hence, their support of a third party.

One of the many problems faced by Governor Francis was a manifestation of the unsettled political situation in southwest Missouri: the case of the Baldknobbers. While it would be inaccurate to label the Baldknobber saga as a strictly political affair, the Baldknobbers did share with the Republicans and Union Labor, Prohibitionist, and other third party movements the frustration of being unable to effect change through normal political and governmental channels.

Baldknobbers emerged first in Taney County, which had demonstrated political and social unrest ever since the end of the Civil War. Hampered by a local economy that was slow to recover from the war and victimized by inefficient and probably dishonest county officials, Taney County residents saw their county taxes and indebtedness mushroom beyond anyone's ability to pay. The traditional political party solutions seemed increasingly not to be solutions at all. Taney County residents quickly left first the political, then the legal, Missouri mainstream. In 1880, when Missourians were delivering 52 percent of their nearly four hundred thousand votes to the Democratic gubernatorial candidate, Thomas Crittenden, Taney Countians gave him only 37 percent of the vote. The bulk of the anti-Crittenden vote in Taney County went to the Greenbacker candidate Brown, who polled more than 23 percent of the gubernatorial votes cast in the county. In 1882, Taney Countians actually elected to the state house of representatives James R. Van Zandt, a Greenbacker, then in his late fifties.

Van Zandt is symbolically significant in that he moved in 1882 from being a symbol of Taney County unhappiness with the political status quo to becoming a Baldknobber in 1884. Van Zandt, like so many of the Baldknobbers, had spent most of his life outside of Taney County. Born in 1824 in Hamilton County, Tennessee, Van Zandt was a veteran of the

Mexican and Civil Wars. He was also a longtime Methodist minister, local supervisor of registration, and justice of the peace.

In 1884, after repeated incidences in which they thought justice had been subverted by the local elected officials, Van Zandt and several others of like mind heeded Nat Kinney's call to form a vigilance committee to right wrongs in Taney County. Over the course of the next four years, Baldknobbers and their opponents, the anti-Baldknobbers, engaged in a number of violent vendettas in Taney County. The dilemma that faced Governor Francis early in his administration was whether or not to commute the death sentences of four Douglass and Christian County Baldknobbers sentenced to be hanged for the murders of Charles Green and William Edens in 1887. The Baldknobbers of Douglas and Christian Counties were unrelated except by name to those of Taney County. In May 1889, four months after taking office, Francis declined to interfere, stating, "The epidemic of lawlessness which has broken out in various parts of the country in the guise of self-styled regulators, and which in this state has found expression in Bald Knobberism, should be suppressed. . . . Being sworn to support and uphold the law to insure protection to peaceable citizens, and to assist in the punishment of the offenders, I cannot grant the commutation desired." The sentences stood and the executions were carried out on May 10, 1889. Thereafter, Baldknobber activity in the Ozarks declined greatly, as did vigilante activity in other parts of the state.

Challenges to the Democratic party notwithstanding, the Democrats maintained political hegemony in Missouri throughout the last quarter of the nineteenth century. The party's dominance held many consequences. For one thing, state government was dominated by people who were genuinely opposed to governmental activism. Indeed, the laissez-faire philosophy, violated only rarely and then ineffectively, played right into the hands of developers, boosters, and modernists. Hence, the state's economic growth was undirected, uncontrolled, and individualized. The beneficence that flowed from the growth was unevenly distributed, and people who perceived themselves to be victimized by the purveyors of progress blamed the powers that were for what was. Thus, at precisely the time that industrialization and urbanization were bringing great changes to Missouri and Missourians, political leaders refused to try to control and direct those changes for the common good. By the time they realized that the common good was not a natural by-product of the changes that were occurring, it was often too late. The result was, among other things, that more and more people became disillusioned and alienated from the existing political parties and even from government itself.

Nowhere was this process more graphically illustrated in Missouri than in the black community, and especially in the life of black political leader James Milton Turner. The immediate postwar period had been a time of gleeful optimism for blacks and for the Radical Republicans they supported. Radical Republicans, of course, had supported emancipation, but they also supported the black vote and other black civil rights. Turner was the state's preeminent beneficiary of that atmosphere. Heavily involved in the Missouri Equal Rights League and black educational efforts immediately following the Civil War, Turner became a power broker in the 1870 election by delivering twenty thousand black votes to the Radical cause. In return, state Radicals strongly endorsed him to President Ulysses S. Grant for a patronage position. Grant appointed him Minister Resident and Consul General to Liberia, making him the second African American in the country's history to become a diplomat.

Turner spent the bulk of the next seven years out of the United States. When he returned in 1878 he discovered quite a different atmosphere from the one he had left. At the national level, blacks had been abandoned by Republicans in the Compromise of 1877, which drew the few remaining federal troops in the South out and allowed Southerners to restore home rule. Turner, who had left the country a "somebody," came back a "nobody" and spent the remainder of his life (which ended in 1915) trying to recapture the power and privilege he had once known. The first truly rude awakening he experienced had to do with the tragedy surrounding the so-called Exodusters—the blacks who fled the South in 1878 and 1879 after the restoration of home rule. He even flirted with the Democratic party, actively campaigning in 1888 for Democratic candidates and urging fellow blacks to do the same. Despite his efforts, Democratic hegemony precluded any need to respond to black requests, leaving Turner, and many blacks like him, without a voice in government.

Blacks, of course, were not the only Missourians without a political voice in post-Reconstruction Missouri. Women were denied the vote, even in principle. As early as May 1867, Missouri women had carried on an organized fight for the franchise under the auspices of the Missouri Woman Suffrage Association. In 1872, Virginia Minor, an MWSA founder and its first president, spoke to a national suffrage convention held in St. Louis. In her speech, she asserted that the Fourteenth Amendment to the U.S. Constitution entitled women to "every right and privilege to which every other citizen is entitled," including the right to vote. In the fall of 1872, Minor attempted to put her philosophy into practice by trying to register to vote. Denied the opportunity to do so by the St. Louis County clerk, Minor, with the assistance of her lawyer-husband, filed suit in a case that wound its way to the United States Supreme Court. In 1875, in the case of *Minor v. Happersett,* the high court ruled that Missouri's refusal to allow women the exercise of the vote was constitutional.

Missouri women tried to get the members of the 1875 Constitutional Convention to look favorably upon the female franchise. In April of 1875 the Women's Suffrage Association, represented by Rebeca N. Hazard and four other women, issued a memorial to the members-elect of the constitutional convention, urging them to produce a document that allowed women the right to vote. The editor of the *People's Tribune* predicted that in spite of the fact that "These ladies earnestly present their grievances . . . and honestly . . . think that their sex is greatly oppressed . . . it is scarcely to be expected that [the convention] will be influenced by any arguments they will be able to present." The *Sedalia Democrat* advised, "The convention should not spend much time on this question." On the night of the fifteenth day of the convention, noted suffragist Phoebe Couzins spoke in the state capitol in favor of allowing women the right to vote. Unpersuaded by her arguments, and by those of women's rights advocates who had preceded her, convention members refused even to debate the issue, much less to act favorably upon it. The failure of the convention to consider allowing women the vote enraged one participant, Albert Todd of St. Louis, although Todd's disappointment was peculiarly framed. Rising to protest the silence of his colleagues on this matter, he made it clear that the "argument upon which I base female suffrage is not the usual consideration presented by women themselves." Todd was angry that blacks had been given the right to vote and blamed them for what he argued was the unfortunate election of Ulysses S. Grant to the presidency in 1868 and 1872. Hence, he wanted to give women the right to vote as "a remedy against . . . negro voters precipitated upon us." Unfortunately for Todd, he could not persuade other delegates to take up the issue. Early the next year,

Todd sat on the board of freeholders that drew up a new charter for the city of St. Louis. As historian James Neal Primm points out, this board "heard but did not seriously consider a request from . . . Virginia L. Minor that all property of women be exempted from city taxes as long as they were disfranchised."

But if women could not exercise formal political power by voting for and serving as elective officials, they found informal ways to exercise influence. Perhaps the most effective vehicle was the Women's Christian Temperance Union, a national organization formed in Chicago in 1873 and first led by Annie Wittenmeyer and, later, by Frances Willard. As historian Nancy Woloch points out, under Willard's direction, the WCTU was much more than an antiliquor organization: it worked "to erase all evils for which men were responsible, from prostitution to political corruption." Clara Cleghorn Hoffman of Kansas City, the first president of the Missouri WCTU, was the dominant force in the organization in the state for nearly twenty-five years.

The Democratic party in Missouri had a long tradition of opposition to centralized rule and expansive governmental power. That tradition was rooted in a fundamentally Jeffersonian commitment to the notion of that government being best which governs least. The Civil War and Reconstruction experiences in the state had given Democrats tangible and graphic evidence of the frightful results of governmental activism. In creating the 1875 Constitution and in controlling state government thereafter, they acted upon that evidence. And yet, changes were occurring. Increasingly, Missourians and the political leaders they elected were coming to understand that there were some issues facing the state that could be addressed only by strong, centralized action. Outlawry, for example, threatened to drive immigrants away from the state and to diminish respect for the law if it continued unabated, and the railroads were a bigger force than any local government could handle. Hence, as Missourians entered the final decade of the nineteenth century, they did so with an ambivalence about governmental power that left them frankly confused.

CHAPTER II

RAILROADS AS ENGINES OF ECONOMIC GROWTH

No single force changed the lives of Missourians more during the last half of the nineteenth century than did the railroads. The railroads changed people's notions of space. The isolation that Missourians had felt in their overwhelmingly rural state began to lessen in the generation after the Civil War. Distant urban centers of the East, so far away from most Missourians in the 1850s and 1860s that they were only abstractions, were brought closer by the faster and easier means of travel and communication available in the 1870s and 1880s.

The railroads also changed people's notions of time. Indeed, the railroads defined time for Missourians. On November 8, 1883, Governor Thomas Crittenden, following the urging of "the managers of the railroads of the United States to adopt standards of time which shall be uniform," urged Missourians to adopt Central Time as their standard. They did so beginning at noon on November 18, 1883. With the coming of the railroad, trips to the nearest town could be measured in minutes rather than hours; trips across the state in hours rather than days; and trips across the country in days rather than weeks. The interconnectedness of life—the effect of each upon the other—became more apparent. Life in faraway places and at distant times became much less remote, much less abstract, because the places could be reached in much shorter amounts of time.

The railroads changed the way most Missourians made a living. Missourians discovered that they could grow, make, and mine things that were wanted by people outside the state, and that those things could be shipped by rail anywhere in the country. Just as importantly, Missourians discovered that they could receive goods produced elsewhere in return. Missourians began, increasingly, to specialize in the production of those goods and commodities that would bring them the greatest cash profit, and with that cash they became consumers as they had never been before.

But all of this occurred at precisely the same time that another great change was taking place in the lives of Missourians. The memory of the Civil War was still fresh in the minds of most Missourians in the 1870s. The men who had fought and suffered on the battlefields, and their wives and girlfriends who had remained behind, had reached middle age and the peak of their productivity. Fiercely independent and suspicious of circumstances and people they could not control, they nurtured mutually inconsistent aspirations: they wanted the benefits and conveniences of commercial cosmopolitanism as well as the control and isolation of provincial localism.

Railroads, and the changes they brought, could not be stopped. By the 1870s, Missouri was embarked upon a new economic course that inspired hope in the hearts of most of the residents of the state. Ironically, the source of that hope—the railroads and the improved standard of living that they promised—also often brought economic disaster and despair. The future belonged, then, to those who best recognized the reality and nature of the economic changes that were upon Missouri and who were able to capitalize on this knowledge.

Railroads were not new to Missouri in the 1870s, of course. The first "Iron Horses" entered the state in the mid-1850s, and over the next two decades several tracks crisscrossed the state. But in the 1870s and 1880s an ever-increasing number of feeder lines emerged, tying theretofore rural, semisubsistent people into an expanding, urban, commercial economy. In 1870 Missouri had 2,000 miles of railroad completed. By 1880, that figure had nearly doubled, to 3,965 miles.

Communities sought out, solicited, and even bribed railroad entrepreneurs to lay track through, around, or just near their towns. The town of Pilot Grove, in Cooper County, was actually moved to gain access to the Missouri, Kansas and Texas (M.K.T.) Railroad. The current site of the town, about one mile from the previous site, was platted in 1873 by Samuel Roe, who owned a farm on the site. By 1880, Roe's town had grown to more than two hundred people and had become an important railroad, trade, and shipping center. In the early 1880s it featured several general merchandise and hardware stores, a bank, two restaurants, two tin shops, three blacksmith and wagon shops, two combination hotels and boardinghouses, two livery stables, one barbershop, several carpenters, and a number of resident railroad workers. As one agriculturist wrote in 1880, "An important matter for consideration, in computing the value of a country, is the means a country had to place the surplus products in a market where they will command a ready sale at good prices." The most available means for doing that throughout the last quarter of the nineteenth century was the railroad. As the editor of the *Lawrence Chieftain* wrote in 1884, if Lawrence County residents could get a railroad to come to Mount Vernon, it would create "a flourishing, wealthy town beyond the dreams and expectations of the most sanguine."

The railroads also spawned a number of overland commercial roads frequented by freight haulers who carried goods to and from railroad marketing points. The establishment of railroad service to Springfield by the St. Louis–San Francisco Railroad in 1870 and to Ozark and Chadwick in the early 1880s led to the emergence of several commercial roads in the upper White River region. The Wilderness Road, the Harrison-Springfield Road, the Boston Road, the Walnut Shade–Spokane Road, the Lead Hill–Springfield Road, and the Yelville-Chadwick Road extended, as historian Elmo Ingenthron has written, "freight wagon services . . . well over 100 miles across the White River country to the south."

Teamsters from a wide radius spent a week or more on a round-trip carrying wares to or from railroad marketplaces in southwest Missouri. Farm produce of all sorts was carried to Springfield, for example, and on the return trip, manufactured goods were transported to local merchants, who in turn sold them to area residents. In some instances, fifty or more wagons would pass over a road in one day. Enterprising residents discovered that money could be made by charging a small fee for minimal services to traveling teamsters. Ten to twenty-five cents would usually buy a teamster a place indoors to at least lay his bedroll and feed and care for his horses. Villages and hamlets often emerged out of the campgrounds where teamsters stopped for the night. The town of Reno in southwestern Christian County, for example, became a thriving community in the 1880s thanks to the freight traffic. Teamsters and others using the Harrison-Springfield Road created enough business to sustain two hotels, three stores, a post office, a gristmill, a blacksmith shop, a sawmill, a dance hall, and a saloon.

To be sure, most Missourians remained farmers throughout this period. For them and the small towns accepting their goods, the railroads changed both what they produced and how they produced it. For example, in 1890, J. H. Hill, who owned a creamery in Edina, produced 43,500 pounds of butter, "all of which he sold in eastern markets," an impossibility before railroads connected Edina with the East. But not all Missourians saw railroads as an unmitigated good. Agriculturists who had become accustomed to guaranteed local markets found that the railroads ran both out of and into their communities. The same train that carried produce to a distant market returned with competitive goods for the local market. W. M. King of St. Louis summed up this change and its adverse effects on Missouri fruitgrowers in his January 1876 presidential address to the Missouri Horticultural Society:

> From 1850 to 1860, our views of transportation markets—the influences controlling production, consumption, supply, demand, restrictions on trade, on mediums of exchanging commodities . . . were limited, untried. At that time all these relations bore less on our crops and planting in the entire State, than they now do in almost any one county. Then the measure of planting was for the local markets. . . . The St. Louis market, and its supplies, were facts almost alike fixed; but the railroad era changed all this, and of itself practically obliterated in a sense never to be forgotten by the fruit-grower north and south, east and west, and those plantations made, and crops raised, were changed in their value as by the wand of a fairy. Thus the grand agency crowning our civilization upset many a plan, blighted many a well-founded hope, and put the balance of the growers' account to the wrong side. Now [other parts of the country] are as near St. Louis as Franklin, Jefferson or St. Louis counties were in 1850. What an element in our calculations of risks; what a disturbance in our conceptions of probabilities. . . . A full sense of the vital importance of the whole question of transportation presents itself; we are brought face to face with it as upon an issue of life and death. We must aim at bringing the producer and consumer, the raw material and manufacturer, into the very closest proximity possible, and thus create local markets and local centers of industry, especially to save our perishable products and to curtail the cost of transportation.

There was very little chance, however, that local markets for agricultural products could be protected against the competition provided by outside producers. Those who realized this fact urged farmers to accept the railroads as their friends and to specialize in the production of agricultural commodities in demand in distant urban markets. Henry Clay Dean put it this way in a November 1879 speech before the State Board of Agriculture: "We must penetrate every accessible part of the State with railways, until everything we have to sell is brought to the door of the market. Our wetlands must be drained and our uplands fertilized, and skilled farmers of other states invited to make their homes among us."

Agricultural reformer Norman J. Colman criticized railroad rates while urging farmers to adopt scientific agricultural techniques and to use the rails to market their goods. Appointed to the Missouri State Board of Agriculture in 1867, Colman served on it for nearly forty-five years. As early as 1869 at a meeting of the board, he spoke against "excessive freight rates." Nationally known through his magazine *Colman's Rural World,* he consistently recognized the necessity of railroads, while arguing that they should be regulated in the public interest. He also advocated that Missouri's rivers be developed for better navigation and led in the fight for good roads that connected farms to towns and cities. When Missouri voters turned down a constitutional amendment in 1886 to permit the levying of a large road tax, Colman bitterly editorialized against the action. Four years later, the state's Board of Agriculture led efforts to try to persuade Missourians to develop a system of good roads.

Colman's concentration on good transportation facilities fit a larger pattern of agricultural production for markets, a pattern that existed in the Boonslick before the Civil War but that did not extend to most of Missouri until much later. Colman's thrust included advocacy of scientific training for Missouri farmers. As early as 1869, Colman suggested that farmers be taught better methods in farmers' institutes. In 1870 while he served on the University of Missouri Board of Curators, the state went beyond the institute idea, establishing a College of Agriculture at the state university. According to James Olson, a historian of the university, farmers had desired "specialized scientific training" for years. It took the passage of the Morrill Act in 1862 and the political skills of James S. Rollins, who served in the legislature and as president of the board of curators, and Colman, who supported Rollins, to secure the school for Columbia. The college recruited Jeremiah W. Sanborn, a well-known agricultural researcher, as its second dean in 1882. The next year, Sanborn used the college's professors and the financing of the state's Board of Agriculture to organize three farmers' institutes, and within three years what amounted to agricultural extension courses had been firmly established. According to George S. Lemmer, Colman's biographer, "Sanborn had far more requests for meetings than the board's finances would permit." In those early years, College of Agriculture faculty conducted more than fifty institutes across the state. In 1889 the legislature appropriated $3,600 to support the institutes, a figure Colman claimed was insufficient since Wisconsin invested $12,000 per year and Illinois spent $10,000 per year on them.

In 1885 Colman was appointed United States commissioner of agriculture by President Grover Cleveland. In that position, Colman worked with U.S. Representative William Henry Hatch of Hannibal to pass legislation creating agricultural experiment stations. Called the Hatch Act, it passed Congress in 1887 and provided for federally financed experiment stations to be established in each state. The next year Congress elevated the agriculture department to cabinet status, and Colman became the first secretary of agriculture. In 1889 the department began issuing weekly agricultural bulletins free of charge to farmers. By 1900, both elementary and secondary school curricula offered courses in agriculture, spreading the influence of scientific production even more widely. Norman J. Colman and his apostles could be proud of their efforts.

By urging better transportation and more scientific agriculture, Colman fostered expansion of markets and increased production. Following his and others' leadership, farmers brought previously unused and often marginal land into production. Often they could do this only by borrowing money that they hoped to repay with the profits they assumed would result from their ever-increasing productivity. Hence, Missouri farmers became debtors as never before, a situation that made them dependent on and often hostile toward their creditors. The 1870s and 1880s witnessed tight money supplies and massive deflation, which hurt debtors. Farmers were always supportive of ways to inflate the currency during this era through such means as the use of greenbacks and silver as legal tender. Such inflationary measures, however, were always opposed by creditors. The degree to which Missourians succeeded in expanding their production is evidenced by the growth in the number of farms and acreage under cultivation. In 1870 Missourians cared for 148,328 farms and had 9,130,615 acres under cultivation. By 1880 those figures had jumped to 215,575 farms and 16,745,031 acres under cultivation.

Dramatic examples of increase occurred all over the state. Wayne County in southeast Missouri had no access to a railway prior to the early 1870s. But after the small town of Piedmont was made a division point on the Iron Mountain railroad, agricultural production boomed. In 1870 the county had 27,489 acres under cultivation and produced 293,569 bushels of corn. By 1880, 47,234 acres had been brought under cultivation and 524,126 bushels of corn were produced. By 1890, 66,008 acres were being cultivated and 617,267 bushels of corn was produced.

Piedmont, which was not platted until 1871, grew to a town of approximately seven hundred people by 1880. The census for that year clearly illustrates the occupational differentiation that came with Piedmont's status as a commercial center. Railroad workers abounded in the town, and occupational alternatives to farming were evidenced by the many blacksmiths, merchants, wagon-makers, seamstresses, lawyers, physicians, and general laborers, many of whom were residing in the town's half dozen hotels and boardinghouses.

Just south of Piedmont, also on the rail line, the town of Clearwater prospered by concentrating on one industry: the timber of the Black River drainage area. Timber was floated down the Black River and its tributaries to Clearwater, where sawmills turned the logs into a variety of wood products to be shipped all over the United States. The land cleared, of course, was placed into agricultural production.

While the number of Missourians living on the land increased, the state's urban population grew even faster. Indeed, Missouri's rural population actually declined from 74.8 percent of the state's total population in 1880 to 68 percent in 1890, as an increasing number of farm implements displaced agricultural laborers. President John Walker, speaking to the annual gathering of the State Board of Agriculture in 1882, lamented the fact that he "came too soon to get the benefit of recent inventions." Addressing the younger men in his audience, "who are aided by the genius of modern inventive skill," Walker told them they had "a more inviting field before you than we older pioneers who have constructed your roads and cleared your fields with the ruder implements then at hand. Those were the days when we walked after the plow and held it. Now you ride." J. R. Estill of Howard County encouraged his fellow farmers to raise more hay in 1880, arguing, "The great improvement in machinery within the last few years for cutting and saving hay has produced a revolution in this crop. Now a hundred acres of heavy grass does not look so formidable in labor as twenty did a few years since. With a good machine fifteen acres can be cut in a day; three men and four boys provided with long rakes and a stacker can save it, thus making forage faster than by any other process."

Colman's Rural World noted in 1879 that "with the improved implements and machines which we now have, a farmer with one hired man can carry on farming on a larger scale than he could a generation ago with half a dozen hired men." The State Bureau of Labor Statistics, in its Sixth Annual Report (1885), noted, "The barshare plow, requiring three to four men per acre a day of plowing, has given place to the sulky plow, asking for but one man per day for three acres of plowing. The corn planter has replaced ten men; the mower, four to five; the reaper, ten men; and so on for other field operations." The result: "expansion of labor-saving machinery on the farm has forced the laborer to seek other employment."

Farm laborers not only were being pushed from the farm by increased use of labor-saving devices but also were finding more opportunities in the towns that were emerging and the cities that were growing. Whole towns grew up because of the railroads, as was the case of Helena in Andrew County. "This prosperous village," according to a writer in the 1880s, "derived much of its growth and importance from its location on the Chicago, Burlington & Quincy Railroad—in fact, it owes its existence to the construction of the said road." In 1878, two Rochester Township farmers, Henry Snowden and H. C. Webster, learned that a narrow-gauge railroad being contemplated from St. Joseph to Albany would run through their farms. Hopeful that the coming of the railroad would bring economic prosperity, they plotted a town site on portions of their land. The railroad was completed through the "town" in the summer of 1879. Snowden became the town's first depot agent, largely the result of his donation of a depot site to the railroad. Webster donated a tract for a city park. The 1880 census reveals that in that year thirty-one people were living in Helena, including thirty-six-year-old William Coy, his wife Martha, and their two sons. Coy, identified in the census as a "Grain Dealer," was the first person to take advantage of the railroad by establishing a business. His general store was quickly followed in the 1880s by a saloon, a drugstore, a feed mill, and a hotel. The establishment of these businesses also attracted mechanics, carpenters, and a blacksmith. In 1885 a large Elks Lodge was built, and by the end of the decade, after the purchase of the narrow-gauge line by the Chicago, Burlington and Quincy Railroad, Helena's population rose to approximately three hundred.

Central Missouri towns along the Pacific Railroad that were made into section points soon provided jobs for workmen who maintained the railway and for merchants and middlemen who bought and sold produce transported on it. Tiny villages such as Chamois and Bonnots Mill in Osage County prospered in this fashion during the 1870s and 1880s. Chamois was a sleepy little village along the Missouri River and Pacific Railroad tracks in northern Osage County. So small that it was not distinguished separately in the 1870 census, the town grew to 562 residents in 1880 and then to 769 in 1890. A contemporary observer noted that the town's growth peaked during the 1870s, when the railroad located a freight division there that included a roundhouse, repair shop, tanks, stockyards, coal chutes, and a ballast crusher. Most of the gainfully employed laborers in the town held jobs that either were directly associated with the railroads or were in commercial activities resulting from the railroad's presence.

Even farmers in the outlying area of Benton Township found that the railroad's activities changed their lives. Not only did they begin shipping more cash products out of the area by rail and buying more "store bought" goods than ever before, but they also discovered that their own slack periods were good times to cut the ever-in-demand railroad ties needed by the repair crews or to haul the always-needed rock that was crushed into ballast, thereby providing themselves and their families with the ready cash that enabled them to become greater consumers.

The 1880 census reveals the complexity of occupational differentiation in Chamois. More than twenty adult males worked directly for the railroad, with many of them living in one or the other of the two hotels in town. There were nine blacksmiths, a number of teamsters and draymen, carpenters and craftsmen of great variety, two "veterinary surgeons," two physicians, and at least one lawyer. By 1880 there were also two newspapers: a temperance paper called the *Battle Flag* and published by W. J. Knott, and a liberal Democratic paper, the *Chamois Liberalist.*

In Missouri's capital city, a neighborhood surrounding the Pacific Railroad roundhouse prospered during the 1870s and 1880s, and a German immigrant named Gerhardt Dulle became one of the first residents of the city to recognize the wealth to be gained by producing a product that could be marketed nationwide. Dulle, who came to Jefferson City from Germany in the 1850s, established a small gristmill in the area west of the capitol building where the roundhouse was located. By the late nineteenth century, the Dulle Mills were producing five hundred barrels of flour a day and serving a national market.

The Dulle Mills, and other employers in the neighborhood (the Jefferson City Gas Works, the Jefferson City Produce Company, and the Pacific Railroad roundhouse), provided residents in the Millbottom area with places of employment two or three blocks from their homes. The concentration of people living in the neighborhood created business opportunities in the service industries. Millbottom residents, for example, could shop for foodstuffs at the Richmond Hill Grocery in the 600 block of West Main. They could buy baked goods at the McKinney Brothers Bakery just down the street. Next door to McKinney's was the H. A. Swift Ice and Fuel Company. Nearby also were a shoe shop, a couple of restaurants, and several taverns. The neighborhood doctor, Joseph P. Porth, lived across the street from the Richmond Hill Grocery. On Sunday, Millbottom residents, the majority of whom were German Catholics, could simply walk up the hill to St. Peter's Church, the same place that they sent their children to school. In short, there was little need for neighborhood residents to go more than a few blocks from their homes.

Sedalia was another town that prospered in the 1870s and 1880s because of the railroads. The Pacific Railroad had been the major reason for George Smith's platting of the town in 1857. Sedalia grew by leaps and bounds thereafter. From a population of approximately 300 in 1860, the town grew to 4,560 in 1870 and 9,561 in 1880. One of the key elements in the growth of Sedalia in the 1870s was the presence of the Katy, or M.K.T., rail line, including its general offices, in the early 1870s. By 1873, Sedalia was connected directly to markets as far south as Denison, Texas, and as far east as the burgeoning metropolis of Chicago. By 1876 more than 200 resident railroad employees made their homes in Sedalia, and another 100 itinerant workers (conductors, engineers, and brakemen) spent a great deal of time and money in town.

Rail traffic flowed constantly through Sedalia. Trains carrying would-be western migrants stopped routinely, providing Sedalia merchants and hostlers with abundant opportunity to serve a somewhat captive market. More than 23,000 persons purchased train tickets in Sedalia in 1875, and more than 90 million pounds of freight were either shipped or received in that year. Such traffic spawned employment and business opportunities for many Sedalians. By the mid-1880s, Sedalia had four banks, five building and loan associations, and at least seven hotels; the largest of the hotels, the Garrison House, contained fifty-five rooms and was owned by the Missouri Pacific Railroad.

Additionally, the railroad, and the activity that it generated, encouraged manufacturing and commercial ventures of great variety. Mills and elevators, for example, did a booming business. The Farmers Mill, which added a three-story brick elevator in 1881, did $200,000 worth of business in that year. It vied for control of grain handling in the city with at least three other mills. Brunkhorst's Saw Mill, established in 1881, sought to keep up with the lumber demands of a growing town by sawing native Missouri hardwoods; within a short time the mill was sawing eight thousand feet of lumber a year. Likewise, two brick-making establishments in the city provided the bulk of the three and a half million bricks used per year by Sedalians in the early 1880s. Merchants, grocers, butchers, bakers, milliners, jewelers, and tailors likewise prospered, drawing, as they did, from a seemingly endless supply of potential customers.

The frequent presence of large numbers of itinerants in Sedalia and other railroad communities created money-making opportunities for another growing class of entrepreneurs: prostitutes. Prostitution had become so common in St. Louis by the early 1870s that city officials embarked on a short-lived and unsuccessful experiment of legalizing and regulating it. In Sedalia, the escapades of prostitutes became common front-page material for local newspapers. In August of 1875, for example, the *Sedalia Weekly Bazoo* reported on the activities of several local prostitutes, described as "The ugliest, most repulsive looking lot of females that the *Bazoo* reporter has gazed on in many days." An 1886 incident in Carthage involving a prostitute revealed both the treacherousness of prostitution as a "profession" and the public's attitude toward those who engaged in it. According to the *Jefferson City State Times,* Sue Robinson, "a notorious colored street walker," accused Charley Brown, a hotel porter, of robbing her. Brown responded to the accusation by striking Robinson on the head with a baseball bat, fracturing her skull and killing her. Although Brown was arrested, the newspaper reported that "public sympathy is somewhat in his favor."

The arrival of the M.K.T. Railroad in southeast Bates County in 1880 drastically changed the lives of many west-central Missourians. The population of Bates County jumped from 15,960 in 1870 to 32,223 in 1890, an increase of more than 100 percent. The bulk of this population found employment in nonagricultural pursuits, as the number of farms in the county grew by only 291, or less than 9 percent. Not surprisingly, the value of this farmland grew in direct proportion to the population increase: from $5,023 per farm in 1870 to $11,428 in 1890, an increase of 128 percent.

The major new form of employment in Bates County was mining the rich coal deposits that became the county's major export. Prior to the coming of the railroad, the overwhelming majority of coal taken from Bates County soil was used within the county's borders, or, as County Mine Inspector M. L. Wolfe wrote, "Quite a number [of mines] are worked on a small scale for neighborhood consumption." After the railroad arrived, the amount of coal mined increased dramatically, with most of it shipped to consumers in faraway markets. In 1886 Wolfe reported to the State Bureau of Labor Statistics that he estimated twelve hundred men were employed in the county "one way and another in running the mines."

The actual work of the miner was dirty and dangerous, so much so that in the mid-1880s the legislature passed a law stipulating that "No young person under 12 . . . or woman or girl of *any* age shall be permitted to enter any coal mine to work therein." County Inspector Wolfe described the job of the miner as follows: "The tools of a miner consist of a sledge, several steel wedges, four or five picks, a drill, tamping bar, scraper and needle; this necessitates a keg of powder and a box of squibs. Two men work together in a room or entry to keep each other company in their dark abode. They are now called buddies and share alike their profits; one of them watches while the other works in dangerous places, and if anything happens to one, such as roof failure, the other raises the alarm."

The danger of life in the mines was only part of the miners' precarious existence. At first optimistic about the "better life" they thought working for cash would bring, the miners felt victimized before the decade's end. In many instances, mine owners deducted fifty cents to a dollar from the paychecks of miners for payment of a "company doctor," whether or not the doctor's services were used. Secondly, in most instances, miners were faced with the choice of working under antilabor union contracts or not working at all. In Macon County, for example, miners agreed that they would not "stop work, join any coal federation, Knights of Labor, miners' mass meeting, strike or combination for the purpose of obtaining or causing the company to pay their miners an advance in wages," under penalty of a hundred-dollar fine.

But the condition that caused the greatest unhappiness was the company store, or, as some miners called it, the "Pluck-Me" system. Owners of mines often paid wages in the form of "script," or "pasteboard money," redeemable only for merchandise at a store owned by the mine owner. Prices at these company stores were notoriously high, resulting in a 24 to 40 percent reduction in real wages for the mine workers. S. C. Pierce, a miner from Bevier in Macon County, best summed up his coworkers' attitude toward this system in an 1889 letter to Missouri Labor Commissioner Lee Meriwether:

> I think that a store run by a mine operator is a 'pluck me.' It is a system that plucks me of my civil rights, and one of the dearest privileges of my life, that of having the dollar that I have earned by the sweat of my brow, to go with it to the place I like, to trade it for food to put on the table and clothes to put on my children's backs. When I am forced to go to a company's store to buy the necessaries of life, Mr. Skinner, on the other side of the counter, forces me to pay enormous prices for the goods.

Joplin, in the southwest corner of the state, enjoyed the most spectacular growth of any outstate Missouri town during the period from 1875 to 1890. Joplin's growth started in the early 1870s when iron ore was discovered by Eli R. Moffet and John B. Sergeant. Miners quickly gathered at the sight of the strike and dug for ore with pick and shovel in the absence of more sophisticated equipment. The real impetus to the growth of the mining industry in Joplin, however, was the establishment of the Joplin and Girard Railroad in 1877. Efforts to establish the railroad had begun in the winter of 1875–1876 with the creation of the Joplin Railroad Company, composed of seven stockholders, two of whom were Moffet and Sergeant. Early in 1876, Moffet and Sergeant bought out the other stockholders and continued planning their thirty-nine-mile-long railroad that would link Joplin to the Gulf Railroad at Girard, Kansas. Moffet and Sergeant hoped that this line would provide the Kansas coal necessary for the Joplin smelters while allowing Joplin miners a market outside the state of Missouri, especially in the north. The Joplin and Girard Railroad, completed in 1877, was sold by its owners to the St. Louis and San Francisco Railroad Company in 1879. Soon other railroads joined the scramble for Joplin's precious ore.

Joplin, which had not existed in 1870, saw its population soar to 7,038 in 1880 and to nearly 10,000 by 1890. That dramatic rise in population created opportunities for a host of businesses to serve a variety of miners' needs. The *Joplin Daily News* reported in 1875 that there were 225 business establishments in the community, one-third of them saloons. The Joplin Hotel, completed in April 1875, provided temporary housing for many residents of the city. The Banking House of P. Murphy, organized in 1877 and known as the Miners' Bank after 1878, was joined in 1882 by the Bank of Joplin in providing the financing necessary for the city's growth. Other businesses that flourished as a result of Joplin's rapid growth included the Fourth Street Stable (1875), Southwestern Livery, Feed, and Sale Stable (1877), Southern Livery, Feed, and Sale Stable (1880), Joplin Wagon and Carriage Works (1876), Joplin Floral and Vegetable Gardens (1875), Joplin Woolen and Flouring Mills (both in 1882), and Harmony's Foundry (1877). These establishments provided hundreds of Missourians with alternatives to agricultural employment, thereby nurturing Missouri's movement toward the mainstream of a national commercial economy.

In southeast Missouri, the colorful Louis Houck identified and promoted the railroad as the key to economic vitality for the region and for Cape Girardeau in particular. Houck, the son of a Bavarian father and a Swiss mother, lived in Illinois until 1868. He then moved to St. Louis, only to move again to Cape Girardeau the next year, because, as he said, country living was preferable to city living, and nowhere, in his judgment, was the climate, the fertility of the soil, and the richness of mineral resources greater than in southeast Missouri. Working as a newspaper correspondent for the *Missouri Republican,* Houck assessed southeast Missouri's fortunes as follows: "Business here, as everywhere else, I suppose is dull. Money is scarce." The solution to the region's prosperity was the railroad. In 1869, when the Iron Mountain railroad entered Charleston, Houck wrote, "It is of course useless to expatiate on the utility of a railroad. Everybody knows that a railroad is a good institution. It will make this county the garden of vegetables for St. Louis and Chicago."

Prompted in large part by Houck's boosterism, Cape Girardeau's officials courted the Cape Girardeau and State Line Railroad, only to find themselves deeply in debt with no completed railroad as a result of the Panic of 1873. Things became so bad during the mid-1870s that many Cape Girardeau County residents refused to pay railroad taxes, which resulted in default on bonds. Subsequently, Houck was retained as a lawyer to straighten out the troubled company's finances. He eventually emerged as the president and director of the newly formed Cape Girardeau Railway Company. Testifying before a House committee in 1887, Houck explained how he had gotten into the railroad business: "Public opinion, to a certain extent, and my own inclinations, being a large property holder in that territory, compelled me to take hold of that enterprise in order to secure and afford our town its benefits as well as develop the material resources of that section."

From the time Houck took over the Cape Girardeau Railway Company on August 10, 1880, until January 1, 1881, he directed a frenzied effort to complete a 14.4-mile stretch of rail from Cape Girardeau to the Iron Mountain railway. Over the course of the next four decades, Houck was instrumental in constructing roughly 500 miles of railroad throughout southeast Missouri. Unfortunately, Houck's eagerness to see the railways completed as quickly as possible, coupled with his desire to realize an immediate return on his investment, caused him to be inattentive to accepted construction practices. Indeed, the shoddiness of his lines became legendary across the state. As was noted in the Annual Report of the Railroad and Warehouse Commissioners of Missouri in 1891, one of his lines

> was known locally as the "peavine," because it was so crooked, and sometimes for days at a time there would be no trains, because the one engine and coach would jump the track. . . . At one place just south of Benton, Houck had felled two trees and laid them across a small creek, building his track on this structure instead of the regulation trestle. This caused the track to rise up in order to get on the trestle, and we recall the warning which the conductor always gave the passengers: "Look out, she's going to jump!" in order that they might prepare themselves for the sudden change in the roadbed.

Missourians in all parts of the state prospered to the degree that they understood and took advantage of railroad connections to national markets. The Missouri Meerschaum Company of Washington, in east central Missouri, is a case in point. Henry Tibbe began making corncob pipes for the local market in 1869. His son Anton joined the business in 1872. In 1879 the two men were joined by George H. Kahmann, and the three of them incorporated under the Meerschaum trademark. Kahmann contracted with a St. Louis jobbing firm known as Hirschland Behdheim, which provided the company with a nationwide outlet, causing it to turn to mass production.

Missouri's largest city, St. Louis, grew dramatically during the generation after the Civil War. Long an important trade center because of its location on the Mississippi River, St. Louis became even more important in the mid-1870s, after the completion of the famous Eads Bridge, which spanned the river in 1874. The Eads Bridge served as a symbolic and physical link between the city and the vast urban markets of the East. The value of manufactured products produced in St. Louis leaped from an estimated $27 million in 1870 to $114.3 million in 1880, and then doubled again by 1890 ($228.7 million). The amount of capital invested in manufacturing in the city rose from $50.8 million in 1880 to $171 million in 1890. The number of industrial establishments grew from 2,924 to 6,148 during that same period. Industrial workers in the city totaled 41,824 in 1880 and 93,610 in 1890. Aggregate wages paid these workers jumped from $17.7 million in 1880 to $53.1 million in 1890.

The growth of the Anheuser-Busch brewery epitomized the city's ability to fill the need of distant markets by rail. Adolphus Busch, the business patriarch, immigrated to St. Louis from Germany during the decade preceding the Civil War. In 1861 he married Lilly Anheuser, daughter of Eberhard Anheuser, also a German immigrant. Anheuser operated a small brewery in the city and in 1865 he made Busch president of the firm. Busch's genius was his ability to combine advances in science and technology with the convenience and efficiency of the railroad to ship quality-brewed beer to the South, particularly Texas. It was Busch who experimented with and pioneered in the use of refrigerated cars, and it was Busch who introduced pasteurization to the brewers' art in the mid-1870s, thereby making available to a large Southern market a quality of beer that its climate would not otherwise allow.

Busch's introduction of Budweiser in 1876 signaled his domination of the industry. Budweiser's clarity and taste made it a huge success. Astute at marketing, Busch purchased a painting called "Custer's Last Fight" from the artist Cassilly Adams. Prints of the large canvas with the name "Anheuser-Busch Brewing Association" in large letters across the bottom soon adorned bars across the country.

As the historians of the brewery have written, "He [Busch] shrewdly decided that a great market was his for the taking in the southern states. The climate was conducive to thirst and unfavorable to proper fermentation in cool cellars. So, he built his trackside ice-houses and tackled

Texas." When Anheuser-Busch incorporated in 1875, the company was producing 34,797 barrels of beer per year. By 1880 that figure jumped to 131,797 barrels of beer per year. By 1890, it was 702,075 barrels. The small company, which occupied a single lot with a twenty-five-foot street frontage when it began, covered one hundred acres by 1893.

No Missouri city grew as spectacularly as did Kansas City during this era. The city had begun to grow exponentially immediately after the Civil War, with its population increasing from 3,500 in 1865 to more than 32,000 in 1870. A principal reason for this growth was the foresight of Joseph G. McCoy and others, who envisioned Kansas City as a railhead for Texas cattle drovers who wished to ship their beef by train to the Eastern urban markets. This focused marketing venture spawned two incredibly explosive growth industries: meatpacking and milling. Plankington and Armour Company emerged as the major packer in the 1870s, slaughtering thousands of head of cattle and shipping beef initially in canning tins and later in refrigerated cars to distant markets. Kansas City canned beef rose from 778,720 tins in 1880 to more than 4 million tins in 1885. Likewise, a similar growth occurred in the volume of wheat received into the city. Wheat receipts for Kansas City stood at 678,000 bushels in 1871; that figure rose to more than 9 million by 1878.

By 1880 eleven railway lines ran through Kansas City, and the burgeoning metropolis was attracting aspiring workers from all parts of Kansas and Missouri. In particular, many plains farmers who had never recovered from the grasshopper plague of the mid-1870s and the depression and poor crop prices of those years saw Kansas City as a mecca of opportunity. They imagined the wealth that could be gained working in the slaughter and packinghouses.

Real wealth, however, was within the grasp of land brokers and real estate speculators who served as agents of change in the conversion of western Missouri prairie land into subdivisions with paved streets. Between 1873 and 1876, only ten additions to the Kansas City metropolitan area were platted—little more than two a year. In 1879 alone, however, thirteen new subdivisions were platted, and that figure more than doubled, to twenty-seven, in 1880. The need for land on which to settle new residents and build new buildings where they would work drove land prices ever higher. In the mid-1870s, land transfers in Kansas City amounted to less than $2 million annually. By 1879, that figure had risen to $3.5 million. The next year it jumped to $5.5 million, and the rise had only begun.

The secret for the speculator, of course, was to be able to predict the direction of future growth before anyone else did and to buy up land as cheaply as possible in the projected growth area. The person who did this better than anyone else in Kansas City in the 1880s was Willard E. Winner, who came to the city in 1858 at the age of nine with his father, a tailor. After working at a variety of retail jobs, Winner began selling real estate in 1880. In 1883 he established a partnership with his brother and others that he called Winner Investment Company. The firm prospered, as it took a large share of the $11 million worth of land transfers that occurred in 1885. In 1886, when land transfers rose to $40 million, Winner and his associates embarked on an ambitious venture of buying up a tract of land for $480,000 and subdividing it into a residential neighborhood called Pendleton Heights. Within three years, this speculative venture netted the company $110,000 profit. Encouraged by this success, and by a market that saw land transfers rise to $88 million in 1887, Winner bought thousands of acres to the east toward Independence and more land north of the Missouri River in the hope that the boom would continue unabated. Unfortunately for him, it did not. The level of speculation, and the increase in land prices which it nurtured, had risen too high. The land bubble burst, and with it in the early 1890s went the quickly accumulated Winner fortune. By 1897, even Winner's personal residence had to be sold to satisfy creditors. By this time, Kansas City's growth achieved a more orderly, if less spectacular, period of development.

Not all Missourians, of course, saw their lives dramatically changed by railroads during the period from 1875 to 1890. Indeed, many continued to live the same type of subsistence life that they and their families had experienced for generations. This was particularly true of whites in interior Ozarks counties and rural blacks who were still experiencing their first generation of freedom.

In Saline County, a freedmen's hamlet grew up south of Marshall, Missouri. This hamlet came to be known as Pennytown, named for the black Kentuckian who moved to Missouri in search of cheap land and a new way of life in the late 1860s. Joseph Penny worked as a tenant farmer in the area for several years until, in March of 1871, he was able to purchase eight acres of land for $160 from local white landowner

John Haggin. Penny's purchase in 1871 was the first of eleven during the 1870s at the emerging hamlet. Penny held his land for only two years, selling it in March 1873 to stepdaughter Evaline Butler, but the Penny family continued to live in the same house together. The average parcel purchased was six and one-half acres, and the tracts ranged from one and one-fourth to twenty acres. The sale that seems to have been a particular catalyst for the concentration of several black families at the new freedmen's hamlet was Edward Railey's and Daniel Lewis's purchase of twenty acres in 1875.

By 1880 blacks owned almost 64 of the 160 acres in section twenty-four of Salt Fork Township. They had organized a distinctive, self-subsistent community. The agricultural census of 1880 suggests division of labor and sharing within the black settlement. Of eleven landowners, three had some machinery, eight had a horse or two, six had milk cows (although only four produced butter), seven had swine, three raised wheat, seven raised corn, two raised tobacco, three raised Irish potatoes, three raised apple trees, six cultivated peach trees, apparently all had poultry and eggs, six produced molasses, seven cut cordwood, and three had built some fencing. Dick Green, long recognized as an expert sorghum maker, produced eighty gallons of molasses, the highest in that category. Owners managed a median of seven acres valued at forty dollars per farm.

In short, Pennytowners practiced communal cooperation in getting their work accomplished. Each family kept a "hog killing book" that had the dates and number of swine that each family intended to kill that fall. As the proper times approached Pennytowners gathered at each family's hog killing. Dogs guarded the smokehouses from intrusions of oppossums and other varmints. Throughout the year families accumulated woodpiles near their homes. During Christmas week the men of the hamlet traveled from house to house with axes, breaking up each woodpile into stove wood for the winter.

Residents built a community icehouse that they filled by hauling ice chopped from the Blackwater River. After this supply ran out they drove wagons to Marshall to purchase ice, covering it with blankets until they arrived home with what had not melted. In warm weather women spent a great deal of time hauling water. Women did laundry in the Davis hole of Blackwater River, using limbs of trees in Pennytown as clotheslines. Others filled water cans for home bathing and for watering the chickens. Although there were a few hand-dug wells, a small spring, and catchment-barrel cisterns that stored rainwater from the roofs of houses, the water supply never lasted into hot weather, and its volume never satisfied the needs of people and animals.

Men hunted and trapped small game; they used muzzle-loading shotguns and rifles, and, most commonly, clubs and dogs. Large game had long since disappeared, but squirrel, rabbit, raccoon, oppossum, and ground hogs provided meat for their families. They sold the pelts in Marshall. Fishing at Blackwater River, and occasionally at Salt Fork River, proved a regular duty and pastime. Men fished mostly at night since they had time then, using seines for larger harvests. They fished often, as they lacked refrigeration to keep the harvest; occasionally someone canned fish. Fishing continued as a year-round activity.

Pennytowners became expert gatherers. In season they collected large numbers of gooseberries, walnuts, and hazel and hickory nuts. Nearby woods provided mushrooms and wild greens—lamb's quarter, carpenter's square, wild tomato, lettuce, mustard, polk, dandelion, narrow dock, thistle, and more. Women stored dried fruit in paper bags and in stone jars; they protected some food in small cellars for long-term storage. Everyone raised chickens, and the more prosperous added ducks, geese, turkeys, and guinea fowl. Men traded work to white farmers in exchange for runt pigs. Some traded for males, others for females. After raising them to maturity, neighbors bred the swine and later divided the brood.

If some Missourians, like the Pennytowners, saw their lives remain relatively unchanged by the railroads, others found the railroads, and the transformation from a predominantly subsistence economy to an increasingly commercial economy, to be less than an unmitigated good. Indeed, the vagaries of the market meant for many Missourians a real or at least relative decline in their standard of living. Farmers, eager to reap large profits from distant markets for their goods, concentrated on producing ever-increasing amounts of a limited number of cash crops. But they found themselves in the quixotic position of receiving less and less for their efforts.

Even more than farmers in the generations before them, Missouri farmers of the period could neither control prices they received for their products nor the weather conditions that so importantly influenced their successes or failures. Farm prices generally declined after 1873. The price of corn, for example, went from sixty-seven cents per bushel in 1874 to twenty-four cents per bushel in 1875 and remained in the twenties and thirties for thirteen of the fifteen years between 1876 and 1890. Livestock prices varied in a similar fashion, ruled by the iron law of supply and demand because agriculture operated in a truly and increasingly competitive market. Despite the fact that Missouri agriculturists increased the acreage they farmed from slightly over nine million acres in 1870 to nearly seventeen million in 1880, the value of the products they produced actually declined from $103,035,759 in 1870 to $95,912,666 in 1880. Looking at figures such as these, farmers reasoned that something was terribly wrong; someone must have been to blame for their declining fortunes. Historian Floyd Shoemaker wrote, "The farmer's discontent was heightened when he saw how fortunes were being made in other enterprises."

In 1880, Boone County residents witnessed a graphic illustration of the agriculturists' relative decline when the 1,465-acre "Model Farm" of John Woods Harris, twelve miles northwest of Columbia, was divided and sold in an estate sale. Harris, who served on the State Board of Agriculture, had long been an innovator. He reportedly brought the first Alderney and Jersey cattle into the state, and his spacious farm had been designated "the model Missouri Farm" at the 1873 fair. According to the *Columbia Herald,* Harris's land was "much improved." Even so, "The prices realized were less than even those best acquainted with the depreciated value of lands in this section had been led to expect." One 355-acre plot, "the home tract," sold for $30.10 per acre; Harris had purchased it "10 or 30 years ago" for $37.50 per acre.

Not surprisingly, farmers expressed displeasure with their plight. One manifestation of the farmer's discontent was the formation of chapters of the Patrons of Husbandry, commonly referred to as the Grange. Initially begun as a social entity designed to instill variety and diversion into the somewhat drab and isolated lives of farmers, the national Grange turned increasingly in the 1870s to efforts designed to alleviate the economic woes of agriculturists.

The first Missouri Grange was established in 1870 by Oliver Hudson Kelley, a former United States Bureau of Agriculture employee who had come to the state at the request of Norman J. Colman. Although the Grange began slowly, by 1875 there were two thousand chapters in the state, the most granges established in any state. Ostensibly apolitical from the beginning, the Grange sought to organize farmers into buying and trading collectives that would allow them to barter with businessmen from positions of strength. Granges held local fairs, for example, where farmers could come and display their produce and sell it to area consumers without the cost of rail transport or middlemen. The fairs also drew manufacturers and distributors of agricultural implements, enabling farmers to deal directly with them. Grangers also tried holding Saturday auctions that would serve the same purpose.

Additionally, some Granges established cooperative, member-owned stores where goods could be purchased in quantity by owners and distributed at fair prices to all members. Cooperative stores were established in some of the communities where commercial agriculture was the strongest: Appleton City, New Palestine (Macon County), Montgomery City, Paris, La Grange, Otterville, Mason, and Boonville. The store at Otterville was particularly successful, at least for a short time. But the Grange was no match for the system it fought, and in 1890, when a history of the Farmer's Alliance was published, a preface by the editor of Missouri's *Journal of Agriculture* summed up Missouri farmers' views when he wrote:

> Commercial developments in the last quarter of a century have placed it so completely within the power of capitalists to obtain such absolute control of the purchase and sale of agricultural products, that the toiler, the creator of wealth has no voice whatever in controlling the market for his produce. This condition of affairs has transferred the profits wholly from the pockets of producers, and placed them in those of the capitalists. The result has been unparalleled increase in the wealth of the rich; and an equally unparalleled increase in the poverty of the poor.

Still, the emergence of a national market brought with it the desire to produce more at a continually reduced cost. In manufacturing and industry, as in agriculture, machines that could perform simple, repetitive jobs took the place of highly skilled artisans and craftsmen. Additionally, women and children were used increasingly to displace higher-paid, more highly skilled male workers. This was particularly true in the clothing, shoe, and tobacco industries. Census figures reveal that there were 8,592 manufacturing establishments reporting in Missouri in 1880 and that they employed 63,995 workers who received salaries totaling $24,309,716. Nearly 84 percent of those workers (954,200) were males above the age of sixteen. About 8.5 percent (5,474) were females above the age of fifteen, and 6.8 percent were children. The cost of materials used by these manufacturers was $110,798,392, with the value of finished products $165,386,205, or a value added of $5,458,781.

By 1890, those figures had changed substantially. In that year, there were 14,052 manufacturing establishments reporting with 143,139 workers who received salaries totaling $76,427,364. Again, nearly 84 percent (119,790) of those workers were males above the age of sixteen. But this time, 14.8 percent (19,858) of the workers were females above the age of fifteen. Indeed, the increase in the number of women working in factories had led the legislature to pass a law in 1885 that required factories "To provide and maintain suitable seats for the use of such female employees at or beside the counter or work bench where employed and to permit the usage of such seats by employees as may be reasonable for the preservation of their health." Despite the harshness of working conditions in the factories, some women clearly enjoyed the chance to be wage earners for the first time. In 1893, for example, the Bureau of Labor Statistics asked a number of women working in the manufacture of chewing and smoking tobacco if they preferred their present occupation to housework. Overwhelmingly, they said they did. One woman's response seemed to sum up the feelings of others: "At this occupation I am more independent than if doing house-work. I commence work at a certain hour and at a certain hour I quit. All the work is by the piece, and there is no fault-finding and scolding. My Sundays and evenings are my own. My services are appreciated, and my pay is according to the work done." By 1890, the number of children working in manufacturing had been reduced to 1.4 percent of the total labor force. The cost of materials used by manufacturers in 1890 was $177,582,382, with the value of products $324,561,993, for a value added of $146,979,551.

Perhaps the ultimate example of low-cost production of goods for a mass national market during this era came from the state of Missouri itself. Concerned since the 1830s with the expense of maintaining the state prison, governmental officials turned in the late 1870s to a scheme designed to force inmates to finance their own incarceration. Governor John S. Phelps best expressed the prevailing sentiment when he noted in his 1879 message to the General Assembly, "it would seem reasonable to expect the prisoners would not only be able, by their labor, to earn an amount sufficient to support themselves, but also to pay the salaries and wages of the officers and guards." Phelps's suggestion for accomplishing this goal was to have the state construct factories inside the prison, and then negotiate multiyear contracts for the use of convict labor. It was a suggestion that entrepreneurs welcomed with great delight.

Convict labor was used most profitably in the boot and shoe industry. Manufacturers could, with little capital investment, mass-produce footwear for distribution in the inter- and intrastate market while paying the state of Missouri only forty to fifty cents per day for the use of an inmate's labor. In the 1880s, shoemakers were averaging $11.50 per week for nine-and-a-half-hour days in private manufacturing establishments all over the state. So profitable for the businessmen was the prison-labor system that some of them moved their operations from other parts of the state, and even from out of state, to take advantage of it. The August Priesmeyer Company was a good example.

Priesmeyer, a native of Westphalia, Germany, came to Jefferson City from St. Louis in 1874. He had been in the shoe retail business in St. Louis for many years until he decided to manufacture shoes in the state capital with the help of convict labor. He began in the mid-1870s, using approximately 35 men. By century's end more than 250 men were involved, and the Priesmeyer Company employed 18 traveling salesmen operating primarily in the South and the West. In 1890, the Missouri Department of Labor Statistics reported that 516 convicts at the state penitentiary and 85 inmates at the St. Louis City Workhouse had been used to manufacture 532,000 pairs of shoes valued at $915,000.

Thus, the railroads, and the entrance into a national market that they encouraged and facilitated, dramatically changed the Missouri economy. But some communities that turned optimistically to the railroads later regretted doing so. St. Clair County was a case in point. In January 1870 a petition signed by 768 residents asked the court to issue bonds totaling $250,000 to the Clinton and Memphis branch of the Tebo and Neosho Railroad. Within five years the railroad company had gone bankrupt, and the railroad remained unbuilt. A fight over the redemption of the bonds, which continued until 1938, had begun. Residents of the county felt betrayed and resisted paying for a railroad that had never been built. No doubt many residents of the county shared promoter DeWitt Stone's sentiments when he reportedly said, "I wish to God I had never had anything to do with that railroad, and I would give all I am worth if I never had."

Significantly, the experience did not sour Stone's attitude toward all railroads, just the irresponsible, fraudulent ones. A contemporary writer summed up what he believed to be the pervading opinion when he wrote, "Even at this day could a railroad be constructed from this point to Kansas City the people of St. Clair County would be willing to pay the original amount of their subscription, but they are determined not to pay the demand of the bondholder if it costs years of litigation. Such a road would in itself add greatly to the taxable wealth of the county and aid materially in developing its resources; but to have given the money and have nothing at all for it is what makes the burden so grievous."

Things were not as Missourians thought they should be twenty-five years after the ending of the Civil War. All around them Missourians saw possibility and promise, and yet the possible seemed always to remain just out of reach and the promise to go unfulfilled. If one word could summarize the attitude of many Missourians by 1890, that word might well have been "confused." Why was prosperity so elusive? Why did traditional values of hard work, frugality, and sobriety often seem to count for so little? Who or what was to blame for such an unpredictable turn of events?

A growing number of Missourians must have felt like the person who signed his name "A Farmer" to an 1886 letter to the editor of the *Lawrence Chieftain*. He complained, "The farmer is looked down upon now days by the high toned just about the same as the Negro in time of slaves, and it is growing worse all the time." He asked for opportunity, not privilege: "All we want is to be put on equal footing so everybody will have the same chance." What would achieve such a result? The answer seemed to be organization and regulation. "A Farmer" blamed the government for allowing itself to be run by "the hands of the monopoly." The "death grip" of monopolists could be escaped only "if we organize like other classes do and stick together. . . . We farmers pay it all. Now if we can work together and regulate these things times will get better." It was a sentiment becoming more and more popular among Missourians as they entered the last decade of the nineteenth century.

CHAPTER III

SOCIAL AND CULTURAL CHANGE IN POST-RECONSTRUCTION MISSOURI

Missouri's increased exposure to the rest of the country during the 1870s and 1880s brought many social, cultural, and educational changes to the state. Society became more complicated. In a primarily agricultural, subsistence economy, training children for adulthood was a fairly straightforward process. Children spent little time receiving formal education and a great deal of time emulating the role models whose lives they would one day mirror: their parents. Little girls learned how to take care of babies by tending to the needs of young siblings. They helped their mothers plant and harvest gardens and preserve and prepare the produce; they learned how to clean house, do laundry, and make and mend clothing. They stirred hot kettles of lye soap and learned to weave baskets from the bark of freshly cut hickory saplings. Reading, writing, and arithmetic were fairly meaningless to them.

At the same time, little boys followed their fathers on daily rounds of chores and learned to care for livestock, plant and harvest crops, build fences and buildings, and hunt and trap. But the railroads, the increased reliance on a market economy, the flight from the farm, and increased urbanization and industrialization changed all that. More and more people ended up in jobs requiring skills that could no longer be learned at home. Clerks working in the stores of Missouri's burgeoning towns and villages had to know their three R's. Factory workers needed at least a modicum of training, which was greatly facilitated by formal education. Even farmers found that being able to read and to cipher decreased the chances of their being duped by unscrupulous entrepreneurs.

Still, revision of Missouri's public education law in 1874 reflected the sentiment for localism that would be enshrined in the new constitution of the next year. School districts were to be managed by locally elected, three-member boards. Each board member was to be elected annually. School boards were given great latitude in their control over schools.

They assumed control over school property and established rules and regulations for the school's internal operation, including the curriculum and all academic standards. Voters of each school district retained the power to determine the length of the school year and the rate and amount of taxes to be collected for the district. Such a disparate, uncoordinated, decentralized system made for a great variety of educational experiences throughout the state, in spite of efforts to the contrary by Missouri Superintendent of Education R. D. Shannon.

Indeed, great variety could occur even within a single county. Liberty Number Two school district was established in 1875 in the south-central portion of Cape Girardeau County. The school term was four months long throughout the 1870s, usually beginning after the harvest was completed near the end of October and ending in time for spring planting in early March. In spite of the four-month session, however, the average district pupil attended only twenty-one days, missing nearly one-fourth of the session. Nearby Liberty Number One school, however, which had a school session of the same length, saw its students attend classes nearly twice as often, but still miss almost half the session. Obviously, while many parents saw the establishment of schools as important enough to merit their payment of taxes, some still felt as though going to school was less important to the family than the work that needed to be done at home.

One result of the growing recognition of the need for more formal training was a tremendous expansion in the number of schools available and the number of students attending them. Missouri newspapers of the period were filled with comments about and celebrations of new community schoolhouses, such as this one offered by Thomas Callahan in the *Iron County Register* in 1881: "The building is an honor to Southeast Missouri, and compares very favorably with those at Salem and Rolla, and is such a great advance on anything hitherto attained in this district that Suggestion is silenced and Criticism disarmed." Historian Duane Meyer has written, "During the late 1870s an average of 250 school districts were organized each year in Missouri." Although the trend slowed somewhat in the 1880s and 1890s, far more children in Missouri had the opportunity to attend at least a grammar school. And more and more young people availed themselves of the opportunity. Census figures reveal that in 1870, less than half of Missouri's school-age population (46 percent) was attending school. By 1880 that figure had leaped to

65 percent. By 1890, almost 571,000 Missouri children were enrolled in schools, nearly 25,000 of them African American children in racially segregated schools. By the century's end more than three-fourths (76 percent) of the state's school-age children were attending school.

Often the schools were still somewhat primitive, especially in the rural areas. Few schools could afford books, paper, or pencils for all students, so learning was still by rote. One-room schoolhouses were common with a single teacher hired to instruct students who might range in age from six to twenty. Often teachers were barely as old as their students, and sometimes they were even younger. Often, also, especially in rural areas, teachers were forced to serve as janitors or the supervisors of student/janitors whose help they could enlist or coerce. Coal or wood had to be carried in during cold months and water had to be brought in from a spring, stream, or cistern nearby. The cleanliness of the schoolhouse was the teacher's responsibility as well. One Dent County resident remembered his schoolhouse of the mid-1870s as follows:

> The seats were about 16 feet in length, were of split logs and excepting two, were mounted on large flat logs for legs. The two which had legs of their own were called "Old Slabsides" and "Racer." "Old Slabsides" was made of a twisting log which made a sort of back for the pupils at one end. On the other end it was difficult for the pupils to keep from sliding off while studying their lessons. When ice covered the slope west of the house the seats were used as toboggans or sleds by the pupils. "Racer" was level and slick and always won the races with "Old Slabsides."

A visitor to a Moniteau County school in 1877 described the schoolroom furniture as "the most outlandish of any we have seen for twenty years. Old slab benches still remain in the house and furnish the only seat for the teacher to occupy." More money did become available for public schools in the state after an 1887 statute changed the percentage of the state budget devoted to education from one-fourth to one-third.

Another consequence of the increased attention given to public education in the state was an increased concern for uniformity of standards and improved quality of education. The Missouri State Teacher's Association (MSTA) began to push for a lengthened school term in the mid-1870s. In 1877 the law was changed to provide for a public school term of five months. This law was designed to improve upon situations such as the one that existed in 1875 in Dent County, where the average number of days students went to school was only thirty-eight. The school year was lengthened by two more months in 1889.

The most cosmopolitan and "interconnected" of Missouri's cities, St. Louis, had, not surprisingly, the most elaborate and extensive educational system during the 1870s and 1880s. St. Louis reached the peak of its national influence as Americans gathered to celebrate the one hundredth anniversary of the Declaration of Independence in 1876. Fourth in population among America's cities in the 1870s, St. Louis hoped that it would soon replace Washington, D.C., as the federal capital.

A city with such an exalted self-image, and such ambitious hopes, required an educational system that would promote knowledge and training as vehicles for progress. Not coincidentally, St. Louis began the process of greatly expanding the time children spent in school and in formalizing the experiences they encountered while they were there. Perhaps the most innovative, and most controversial, of these changes involved starting youngsters in school at an age that most Missourians had theretofore assumed was unnecessary. This was the beginning of the kindergarten movement.

Private kindergartens had begun in Europe in the 1830s and had come to St. Louis in the 1850s. But it was not until 1873 that St. Louis Superintendent of Schools William Torrey Harris and Susan Elizabeth Blow were able to establish the state's first publicly supported kindergarten. From the beginning, children from the city's slums were Harris's and Blow's target, since it was believed that they were particularly susceptible to lives of crime and waste.

The kindergarten program began tentatively enough in 1873 with Susan Blow as the teacher, assisted by three unpaid helpers, teaching an experimental group of sixty-eight students. Support for the notion of the public financing of a kindergarten was by no means unanimous and, indeed, in the early years the St. Louis school board was frequently urged to close down the program to save money. In 1875, however, support for the program was reflected in a petition to the board signed by fifteen hundred city residents and by letters to the *St. Louis Globe-Democrat,* such as one that stated, "So thorough and efficient had been the work so far, that the children who, six months ago, were timid, untutored and probably in some instances 'unwashed,' now present a tidy, brightened, cultured appearance far beyond their years."

So eager were parents to take advantage of the kindergarten that the board found it impossible to continue financing its unrestrained expansion. During the 1876–1877 school year the board began collecting a fee of one dollar per quarter from students whose families could afford to pay. Forty percent of the students enrolled during that year were admitted free. By 1878 the kindergarten had proved its worth to the board, which ended its experimental status, along with the fee, and made the kindergarten a formal, permanent part of the public school system. By 1880, the kindergarten had grown to a total of 7,828 students taught by 166 teachers and 60 unpaid assistants. The next year the program again grew dramatically when kindergarten opportunities extended to the city's black children, who attended segregated schools.

Another change that occurred was that more emphasis was placed on postgrammar school eduction than ever before. At the outbreak of the Civil War, only St. Louis had a public high school system. By 1870, high schools had spread to the major metropolitan areas. But over the course of the next twenty years, thirty-some Missouri towns developed full four-year high schools and more than one hundred towns developed two- or three-year high schools.

The Jefferson City public school system graduated its first class from a four-year high school on June 24, 1875, amid a great bit of fanfare for the three students who had completed the course of study. But the continuation of the program was destined to be short-lived. The value of a high school education was highly controversial in a town the size of Jefferson City in the 1870s; the question of whether it should be publicly supported was even more problematic. Not everyone in the city agreed with the newspaper editor who wrote in 1875 that "our High School is as much a part of the school, a necessary part, as the doxology is of divine services, as a roof is of a house." Even a prominent former president of the board of education, Judge Arnold Krekel, admitted to ambivalence when, addressing a meeting of the State Teachers Association in December 1874, he said the way in which a high school "should be connected with our public schools is a matter of grave inquiry."

When the school year began in Jefferson City in the fall of 1875 there were only fifteen high school students enrolled. By year's end, the number had fallen to four. In September of 1876, School Superintendent F. A. Nitchy issued a report in which he wrote, "High School classes with classical or scientific course for one, two or more years should not be maintained . . . [There is] not sufficient number of scholars to justify expense. The course of study in our High School must be confined to one year, one grade or class."

A decade passed before another commencement was held for a graduating class of Jefferson City High School students. In 1884 a report on the status of the high school was included in a report on school conditions:

> A high school organization has been effected. . . . The course of study is not yet what we desire but before we can have a symmetrical system of classes, the schools must grow towards it, and this requires time. There are three years in the course. The juniors have arithmetic, grammar, history, algebra, with spelling and writing. The middle class has advanced arithmetic, grammar, history, algebra, with spelling and writing. The senior class has English literature, modern history, geometry, algebra, and they will finish the year with civil government and higher arithmetic. German and Latin are optional studies. The conditions are all favorable for splendid work in the high school this year. The graduating class has 23 members, with scarcely an exception, capable young students.

The graduating class was reduced to fifteen by commencement time the next year. But from 1885 on there would at least be a graduating class. Although a debate raged again near the century's end over whether or not the city could afford the luxury of a high school, the high school was destined to stay.

Hannibal High School graduated its first student in 1873, but lack of community support closed the school in 1877. It reopened in 1881. High school programs were especially slow to develop in Missouri's Bootheel. As regional historian Robert Sidney Douglass has written, "Up till about 1895, very little attention was paid to public high schools; they were practically unknown."

Not every child who attended school during these years, of course, attended public schools. Most of the state's private colleges maintained an academy where students could obtain an education during the late nineteenth and early twentieth centuries. In addition, many religious denominations established their own schools for the orthodox instruction of their members' children. In September of 1883, for example, the School Sisters of Notre Dame established a parochial school in the small Osage County community of Rich Fountain. The School Sisters of Notre Dame were members of a Catholic teaching order that had been founded in Bavaria in 1833. Students in the Rich Fountain school, themselves of Bavarian ancestry, numbered forty-five in 1883, although the numbers fluctuated greatly with the demands of rural farm life. An 1886 cholera epidemic in the community also had a negative effect on attendance.

In nearby Linn, the county seat of Osage County, four Notre Dame sisters established a school also in 1883. The nuns taught forty-eight children the first year, four of whom boarded at the combination convent and school. This building, a two-story structure measuring forty-eight feet by forty-two feet, had been completed earlier in 1883 at a cost of $4,500.

Public schools in Missouri were racially segregated by the 1875 Constitution. Missouri law required school districts to establish separate school facilities for black children when the number of African American school-age children reached fifteen. Black schools named either for the slain sixteenth president of the United States or for famous black leaders sprang up all over the state. Schools named for Frederick Douglass, the black abolitionist and civil rights activist, were especially popular. Hannibal, Missouri, residents built a Douglass School in the mid-1880s with money raised by an 1884 bond issue. The school cost $8,856 and consisted of eight rooms. Columbia, Missouri, also had a Douglass School. Not long after Frederick Douglass's death in 1895, African Americans in the northwest Missouri town of Maryville gave their school, which served approximately thirty students, the name "Douglass."

African American students who wished to attend school beyond the eighth grade in Missouri had very limited choices during the 1870s and 1880s. When Sumner High School opened in downtown St. Louis in 1875, it was the only black high school west of the Mississippi River. Lincoln Institute in Jefferson City became a state-supported normal school during the 1870s and, as such, became the major provider of black teachers for the state's segregated schools. A preparatory department provided high school–level courses for students, and in 1887 a college department was added that provided black Missourians with their first opportunity for higher education in the state.

The person who most shaped education at Lincoln Institute during the 1880s was Inman E. Page, who was born a slave in Virginia in 1852.

Page's family moved to Washington, D.C., sometime before the Civil War. There he was educated in private schools and at Howard University. He also attended Brown University in Rhode Island. Page came to Lincoln in 1878 as an assistant to white principal Henry M. Smith. Indeed, as the historian of Lincoln University, W. Sherman Savage, points out: "Page was the only Negro on a faculty completely manned by white teachers." In 1880 Page became the first African American to be named president of the school. One of Page's first priorities was to replace all of the white teachers with black teachers, bowing to the commonly held notion that black parents and students preferred black teachers over white. One of the first black teachers Page hired was Josephine A. Silone, a native of New York who was educated at the famous Philadelphia Institute for Colored Youth and the Rhode Island State Normal School. She taught "Chemistry, Elocution and English Literature" and served as an adviser to women. In 1889 she married W. W. Yates, a school principal in Kansas City, and, as Josephine Silone Yates, she gained notoriety as a writer in such publications as *Southern Workman, Voice of the Negro, Woman's Era,* the Indianapolis *Freeman* and the Kansas City *Rising Son.* In 1901 Yates was elected to the presidency of the National Association of Colored Women; she held that position until 1906.

White women who sought higher education opportunities during the last quarter of the nineteenth century had more options than black women. The University of Missouri admitted its first woman student in 1868, and the state's normal schools accepted women. Phoebe Wilson Couzins and Lemma Barkeloo entered St. Louis Law School in 1869. Miss C. C. Smith was among the first class of students admitted to the Missouri School of Mines and Metallurgy at Rolla when it opened in 1871. Florence E. Whiting was the first woman to complete the course of study at Rolla, but, as historian Lawrence O. Christensen has pointed out, "Despite her academic performance, Whiting failed to earn a degree. . . . Instead, she received a certificate of proficiency, a designation reserved for special students or those not enrolled in the 'regular engineering course.'" Women such as Whiting endured such discriminatory treatment in exchange for educational opportunity. Ironically, the School of Mines might not have survived its first quarter century had it not been for its tuition-paying female students. The school struggled especially during the mid-1870s when an economic depression and a decline in legislative funding saw the student enrollment drop from

101 in 1875 to 66 in 1876. Women were heavily recruited to make up the shortfall.

Women and men had a growing array of choices among higher-education institutions in the state by the late 1880s. In 1889 there were 580 students enrolled at the state university in Columbia and another 1,605 studying at the three state normal schools in Kirksville, Warrensburg, and Cape Girardeau, more than half (52 percent) of them women. In addition, there were fifteen private colleges in the state with 200 or more students, seven of which admitted women.

The education of Missouri's juvenile delinquents became a matter of some concern also during the late 1880s. In 1887 the state legislature authorized the building of a reform school for boys on a 168-acre tract of land at the eastern edge of the city of Boonville. The law specified that boys between the ages of ten and sixteen could be sent there and, while there, they were to be given "physical, intellectual and moral training." Superintendent Lyman R. Drake reported that seventy boys were in residence at the facility by the end of the first year. By 1891, the school's enrollment doubled.

A state reform school for delinquent girls was also opened in 1889. Erected just outside of Chillicothe, Missouri, the school was to be "conducted on the family or cottage plan" and was to be a place "where girls from seven to seventeen years of age, removed from vicious associates and evil influences, may receive a careful, physical, intellectual, and moral training, and such non-sectarian religious instruction as may be prescribed by the Superintendent; participate in the enjoyment of a true home life; be reformed and become good domestic women, prudent in speech and conduct, cleanly, industrious and capable housekeepers." By the end of 1890, Superintendent Emma Gilbert reported, the Chillicothe facility had only eleven residents. Gilbert attributed the small number of girls being sent to her school to "an idea that is very ancient . . . that a girl or a woman that has once gone wrong can never be redeemed."

Schools provided more than educational opportunities for the students who attended them: they also provided opportunities for social interaction as well. One of the most important social events of any year was the "Closing of School Program." It was a chance for teachers to show what they had taught, for students to show what they had learned, and for parents and friends to enjoy both. Such was the case, for example, with the "Annual Examinations" held at the Cooper Institute in Boonville in June of 1878. According to the *Boonville Weekly Advertiser,* the examinations were to continue for three days with the public invited. Likewise, in 1886 the same newspaper reported on a "Public School Closing Exercise" with the following comment: "The annual recurrence of school exhibitions, examinations and closing exercises always presents new features of interest to the visitors eye. Of course, there is always a crowd of eager, expectant scholars and anxious parents, decorated rooms and showy exercises." The exercises included a musical presentation, a recitation, the reading of an essay, and a debate on the topic "That women ought to be allowed to vote."

In Edina the local paper reported on February 19, 1875, that the Canada Baker school had recently closed and that an end-of-session exhibition had been held before a "house . . . crowded with spectators." The exhibition consisted of a variety of performances by individuals and groups. The local newspaper concluded, "Those in attendance pronounced the exhibition a success, and say that credit is due the teacher, Mr. Perry Halloway, for the manner in which he has conducted the school." In June of 1875 the Jefferson City public school arrived at a unique closing exercise: it issued a challenge to members of the constitutional convention, gathered in the state's capital since the previous month, "to cross swords in the spelling arena at the corner of High and Madison." An admission fee of ten cents was charged spectators, who were also treated to "strawberries and ice cream in abundance." Twelve school children defeated twelve "Con Coners" before a large audience. In 1888 in Lawrence County, Miss Sadie Brayshaw closed her school in February after "a successful term of five months." Declamations and dialogues dominated the exhibition, providing, as one school official noted, "the board of directors and public in general the opportunity of assembling . . . in order to witness and judge for themselves, as to the manner in which the school has been conducted."

Debating societies for adults were very common during the 1870s and 1880s; their activities provided "home grown" entertainment for participants and spectators alike. In 1886, the Mount Vernon newspaper invited the public to a Saturday night debate at schoolhouse Number 7, "near T. B. Turk's," where Joseph Owens and T. B. Turk would debate the following popular political question: "Resolved that high protective tariff is [in] the best interest to American people."

Often local communities had dramatic clubs and bands. In Edina on March 19, 1875, the town's Cornet Band celebrated the coming of spring with a concert of "some very choice music" on the courthouse square. Three weeks later, the Kirksville Dramatic Association entertained Edina residents with a performance of *Hamlet* in the public school hall. In Jefferson City, the Evening Star Quartet, a group of African American musicians, played and sang nearly every Saturday night for white audiences at the Madison Hotel.

Entertainment changed greatly once access to the railroads increased. Sometimes the railroads took people to new forms of entertainment, or to new places to enjoy old forms of entertainment. Historian Richard West Sellars has pointed out that as railroads made remote areas of the state accessible to urban dwellers, sportsmen and vacationers from St. Louis and Kansas City as well as from out-of-state areas began penetrating scattered parts of Missouri. The Missouri Pacific Railroad, for example, promoted the area around El Dorado Springs as an area to be used by Kansas Citians who wanted to enjoy the bucolic beauty of rural Missouri. John Canon O'Hanlon wrote in 1890, "Excursion parties by train [into the Ozarks] are now all the rage in St. Louis." During the mid-1880s, the Nashville, Chattanooga, and St. Louis Railroad arranged to bring a group of Nashville businessmen into southeast Missouri for a "deadly raid" on game.

Sometimes the railroads brought new entertainment to people, especially with the emergence and growth of railroad-spawned towns. Towns such as Boonville, which was on both the Missouri River and the M.K.T. Railroad, had far more entertainment possibilities than did more remote rural communities. Boonville's Thespian Hall regularly played host to such diverse entertainers in the 1870s and 1880s as "Prof. Hart, magician," the Oakes Elite Concert and Specialty Company, the New Orleans Minstrels, the Chicago Theatre Company, the Julia A. Hunt Theatre Company, Billy Rice and Hooley Minstrels, and many, many others.

Often, however, the entertainment was not open to everyone in the same way. A mid-1870s incident in the capital city graphically illustrated this point. In February 1874 a Lincoln Institute instructor named Lizzie Lindsey and several of her students attempted to attend a literary reading by Mrs. Scott Siddons. They had purchased reserved-seat tickets in advance, but upon presenting those tickets at the door, they were told that they could not sit in the reserved section but would have to "take the seats in the gallery, which were provided for colored people."

Lindsey and her students refused to move to the gallery; hence, they were denied admission to the theater. Soon thereafter, Miss Lindsey addressed a letter to the editor of the local *Daily State Journal* and summarized her case against local social standards when she wrote: "These were students thirsting for knowledge, and hearing that Mrs. Siddons' readings were worth attending, they went for the purpose of gaining instruction, yet were subjected to insult merely on account of their color. The cry is heard from the Lakes to the Gulf, from the Orient to the Occident, educate the colored people: and how are they to be educated advantageously if colored teachers, students and persons of culture and intellect are insulted and outraged by those who *consider* themselves their superiors?"

The great irony of this situation was that whites in Jefferson City often turned to black Lincoln Institute for social entertainment and cultural enlightenment. This irony was not lost on the *Journal* editor, who commented in 1877, "It seems incredible, but it is none the less a fact that must be admitted, that the dependence of Jefferson City, the capital of the old slave state of Missouri, for literary entertainments, is Lincoln Institute."

The fondness of whites for black entertainment was part of the fiber of late-nineteenth-century Missouri, indeed, of late-nineteenth-century America. One of the most popular black musicians of the period was John William "Blind" Boone. Boone was born in 1864, the son of a former slave named Rachel who had fled to the safety of a military encampment at Miami, Missouri. His father was a soldier of the Seventh Missouri Militia. Soon after young Boone's birth his mother moved to Warrensburg and found work as a domestic. At six months of age the baby contracted "brain fever." A local doctor persuaded Rachel Boone that the only way to save her child's life was to remove his eyes. The operation was performed and the baby lived, sightless.

Warrensburg provided little opportunity for education or training for a blind child, so at age nine John was sent by his mother to St. Louis to attend the Missouri School for the Blind. Except for a very limited exposure to piano classes, John's time at the School for the Blind was quite unpleasant. He disliked the regimen of formal education and he found himself, as one of only a few blacks in the school, to be the victim of constant racial jibes and comments. He sought escape and solace in the saloons and dives of the "tenderloin district." Eventually his truancy resulted in his expulsion from the School for the Blind, and John finally found his way back to Warrensburg. For some time thereafter he wandered alone around central Missouri playing in, among other places, churches whose ministers promised him board in return for his performances. Eventually Blind Boone was "discovered" by a black Columbia contractor named John Lange and another black blind musician of the period named "Blind" Tom Bethune. With Blind Tom's encouragement, and John Lange's financial backing, Blind Boone began touring Missouri playing concert halls and churches all over the state.

Another black group that toured Missouri to sellout crowds during this period was the Jubilee Singers of Fisk University in Tennessee. The *Boonville Weekly Advertiser* reported on a concert by the singers in 1882 as follows: "The Jubilee Singers, all colored, drew a large house at their concert here last week and will be able to draw a crowded house if they ever visit this city again. Their opening piece was the chanting of the Lord's prayer, which held the house spellbound. You could have heard a pin drop; the double quartette chanted it so low and solemnly that it filled the audience with reverence and the most undivided attention was given. . . . Everybody enjoyed it and will be glad to see them back again."

That the performance by blacks before a white audience did not mean any lessening of social distance between the races was tellingly revealed by the following comment in the *Advertiser's* coverage of the Jubilee Singers: "The troupe seemed to know and appreciate their place socially and acted in a most becoming and respectful manner towards the cultivated and refined audience which sat before them."

Baseball was a popular warm-weather diversion both for the men who played it and the women who watched them. Baseball during the 1870s and 1880s was as much an adult game as it was a child's. Grown men formed town and community baseball clubs and issued challenges to teams from other towns, as was the case with the "Bethany Blues" in 1881 when they issued a newspaper challenge to "any club in Harrison County." Towns that had a large enough population could field two or more teams that engaged in "match games." In Boonville in June of 1882 the Boonville White Stockings defeated the Eclipse by the lopsided score of 57–10. According to the article that reported the game, the ball grounds were under the management of the White Stocking Club, "and some valuable improvements are being made. Seats are being arranged with covering over them to protect spectators from the sun. Tickets will be issued which will be good for the entire season, at the small cost of 50 cts., boys 25 cts., for sale by members of the club. Arrangements are being made for quite a number of games which will be played along during the summer all of which will no doubt prove of interest to lovers of the national game."

Professional baseball came to Missouri in the form of the St. Louis Brown Stockings in 1874. The next year, on May 6, 1875, ten thousand fans turned out to watch their club beat the Chicago White Stockings by a score of 10–0. The *St. Louis Republican* boasted, "Time was when Chicago had an excellent baseball club, the best in the West, but that was before St. Louis decided to make an appearance on the diamond field and there, as everywhere else, attested her supremacy."

When the National League was formed in 1876, St. Louis's Browns joined teams from Chicago, Cincinnati, Philadelphia, Boston, Brooklyn, Louisville, and Hartford. St. Louis lost its team in the late 1870s, and then baseball returned in 1882, when a new league, the American Association, was formed. Chris Von der Ahe, a saloon keeper whose business was near the ballpark on Grand Avenue, was one of the franchise owners. With Von der Ahe's financial support, and with the playing ability and managing skills of Charles Comiskey, the Browns won four successive pennants from 1885 through 1888. In 1886, led by Bob Caruthers, who was the team's pitching ace and batted .334 in 1886, and third baseman Arlie Latham, the Browns won the world championship. The final game of the series, played before a crowd of ten thousand, was a come-from-behind clutch effort keyed by Latham.

Baseball, like so much else of late-nineteenth-century Missouri social life, was racially segregated. At Edina in 1875, the Sampsons, "a colored baseball club of Newark," traveled to Edina to play the local black team, the "Blackhawks." Unfortunately, according to a local paper, the game had barely begun when a fight erupted between the two teams "which busted the game 'higher than a kite.'"

Horse racing remained a popular amusement in Missouri during the 1870s and 1880s. Racing clubs in St. Louis during that era included the St. Louis Jockey Club (organized in 1877) and its successor the Cote

Brilliante Club, and the Gentleman's Driving Club (1881). Horse racing was a featured attraction at the annual St. Louis fair, where crowds of fifteen thousand or more looked on. The annual fair at Ridgeway in 1882 featured horse racing as a major attraction. In 1882, also, the Lawrence County Fair in southwest Missouri featured races by the "fastest horses" of the southwest. In the southeast Missouri town of Kennett in 1890, the local paper described the large crowd that had come to the small town to witness a horse race and summarized the views of the spectators by writing that it had been "a 'L' of a race."

Fourth of July festivities were common community celebrations that often lasted an entire day. Work was suspended so that area residents could travel to a nearby gathering place, often the county seat, to visit with friends, hear patriotic orations, and indulge in generous portions of food and drink. In Jefferson City, according to reminiscences of Julius H. Conrath, born in the capital in 1863, the Fourth of July was always a big event and a parade was always formed: "In a large red and gold bandwagon rode some of the participants, dressed in Continental uniforms, and they were followed by wagons and carriages decorated with flags and bunting; then followed men on horseback and afoot to some meeting place where patriotic speeches were made. In this parade the fire company took a leading part. The day was always ushered in with a salute from the old Mexican guns in the capitol grounds, and at night there was a display of fireworks."

The *Kennett Clipper* reported in 1888 that a Fourth of July celebration held in that Dunklin County town had been a "grand success": "About 1200 people assembled at Wrights grove early in the morning and proceeded to enjoy themselves each after their own fashion. While the young folks tipped the light fantastic toe, others old and young seemed to enjoy themselves hugely on the different swings. At noon all partook of a bounteous dinner. After dinner speeches were made by H. N. Phillips, R. M. Finney, and W. D. Penny." Often Fourth of July celebrations were times when local politicians could appear before large audiences and promote their political fortunes. On July 4, 1890, the *Boonville Weekly Advertiser* reported that "bills are out for a grand picnic at Hedge's Pasture, near Clifton . . . to which county candidates from Cooper and Pettis counties are invited."

Perhaps the most elaborately celebrated Fourth of July commemorations came in 1876, on the centennial observance of the signing of the Declaration of Independence. In Boonville, a torchlight procession on the night of July 3 touched off a twenty-four-hour celebration that included a recitation of a commemorative poem written by a local lawyer, Horace A. Hutchison, and a lengthy oration by Colonel John Cosgrove.

Missouri blacks often chose to celebrate Independence Day on August 4 instead of July 4, in commemoration of black independence in the West Indies. In 1890 the *Boonville Weekly Advertiser* reported on one such celebration as follows: "There was an immense crowd of colored people in town on Mon., the 4th of August. They had a picnic near town during the day, and at night indulged in festivities at the Thespian Hall until a late hour." In Osage County, blacks traveled by special train from as far away as St. Louis and by ferryboat from across the Missouri River to attend the "Colored Picnics" on August 4 at Chamois. Eating, drinking, and dancing lasted all day and through much of the night, with large crowds of whites gathered around the perimeter of the celebration as curious onlookers. Blacks in Wright County's Hartville celebrated similarly.

Closely related to Fourth of July celebrations were community gatherings to commemorate political victories. Indeed, politics provided entertainment in a way that Missourians born since the advent of radio and television might find difficult to comprehend. In 1884, for example, the Democrats of Bowers Mills in Lawrence County gathered to celebrate the nomination of Grover Cleveland and Thomas A. Hendricks to the offices of president and vice president respectively. The announcement of the event came by means of a horseman "dressed in a starbangeled [*sic*] banner suit with a bugle hung around his neck" who rode about the county distributing handbills. The celebration attracted a crowd of five hundred people, who were entertained with a seventy-five-minute oration delivered by the Honorable A. L. Thomas.

The coming to town of a circus was always a welcome event for young and old alike. In June of 1881 the *Bethany Republican* excitedly reported that a new circus had come to town: "The New Great Pacific made its grand *entree* in Bethany last Thursday, and it was greeted by expectant thousands. The show was by far the best of the kind ever exhibited in this city. The street parade, with its large and glittering train, 3 bands and steam piano, was a glorious spectacle, while the arenic attractions were novel and varied." In May of 1882, the Mount Vernon newspaper advertised that James T. Johnson's "World Renowned Circus," featuring thirty acrobats, gymnasts and athletes, four clowns, and "troupes of the best educated animals ever placed before the public," was in town. The "Great Forepaugh's Circus" appeared in Boonville in September 1878 and was described by the *Weekly Advertiser* as being a performance "as good, if not better, than any that travels." The five trained elephants, the newspaper assured its readers, were "without a doubt, the best in America and probably in the world."

One macabre form of entertainment for rural and small-town Missouri was the public hanging. Often people came from miles around to witness the grisly proceedings. Hangings were community events, even community catharses. On April 21, 1883, the *Rolla Weekly Herald* reported on the hanging of George Bohannon, who had been found guilty of murdering William Light. Bohannon's execution took place "in the presence of an immense concourse of people." The *Herald* estimated the crowd at three thousand spectators. The day was commemorated by a proclamation issued by Rolla Mayor W. C. Pomeroy, who ordered "that the First National Bank be closed, that saloons be closed, and that schools be turned out. Peanut hucksters on the scene did a thriving business. Rolla's streets were deserted."

In Mount Vernon, in Lawrence County, in May of 1877, the county executed a man named Sam Orr. A large crowd began to gather in town the evening before the event. "Early next morning," the local newspaper reported, "people could be seen coming in by droves from this and adjoining counties, until 4,000 were present to witness the execution."

One of the most gruesome of the era's hangings occurred in Cooper County in 1879. John Isaac West of Illinois was arrested near Arrow Rock for the murder of a man near Pilot Grove. West admitted killing the man but contended that he had acted in self-defense. Eventually West was found guilty and sentenced to be hanged in a trial moved to Boonville because of lynching threats.

West tried unsuccessfully to escape in March of 1879, two months before his scheduled execution. Following his unsuccessful escape attempt, West began to seek publicity about himself and his case. By the time the execution date approached, West had become something of a local celebrity. A large crowd gathered on the eve of the execution. The next morning, the atmosphere and theatrics surrounding the execution included a long speech by West, who admitted his guilt and expressed regret at his actions: "I chose darkness rather than light and this is my end. I trust to almighty God that it may be to you a warning. . . . The leaves are putting out, the flowers are blooming, everything is bright, but I must go." The execution finally occurred in front of a crowd estimated at six thousand, many of whom had brought with them picnic lunches for the festival-like occasion.

An even larger crowd gathered to watch the hanging of Edward F. Clum in Barry County in 1887. According to the *Lawrence Chieftain,* southwest Missourians numbering seven thousand traveled as far as fifty miles to witness the execution. Before climbing the scaffold, Clum listened to a rendition of "Nearer My God to Thee." From the scaffold, with a rope around his neck, Clum told the assembled crowd, "nearly one-third . . . women and children," that he was guilty of the double murder of which he was accused and that he was ready to die for his crime. His last words were, "Friends of earth, farewell, I'm going to Jesus; come and meet me. Farewell."

Religion, of course, continued to play a socializing and supporting role for masses of Missourians. Indeed, although statistics on church membership and other indices of religious involvement are difficult to ascertain for the period preceding 1890, it seems likely that many people whose uncertain lives were further destabilized by the rapid changes of the 1870s and 1880s turned more and more to religion. According to Bureau of the Census figures for 1890, Missouri had 8,064 religious bodies in the state worshiping in 6,121 edifices. There were 735,839 church members in the state, which represented slightly more than one-fourth (27.47 percent) of the state's total population. There were more congregations of Methodists (2,412) in Missouri than of any other denomination; 1,230 of the congregations were Methodist Episcopal, South churches. There were 2,355 Baptist congregations, with Southern Baptists being the most dominant (1,636). Missouri's African American Baptists organized their own state convention during a gathering at the Second Baptist Church of Chillicothe on October 8, 1888. The Reverend J. J. Caston was elected the group's first president and served in that position for thirty-four years. Presbyterian congregations outnumbered Roman Catholic groups 776 to 442.

Religious revivals known as "tent meetings" were common in the 1870s, 1880s, and 1890s. Itinerant preachers such as the Reverend Enoch Hunt of the M. E. Church in Henry County drew crowds wherever they preached. Sometimes the "tent" was nothing more than a brush arbor designed to deflect the hot summer sun's rays. Revivals often went on for days, requiring tents to be fitted with furniture and cooking utensils and sometimes sending revivalists back to their farms for additional supplies.

Churches often resorted to socials as a way of raising money. In February of 1875 the Friendship Sunday School of Pierce City sponsored a musical program, festival, and oyster supper in an effort to raise money for its Sunday school classes. On February 15, 1881, a "grand vocal and instrumental concert" was held at the Prairie Chapel, six and one-half miles east of Bethany. The ten cents admission charged for the concert was collected in the hope of paying for the church organ. In 1882, the Boonville M. E. Church held an International Tea Party at Thespian Hall. According to a local newspaper, "The Thespian Hall was literally metamorphosed from a public hall into a bazaar of nations and one could readily imagine themselves [sic] on a miniature tour of the world." The event earned two hundred dollars for the church. Often entertainment for church socials came from a distance, as was the case when Mr. and Mrs. John Petit of Chicago gave a "grand concert" at the old Baptist Church in Boonville in March of 1890. The concert, described by a newspaper as "the musical event of the season," was held to finance the installation of a new pipe organ in the church.

Supplementing the schools and churches as places of entertainment and social interaction were fraternal and sisterhood organizations such as the Masons, the Ancient Order of United Workmen, the Daughters of Jericho, and a host of others. In addition, groups such as these provided burial insurance for members and their families and financial assistance for widows and orphans. In 1890, for example, the Ancient Order of United Workmen boasted that there were 450 lodges in the state with membership of nearly twenty-five thousand. Over the course of two decades, United Workmen spokesmen claimed, the organization had paid out more than $5 million in benefits.

Ethnic groups also came together for social interaction and celebration. Among the most prominent of such late-nineteenth-century groups was the Turn Vereins, whose roots extended back to the antebellum period when German immigration to America began in earnest. In Boonville, Missouri, for decades after the Civil War, the "Turners," as they were called, held monthly entertainments in Thespian Hall. According to historian Robert L. Dyer, these gatherings, called "Kraenzchens," included "gymnastic exhibitions, music and recitations, and closed with a dance." During the mid-1890s, the Boonville Turners purchased an old Baptist Church on Vine Street, renamed it "Turner Hall," and continued their social gatherings, including the dances.

As historian Floyd Shoemaker has written, "the 1870s ushered in the golden years of the theater in Missouri." The railroad played a critical role in making it easier for traveling groups to arrive at their destination. A number of new theaters were erected in St. Louis during the 1870s and 1880s, including Pope's Theater, the Pickwick Theater, the Grand Opera House, Haulin's Theater, and the Standard Theater. St. Louis also got its first symphony orchestra in 1880 when Joseph Otten, a twenty-eight-year-old German organist, led an effort to found the St. Louis Choral Society, the precursor of the modern St. Louis Symphony Orchestra.

In Kansas City, the Gillis Theatre opened in 1883, the Ninth-Street Theater in 1887, and the Warder Grand Opera House in 1883. The Tootle Opera House brought many famous stars and productions to St. Joseph after its opening in 1873. Smaller towns and cities also featured opera houses in which were presented "lectures, traveling shows, stock companies, dances, and just about any form of community entertainment." In Hannibal the Park Theatre and Opera House was built in 1882 and opened with the production of a play entitled "Hazel and Kirk." It had a stage sixty-five feet long and forty-five feet deep and seated eleven hundred people. Hannibal's Mozart Hall, constructed during the early 1870s, featured a roller skating exhibition in 1877. As local historians J. Hurley and Roberta Hagood point out, Hannibal's location as a railroad center between Chicago and St. Louis and between Chicago and Kansas City made it "a convenient stop-over for troupes traveling by train" and "a favorite place for entertainers." Jefferson City's Lohman Opera House opened on October 5, 1886, with a performance by Patti Rosa. Columbia had the Haden Opera House (1884), described by historian John Crighton as "The center of Columbia's cultural life. . . . Here during the season was staged a wide variety of entertainment features, including musical comedies, vaudeville, drama, music recitals, university commencement programs, and fraternity dances." Clinton (1877), Richmond (1880), and California (1884) had similar facilities. Thespian Hall, built in Boonville prior to the Civil War, enjoyed great success during the "golden years" of the 1870s. One of the frequent performers on its stage was George T. Ferrel, a local newspaper man widely referred to as the "Poet Laureate of Missouri." Ferrel's first statewide recognition as a poet and journalist came in May 1875 at the ninth annual convention of the Missouri Press Association, held at Thespian Hall.

Although the railroads had become a major source of travel in Missouri, rivers and streams continued to provide a great deal of entertainment during the 1870s and 1880s. Sunday excursions on the Missouri and Osage Rivers were especially popular. In March of 1884 a Chamois, Missouri, newspaper reported on an excursion to its town as follows:

> Our town was visited last Sunday by an excursion party from Hermann, consisting of a large crowd of the inhabitants of that town. They came up on the *Steamer Fawn,* landing here about two o'clock in the afternoon. Louis Rincheval with his famous Apostle Band was among the excursionists. The excursion party immediately repaired to Shobe's pasture, where the grounds had been prepared for the occasion and a game of baseball between the Hermann and Chamois nine was begun. The game was rather interesting so far as it was played, yet it was not played out. The boat whistle sounded about 5 o'clock and put an end to the game. . . . As the game progressed the band played several pieces of nice music.

Winter sports included hunting and ice fishing. In 1884 a writer for the *Gasconade County Advertiser-Courier* described what he called "A 'Gar' Picnic" on the Gasconade River:

> While the Gasconade River is covered with ice it is fine sport to 'gig' gars through the ice, and your correspondent in company with several other parties went up from here last week and had some rare sport. There were probably twenty other persons at the place when we arrived there and the ice was already covered with a wriggling mass of gars. We were not long selecting suitable places and cutting holes about 2 by 4 feet through the ice. We were soon at work and during a few hours killed about 200 gars. There were from 2,500 to 3,000 killed that day and at least 10,000 during the winter at this one point. When we consider that the gar is the greatest enemy of all small fish, there certainly is some satisfaction in seeing them exterminated at this rate, and besides the sport is quite exciting.

Arguably, the height of intellectual discussion and interaction occurred in the place where the greatest number of ideas and cultures clashed: St. Louis, the Gateway to the West. In the late 1860s a philosophical movement that eventually gained international attention began in St. Louis. It revolved around Henry Brokmeyer and, later, William Torrey Harris. Brokmeyer had studied at Brown University before moving to Warren County, Missouri, and then to St. Louis in 1858. In 1866 he founded the St. Louis Philosophical Society, and in 1867 he began publishing the *Journal of Speculative Philosophy.* Harris later became editor of the *Journal.*

By the mid-1870s, the movement had established another journal, called the *Western,* and eventually established clubs and discussion groups for men and women where philosophy, history, literature, and languages could be studied. Evenings were often spent discussing such topics as the true nature of man, with a common reference point being a commitment to Hegelian dialectics. In Brokmeyer's and Harris's views, and thus in the views of their followers, man was perfectible if he would but use his reason. Indeed, it was in a reasoned analysis of the clash of agrarian and industrial culture that followers of the St. Louis Movement saw hope. In their minds, the clash of the old agrarian order, with its moral values, against the amoral world of emerging industrialism, would result in a new order that was at once more efficient, more bountiful, and more free. An altogether idealistic movement, the St. Louis Philosophical Society declined in numbers in the early 1880s after Harris left the city for Concord and Brokmeyer, disillusioned by his exposure to practical politics as Missouri's lieutenant governor from 1877 to 1881, moved to Indian Territory to live among the Osage and Cherokee tribes.

The interconnectedness with the outside world, and the accompanying prosperity enjoyed by the few at the top, manifested itself in many ways. One was in housing. The nouveau riche of the 1870s and 1880s built homes not only for the practical purpose of shelter and comfort from the elements but also for show, an ostentatious display of their awareness of the ways of the world and of their means to emulate the lifestyles of the rich and famous in other parts of the country.

Nowhere did this phenomenon occur with a greater flair than in St. Louis, where prominent eastern architectural firms such as Peabody and Stearns and Henry Hobson Richardson began to influence public and private building styles. Design critic William R. Hodges welcomed the transition. In 1883 he wrote an essay juxtaposing the "old" style prevalent in St. Louis against the "new" style that was emerging there: "The old, obsolete and utterly ridiculous, inexcusable and ugly school is that one which prevailed in St. Louis without any interruption from the first American invasion of St. Louis to the first glimmering notion of taste in architecture ten or twelve years ago [in the early 1870s]."

Hodges offered as examples of the welcome, eastern-influenced new styles some of the houses recently built in Vandeventer Place, a private residential area in St. Louis laid out in 1870. A magnificent Queen Anne residence was designed for Watson B. Farr by Burnham and Root of Chicago in 1882. The prestigious Boston firm of Peabody and Stearns ultimately designed at least four homes in Vandeventer Place. Peabody and Stearns began doing work in St. Louis in the late 1870s. Among the first St. Louis buildings designed by the firm was the white limestone, High Victorian Gothic, Unitarian Church of the Messiah, built at the corner of Locust and Garrison in 1879. The botanist Henry Shaw, owner of Shaw Place, had ten houses built between 1878 and 1883. All were modeled at least in part after Vandeventer Place. All of the houses were designed by English architect and Shaw associate George I. Barnett.

In outstate Missouri, other newly rich entrepreneurs sought also to demonstrate an awareness of styles in distant lands through the houses they built. One of the most distinctive styles to appear on the cultural landscape of outstate Missouri during the generation after the Civil War was the "Italianate," described by one historian as "the dominant expression of the post Civil War housing revolution." A good example of this type of structure was a home built during the early 1870s in Moberly, Missouri, by a railroad entrepreneur, Joseph Burkholder. Moberly was a major junction point for the Wabash and Katy Railroads, and it was the railroads that brought pine lumber, probably from Minnesota, to substitute for local hardwoods that would have been used in an earlier generation. Likewise, the railroads brought factory-produced ornamentation and decorative items, such as brackets, cornices, and mantel blocks, which mitigated against the need for local craftsmen. Hannibal, Missouri, was the site of dozens of Italianate structures built during the 1870s and 1880s, including the home of John T. Holme, who operated an insurance and real estate firm, and the home of Wilson B. Pettibone, a prominent lumberman. In 1884 J. H. McVeigh, another wealthy lumberman, built an Italianate house at 512 Center Street and sold it the next year to John C. Woodworth, manager of the local Singer Manufacturing Company. The lumber baron Sumner McKnight built a magnificent Italianate mansion overlooking much of the town at 1001 Hill Street in 1877. The architect for the McKnight home was John

Oliver Hogg. It was built by H. W. Shedd for the then-considerable sum of $13,000.

Less grandiose, but no less illustrative, were the houses built by second- and third-generation German Americans in central Missouri's Maries River Valley (Osage County), at the western edge of what has been called the Missouri Rhineland. In the first generation, German immigrants tended to live in the log houses that had been built previously by old-stock Americans. When they did build houses of their own, the houses tended to be of distinctive European design, as was the case with the wealthier Bruns and Dohman families in the valley. For the most part, however, it was not until the 1870s and 1880s that the sons of the German settlers built substantial stone and brick houses to withstand the ages. When they did, as in the case of the Hubers, Schauweckers, and the Plassmeyers, the houses reflected an interesting blend of European and American traditions: in craftsmanship and attention to detail, the houses were distinctively German; in design, the houses reflected patterns that had been made popular over the entire Midwest. The Huber house in particular was a marvelous example of the Second Empire style adopted and adapted by mid-Missouri German craftsmen.

The houses Missourians built during the 1880s held slightly fewer residents per dwelling than their predecessors. Between 1880 and 1890 the average number of persons to a dwelling in Missouri dropped from 5.87 to 5.52. Missouri had 528,295 families in 1890, with an average of 5.07 persons to a family. Increasingly during the 1880s, home dwellers could expect to live in houses that had at least some "modern" conveniences, especially if they lived in one of Missouri's towns or cities. Boonville's first waterworks was constructed in 1883. Electricity came to Hannibal in 1886 and to Jefferson City in 1887 when a power plant costing $18,000 was built. The next year, German immigrant Henrietta Bruns wrote to Auguste Geisberg, her sister-in-law, telling her, "There are a lot of new things here in our city. Approximately two hundred paces from our apartment a big tower for the water line has been completed." Henrietta also boasted that "we even have a streetcar that goes down the main street every hour."

Most Missourians stayed abreast of local, state, national, and world events during the late nineteenth century by means of newspapers. According to the Bureau of the Census, there were 530 newspapers and periodicals published in Missouri in 1880, 43 of which were printed daily. The vast majority (415) of these publications were printed weekly. The circulation of daily newspapers was 122,660 and of weeklies, 842,625. The majority of the newspapers and periodicals (425) were devoted to news, politics, and family reading. Twenty-eight publications were devoted principally to religion. Thirty-four of the 530 periodicals were printed in German, a reflection of Missouri's large German population, especially in St. Louis and in communities along the Missouri River.

As historian Robert Gilmore has pointed out, "Much of the newspaper was made up of 'boiler plate'—syndicated, ready-to-print copy shipped in to the newspaper from outside sources. This boiler-plate might consist of serialized fiction, sermons, Sunday school lessons, homemaking and fashion articles, historical essays, reprints of lectures, etc." The newspaper was a source of not only information but also literature at a time when books were scarce and public libraries were all but nonexistent. Not only could one read the political reporting of a journalist such as St. Louis native Eugene Field in a paper such as the *Kansas City Times,* but one could also read Field's early poetry and literary criticism. When the Free Public Library was established in Hannibal in 1889 as the result of a special municipal tax, it was the first such library in the state. Presumably, one could find in the library the first novel of St. Louis native Kate Chopin, a book called *At Fault* (1890), which preceded her more famous second novel, *The Awakening* (1899) by nearly a decade. No doubt one would have had no trouble in finding there a copy of Mark Twain's *Life on the Mississippi,* a book that the famous Missouri author was able to complete only after returning in 1882 to the Mississippi River town that he had abandoned with some disgust so many years earlier.

One of the most popular newspaper sections during the 1870s and 1880s was "Old Times" reminiscences of people such as Jerome Berryman, Theodore Pease Russell, and Silas Turnbo. As historian Lynn Morrow notes, these columns "became the place for Missourians to record their collective memories." In a transitional period, when "frontier life" was increasingly only a memory, writers such as Russell, whose articles appeared in the *Iron County Register* from 1883 to 1898, connected the experiences of preceding and succeeding generations to each other. Travelogues of local prominent citizens, who always had an interested audience back home for their correspondence, were also common. The travel accounts of people such as John Emerson and Eli Ake always found an interested readership.

By the last decade of the nineteenth century, Missourians were more aware than ever before of the diversity of life in America. Newspapers contributed to that reality, as did the increased ease of travel provided by the railroads. New ideas were also introduced through the schools, in which Missourians were spending unprecedented amounts of time.

These developments had multiple effects upon Missourians, especially those who still lived in rural areas. For one thing, they eased the boredom and loneliness of farm life. Social gatherings disrupted the dispiriting monotony of life in rural Missouri, and travel, whether real or vicarious, allowed Missourians to nurture their social instincts. But social and intellectual interaction with an ever-growing number of people had an unsettling effect as well; often it made people dissatisfied with their own circumstances and eager for the better life they thought they saw in the world beyond. The world, indeed, was changing, and Missourians were caught in the vortex of that change.

CHAPTER IV

A DIVERSE AND SOPHISTICATED
ECONOMY

Missouri's economy became increasingly diverse and sophisticated by the last decade of the nineteenth century, a process that only increased as the twentieth century moved into its first decades. From 1870 to 1890 Missouri's railroad mileage had nearly tripled, increasing to 6,887 miles. By 1904 Missouri had approximately 8,000 miles of track that linked almost all parts of the state together and made it possible for goods produced anywhere in the nation to reach the center of the country. Only Ozark, Dallas, and Douglas Counties did not have access to rails.

Population growth matched the increase in railroad mileage. Between 1880 and 1900, Missouri's population increased by almost a million residents, from 2,168,000 to 3,106,665. Each decade saw an increase of about five hundred thousand people. During the 1890s, 60 percent of the growth occurred in rural Missouri, with practically every county registering an increase. Indeed, with the exception of southeast Missouri, where the drainage of swamps would produce significant population growth between 1900 and 1920, and the most isolated part of the Ozarks, which awaited the mid-twentieth century to be discovered, rural Missouri reached its population peak during the 1890s.

Small towns in Missouri provided the connecting link between farmers and their markets, and between rural Missourians and the suppliers of consumer goods that farmers purchased. Lucy Routt Bradford Duncan remembered her early years in Phelps County and how railroads changed her life. Born in 1844 and still living in the same rural area near Rolla when she wrote in 1924, Duncan observed, "Since the Civil War times have changed wonderfully. There is now a railroad near and a market for all the farmer can raise. The loom, spinning wheel, and all old style handmade work are things of the past, modern inventions have so excelled them that life is not so burdensome for the one who labors."

79

During the 1890s, Missourians became both producers and consumers as never before. In such towns as Bethany, Edina, Boonville,
Mount Vernon, and Kennett, one could buy almost anything in 1890.
Their weekly newspapers indicated the possibilities of goods and services
available. In Bethany, a town of slightly more than one thousand people,
a person in need of legal counsel could choose from five lawyers, who
advertised in the newspaper. Two dentists and eight physicians offered
their services to the public. You could buy "seamless vamp shoes" for
three dollars a pair; sell your chickens to Alex Harrison; purchase the
"finest French effects" (satins) at seven and one-half cents per yard; and
treat your rheumatism with St. Jacob's oil. If you lived close to Ridgeway,
a small town nearby, J. H. Goodwin would sell you dry goods, boots
and shoes, clothing, and groceries, and he would buy your produce. You
could buy a new wagon, carriage, or buggy from Bethany manufacturer
J. A. Cushman or from W. S. Eads. Cushman produced from 150 to
200 wagons a year. Hart's Implement sold Deering mowers and Moline
Buggies. D. C. Wood offered the "New Vibrator-threshing machine."

A consumer in need of liver pills could choose between Carter's
Little Liver Pills or Dr. C. McLane's variety. Newburn and Company
sold drugs, wallpaper, varnish, paint, stationery, and books. One could no
doubt purchase a number of remedies such as Ozmanlis Oriental Sexual
Pills, a cure for impotence that would make a man strong and vigorous.
If Newburn failed to have an item, one might find it at C. B. Shearer
and Son, another druggist. Women with "female complaints" could go
there for Dr. Dromgoole's Female Bitters, "a powerful uterine tonic and
Female regulator for the cure of all female complaints." Beecham's Pills
claimed to cure those suffering from bilious and nervous disorders or
sick headaches, weak stomach, impaired digestion, constipation, or a
disordered liver. Tutt's Pills had almost as much range, addressing "sick
headache, torpid liver, piles, malaria, [and] dyspepsia." A medicine called
"Syrup of Figs" acted promptly on kidney disease and problems of the
liver and bowels. Dr. Owens Electric Belt corrected kidney problems,
among other things. And if these failed, one of the advertising physicians might effect a cure. The manufacturers of these patent medicines
produced them for a national market and advertised across the nation,
including in the weekly newspapers of Missouri.

Those in need of lumber in northwest Missouri could buy from Miner
and Frees in Bethany. The musically inclined could find a piano or organ

at A. J. Barber's establishment. Tailors, shoe stores, hardware stores, pipe fitters, clothing stores, livestock commission agents, a woolen mill, a cooperage firm, and three banks advertised their services in Bethany newspapers.

In southwest Missouri, Mount Vernon counted only 782 people in 1890, but claimed the talents of seven lawyers. Physicians did not advertise in the Mount Vernon newspaper. E. W. Mcfarland, however, asked the public to come to him for dental treatment. Two hotels met travelers' needs in the little town. Mount Vernon had two livery stables, a flour mill, an implement dealer, a lumberyard, one bank and a couple of loan agents, plus Robert Crump, "fashionable barber and hair dresser," as members of the business community. A full array of patent medicines were advertised in the *Fountain and Journal,* as were the Kansas City, Fort Smith, and Southern Railroad, the Missouri, Kansas, and Topeka line, and the Northern Pacific. Harper publications of Boston, Massachusetts, devoted a full column to making readers of the weekly newspaper aware of its magazine and other offerings.

With only 302 people, Kennett's businesses provided fewer services to farmers and residents than did Mount Vernon's. At T. E. Baldwin's drugstore, one could buy medicines, books, stationery, paints and oils, and fancy goods. Tatum Brothers ran the big general store, selling dry goods, groceries, hardware, tinware, boots and shoes, clothing, sash doors, "and everything else in proportion." Kennett subscribers learned of the wonders of patent medicines, including Smith's Bile Beans, a cure for sick headache, constipation, malaria, and liver complaints. Kennett grew by 400 percent in ten years, and the citizens installed electricity. Factories that produced barrels, buggy spokes, and brooms sprang up. A machine shop, a couple of cottonseed oil mills, three cotton gins, two planing mills, an ice plant, and a bottling works added to the town's employment opportunities and its services to agriculturists.

A town such as Boonville with more than four thousand people not only had everything available locally but also attracted merchants' advertisements from St. Louis. The Elleard Floral Company, Nies and Straub, tailors and drapers, and the William Barr Dry Goods Company, among others, ran ads in the appropriately named *Boonville Weekly Advertiser.*

Edina's 1,456 people had a vigorous business community. One of the more interesting establishments dealt in furniture of all kinds, sold and repaired sewing machines, sold pianos and organs, framed pictures, offered "a large stock of Fancy and Staple *Groceries,*" and embalmed the dead. The fact that the newspaper emphasized the availability of groceries as opposed to supplies suggests the growing popularity of purchasing rather than raising foodstuff. Three jewelry stores in Edina competed with one in Quincy, Illinois, for local business. In addition to makers of patent medicines who advertised nationally, businesses from St. Louis, Chicago, and West Grove, Pennsylvania, placed advertisements in the paper. Rose's shipped their plants and bulbs from West Grove to Edina. Eight local lawyers advertised for business, as did Patrick O'Farrell, an attorney from Washington, D.C., who specialized in patents, pensions, and claims.

Four physicians asked the public to see them, including a Doctor Lanoix from Quincy, Illinois. He claimed twenty years of experience "in the treatment of all the chronic diseases of male and female. Diseases of the skin, nervous debility, arising from excesses producing weakness, nervousness, loss of memory, pimples on the face, loss of ambition, [and] unfitness for marriage." The usual drugstores (four), grocers (three), realtors (two), and other businesses provided for citizens' needs. Edina had a photographer, an implement dealer, a music store, a butcher, and a store that sold stoves. P. Miller manufactured farm machinery, and W. J. Slaughter dealt in pine lumber, laths, shingles, pickets, doors, moldings, and other items. J. Long and Son sold groceries and bought country produce.

The Edina of the 1890s reflected its rural foundations. The editor of the *Knox County Democrat* complimented the "young town council" for its energy and then suggested, "Now gentlemen if you wish to gain the everlasting respect of those who have some pride for the looks of the city, pen up the hogs and put a stop to their tearing up sidewalks hunting for something to eat." Edina lacked a sewer system in 1890, but the town purchased a quantity of pipe "to be put down at the crossings and other places where needed." The mayor forbade throwing garbage and slops in the streets and alleys. By 1900 Edina had electricity, a waterworks, and "telephone connection with every corner of the county."

Boonville residents voted 422 to 158 in January of 1890 to erect an electric plant. The city had made contracts with the Sperry Arc Light Company of Chicago and the National Incandescent Light Company of Michigan for all of the necessary equipment by May 1. On July 1 the lights went on in Boonville as the town band played. The local editor projected that many businesses would "attach to the generators." With a population of 4,377 by 1900, Boonville had brick-paved streets and "other modern improvements."

Fire always threatened these mostly wooden towns, and thus fire insurance was important. In March of 1890 a blaze destroyed three buildings in Edina's business section, burning to the ground Philip Miller's wagon and carriage factory. Miller lost all of his equipment, but promised to rebuild with his fifteen hundred dollars in insurance money. In December of the same year, fire struck Bethany. Four buildings went up in flames. The fire started in a grocery store and then spread eastward to an implement store and the Simon King building, which housed a produce dealer, a meat market, and Mrs. Thomas's dressmaking establishment in the upper story. The Athenaeum block, presumably brick, and with iron shutters over windows and doors, stopped the fire's progress, but the Athenaeum suffered a cracked wall and other damage. Professor Bachelar, the high school principal, fearlessly endured "scorching heat [and] remained seated on the roof of Robert Good's residence and assisted by others succeeded in keeping the building so wet it was saved." A newspaper editor praised all of the town's citizens for doing all possible to "stay the progress of the fire." He called upon the community to learn the appropriate lessons from the fire. Bethany needed a waterworks of greater capacity and a well-organized "hook and ladder company" with the equipment to protect the city.

Grandin, in Carter County, represented a different kind of small town. It epitomized the lumber industry that developed in the Ozarks between the 1880s and the first decade of the twentieth century, providing scores of local residents with employment alternatives to farming. Experienced lumbermen from Pennsylvania created Grandin, building it from scratch in 1889 as a sawmill and planing mill town. At its peak, Grandin had 1,211 men working its mills, sawing and planing hundreds of thousands of feet of lumber daily.

In 1900 Grandin had a public school system, including a three-year high school offering advanced courses in mathematics, science, and literature. It had a hospital, a library that opened seven days a week, electric lights, and an elaborate telephone system. Most workers earned between $1.25 to $1.35 per day for eleven hours of work, six days per week for a minimum of $30 per month. This was slightly more than the average for Missouri's industrial employees, who worked approximately nine hours per day for slightly more than $27 per month in 1900. Skilled workers and managers earned considerably more. A high percentage of skilled workers in Grandin's mills came from the East, where they had gained experience in the business. While the high school and library offered unusual advantages to the people of the area, both operated on a subscription basis. The hospital required payments of $.75 per month for single people and $1.25 per month for families. In its first year, the company made a profit of $153,000.

The Missouri Lumber and Mining Company created the town and named it after E. B. Grandin, partner in the company and son-in-law of O. H. P. Williams, the Pennsylvanian who bought the first 30,000 acres of Ozark timberland for $30,000 in 1871. By 1900, the firm owned 324,000 acres, much of which it bought for less than a dollar an acre, and for some of which it paid only 25 cents per acre. Williams, Grandin, J. B. White (another partner and manager of the operation at Grandin), and other partners raised the capital to make the operation possible. Besides the investment in land, the company eventually built and maintained 66 miles of railroad track and owned 5 locomotives, 156 logging cars, 4 passenger cars, and the mills required to saw and plane a couple of hundred thousand feet of lumber every day. By 1903, the company had cleared more than 65 percent of its land holdings, or more than 213,000 acres.

Two other firms in Shannon County, the Ozark Land and Lumber Company of Winona and the Cordz-Fischer Lumber Company of Birch Tree, owned an additional 215,000 acres that they exploited in the same manner. The Birch Tree mill capacity reached 130,000 feet and the planer capacity reached 85,000 feet by 1900. The Winona facilities could process about 150,000 feet of lumber a day. These companies owned land in Carter and Oregon Counties as well as in Shannon. In Ripley County, Doniphan served as the center of the industry, with three sawmills. Making railroad ties also occupied the residents of Ripley County. The *Prospect-News* of Doniphan estimated that about two thousand ties left Doniphan daily, producing revenue of $750.

The industry quickly declined after 1910. In Ripley County by 1920, even the machinery of the industry had disappeared. Thomas Gage, a historian of the industry, noted that lumbering brought the region thirty years of prosperity, but in discussing Ripley County observed, "if anything, the county exited those decades even poorer than it had entered into them, and faced the future without a primary resource." Worse, the manner of cutting led to soil erosion and the silting of the area's streams and rivers. Scrub oak and brush replaced the stately pines and hardwoods that once graced the rugged hills. The evidence suggests that the residents of the counties affected welcomed the development of the timber industry. Land-poor and without capital, the citizens had no means to improve their conditions without outside influences. That the timber companies bought the land for so little provides eloquent evidence of the impoverishment of the region.

Like the state's timber resources, its minerals proved important to local areas and demonstrated the variety and richness of nature's endowment. During the decade of the 1890s, lead production rose from 47,000 tons to 80,000 tons, and then jumped to 142,000 tons by 1903. The value per ton varied from a low of twenty-seven dollars in 1897 to a high of forty-nine dollars in 1903. The St. Joseph Lead Company introduced the diamond drill in 1869, which revolutionized the industry. The company continued to be the most important producer of lead in the state and the nation at the turn of the century. That firm, the Doe Run Lead Company, and the Desloge Consolidated Lead Company, all three centered in southeast Missouri, produced the bulk of the product. Southeast Missouri's contribution made up more than 80 percent of the state's total.

Zinc usually appears with lead ore. Southeast Missouri produced zinc, but the center of the industry developed in southwest Missouri. Jasper, Newton, Lawrence, Greene, Ozark, Barry, and Christian Counties all produced commercial-quality ore, with Jasper, Newton, and Lawrence leading the others. Jefferson County, just south of St. Louis, and Moniteau County, in central Missouri, mined enough zinc to make it profitable. Zinc production almost doubled between 1890 and 1900, going from 100,000 tons to 186,000 tons. The price per ton increased from twenty-two dollars to thirty dollars. As with lead, Missouri produced about 80 percent of the zinc mined in the United States in 1900.

About one-half of Missouri's counties mined coal in 1900. Thirty-eight counties produced coal commercially, and during the decade, the tons mined increased from 2.4 million selling for $1.32 per ton to 2.995 million selling for $1.21 per ton. By 1903, production had zoomed upward to 4.6 million tons and the price had increased to $1.46 per ton. Bituminous coal made up the bulk of the production and steam locomotives used most of it, followed by steam-powered manufacturing establishments.

Fire and other clays, Portland cement from shale and limestone, building stones, iron ore, barite for making paint, silica for making glass, all added to Missouri's storehouse. St. Louis and Kansas City led in the making of clay products, from bricks to tiles to flower pots. Crystal City and Pacific manufactured high-quality glass; Carthage produced excellent limestone building materials, some of which it displayed in its lovely 1890s Jasper County courthouse. Later, Carthage stone was used in the construction of the state capitol.

In 1900 Missouri's coal, lead, and zinc mines produced almost $14 million worth of goods. To put that figure in perspective, in the same year St. Louis's manufacturers produced $233.6 million worth of goods, according to one source. Another researcher placed the figure at $300 million in 1897. Accounting technique may explain the differences, but whatever the case, St. Louis's manufacturing added greatly to the economic activity of the state and nation. St. Louis had the largest brewery in the world, Anheuser-Busch. The brewery employed twenty-two hundred people and produced more than one million barrels of beer in 1900; the Lemp Company made five hundred thousand barrels that year, making a total for the two breweries of $10 million worth of product. St. Louis's seventeen other breweries added a like value, so that a total of $20 million worth of beer was produced in the city. Still, St. Louis ranked fifth among U.S. cities in beer making, dropping from second in 1890. New York, Chicago, Milwaukee, and Philadelphia made more beer than St. Louis.

St. Louis's place in flour milling also declined during the 1890s. Minneapolis had replaced the Mound City as the nation's leading producer of flour and gristmill products during the 1880s, and in the 1890s the value of mill products dropped from $12.5 million to $4 million. Almost half of St. Louis's mills closed, and at the end of the decade the city ranked fifth in flour and gristmill production.

St. Louis industrialists offset declines in milling and in the manufacture of men's clothing, food processing, construction, machinery production, and lumber processing with gains in women's clothing, furniture making, various forms of publishing, the manufacture of boots and shoes, and tobacco products to post a 2 percent increase during the 1890s, while such other mature cities as Boston and Cincinnati experienced substantial declines. Long established in processing tobacco, St. Louis firms produced twice as much plug tobacco as any other city in 1890. Liggett and Meyers led the world in the production of chewing tobacco. The Lorillard Company of New York and the Drummond firm of St. Louis offered the most competition. Two other St. Louis firms, the Brown Company and the Catlin Company, added substantially to chewing tobacco and snuff production. A number of firms made cigars.

James B. Duke's American Tobacco Company soon changed the industry. Using his enormous profits from cigarette sales during the 1890s, Duke purchased all of the chief St. Louis tobacco companies except Liggett and Meyers. Still the leader in plug tobacco production but now facing disastrous price wars, Liggett and Meyers eventually succumbed, and by 1904 the American Tobacco Company had a virtual monopoly on the industry. The United States Department of Justice brought an antimonopoly suit against the Duke company, and in 1911 the Supreme Court ruled against it. The government required a reorganization of the industry, and Liggett and Meyers became one of four successor companies. Its plant in St. Louis continued to lead the world in making plug tobacco, but its offices and ownership left for North Carolina and New York, respectively.

Along with brewing beer and processing tobacco, St. Louisans distilled and distributed other alcoholic products. The Rebstock Company marketed its "Old Stonewall" whiskey in the South and Southwest. Charles Scheele made rye whiskey that he sold under the names of "Autocrat" and "Geisha Malt." The Stracke and Caesar Company distributed "Old Crow," the nation's best-selling bourbon. The Bardenheir Company sold sour mash whiskey and wines made from Missouri, Ohio, California, French, and German grapes. St. Louisan Douglas Cook made about ten thousand bottles of champagne a day and sold it as "Cook's Imperial."

St. Louis shoe companies numbered thirty-eight in 1897. The Brown Shoe company made about $5 million worth of shoes that year in the largest shoe factory in the world. During the decade of the 1890s, St. Louis doubled the value of boots and shoes produced, to more than $8 million. The city ranked fifth in that category in 1900. St. Louis also had the world's largest streetcar factory, sending cars throughout the country and overseas. With more than 70 percent of the value of manufactured products of the state's twenty-five leading cities, St. Louis produced about everything, from patented medicines to sewer tile. Clothing manufacturers included S. and J. Friedman, a firm employing some five hundred workers producing skirts, cloaks, suits, and fur garments. In 1901 the Marx and Haas Jeans Company employed two thousand people in making its nationally marketed Rabbit Brand jeans and corduroy trousers. Other manufacturers in St. Louis turned out watches, clocks, jewelry, china, and glass.

St. Louis's inventive wholesalers marketed the products of the city's and the world's manufacturers. The Norvell-Shapleigh Hardware Company did more than $1 million worth of business annually, selling cutlery, guns, mining machinery, nails, chains, and any other product in the hardware line. St. Louis grocery wholesalers did between $70 million and $80 million a year. In 1901, they handled 150 million pounds of sugar, 37 million pounds of coffee, 20 million pounds of rice, and quantities of flour, soap, tobacco, wooden ware and silverware, and other products.

The Moll Company handled more goods than other wholesalers, and like many of them occupied space in Cupples Station. Built by Samuel Cupples and Robert S. Brookings in 1891, the station provided 1.5 million square feet of floor space with its seven-story buildings, constructed on thirty acres in south St. Louis. A tunnel connected the warehouses with the railroads so transporting the millions of pounds of goods from storage to the trains never clogged the city's streets.

Wholesalers of dry goods produced between $50 million and $60 million worth of business annually. Wayman Crow and Samuel C. Davis pioneered in the business in St. Louis, starting in 1835. Davis continued into the 1890s. Leading firms by that decade included Carleton's, which did about one-third of the business, Ely and Walker, Rice-Stix, and Hargadine and McKittrick. Each firm stationed buyers in New York, Paris, London, and Brussels.

While continuing as wholesalers in the twentieth century, these firms also moved into retailing through department stores or into manufacturing, or they did both. Rice-Stix made men's and women's clothing; Hargadine and McKittrick bought St. Louis's largest and original department store, the William Barr Company. In 1911, Hargadine and McKittrick had to sell out to the May Company of Cleveland because of losses in building the twenty-story "Railway Exchange" building. The May Company had already purchased the Famous store, another department store, and when it became owner of the Barr store it simply merged the two, making the huge Famous-Barr department store. By 1920, four firms dominated St. Louis's wholesale dry goods market: Ely and Walker, Rice-Stix, Carleton-Ferguson (the result of merger with another large St. Louis firm), and Butler Brothers (a branch of a Chicago business).

As an enthusiastic writer pointed out in 1903, St. Louis had many advantages as a trade and manufacturing center. Within a radius of five hundred miles lived some thirty-seven million people. As a terminal point for twenty-four railroads, St. Louis had access to eighty thousand miles of track. It completed its second bridge across the Mississippi in 1890, the Merchants Bridge. In 1889, electric streetcars began operating, moving workers and shoppers around the city cheaply and efficiently. A year later, the city lighted its streets and alleys, having built the world's largest electric works. It had a vigorous workforce that numbered more than 245,000 individuals over the age of ten. More than 37 percent worked in manufacturing; 31.8 percent in retail and wholesale trade and transportation; 24.5 percent in domestic and personal service; 5 percent in professions; and 0.9 percent in agriculture. Women made up 23.3 percent of workers, contributing 40 percent of those in domestic and personal service and 28 percent of those in the professions. St. Louis had the lowest tax rate among the nation's cities, which many argued was one of the reasons it had attracted so many businesses. Its more than 575,000 residents contributed a hefty share to the economic activity of the state. The city had grown in population in the decade of the 1890s by almost 115,000.

Kansas City grew by about one-third as much, going from 132,416 to 163,752. Its population made it the second-largest city west of St. Louis, surpassed only by San Francisco. Kansas City looked to the West, and a publicist summarized the city's chief economic activities by writing: "To her markets are brought the cattle, the sheep and the hogs; and to her mills and elevators the wheat and corn and rye and oats and rice from fifteen states and territories."

Only Chicago surpassed Kansas City as a livestock center. Thirty-nine rail lines ran through the city, bringing in livestock from across the West and Midwest. By 1900 the livestock industry had surpassed all others in attracting capital, employing people, furnishing tonnage of rail freight, drawing supplies from a greater territory, and selling its products to a greater market. From their beginning in 1871, Kansas City's stockyards had grown from fifteen acres to two hundred acres. Between 1891 and 1901, the number of cattle received increased from 1,347,487 to 2,126,575. Hogs went from 2,599,109 to 3,716,404; sheep from 386,760 to 980,078; and horses and mules from 31,740 to 96,657. Kansas City's packinghouses processed many of these animals. Eight companies, including Armour and Swift, had plants in Kansas City by 1890. In that year Kansas City packinghouses slaughtered 581,520 cattle, 2,348,073 hogs, and 199,000 sheep. Ten years later the number of cattle slaughtered had grown to 1,139,246, hogs to 2,854,281, and sheep to 629,918. In 1900 the value of products processed in Kansas City packinghouses totaled $73,205,027.

Farm implement manufacturers took advantage of Kansas City's location, population, and railroad facilities to locate their factories in the Missouri city. Kansas City's implement trade area covered two hundred thousand square miles. Implement sales reached $25 million annually by 1900, which meant that about one-fourth of all agricultural implements manufactured in the country came from Kansas City.

The city developed into the nation's ninth-largest flour and grist-mill center, with twenty-eight elevators that had a storage capacity of 6,320,000 bushels. Kansas City also served as a market for fruit, eggs, butter, poultry, and other farm commodities. Kansas City had about one hundred lumber companies and consumed some four million tons of coal per year, with more than half of that used by railroads operating out of the city.

Kansas City's industrial production placed it fifteenth in the nation. It had extensive wholesale dry goods and grocery operations, and while it was twenty-second in the nation in population, it ranked eighth in bank transactions. All of this growth changed the city, but nothing had a more important impact on its future than voter authorization for the City Beautiful Movement. In 1880, Kansas City had eighty-nine miles of streets, with only five hundred yards of them paved and sixteen miles of them covered with broken limestone. Public transit moved by horse power. Privately collected garbage simply went into the Missouri River. Only 5 percent of residents had water closets, and only one-third of them dumped their waste into a sewer system. "In sum, Kansas City was ugly, dirty, and boisterous: its police force made 3,877 arrests in 1880, principally for intoxication." Kansas City needed to improve, and the City Beautiful Movement did exactly what its name implied. William Wilson's history of the movement summarized its impact in these words: "It remade an ugly boom town, giving it miles of graceful boulevards and parkways flanked by desirable residential sections, acres of ruggedly beautiful park land dotted with recreational improvements, and several neighborhood playgrounds in crowded districts."

Wilson credited William Rockhill Nelson, owner of the *Kansas City Star,* and George E. Kessler, landscape architect, with making the most important contributions to Kansas City's development into a model for other cities. Nelson joined early editors in campaigning for parks, and after 1880 he took the lead as a constant promoter. He became an important land developer and incorporated the themes of open space, rock walls, and plenty of trees in his properties. George Kessler created the comprehensive plan that the city adopted. His parks and boulevards divided the city into residential, commercial, and industrial districts. In 1895, voters gave the planners a green light after the planners amended the city charter providing for the condemnation of land, issuance of long-term bonds, and establishment of a supervisory board. Not all agreed with the change. Kessler's careful planning offended some business and professional people, while appealing to others in the same groups. That division kept officials from executing the plan until the turn of the century.

Wilson captured the impact of Kessler's plan, writing: "It reached into every part of the city establishing unity through its own pervasiveness. In later years another set of city planners would find the much maligned City Beautiful architects had willed them a boulevard grid to ease the mounting loads of automobile traffic, had pointed the way to greater use of the park and boulevard system's recreational opportunities, and had left to them a precious legacy of urban beauty." In 1920 the city enjoyed 1,992 acres of parks, 676 acres of parkways, and almost 90 miles of boulevards and drives. Today's Kansas City continues to reflect the brilliant planning of George E. Kessler.

Missouri's third-largest city almost doubled its population between 1890 and 1900, registering as impressive an increase as Los Angeles. St. Joseph went from 52,324 people to 102,979. Enormous strides in commerce and manufacturing accompanied the city's population growth. Its most important industry remained livestock processing, with Swift, Nelson-Morris, Hammond, and Krug operating plants there. Its stockyards had a daily capacity of 15,000 cattle, 20,000 hogs, 15,000 sheep, and 2,000 horses and mules in 1903. It employed 275 men. The packinghouses' slaughtering capacities reached almost 8,000 cattle, 20,000 hogs, 5,500 sheep, and 10,000 poultry per day. Packers had invested more than $2.6 million in plants, and in the five years between 1898 and 1903 their expenditures for work done and for livestock increased by 84 percent, and their use of railroad cars to ship their products went up by 98 percent.

St. Joseph also did a flourishing wholesale business in dry goods, hardware, boots and shoes, and groceries. In 1900 it ranked fourth in the nation in wholesale dry goods sales. Four large houses employed two hundred drummers hawking goods from Kansas to Canada and from Alaska to Mexico. St. Joseph milliners employed five hundred people in making hats and another thirty-eight in selling them. Wholesale drug companies included the C. D. Smith and Van Natta-Lynds firms. St. Joseph salesmen marketed paint across the country, and the Sheridan-Clayton Paper Company specialized in making tablets. Other manufacturing included five boot and shoe factories and the Buell Company, which made blankets, robes, and flannels. St. Joseph companies made hats, duck and denim trousers, and woolens. The National Biscuit Company owned three large flour mills in the city, and three large breweries made beer. St. Joseph had two hundred manufacturing firms employing some eight thousand workers.

As discussed earlier, Joplin, Missouri's fourth-largest city in 1900, started and grew as a mining town. Lead was responsible for its existence and zinc helped it to flourish. During the decade of the 1890s, Joplin's population more than doubled from 9,909 to 26,023. To supplement its main activity, the town had ten wholesale houses, eleven foundries, six factories, six banks, and a building and loan association. Saturday nights in Joplin, however, indicated how much mining and miners dominated the town. Banks opened their doors from seven until eight o'clock and on a typical Saturday paid out more than $100,000 by cashing miners' checks. "From 8 o'clock until midnight the stores are crowded with people making purchases, paying the week's grocery bill, laying in supplies for the next week. . . . Fully one-fourth of the week's business in the stores is transacted on Saturday night."

In the 1890s, Springfield grew by only 2,000 people to 23,267, but its eight banks held two times the deposits of Joplin's banks. Springfield served as the division headquarters for the St. Louis and San Francisco railroad, which employed 2,000 workers there. Fruit-producing Ozark farmers made Springfield their leading market. Trainloads of apples went from Springfield to the East Coast and on to Europe. The town's two cold storage houses could hold 65,000 bushels of apples at a time. A poultry center, Springfield also did a brisk wholesale business in groceries, hardware, hats, dry goods, clothing, seeds, and other goods. Manufacturers produced wagons, furniture, and iron products. Like every town of any size, Springfield milled wheat into flour.

Other important towns included Sedalia, a railroad shop town with an agricultural base; Hannibal, a Mississippi River town with 4,000 workers in its factories and railroad shops; Carthage, in the heart of southwest Missouri's lead and zinc area and a railroad center, but best known for its wonderful white limestone; and Jefferson City, the seat of state government, but with five shoe factories, brickyards, flour mills, an overall factory, and five banks. Hannibal lost population in the decade of the 1890s, declining from 12,816 to 12,780, while the rest of these towns experienced some growth. Sedalia went from 13,994 to 15,231; Carthage grew from 7,962 to 9,416; and Jefferson City increased its population from 6,732 to 9,664, registering the highest percentage growth and the largest increase in numbers as well. In all, Missouri had forty towns with populations of 3,000 or more in 1900, and more than one hundred other towns with populations of between 1,000 and 3,000.

No doubt the Panic of 1893 affected virtually all Missourians, but its impact differed throughout the state. James Neal Primm attributed St. Louis's relatively slow growth of 2 percent in manufacturing during the decade to the Panic, and the 1894 report of the Bureau of Labor Statistics supported his position, noting a reduction of workers in a variety of industries. Nevertheless, Susan Fitzpatrick in her study of the city noted that no St. Louis bank failed between 1885 and 1900. Kansas City experienced more than a 14 percent increase in manufacturing; Springfield registered a 34.8 percent increase; and St. Joseph gained by a whopping 165.9 percent between 1890 and 1900. In their study of Kansas City, A. Theodore Brown and Lyle W. Dorsett did not even mention the Panic. By contrast, in her work on Scott Joplin and Sedalia, Susan Curtis noted, "Like other Americans in 1893, Sedalians survived the economic panic and ensuing depression with little of their Victorian faith intact." She cited store closings, and a reduction in size and two-month cessation of publication of the *Sedalia Bazoo*, as examples of the Panic's effect. Yet the 1894 report of the Bureau of Labor Statistics noted no significant changes in the work patterns in Sedalia, Carthage, Independence, Chillicothe, Warrensburg, California, or Louisiana. In St. Charles, only the car shops seemed adversely affected. From local newspaper comment in Edina, Boonville, Bethany, Mount Vernon, and Kennett, the Panic had little impact. Likewise, in the small towns, the Panic seems to have had minimal effect. One store in Kennett moved to new quarters because its location seemed too large "for hard times." But in the same week a new butcher shop opened and W. H. Napper returned from St. Louis with a "new stock of goods" for his store. The Edina paper noted:

> The year 1893 will have gone down into history as one of growth and prosperity for our city and county, and while it has been an era of depression in money matters throughout manufacturing districts of the east and silver producing states of the west, it is also a fact that Missouri, the garden spot of the nation, is in the best shape of any state in the sisterhood. . . . The past two years have been years of growth and prosperity for Edina and Knox county; in fact, Edina's growth and advancement during these years was of a character more solid and substantial than for many years previous.

It would appear that the 1890s depression affected most significantly those industries, markets, and places tied to the credit system of eastern banking houses, as suggested by the Edina editor. For example, the mining districts of the state suffered serious problems. At the Doe Run lead mine in southeast Missouri the company tried to protect its workforce by giving a number of men part-time work. An investigator noted that 206 men could do the work, but the company kept 705 men working a limited schedule. The company paid the wages of an injured employee and gave preference to married men when assigning work. In the Centre Creek Mines near Webb City in southwest Missouri, 161 miners worked although 71 working full-time could have performed the tasks. An extreme was set by the Victor Mining Company. The investigator reported dissatisfaction among the miners because 411 men remained on the payroll while 40 could have done all of the work required. Average days worked at that mine numbered only 30 for the year; at Doe Run miners worked 90 days; and at Centre Creek they averaged 137 days. Conditions in the mines left much to be desired.

Centre Creek miners earned $1.82 for a day's wages. Doe Run miners received only $1.19 per day, and Victor miners took home $1.29 for a day's pay in 1894.

Despite whatever impact the Panic had on St. Louis, wages there proved better than in the mining districts. For example, bakery employees earned between $2 and $2.25 per day, while those delivering bakery goods received between $1.50 to $1.75 per day. Foremen earned $3 per day. Labor investigators surveyed ten bakeries in 1891 to calculate these averages. Wages in St. Louis beef and pork packing establishments in the same year ranged from $1.75 to $2 per day for laborers and rose to $3.33 per day for engineers. Laborers in the city's breweries earned an average of $1.75 a day; brewers and cellar men received between $2.10 and $2.75; drivers earned $2.10 to $2.15; maltsters earned $2.15 to $2.50; and engineers received from $3.25 to $5 a day. St. Louis industrial workers worked an average of about 60 hours a week, with a few working as many as 72 hours or as few as 54 hours. The Laclede Gas Works required employees to put in 77 hours a week. Workers in Kansas City had about the same hours, with most of them working 60 to 72 hours a week.

At least for industrial workers in Missouri, the cost of living fell during the 1890s. Steven Piott in his *Anti-Monopoly Persuasion* placed the decrease at 9 percent between 1891 and 1897 and noted that it remained almost stationary during the period from 1898 to 1902. A decline in food prices of more than 5 percent between 1891 and 1897 helped the urban dwellers and no doubt injured farmers. But food prices rose by more than 8 percent between 1898 and 1902, and that helped farmers.

An analysis of the two cities' workforces revealed relatively little dependence on child labor but a somewhat heavier reliance on women workers, who made up more than 20 percent of the total. In 1891, 53,770 employees worked in 1,072 factories in St. Louis investigated by the state labor bureau. Adult males numbered 43,733; boys under twelve years of age, 573; women, 9,345; and girls under fourteen years of age, 119. In Kansas City, the investigator went to 110 factories, where adult males numbered 3,782 and women numbered 461. No boys under twelve and no girls under fourteen worked in those factories.

Of the 2,058 industrial workers in St. Joseph, women made up more than half the total: there were 1,190 women and 835 men. Only 2 boys and 31 girls worked in those thirty factories. A large percentage

95

of St. Joseph's factories made clothing. The Bureau of Labor Statistics reported that the most "numerous class of working women are those engaged in the manufacture of clothing and underwear." Springfield's thirty-three factories employed only 288 people in 1891. Adult males numbered 107; boys under twelve, 78; women, 38; and girls under fourteen, 15. Labor Bureau reports for Marion, Pettis, and Jasper County factories revealed similar breakdowns.

Women workers received less pay for their efforts and often spent long hours at their labor. For example, women working in St. Louis clothing factories earned from $.35 to $1.25 a day for ten hours of work. Of those engaged in making clothing, the Labor Bureau estimated that only 25 percent worked in factories; the remainder toiled at home earning an estimated $.50 for a seven-hour day. Native-born women made up the bulk of factory employees, followed by German-born, with only a few Irish-, Scotch-, and English-born. In the city's large shoe factories, about an even number of men and women worked. There the "piece system" prevailed, where one received pay based on the pieces completed. Women usually sewed the upper part of the shoe or packed them for shipment. They received on average pay of $1 for a ten-hour day.

Large tobacco factories also employed women; in St. Louis about 2,500 women worked in them in 1891. The women ranged from ten-year-olds to "gray-haired matrons" of sixty years of age. The youngest worked as stemmers, removing stems from leaves. Native-born women made up only 10 percent of the female tobacco workforce, with eastern European women providing the bulk of it. At one tobacco factory, about one-third of the women employed were blacks. Stemmers and wrappers earned about $.85 per day and lump wrappers received $1.65.

Another one thousand St. Louis women toiled in candy factories. They earned an average of $.75 for a ten-hour day. Most of these workers ranged in age from thirteen to twenty and traced their ancestry to Germany. Women worked in paper box factories, in the printing and book binding industry, in cotton mills and bagging factories, in cleaning peanuts, and in sorting rags and paper. Everyone considered these last jobs the worst. Girls started in these jobs at age eight; the average age of female employees in these jobs was only twelve. A labor official made the following observation in 1891: "While it is claimed that there is nothing connected with the work performed that can be detrimental to health, it must at least be doubted whether the constant buzz of machinery will not affect the hearing, and the inhalation of dust and lint must ultimately affect the lungs and plant germs of consumption."

Single women dominated the female workforce. Of some 871 working St. Louis women studied, only 22 had husbands and only 51 had ever been married earlier, leaving 798 as never having married. Kansas City's women workers reflected the same pattern. Of the 871 in the 1891 St. Louis study, 668 worked to help support their families and 813 of them lived with their parents. Of the 58 who did not live at home, 35 lived in boardinghouses and 23 rented single rooms. In Kansas City, 84 percent of the 413 women studied lived at home. Of the 45 who boarded, most lived with a relative. In St. Joseph, 78 percent of the group interviewed lived at home and 91.4 percent had never married.

A labor bureau official placed blame for the child labor that did exist on employers, but heaped even more blame on parents, who "bring their children to the factories and beg that they be taken, pleading extreme poverty and often no other means of support . . . [;] some want them in factories to get them off the streets." In 1897 the legislature passed a child labor law that prohibited children under fourteen years of age from working in shops that used mechanical, steam, or water power or in any place declared by a doctor to be harmful to health. In 1905 the legislature passed a compulsory education law in Missouri that made it even more difficult to employ children. All children from six to fourteen years of age had to remain in school for at least half the academic year. Those ages fourteen to sixteen not gainfully employed had to attend school also. Loopholes in the law caused the legislature to pass another regulation in 1907 that required parents to send their children to school the full term. Employed children between ages fourteen and sixteen had to supply employers with affidavits, signed by the child, certifying age, color of hair, and eyes. Impoverished children could get exemptions, but they had to attend evening classes.

Lee Meriwether, Missouri's first state labor commissioner, reported that "as a special agent of the Department of Labor at Washington," he "visited factories in a great many parts of the United States. . . . [He felt] warranted in saying that the condition of Missouri factories and workshops is as good, if not better, than the condition of factories and workshops in the East or in any other part of the country." Nevertheless, Meriwether found much to correct in Missouri labor practices. Employers in some industries withheld worker's pay as a means of keeping them on the job and forcing them to use credit at a company store. Some paid workers in script, redeemable only at a company store. In Bevier, the Loomis and Snively coal mine kept twenty days of pay from their workers in violation of an 1889 law. When confronted, the mine owners dismissed those making complaints. A report summarized the perspective of the workers: "A miner with cash can select his store, can buy in the cheapest market. But the miner with nothing but unpaid wages is compelled to buy at the store of his employer, whether prices there be reasonable or extortionate."

At the Crystal City Glass Company, a worker beginning employment on August 1 would not be paid until September 15 or 20. In addition, the cashier kept his window open for only two hours. Those unable to get there waited another week to be paid. According to Meriwether, "the manager of the glass works justifies the company's infrequent pay-day on the ground that the men get drunk on Sunday, and on Mondays break thousands of dollars worth of glass; that by the present system there is only one such drunken Sunday once in four weeks." Such delays in pay required workers to get credit; Meriwether concluded that credit increased workers' cost of living by 25 percent. Railroad tie hackers in Miller County complained that they sometimes waited months to get paid. A system of acquisition and collusion caused the delay. A railroad agent contracted for the ties and the railroad only paid him when an inspector of the company approved the product. The railroad agent, however, frequently owned a store and willingly advanced credit to the hackers. Evidence indicated that the agent also directed the inspector to approve speedily the wood of those who traded at his store.

Organizing workers into unions aimed at improving pay and working conditions achieved little success during the 1890s. Gary Fink in *Labor's Search for Political Order: The Political Behavior of the Missouri Labor Movement 1890–1940* noted that only forty thousand Missouri workers held union membership in 1900, and most of these workers were concentrated in St. Louis. As late as 1899, two-thirds of the delegates to the annual state convention came from St. Louis. And even in St. Louis, Fink found that there "was little consensus in social and cultural values, political philosophy, or in the economic thought of its working class. The absence of homogeneity is strikingly illustrated in the development of the city's labor movement."

Labor organizing gained ground during the next fourteen years, and by the eve of World War I, labor unions counted 114,000 members in Missouri. More than half of them still lived in St. Louis; Kansas City held 16 percent. Still, the 114,000 union members represented less than 8 percent of the state's 1.5 million workers. Only about 20 percent of manufacturing and construction workers joined unions, while 50 percent of miners and 46 percent of railroad workers had joined. By then unions had organized only 2 percent of the 250,000 women in the workforce, and almost all of them were in the clothing and shoe industries in St. Louis and Kansas City. Nevertheless, in 1890 women in an overall factory in Mount Vernon successfully struck, winning wage increases of from fifty-five and eighty cents a day to sixty-five and ninety cents a day.

Shorter hours, more pay, and less stringent work rules dominated worker demands. In 1891, St. Louis's Furniture Workers' Union struck because company rules caused a deduction of one hour's pay when workers arrived for work even one minute later than seven o'clock and required all employees to report to an official whenever they entered or left the factory. The company changed the work rules after a two-month strike. Black marine firemen also gained their strike demands in 1891. Organized as Marine Firemen's Protective Union No. 1 in March of 1891, they won an advance in wages from thirty dollars to forty dollars per month and recognition of their union after conducting a month-long strike. Employees of the Central Type Foundry Company opposed a change in compensation incurred by a change in power sources from coal to gas, the dismissal of an employee, and the practice of locking workers' coats and hats in closets during work hours. In addition, one of the owner's sons treated workers to certain indignities. Twenty-two workers struck, and after twenty-four days the strike ended with eighteen of the men losing their jobs and the plant operating as before. So while organized labor remained in its infancy, those organized achieved success, at least some of the time.

The professions enjoyed limited success also in their efforts to organize during this period. They sought to organize for many of the same reasons that labor sought organization: to limit competition, to maintain standards, to ensure competency, to control entrance into the occupation and hence remuneration, and to influence decisions that affected the profession. Although Missouri teachers had formed their state association in 1856, its membership totaled only 395 as late as

1906. The Missouri Bar Association, begun in 1880, had only 357 of Missouri's 5,500 practicing attorneys as members in 1905. The Missouri Medical Association, begun in the antebellum period, was the most successful at organizing members of its profession. Even Missouri's bankers created an association in 1890. When the Missouri Bankers' Association held its first annual meeting in 1890, 82 of the state's 585 banks were represented. John Caro Russell, a St. Louis banker, listed as the first object of the organization, "The bringing together the Bankers of our State, thereby forming friendship and good feeling which will be the cause of eliminating many ruinous practices, destroying unjust competition." Russell added that "there is too much of this knifing business in the world."

Both the Missouri Bar Association and the Missouri Medical Association lobbied the state legislature to establish requirements for entry into their professions. In 1901, the Missouri Medical Association succeeded in establishing the State Medical Examining Board. The board became the licensing agency for doctors, and according to historian David Thelen, failed "36 percent of the applicants who appeared before . . . [it] in its first two years." The Missouri Bar Association began lobbying for a common bar examination in 1899, and in 1905 the legislature provided that means of licensing lawyers in the state. Thelen claimed that in 1908, "18 candidates failed the new bar examination among the 135 who took it."

The least organized and most numerous workers in Missouri during the late nineteenth and early twentieth centuries remained farmers. Despite the fact that the growth of cities and towns provided thousands of Missourians with new opportunities to make a living and to become consumers, agriculture was still the backbone of the state's economy. During the 1890s, the number of farms in Missouri increased from 238,043 to 284,886. The number of improved acres increased from 19,792,313 to 22,900,043 acres. Even with that increase, about half of the state's farmland remained unimproved, since total acreage exceeded 45 million acres. Surprisingly, in 1903 the state still had 422,536 acres of vacant public land available for homesteading. That figure had declined from 2,254,000 acres in 1880. All of the unclaimed land lay south of the Missouri River, for all federal land north of the river had been claimed by 1886. The federal government still operated land offices in Boonville, Ironton, and Springfield in 1903.

While the number of farms greatly increased during the decade of the 1890s, the average size of a Missouri farm declined from 129 acres to 119 acres. In 1900, more than two-thirds of Missouri's residents lived on farms and earned their living directly from the land. More than two-thirds of Missouri farmers owned houses, but in both 1890 and 1900, 31 percent of farm families rented houses, indicating a somewhat high rate of tenancy.

Farmers continued to devote much of their acreage to corn. They planted more than 6 million acres of corn in 1890 and more than 7.5 million in 1900. Even though they improved their acres, farmers brought into cultivation less fertile soil over the years in their ever-increasing effort to make more money. Thus, corn yields per acre consistently declined, going down to 27 bushels per acre in 1909. Both the number of acres devoted to wheat production and the number of bushels per acre varied more than did corn. In 1881 Missouri farmers had sowed more than 2.3 million acres of wheat and averaged only 8.6 bushels to the acre. In 1891 they reduced the number of acres to about 1,999,000 and reaped a harvest of 13.6 bushels to the acre. In 1900 they sowed more than 3.1 million acres in wheat and harvested an average of 19.2 bushels per acre. Corn made up about half of all crops and wheat about one-fifth of crop production.

Livestock production consumed a good part of the corn produced in Missouri and accounted for the large number of acres in hay and pasture. Hay fields covered almost 3 million acres of Missouri's farms, and pasture land took up more than 7.5 million acres. Livestock sales produced more than 55 percent of farm income in 1900. Missourians earned $219 million from all farm products, and $142 million came from livestock operations. Capital investment in Missouri's livestock and dairy farms at the turn of the century, including land and machinery, totaled $646,380,516. That figure made Missourians' investment in livestock farming three times greater than the investment of Massachusetts in textiles, that state's most important industry.

In 1899, Missourians owned 3 million head of cattle, about 700,000 more than they had fed in 1890. About 50,000 head carried pedigrees, reflecting the fact that sophistication had come to Missouri agriculture just as it had to other areas of the economy. Purebred Short Horn cattle made up one-half of the pedigreed cattle in the state in 1899, with Herefords contributing 18,000 head. Nathaniel Leonard of Cooper

County had bought a purebred Short Horn bull and heifer in 1839 for $1,100 and from those two created the famed Ravenswood herd. Other important Short Horn cattle operations in 1900 included those of J. H. Kissinger, K. W. Towne, T. J. Wornall, and George Bothwell. They frequently sold animals for as much as $2,500 each. T. F. B. Sotham, who raised Herefords, sold one for $5,100 and another that certainly upheld its name of Sir Bredwell, for $5,000. Overton Harris's best Hereford bull, Benjamin Wilton, sired 200 calves that sold for a total of $75,000 during his very productive life.

Aberdeen-Angus cattle numbered only three thousand in Missouri in 1899, with some of the prominent owners living in Carroll County. Missouri Angus quickly established themselves as top show cattle, winning "the best prizes more continuously than any other breed in this State." Wallace Estill's bulls bred more championship Angus during the 1890s than any other American Angus bulls. During the Chicago World's Fair of 1893, Estill's animals won nine of the thirteen first prizes offered. He sold his Black Knight for $2,100 and his Lucia Estill for $2,800, making the two among the highest-priced Aberdeen-Angus sold in the United States at that time.

Missouri also produced some purebred Holstein and Jersey cattle, but failed to lead in dairying as it did in beef cattle. For example, the butterfat that Missouri dairy cows produced provided less than one-third of the butter that Missourians consumed during 1900. In 1902, the Blue Valley Creamery began operation in St. Joseph. It used cream separated by farmers employing hand separators, a new trend in the industry, and it made more than six million pounds of butter in 1902, making it one of the largest creameries in the country producing only butter. All told, Missouri had fifty creameries and twenty-nine cheese factories in 1901.

Swine production declined during the decade of the 1890s, going from 5,200,000 to 4,524,664. Nevertheless, Missouri accounted for 7 percent of all hogs produced in the United States, and only Illinois and Iowa held more hogs in 1900. Poland-China, Berkshire, and Duroc-Jersey dominated the breeds of hogs in the state, with Poland-China being by far the most numerous. F. M. Lail of Marshall led other hog farmers in the quantity and quality of Poland-Chinas produced. In twenty-three years of raising Poland-China hogs, he sold more than 2,000 of them for $40,000. The Poland-China breed matured and finished quickly; Berkshires gained much of their sustenance by grazing. N. H. Gentry of Sedalia earned a reputation as one of the nation's most successful producers of Berkshire hogs. At the Chicago World's Fair, his livestock won ten of the eighteen first prizes. Durocs became known for their hardiness and numerous offspring. In 1890 few Missourians raised them, but by 1900 more than one hundred Missourians produced Durocs. S. Y. Thornton and J. D. Stephenson became well-known Duroc farmers.

In Edina, H. R. Parsons and Son advertised their Poland-China hogs. They noted, "It takes rooting to make money. Parties desiring rooters should call on us, as we have at present a few choice full blood Poland-China of both sex [sic], old enough for breeding purposes, sired by King of Knox. His sire is the famous old hog Moorish King that sold for $300 when a pig."

Neither sheep nor goats made an important impact on Missouri agriculture, although sheep production greatly increased during the 1890s. By 1900 farmers raised a million of them, including Merino, Cotswold, Rambouillet, and Shropshire. Poultry production supplemented many farm incomes. Most farmers raised chickens, and Missouri ranked third in the nation in poultry production in 1900. Leading producing counties included Marion, Pettis, Franklin, and Lincoln. Few Missouri farmers raised turkeys for market.

No state surpassed Missouri in raising mules. Louis M. Monsees of Pettis County had raised mules near Smithton during the late 1870s. The railroads allowed him to market them nationally. His skill as a breeder made his annual mule auctions the largest in the country. During the decade of the 1890s, the number of Missouri mules increased from 196,000 to 248,850. Besides exporting Missouri mules within the United States, especially to the Southern states, Missouri breeders sold more than one hundred thousand mules to Great Britain during the Boer War between 1899 and 1902. The firm of Guyton and Harrington of Lathrop not only supplied the British with mules but also sent them sixty-five thousand horses as well. During the Spanish-American War, the United States government invested more than half a million dollars in Missouri horses and mules. Buyers preferred Missouri mules because the state's breeders chose to produce large, powerful animals by carefully selecting the animals they paired. High-quality mules sold well. In 1890 a Boonville newspaper reported one jack selling for $800 and another bringing $1,000 in February, and a batch of mules selling for between $100 and $140 apiece during April.

By 1900, Missouri saddle horses had become known throughout the nation. In 1886, L. D. Morris, Clark Potts, R. W. Edmondson, Jack Harrison, and G. Tom King brought four stallions from Kentucky named Black Squirrel, Moss Rose, Artist Montrose, and Mark Diamond. They sired a string of fine horses that helped to establish Missouri's reputation as a producer of saddle horses. John Harrison of Auxvasse sold an average of forty horses per year during the 1890s, receiving $1,665 for Rex Denmark, a horse that subsequently sired the famous Rex McDonald. Rex McDonald won first places and sweepstakes from 1894 to 1903 at the St. Louis fair, and in 1903 received designation as the "champion saddle horse in America." Famous horsemen included A. B. Hughes, Moss A. Robertson, A. F. Styles, J. A. Potts, and Ryland Todhunter. None of them matched the record of Tom Bass, a former slave who rode, trained, and raised horses in Mexico, Missouri.

Owners of breeding stock sometimes advertised their animals in local newspapers. J. L. Simpson, residing near Bethany, owned a Norman stallion named Gray Tom. During the spring of 1890, he announced in the *Bethany Republican* that Gray Tom would be at his farm on Mondays and Tuesdays, at John McEver's barn on Wednesdays and Thursdays, and at Jos. Newland's barn on Fridays and Saturdays. Even Gray Tom apparently took Sunday off. The same issue of the paper carried three other advertisements for stud services.

Agricultural specialization and production for a national market drove land prices up slightly during the 1890s, but prices varied greatly across the state. In Howard County, for example, R. T. Kingsbury sold a fine farm of 257 acres in 1890 for $31 per acre, but Rose Smith sold her 231-acre farm in the same neighborhood for $21 per acre. In 1900 farms with good river bottomland sold for $50 per acre; upland farms for $40 per acre; and farms in less-fertile northeastern Howard County for $25 an acre. Both Kingsbury and Smith farmed in southern Howard County. In Cooper County, L. H. Hansberger sold his "fine farm" near Lone Elm for $40 per acre in 1890. It contained 175 acres. Another farm of 117 acres near Billingsville in Cooper County brought $36 per acre. In 1900 Cooper County bottomland brought as much as $70 per acre. Hill and prairie land sold for $45 to $50 per acre, and rough timberland sold for $25 to $30 an acre.

In Knox County, in 1890 Samuel Hunter sold his 400-acre farm to Henry Bell for $18.75 an acre. By 1900, the cheapest Knox County land sold for from $20 to $40 per acre and the best prairie land brought $30 to $50 per acre. In southeast Missouri unimproved land sold cheaply in 1890. A local newspaper listed land at $10 per acre. Some of that stayed on the market in 1900. The 300,000 acres of Dunklin County that remained unimproved could be purchased for as little as $7.50 per acre in the southern part of the county and for $12.50 to $17.50 in the northern half. The more than 100,000 acres of improved land, however, sold for from $30 to $40 an acre in more remote rural areas and for from $45 to $55 near Kennett, Malden, Campbell, Senath, or Cardwell. Land values in Dunklin County and other parts of "swampeast" Missouri rose dramatically after efforts were made to drain the swamps and reclaim marshland for agricultural use. In 1905 Otto Kochtitsky, a lumberman, led the effort, aided by survey and planning funds made available by the state legislature. Kochtitsky began by redirecting the flow of the Little River into the Mississippi and St. Francis River waters. At one-mile intervals in low areas he dug ditches to drain the land and built levees to guard the drained area from runoff. At a cost of $13 million, paid for by assessing owners of the drained land at the rate of from $4 to $40 per acre, Kochtitsky succeeded in making 550,000 acres of land available for cultivation. Others followed his example to make the entire southeast region one of the most productive areas in the state. In 1909, Dunklin County alone produced 31,000 bales of cotton, and in 1918 farmers of the region planted 156,000 acres in the crop. Of course, in such Ozark counties as Phelps, Taney, and Shannon, even improved land brought less than $25 per acre and unimproved land could be purchased for less than $10 per acre. Some Taney County land sold in 1900 for $1.25 an acre. According to one report, one could have purchased 90 percent of Ozark County for between $1.25 and $2.50 an acre at the turn of the century.

Credit made the farm economy work but also caused it serious problems. A Kennett editor warned his readers to use credit with prudence. He wrote, "Be careful how you buy, what you buy and if you have been wise in your purchases and industrious you will have something at the end of the year to represent your toil." Money was not easy to borrow in many parts of Missouri during the last decade of the nineteenth century. Many rural counties entered the 1890s without even one bank to serve their citizens, and there was a pronounced hostility of urban banks toward their country cousins. Moreover, many of the rural banks had limited capital, most of which was committed by the time farmers needed to borrow money for taxes at year's end. According to the *Bankers and Attorneys Register* for 1888, only three banks in Missouri (outside of Kansas City and St. Louis) had "paid-up capital" of as much as $200,000. By contrast, a number of rural banks had only paid-up capital of $5,000. The situation improved somewhat during the next few years, but many Missouri farmers found it necessary to borrow from eastern insurance companies such as Phoenix Mutual Life Insurance Company of Hartford, Connecticut. This company advertised in an Edina newspaper as "the first to introduce eastern money into this part of the state." It noted that, "For years all other companies were afraid of Missouri and afraid to loan money here." Phoenix offered loans with land as collateral at 6 percent interest, with a "small commission charged." Lawrence County farmers could get the same rate of interest on their loans, but the "small commission" turned out to be 2 percent.

According to historian Homer Clevenger, eastern money had been available earlier as well. A cartoon in the *St. Louis Republican* for March 13, 1888, showed "an eastern capitalist" shepherding a line of "chained and handcuffed farmers into a courthouse upon which was the sign, 'Farm Mortgages foreclosed Here.' " By state law interest rates could not be higher than 10 percent before 1891, when another state law reduced the rate to 8 percent. But agents charged commissions above that. For example, Kansas City and St. Joseph loan companies charged as much as 15 percent for a five-year loan to farmers who borrowed to increase land holdings or buy machinery and such household conveniences as sewing machines, steam washers, curtains, carpets, wall decorations, and kerosene lamps.

Many Missouri farmers lost their farms in sheriff's sales during the 1890s. Sheriff's sales took place when individuals could not pay taxes on their property or could not pay some other creditor. The sheriff then sold the property on the courthouse steps. The *Boonville Semi-Weekly Star* for February 2, 1890, reported thirty-eight sheriff's sales. The paper commented on an advertisement in the *Morgan County Leader,* which urged people to settle in that county, asserting, "it is not consistent to invite immigrants in a double-leaded primer article when it is next door neighbor to a nonpareil Sheriff's sale." During the same year, a Lawrence County newspaper in January carried a full column of sheriff's sales, and in an issue a month later it listed sixteen pieces of property subject to the same end. The Kennett newspaper listed sheriff's sales each week.

Among others, Eli T. Anderson and R. R. Bishop had their property seized in favor of the Mulburn Gin Company, with their land to be sold on the courthouse steps. The *Bethany Republican* listed a number of similar sales throughout 1890.

But the *Republican* editor saw hope rather than gloom. He noted that farmers controlled 80 percent of the wealth of Harrison County and that every interest in the county depended upon them. He thought the last twenty years had been good for farmers, and found neither financial nor spiritual depression in their ranks. He observed, "there are those who engage in all lines of business who fail. There is mismanagement, affliction, idleness, bad seasons, etc. that blot out many bright prospects," but they happened to a few, not to the majority.

Still, the regular presence of sheriff's sales for taxes raises the question of just how onerous taxes were in the state during the late nineteenth and early twentieth centuries. Taxes in Missouri remained low during this period. Between 1880 and 1900 the state taxes on property declined from 45 cents per $100 valuation to 25 cents per $100. During that twenty-year period, property became more valuable, so the amount the state received changed little. According to one authority, in 1902 Missouri's tax rate fell 46 cents per $100 below Nebraska's, 37 cents below Kansas's, and 23 cents below Iowa's and Illinois'. Missouri legislators bragged that the state devoted one-third of its revenue to public schools, but failed to note that the tax base remained so low that it provided only 12 cents per pupil per day in 1902.

County taxes varied greatly. In 1902, county officials taxed property owners at rates of from 25 percent to 75 percent of the property's real value. In addition, taxpayers paid county taxes of from 28 cents to $1.30 per $100 valuation. School taxes also varied about as much from county to county. When the average Pike Countian added school tax to his general county tax, he paid only 68 cents per $100 valuation. Pike County charged the lowest taxes in the state. Clay County, Mercer County, and St. Louis County residents paid only 74 cents per $100. Morgan County, a north Ozark county with timber covering 65 percent of its land, had the highest rate of taxation: $2 per $100 worth of property. Among other things, Morgan County shouldered a railroad debt of $124,500.

Morgan County was not alone: at the turn of the century, forty-eight of Missouri's counties carried some form of debt. Cass County led all others with a total debt of $934,000, divided between a county debt of $570,000 and township debts of $364,000. Lafayette had the second-highest, with county and township indebtedness of $790,700. None of the other counties reached a total of $500,000, although Henry County owed $455,000. Still, most counties had no debt at all, and among those that still had bonds in circulation, the vast majority owed limited sums. The building of railroads, the chief cause of the indebtedness, had hardly saddled most Missouri counties with intolerable obligations.

Still, Missourians were unsettled. The growing complexity and diversity of their economy had brought ever-increasing uncertainty to their lives. It was more difficult than ever for individuals to solve their own problems. City laborers worked long, hard hours under conditions and for wages that they could not control. They used their money to buy goods and services that a generation earlier they might have grown or made themselves, and the prices they paid were also out of their control. And farmers found that added to the vagaries of weather and the certainty of taxes was an ever-increasing competition that left them mystified at the process used to determine the prices they received for the products they produced. Moreover, the growing specialization of agriculture meant that farmers needed to look to others for an ever-increasing number of goods and services. And often they could consume those goods and services only by means of borrowed money. Out of necessity, then, farmers and other workers turned increasingly to politics in the 1890s and beyond as they sought stability and order in their lives.

CHAPTER V

THE CHALLENGES AND OPPORTUNITIES
OF A MODERNIZING STATE

In 1890, the United States Commissioner of Education issued a report on Missouri's public schools that confirmed what many in the state had long known: Missouri's public schools were far from adequate for an increasingly industrial society. The commissioner was especially critical of the rural schools, which, he said, reflected little organization. He called the grading classification "loose," commenting that he failed to see any system. He found that half the schools were taught by "inexperienced boys and girls, who should be attending some good schools" instead of teaching.

This rather sorry state of affairs was the logical result of two developments that had occurred more than a decade before. First, much of the decision making about education had been placed in the hands of local school boards composed largely of rural Missourians whose commitment to formal education was often lukewarm. Second, at virtually every level of life, a majority of Missourians had expressed a desire to see their taxes assessed at the lowest possible level.

By 1890, a growing number of people in the state, although certainly not a majority, began to try to improve the quality of education in the Show-Me State. Teacher institutes, for example, became an important vehicle for improving the skills of people already working in Missouri's classrooms. Usually held at the county level, these institutes offered instruction in how and what to teach. In Harrison County, for example, teachers attended two institutes in the fall of 1890. In the one conducted by Butler Tays, teachers received instruction in science, United States history, and music. The institute held in New Hampton featured United States history and primary numbers. Harry Gilbert discussed the teaching of numbers and Miss Jane Young gave a recitation on the "Causes of the Revolution."

While teacher institutes were held in many parts of the state in 1890, they did not run for any specified length of time, and no law mandated that teachers attend them. That changed in 1891, when the General Assembly passed a law requiring teachers in the field to attend institutes conducted by the county superintendent of schools. The law specified that institutes last for a minimum of two weeks. An institute sponsored by the Wright County Board of Education between July 23 and August 2, 1901, attracted a total of ninety-eight teachers, forty-six of them women. Held in Hartville, the institute was conducted by Professor L. W. Rader of Kansas City, described by a local newspaper as "one of the best educators of the state." The board made it clear that one could not expect to receive a certificate to teach in Wright County unless one could demonstrate regular attendance at the institute. "Excuses and modified ignorance," the newspaper reported, "will be remembered against each one so pleading." Five years later, the two-week Hartville institute had expanded into a seven-week summer school that required participants to attend six days a week. The summer school ran from April 23 to June 9 and concluded with examinations required of all teachers who hoped to teach in the county schools during the next academic year. Teachers who needed additional training were invited to enroll in a summer program that began at the State Normal Summer School in Springfield on June 11, 1906.

Some counties attacked the problems of their schools by creating committees to oversee instruction; some went so far as to create a monthly outline for teachers to follow. For January of 1891, for example, a school committee of Harrison County gave general directions about instruction for the different grades and became quite specific about a geography assignment. The committee required students to draw a map of Missouri in which they showed the location of Harrison County and its adjoining counties as well as the state's chief rivers, mountains, and cities. Students had to compare Harrison County with the rest of the state in the products it produced and in other categories; they also had to show the differences between north and south Missouri in topography, resources, and political divisions. The committee urged teachers to get students to do their own research and instructed them to "Drill, Review, Drill, and Review." Students were to do their own written work: "No copying." The committee expected moral values and manners to be taught. It told teachers to choose good examples and to read and discuss them during opening exercises each day. Discipline should allow "each pupil [to] recognize his citizenship of right and duties in the school, but when the rules of good citizenship are willfully violated, punish promptly." In Wright County in 1900, parents simply showed up at the school en masse to inspect the school and watch its operation. The *Wright County Progress* reported on January 5, 1900, that on a Monday afternoon thirty or more parents visited a local school.

Another way in which Missourians sought to improve teacher preparation was to give added support to teacher education programs at Missouri's state normal schools in Kirksville, Warrensburg, and Cape Girardeau. Two more regional teacher training schools were added in 1905 when similar institutions were established in Springfield and Maryville. The Springfield school served twenty-two southwest counties of the state. The Fifth District Normal School in Maryville served nineteen northwest Missouri counties. The University of Missouri also held teacher institutes in various parts of the state, such as one held at Ava in southwest Missouri between June 10 and July 27, 1901. Missouri's private colleges also tried to assist in improving teacher training. Drury College in Springfield, for example, offered a seven-week summer school that ran from late June to mid-August. According to a 1906 newspaper advertisement, the school was "organized primarily for the benefit of teachers who desire to better equip themselves for their work."

In 1911, the State of Missouri passed a new teacher certification law aimed at centralizing the certification of teachers and thereby improving their quality. State Superintendent of Schools William P. Evans hailed the new law as being "among the more progressive" in the country. Although many reformers hoped the new law would move teacher certification out of the hands of local school boards and into the purview of professionally trained educators at the state level, county superintendents and their constituents resisted the move. Evans estimated that in 1911, 85 percent of the state's teachers still taught on county certificates. The 1911 law continued to allow counties to certify teachers in rural Missouri schools who had "scarcely more than completed the eighth grade of the elementary schools."

Teaching was clearly a predominantly female profession in Missouri by the end of the first decade of the twentieth century. The 1911 state superintendent of public schools' report indicates that of the 17,781 white public school teachers employed in the state, only 25 percent were male. Although female teachers greatly outnumbered males, they were paid nearly 12 percent less. The average salary for a male teacher in 1911 was $60.51 per month; for a female, $53.54.

There were also 765 "colored" teachers in Missouri in 1911, almost one-third of them male, a reflection of the more limited job opportunities available to black men. Preparation of African American teachers in Missouri continued to be concentrated at Lincoln Institute in Jefferson City, although the emphasis on vocational training increased during the late nineteenth century. As historian W. Sherman Savage has written, "While [Lincoln's] special mission was to train teachers for Negro public schools of the state, the industrial features were stressed, including instruction given in farming, gardening, carpentry, woodworking, blacksmithing, mechanics, shoemaking, sewing, cooking and laundering." The leader who shaped the institute most during the early twentieth century was President Benjamin F. Allen, a native of Savannah, Georgia, and a graduate of Atlanta University.

Not all African American students who sought postelementary school education attended Lincoln Institute, of course. The most important alternative to Lincoln in outstate Missouri during the early twentieth century was the Bartlett Agricultural and Industrial School, later called the Dalton Vocational School, in Chariton County. This school was founded in 1907 by Nathaniel C. Bruce, a graduate of Booker T. Washington's acclaimed Tuskegee Institute in Alabama. Indeed, Bruce often referred to his creation as "The Tuskegee of the Midwest."

Although Bruce's school struggled through its early years, it achieved notoriety in 1914 when Bartlett students won a corn-growing contest sponsored by the Missouri Corn Growers' Association and the *Missouri Ruralist*. Subsequently, Bruce and his students won other regional and national contests, bringing much favorable attention to the school. When asked to explain his success, Bruce replied, "Place Missouri black boys on Missouri black land, behind the world-famed Missouri mule, and nothing can beat the combination for raising corn or other crops." In addition to operating the Bartlett School, Bruce also sponsored an annual Missouri-Mid-Western States Negro Farmers' and Farm Women's Conference, which sometimes attracted as many as fifteen hundred "country life" blacks to its farm produce exhibits.

Yet another important teacher training school for Missouri blacks at the turn of the century was the George R. Smith College, opened in

Sedalia in 1894. In addition to a normal school program, the curriculum of George R. Smith College included elementary grades, a college preparatory program, a four-year college program, and a one-year Bible study course. The school was founded by the Freedmen's Aid and Southern Education Society of the Methodist Episcopal Church with help from a gift of land by the daughters of Sedalia's founder, the school's namesake. George R. Smith College attracted hundreds of African American students from Missouri and eight other states until a disastrous fire destroyed the school in 1925. It was not rebuilt.

Not all efforts at improving Missouri's schools were focused on teacher preparation. During the last decade of the nineteenth century a movement to enact a compulsory education law began to take shape. That effort culminated in 1905 with a statute that required children between the ages of six and fourteen years to attend a school, either public or private, for at least half the year. The law also required those youngsters between the ages of fourteen and sixteen who were not employed to attend school. In 1907 legislators acted to remove that loophole by requiring the parents of children between the ages of six and sixteen to send their children to school for a full term. There remained an exemption for those children who lived in poverty and were forced to work, although those students were required to attend evening classes.

In his study of the compulsory education law, historian Richard Ives discovered no opposition to the legislation. While civic reform leaders such as St. Louisans Dr. Calvin W. Woodward, manufacturer N. O. Nelson, women's club leader and activist Mrs. Philip N. Moore, Professor Arthur O. Lovejoy, Reverend John W. Day, Rabbi Samuel Sale, and General Secretary of International Building Trades Herman Steinbiss pushed the 1905 and 1907 laws, neither law attracted adverse comment in such diverse publications as the *Catholic Fortnightly, Jewish Voice, Post Dispatch,* or *Globe Democrat.* The Socialist party newspaper of Missouri, *Labor,* editorialized in favor of it. Such agreement on the issue suggests widespread support for the idea of public school education.

But not *universal* support. Many Missourians continued to support private education as an alternative to the public schools, which they perceived to be inadequate. Religious groups continued to operate parochial schools throughout the state, and many communities continued to establish academies for the education of their sons and daughters. On October 1, 1890, for example, an academy was opened in Miller County in the small town of Iberia. Known as the "Iberia Academy," the school operated in a two-story brick building and charged eighteen dollars per year for tuition and two dollars per week for board. The academy held its first graduation exercise in 1893. In 1905 it added a six-room building that served as a "girls' cottage." In 1870 the Christian Church (Disciples of Christ) had established a school in Camden Point for female children orphaned by the Civil War. After a disastrous fire in 1889, the institution moved to Fulton and took the name "Daughter's College." Under its new name it began providing elementary and secondary education programs for young women who aspired to become teachers. In 1900 the school changed its name to William Woods College, in honor of Kansas City benefactor Dr. William Stone Woods. Arguably, the most successful private academy begun in Missouri during the early twentieth century was the School of the Ozarks, established by Presbyterians in 1906 at Forsyth to provide elementary and secondary education for "the financially under privileged." The school was moved to Point Lookout after a disastrous fire in 1915 and since 1916 has remained a leading institution in the region. Most of Missouri's private colleges conducted academies of the sort established by William Woods and the School of the Ozarks throughout the era before World War I.

Postsecondary educational opportunities were available to both men and women in the state in a variety of quarters by the early twentieth century. In addition to the state's five regional normal schools, which altogether enrolled 1,471 males and 2,336 females in 1910, another 2,956 students were enrolled at the state university in Columbia. Major private colleges in the state that accepted both men and women in 1910 included Central College in Fayette, Central Wesleyan College in Warrenton, Drury College in Springfield, Missouri Valley College in Marshall, Park College in Parkville, Tarkio College in Tarkio, and Washington University in St. Louis.

Community school activities, especially in rural areas, continued to provide a major source of entertainment for Missourians during the late nineteenth and early twentieth centuries, much as they had done for earlier generations. Parents, friends, and onlookers in search of entertainment continued to attend closing-of-school exercises, declamatory contests, spelling bees, and other student-centered activities. In 1900, for example, the Bootheel towns of New Madrid, Kennett, and Caruthersville held an "Inter-County Declamatory Contest." Sponsors held the contest at the Opera House in New Madrid. Each town could send two representatives. The *Dunklin County Democrat* editor looked forward to Rue Rice's presentation of an imitation sermon called "The Flood" and Jimmie King's speech called "Our Flag." Neither Kennett orator won, as New Madrid's Miss Josie Hart received first prize. People in the area no doubt took the contest seriously: The *Democrat* editor, in fact, questioned the decisions of the three judges. A few years later, Cooper County students from about forty of the area's rural schools competed in spelling and mathematics contests in Boonville's Laura Speed Elliott High School. Winners in mathematics received cash prizes of fifteen dollars for first place, ten dollars for second place, and five dollars for third place.

Home entertainments continued to make up a significant part of social life during the late nineteenth and early twentieth centuries in Missouri. Residents of the state attended musical evenings, dances, costume parties, discussion groups, and Sunday dinners in each other's homes. Few home entertainments anywhere surpassed the parties held by the Leonard and Stephens families of Boonville. One Tuesday evening Mrs. C. E. Leonard gave a party for one hundred guests at her home on Sixth Street. Susie Edgar, Gertrude Koontz, and Mary Johnson dressed as characters from the "Mikado." Mrs. Lon V. Stephens, wife of the future governor, held a party in March in honor of two women from West Virginia and Miss Edith Leonard of Saline County, Missouri. Professors A. H. Sauter and E. O. Weber of the Cooper Institute provided some of the music. In June, Mrs. W. Speed Stephens honored her daughter, Rhoda, with an evening of music, dancing, and feasting. Her Boonville mansion with "its beautiful grounds" served as the site. Guests came from Marshall, Kansas City, and Sedalia as well as from the surrounding area.

Christmas and New Year's Day offered the most pleasures during the winter season. Skating parties, suppers, and gatherings of various kinds brought people together. On one New Year's Day in Carthage, fifty gentlemen went to a select group of houses decorated and prepared by Mrs. A. H. Coffee, Mrs. I. N. Lamb, Mrs. C. L. Bartlett, and the unmarried Roessler sisters. Inclement weather failed to dampen spirits, and the houses' interiors glowed with gas illumination. The women who received the men wore "full dress" and served refreshments, the men left their cards as mementos of the event, while women in each house gave a favor to the men—a spray of mistletoe at Mrs. Bartlett's, a cigar at

Mrs. Coffee's, and a lapel pin at Mrs. Lamb's. Participants enjoyed the day so much that they committed themselves to do it the next year. The editor who reported the event predicted that the "old fashioned custom of paying and receiving calls" would enjoy a "thorough revival in our city."

Knox County had two organized groups that met in members' homes and sometimes gave entertainments attended by the public. Members of the Mozart Club played music and sang for their own entertainment. At one session, a violin duet and vocal music accompanied by a piano made up the program. The club's name indicated classical music, but a Mrs. Gifford sang "Old Folks at Home" during one meeting of the group. Both men and women joined the Mozart Club. The E. B. Browning Club had only women members, but both married and single women joined. The club met monthly, and at one meeting Miss Alice Stauder read Alfred Tennyson's "The Gardener's Daughter," and members discussed the history of Rome. Mrs. J. D. Wilson read her paper on the Roman Praetorian Guards as a part of the evening's entertainment. On Valentine's Day, the Browning Club offered the public an evening of readings, music, and refreshment in the Edina Seminary building. About thirty-six people came; each received a souvenir valentine.

The Browning Club reflected a growing interest among Missouri women in forming clubs of their own. There were so many women's organizations in the United States that a national group known as the General Federation of Women's Clubs (GFWC) was formed in 1892. Among the more prominent club women in Missouri was Constance Fauntleroy Runcie, who organized the Runcie Club in St. Joseph during the 1890s. Runcie, a granddaughter of Utopian socialist Robert Owen, used money from her recently deceased husband's estate to build a house in St. Joseph that had one great room downstairs, divided only by a fireplace. As historian Janice Brandon-Falcone has written, "It was a room ideally suited for entertaining large groups, hosting lectures, offering classes, holding concerts, or supporting weekly gatherings of twenty-five to a hundred women—exactly the kind of activities Runcie planned." The Runcie Club charged dues of one dollar per month in exchange for which its members were entertained and uplifted with weekly lectures, recitations, and musical performances. By 1894, as Brandon-Falcone points out, "the Runcie Club boasted ninety-five members, mostly from important and well-to-do families of St. Joseph." By century's end, women's clubs began increasingly to supplement their social and entertainment role with an interest in civic reform and societal uplift. In St. Louis, a woman's club known as the "Wednesday Club" formed in 1890 and quickly developed a reputation for intellectual seriousness. Its founding members included the prominent St. Louis writer Kate Chopin and Charlotte Eliot, the mother of poet T. S. Eliot.

African American women, denied membership in white women's organizations, formed their own clubs. Josephine Silone Yates, the educator and writer, served as president of the first black women's club in Missouri, the Women's League of Kansas City, formed in 1893. Among the first projects of the Women's League was the establishment of "an industrial home and school for teaching cooking, sewing and other useful employments." The league also started a kindergarten and, later, purchased a six-room house at 1625 Cottage Street in Kansas City as a "Home for Working Girls." While teaching at Lincoln Institute in Jefferson City during the early 1900s, Yates started a women's club known as the Olive Branch. Between 1901 and 1906, Yates was president of the GFWC's black counterpart, the National Association of Colored Women. During Yates's presidency, the NACW's membership rose to fifteen thousand members spread across twenty-six states and Indian Territory.

To a great extent, entertainment continued to follow seasonal patterns in Missouri at the turn of the century. Like their descendants nearly a century later, Missourians were most active during the warmer months. Summer stimulated interest in riding bicycles, a craze that crossed the nation during the 1890s. In Moberly, riders moved along Reed Street. There, cyclists formed an association, wrote a constitution, charged dues, and adopted costumes to wear. The club met twice a month and claimed fourteen paying members. Reverend J. B. Welty even visited his parishioners by riding a bicycle.

Warm weather in St. Louis often meant playing soccer, especially in working-class ethnic neighborhoods. By 1900, more than 60 percent of St. Louis's residents were either first- or second-generation immigrants. According to historian George Lipsitz, "Soccer came to St. Louis as a consequence of working-class migration from Europe in the nineteenth century." Businesses that employed large numbers of ethnic workers sponsored soccer teams, as did benevolent societies such as the Scottish Thistles and the Irish Hibernians. Indeed, Lipsitz argues that "Soccer fields themselves went beyond service as the site of athletic contests;

at Seventeenth and Jefferson in Kerry Patch, at Jefferson and Cass in midtown, and at Compton and the railroad tracks on the south side, soccer fields became multipurpose centers of social life for immigrants and their families."

Baseball continued to hold a special allure for Missourians. By 1902, the St. Louis Browns had become a part of the American League and the St. Louis Cardinals had organized to play in the National League. Kansas City had no major league team, but before 1900 both the "Plug Uglies" and the "Nose Crackers" represented the sport in the city. Later the Kansas City Blues became a top-flight minor league team, and the Kansas City Monarchs played in the professional black leagues, often compiling an outstanding record. St. Louis fielded a black team named the Giants and carried on a well-followed rivalry with teams from Chicago and Pittsburgh in particular. Later the St. Louis black professional team became the Stars. While professional baseball attracted crowds in Missouri's two large cities, amateur baseball continued to rule in the countryside. In northeast Missouri, the towns of Edina, Kirksville, Clarence, Macon, Canton, and Labelle joined Quincy, Illinois, to form a league, and other communities throughout the state did likewise each summer.

Picnics and swimming provided outdoor enjoyments and helped Missourians escape the heat of summer. Young women in Kennett invited some of the young men on what the local newspaper called a "Mother Hubbard Picnic." Some of Kennett's young men organized a Bathing, Boating, and Outing Club, no doubt in order to attract young women and to enjoy the water in the Varner River. The club officers planned to build a large bathhouse for each sex and a huge platform three feet under the water, "for the benefit of those just learning to swim." Overnight fishing trips with multiple families involved were quite common.

A high point of every summer in many Missouri counties continued to be the annual fair. In 1890, forty-one Missouri counties and the cities of St. Charles and St. Louis held fairs. Indeed, time was often measured by the fair: how long was it until the fair, how long had it been since the last one? Typical of Missouri county fairs during the 1890s was the one held in Randolph County, which lasted five days. For the first day, officials scheduled a two-hundred-yard foot race for boys under fourteen years of age and a beauty contest to choose the prettiest girl under age eighteen.

Officials made it clear that the judges for the beauty contest would come from outside the county to ensure impartiality. The second day encouraged older people to attend; everyone older than seventy received free admittance. Highlights included speech-making and music by a "cupid band," made up of children under age fourteen.

In the exposition hall, fair-goers could see the Cardiff Giant, mummies two thousand years old, and ancient relics from Randolph County. Winners of the various competitions received their prizes, and horses raced on the third day. Organizers promised a huge fox hunt on day four. Two hundred hounds, with twenty blooded dogs coming from Kansas City, would chase twenty-five foxes and perhaps wild deer imported from Indian Territory. On the last day, homely men would compete for a silver cup. Officials thought it unnecessary to promise impartiality in the ugly man contest.

Competitions ranged from best ten pounds of homemade hard and soft soap to best collection of stuffed birds. Randolph Countians competed in quilting, knitting, darning, crocheting, and rug-making. They displayed their drawings, paintings, wood carvings, jellies, jams, cakes, chickens, turkeys, ducks, cattle, hogs, sheep, mules, photographs, and musical instruments. For the horse races, animals came from Nebraska, Illinois, and Kansas as well as Missouri. One year Randolph County's fair featured a daily balloon ascension and parachute jump.

As entertaining and eagerly anticipated as county fairs were, the ultimate fair-going experience for most Missourians at the turn of the century was a trip to the Missouri State Fair at Sedalia. In 1899, Missouri's General Assembly passed legislation to create a permanent site for the state fair. Sedalia, Boonville, Centralia, Chillicothe, Mexico, Moberly, and Marshall all sought the fair. Kansas City and St. Louis could not be chosen because the legislature required a central location. On June 3, 1899, delegations from competing towns appeared before Governor Lon V. Stephens and the State Board of Agriculture to make their appeals. While Marshall and Mexico offered well-structured arguments, Sedalia carried the day. According to Governor Stephens, Sedalia won the fair because of its central location, railroad connections, relatively large population, and the passage of bond issues to bring city water and electrical power to the fairgrounds. The city's electric railroad also promised to give 5 percent of its earnings from the line that went from the fairgrounds to the State Board of Agriculture.

The heart of the fairgrounds was a 160-acre tract of land donated by the J. C. Riper family. In 1918 a campground was added to the original site, and over the next three years fair officials added more land, bringing the total to 236 acres by 1921. This completed the expansion of the fairgrounds until after World War II. The layout and design of the fairgrounds was carried out by George E. Kessler, the well-known landscape architect from Kansas City.

The first fair week in 1901 brought rain on Monday, Tuesday, and Wednesday, turning Kessler's roadways and the grounds into a sea of mud. Nevertheless, twenty thousand people turned out, producing gate receipts of $8,249. Fair Board President Norman J. Colman thought the fair had gone well, indicating income at least matched expenditures. Horse races conducted on the well-banked, oval, one-mile track attracted the biggest crowds, in large part because little else had been completed on the grounds. By the time of the 1902 fair, Kessler had filled the treeless terrain with numerous shade trees. The fair board reported a slight profit. By 1907, the fairgrounds held fourteen buildings, including a large livestock pavilion completed at a cost of $70,000 in 1906. More than nine thousand people could see events. Its floor space took up a full acre. Large barns for cattle, horses, poultry, and mules made up ten of the buildings, with the other three named the Agriculture Building, the Horticultural Building, and the Machinery Building.

While Missourians did continue to seek their social and recreational pleasures according to the rhythms of the seasons, they, like other Americans, exercised growing control over nature, using electricity and gas to transform night into day and cold into warmth. The ultimate demonstration of this increasing power over nature came in the form of demonstrations of technological innovations provided at the 1904 World's Fair in St. Louis.

The great fair's origins can be traced to the failed effort to secure the Columbia Exposition in 1890 by St. Louis civic leaders. In spite of the fact that St. Louisans raised $4 million to attract the quadricentennial celebration of Columbus's founding of the country, the celebration went to St. Louis's archrival, Chicago.

The great success of the Chicago affair spurred St. Louisans to try again. In 1896, Pierre Chouteau suggested to a meeting of the Missouri Historical Society that Forest Park should be the site of a memorial to Thomas Jefferson that could house the documents of the

Louisiana Purchase. He also thought the one-hundredth anniversary of the purchase ought to be celebrated by the creation of a Creole village on the waterfront. St. Louis boosters thought Chouteau's ideas too modest.

In 1899, St. Louis hosted a meeting of delegates from the states carved out of the Louisiana Purchase. The delegates chose St. Louis over New Orleans as the proposed site for a grand celebration of the purchase. To finance the Louisiana Exposition, the name given to the celebration, St. Louisans promised to raise $5 million from private sources and $5 million from bonds issued by the city. Delegates from the other states committed themselves to help Missourians raise an additional $5 million from Congress. The $15 million price tag for the Exposition carried great symbolism since in 1803 Jefferson paid Napoleon that exact sum in the "greatest land deal in history."

In December of 1900, the Louisiana Purchase Company announced the completion of the $5 million fund drive. The company had sold shares of stock at ten dollars per share. State and city regulations had to be changed before the city could meet its own $5 million obligation. Voters approved the changes in 1900, and the city made its bonds available in 1901, providing for their payment with a ten-cent tax levy beginning in 1903. To manage the Exposition, stockholders elected mostly members of the city's social elite, with a smattering of labor and ethnic members, as a 118-member board of directors.

The congressional appropriation took longer and required a strong lobbying effort. According to St. Louis historian James Neal Primm, Missouri Senator George Graham Vest removed the last obstacle when he persuaded South Carolina Senator Ben Tillman to support the measure. Congress appropriated the money on March 4, 1901, with the provision that fair managers could spend the federal money only after the $10 million from St. Louis had been used.

Promoters discussed a variety of sites for the St. Louis Exposition before deciding upon the western half of Forest Park as the central location. In addition, the Exposition directors arranged to lease the new campus of Washington University and to purchase adjoining land to create grounds of 1,272 acres, considerably larger than the grounds of Chicago's Columbia Exposition. Walks and roadways on the St. Louis grounds totaled about seventy-five miles, and a visitor could walk for nine miles in the Palace of Agriculture alone without retracing a step. Good rail connections and roadways connected the fairgrounds with the city.

In preparation for the fair, a new organization called the Civic Improvement League worked for the completion and paving of Kingshighway as a link connecting the various parts of the city. Formed by Mrs. Louis Marion McCall and growing to more than one thousand members, the league attacked a host of city problems in order to improve St. Louis and its image before the anticipated millions flocked to what soon became known as the World's Fair. Improvements in the city's waterworks, street railways, air quality, and the physical appearance of neighborhoods occupied the reformers and their mayor, Rolla Wells. In 1903, McCall published an article claiming that the beautification campaign she led had created a "Moral Awakening" that permeated the city. Roadway projects alone numbered 277, according to Primm, and resulted in more than seventy miles of streets being rebuilt and thirty miles of roads being added. Within a year after the effort to abate the heavy smoke that polluted St. Louis's air began, investigators reported a 70 percent decline in dense smoke.

Meanwhile, under the leadership of former Governor David Francis and the board of directors, construction began on the grounds. Organizers conceived a plan of twelve huge exhibit halls or palaces, with the smallest covering more than four acres. The Agricultural Palace, the largest structure, occupied more than eighteen acres. Ornate, varied, and mostly ivory in color, the palaces impressed those who saw them with their size and magnificence. Because a number of states and nations invited to have exhibits believed they could not meet the April 30, 1903, date for opening, Congress allowed a one-year delay. President Theodore Roosevelt solicited support for the fair from nations around the world, and David Francis toured European capitals in 1903. Columbia newspaperman Walter Williams spearheaded efforts to publicize the fair in the foreign press. Primm wrote that Williams covered "25,000 miles in nine months, visiting one thousand newspaper offices in twenty-five countries in Europe, Asia, Latin America and North Africa."

Ultimately, forty-three nations erected buildings at the fair, joining forty-five states and territories that built pavilions or created exhibitions. Missouri's million-dollar structure led others in size and decoration. The unqualified success of the fair was recorded by David Francis in a massive two-volume work published in 1913 under the title of *The Universal Exposition of 1904*. During the 184 days that the fair was open, 19,694,855 visitors attended.

Arguably, one of the most startling technological innovations show-cased at the 1904 World's Fair was the automobile. The automobile changed the lives of twentieth-century Missourians as much as the railroads had changed the lives of their nineteenth-century ancestors. Indeed, historian John C. Crighton has written, "The substitution of the automobile for the horse as the major means of transportation was one of the most important social changes of the twentieth century." The automobile spawned new roads and the placement of houses along those roads. The automobile gave rise to suburban living and to one-dimensional neighborhoods, where residents lived out their private lives away from their work, the stores where they shopped, and the churches where they worshiped. The automobile suited individualistic Americans, allowing them to travel long distances by themselves or with close family members and to avoid traveling with large groups of strangers.

The automobile was also a status symbol, an item of "conspicuous consumption" as the economist Thorstein Veblen would write in his 1899 book *The Theory of the Leisure Class,* a widely influential book written before Veblen's somewhat troubled tenure at the University of Missouri. Early automobiles were quite expensive. In 1905 a Studebaker sold for $1,350, which was approximately three times the annual salary of an industrial worker, while a Peerless five-passenger car sold for $3,200. Few Missourians could afford such high prices; most had to wait until Henry Ford introduced his Model T in 1907 before they could even begin to consider buying a car. In 1908, a Model T cost approximately $825, a figure that Ford reduced to $350 by 1917.

While the automobile brought many positive changes to the lives of Missourians, it also spawned new challenges and problems for residents of the modernizing state. Automobile accidents began to occur, for example. According to North Todd Gentry, the first automobile accident in Missouri occurred in Boone County in 1911. Miss Pearl Mitchell hit the rear end of a surrey when a dog chasing a rabbit ran into the front wheel of her Model T Ford, causing her vehicle to spin out of control and into the horse-drawn carriage. The accident broke a wheel on the Ford and caused the occupants of the surrey—a farmer, his wife, two children, and a baby—to be dumped onto the ground. In a single week in April of 1915, Lawrence County recorded three automobile accidents with two fatalities. H. B. Pankey and T. R. R. Ely were less unfortunate than those who died in their cars. Those Kennett residents went to St. Louis to buy a new car. On their way home on a Saturday evening in 1917, they smashed into a bridge trestle located just south of Ste. Genevieve. Pankey cut his head and face seriously; Ely escaped with just bad bruises. The accident demolished the car. In addition to accidents, car thefts became increasingly common. The *Bethany Republican* reported in 1917 that "Auto thieves are getting to be about as thick as chiggers in this part of the state. During the last five days probably six or eight cars have been stolen within a radius of thirty miles of Bethany."

Although still in its infancy even on the eve of America's involvement in World War I, automobile travel had a great impact on Missourians. Speed of travel increased greatly. In the winter of 1917, for example, one motorist traveled between Albany, Missouri, and Sutherland, Nebraska, a distance of five hundred miles, in twenty-three hours of continuous driving, for an average of about twenty-two miles per hour. Sometimes people used automobiles for pure pleasure. Geographer Carol O. Sauer remembered, "When the first automobiles came to my hometown there existed a single stretch of eight miles of smooth road to a neighboring town. People who had cars soon formed the habit of evening drives back and forth over this stretch for the sheer exhileration of rapid motion. . . . The American has become habituated to relocating himself beyond the proper call of bettering his position, a new restless nomad."

Another innovation destined to change the lives of Missourians was the moving picture show. According to historian Joe E. Smith, Thomas Edison's kinetoscope made "peep shows" available to Missourians during the early 1890s, although opera houses and live theater were still the dominant sources of entertainment throughout the decade of the 1890s. Indeed, every 1890s town of any size in Missouri had an opera house, with the largest, of course, being in St. Louis and Kansas City; there one could hear performers such as the pianist Jan Paderewsky, Sarah Bernhardt, Oscar Wilde, Caruso, and Adelina Patti.

While rural Missourians could only envy the easy access of their urban cousins to "serious" musical presentations, they occasionally got their chance. In Boonville, for example, the women of the Methodist Episcopal Church, South, sponsored "the great violinist" Joseph Heine; Madame Ada Heine, "the renowned pianist," and Evelyn Heine, "the charming soprano and violinist," in concert. In Edina, Biggerstaff's opera house hosted the Alonzo Hatch Opera Company, which sang the comic opera *Fra Diavola;* a presentation by the Edina Seminary and School of Music; an operetta entitled *Laila,* performed by the girls of a Catholic school; and a week-long appearance by the touring Spooner Comedy Company. In southeast Missouri the Kennett Opera House booked the Dixie Belles Concert Company, a "literary, musical affair, elevating and educational in its effect." The local newspaper editor described the Belles as "refined, polished and finished Southern-bred women."

Initially, moving pictures were often shown in opera houses, although increasingly it became customary to erect new, less ornate and simpler structures for the movie-going public. To a great extent, these new, simpler facilities reflected a new clientele. As Joe E. Smith has pointed out, "The poorer and working class citizens probably could not afford to attend the legitimate theatre." By 1907, St. Louis alone had twenty-seven movie theaters. In Kansas City, an estimated 449,064 persons attended movies weekly at one of the city's eighty-one movie theaters. According to historian Julie A. Willett, "Many of the earliest nickelodeons were converted from empty shops or shacks located behind crowded tenements. . . . Cramped and roughly adorned, nickel theatres nevertheless attracted large crowds of enthusiastic patrons who rarely objected to standing for the relatively short duration of these early films." In 1908, the best seats in a Columbia opera house sold for two dollars. By contrast, one could go to the nickelodeon and watch "the championship Detroit-Chicago [baseball] game" for ten cents. Other movies at the nickelodeon could be watched for five cents.

The cheapness of movies, in fact, prompted a group of University of Missouri students to launch a business venture in 1909: the establishment of a moving-picture theater for Columbia's African Americans. Known as the "Negro Nickelodeon," this theater lasted only a short time, largely because blacks did not have the discretionary income to treat themselves to movies on a regular basis. That fact notwithstanding, a local newspaper writer attributed the failure of the theater to blacks' biological inferiority, which made it difficult for them "to follow the rapidly moving images of the motion pictures."

Although the black movie house closed in Columbia, other movie theaters remained open in the college town, taking advantage of the students' discretionary time and money. There was seemingly no end to the ways in which students could be entertained during the first decade of the twentieth century. One important way was the new sport of college football. The University of Missouri fielded its first intercollegiate football team in 1890. On Thanksgiving Day of that year a varsity team from Washington University defeated the university team by a score of 28 to 0. In spite of this lopsided loss, university curators soon set aside six acres of the college farm for a football field, and by 1891 the University of Missouri football team was playing a full schedule of games. By the early twentieth century the highlight of the season was an annual Thanksgiving Day game against Kansas. A 1905 *Missouri Alumni Quarterly* writer observed, "Socially the Missouri-Kansas game is the athletic event of the year here; financially it is the source of fifty per cent of the income of both the athletic associations concerned."

One of the most dramatic cultural developments in the state was the movement to establish community libraries. Kansas City built its first public library in 1897. Jefferson City began its effort in 1898 by establishing a subscription library. Two hundred and fifty subscribers paid three dollars a year each to belong. The first library facility was a room in the courthouse with approximately 365 volumes, most of them donated. The number of volumes grew to about twelve hundred during the library's first year of operation. In 1900, Jefferson City was the recipient of a $25,000 grant from Andrew Carnegie to build a new library facility. The city's Carnegie Library was dedicated on Christmas Eve, 1902. Sedalia also received a Carnegie grant in 1900 to establish a Carnegie Public Library. The $50,000 given by Carnegie allowed the Sedalia community to complete its library by 1901. The Springfield public library was built in 1905 at Jefferson and Center Streets, strategically located near both the senior high school and Drury College. This library also was made possible through Carnegie funds.

St. Louis residents passed a tax of one-fifth of a mill for the support of a public library in 1893, and the St. Louis Public Library opened for the first time on June 1, 1894. Andrew Carnegie donated $1 million to the St. Louis library system with the stipulation that half the money be used to build a main library facility and the other half to start branch libraries. Carnegie's generous contribution aided in the erection of a magnificent new library structure on Olive Street in downtown St. Louis, which opened to the public on January 6, 1912.

Another important event for reading Missourians during the early twentieth century was the establishment of the University of Missouri

School of Journalism in 1908. The force behind this innovative venture was veteran newspaperman Walter Williams, who had been a part-owner of the *Boonville Advertiser* and an editor of the *Columbia Herald* before becoming the School of Journalism's first dean. Under Williams's direction, the School of Journalism began producing much better-prepared editors and reporters for newspapers throughout Missouri and, indeed, the nation.

And what did literate Missourians read, besides their newspapers? The most popular early-twentieth-century Missouri writer may well have been Harold Bell Wright, whose 1907 book *Shepherd of the Hills* was an enormous success. Many Missourians were introduced to the writings of Laura Ingalls Wilder during this period. Wilder, who wrote initially under the name "Mrs. A. J. Wilder," penned articles about Missouri farm life for the *Kansas City Star* and the *Missouri Ruralist.* Other popular Missouri writers included St. Louis's Winston Churchill, whose first successful novel, *Richard Carvel,* appeared in 1907; Sarah Teasdale, whose first book, *Sonnets to Duse and Other Poems,* also appeared in 1907, and the ever-popular Mark Twain. Without question, the most important literary magazine produced during this era in Missouri was *Reedy's Mirror,* published by St. Louis University graduate William Marion Reedy.

Involvement in church activities formed a large part of many Missourians' social life, just as it had for decades. Virtually all of Missouri's religious groups grew in number during the last decade of the nineteenth century. A 1906 United States Bureau of the Census study reported that more than 36 percent of Missouri's roughly three million residents claimed membership in an organized church (the figure had been 27.47 percent in 1890).

Baptists had the most strength in rural Missouri, although they made up a smaller percentage of church members in 1906 (18.2 percent) than in 1890 (21.7 percent). Methodists made up about the same percentage of church-goers in both rural and urban Missouri, although they too had declined in relative terms since 1890. The denomination that grew the most between 1890 and 1906 was Roman Catholicism. In 1890, Catholics had composed only 22.1 percent of Missouri's church members. That figure jumped to nearly 32 percent by 1906. Although Catholics were well represented in rural areas, especially along the Missouri River and its tributaries where German immigrants had settled, the greatest concentration of Missouri's Catholics was in urban areas. In

1906, Catholics made up 69 percent of church members in St. Louis. In Kansas City they held 31 percent of church membership; in St. Joseph, 39.5 percent of church members went to Catholic churches.

Church strength in Missouri during the early twentieth century manifested itself in a myriad of ways. Especially in rural areas and small towns, church socials and meetings once or more a week were the only form of social interaction available to many Missourians. Summer revivals were often as important as county fairs. In late June 1910, for example, evangelists Steve Burke and A. B. Hobbs pitched a huge tent just west of the Kennett depot and began recruiting souls for Christ. A newspaper reporter observed:

> It is hard for the unbeliever to account for such phenomena as he may witness any night at this meeting. Men who have scoffed at Christianity all their lives, about face and declare they are done with sin. The dance, Sunday base ball, gambling, and various other worldly pleasures have not been directly assailed, yet devotees of these pleasures have voluntarily declared they would no longer indulge in them! The singing and the sermons are highly entertaining. The singer has a strong choir of well-trained singers, and these are led by a piano, organ, cornet, violin, clarinet, and an alto.

A junior choir of children between seven and twelve years old provided "an unusual attractive feature." Hobbs sang and conducted the vocal groups; Burke brought the message. The revivalists had such an impact that Kennett's places of amusement closed and no baseball game occurred on the first Sunday. According to the newspaper, "The religious spirit has gotten hold of the people, and a more righteous reign seems to have dawned." A reported crowd of twelve hundred attended the men's meeting of the revival on Sunday afternoon, and "between 30 and 40 accepted Christ . . . at that service alone." The newspaper reported that preacher Burke, "again and again . . . has swept from under them the sandy footing on which unsaved men stand." Altogether some 150 people accepted Christ.

If the church was important for turn-of-the-century white Missourians, it was even more important for African Americans. In many of Missouri's communities, African American churches doubled as social halls because most places of public accommodation were not open to blacks. In the Pike County town of Louisiana, for example, the Bethel Chapel A.M.E. Church provided a gathering place for hundreds of blacks. Built during the mid-1880s, the sixty-by-thirty-seven-foot brick structure was open to the community seven days a week. Two services were held on Sunday, followed by a church board meeting on Monday night, a women's meeting on Tuesday, prayer and devotional meetings on Wednesday, missionary work on Thursday, and choir practice on Friday. Saturdays were reserved for social events that doubled as fund-raisers, such as chicken or fish frys, ice cream socials, and coon dinners.

Other black churches provided similar opportunities in other parts of the state. In Wright County the African American Cumberland Presbyterian Church held Sunday services and midweek prayer meetings, supplemented by barbecues, picnics, and revivals. The *Hartville Democrat* of October 18, 1901, carried a notice to all interested parties that "A protracted meeting is in progress at the Cumberland Presbyterian Church (col) it will be continued indefinitely."

Church strength in Missouri during the early twentieth century manifested itself in many new church edifices, some of them of the grandest proportions. The St. John's Methodist Episcopal Church, South, in St. Louis, built in 1902; the gray limestone Independence Boulevard Christian Church, completed in Kansas City in 1905; and the First Presbyterian Church, erected in St. Joseph in 1909, among others, all bore witness to the power and strength of Christian religion in Missouri. The grandest of all these early-twentieth-century ecclesiastical structures was the St. Louis Catholic Archdiocese's New Cathedral of St. Louis. The cathedral was a striking expression of Byzantine architecture modeled after the Hagia Sophia in Constantinople. Begun in 1907 and formally dedicated in 1914, it featured one of the largest collections of mosaics in the world.

Church strength also made itself apparent in new services provided by old congregations. There was a growing sense among Christian churches in industrializing America that they needed to do more than they had been doing to respond to the needs of the poor and the immigrants in urban America. A "Social Gospel Movement" emerged, prompting various Christian denominations to reach out in new ways and with increased vigor to the dispossessed. Missouri Baptists, for example, targeted railroad towns as places for missionary work, and they conducted a "Chapel Car" ministry that carried itinerant preachers from town to town to establish churches. In addition, Missouri Baptists sent missionaries to work among the poor in cities. A 1908 report on state missions asserted, "We have in our borders peoples from almost every nation, kindred and tongue under heaven. Germans, Swedes, Bohemians, Danes, Italians, Russians, and Greeks—in all, about one million, making nearly one-third of our population. This brings to our doors a gracious missionary opportunity, from which we may not turn away except at our peril."

Missionary work among Missouri Baptists took many forms, including the dramatic expansion of the Missouri Baptist Children's Home, first established in St. Louis in 1883. This "orphans home" could accommodate as many as two hundred children by 1910. Likewise, the Missouri Baptist Hospital, organized during the mid-1880s, became an important part of the urban ministry by the turn of the century. The Missouri Home for Aged Baptists, established at Ironton in 1913, reflected the denomination's awareness of the growing inability of Missouri families to care for their aged and infirm members. Likewise, Catholic women of Missouri formed an organization known as the Queen's Daughters, or the Daughters of the Queen of Heaven. When first organized in St. Louis in December of 1889, this group pledged itself to "the industrial education of the children of the very poor, the improvement of the home life of the poor and assisting the unfortunate in every possible way." In 1897, the Queen's Daughters established a home in St. Louis for working women and girls.

Although Missouri's religious groups agreed upon many issues of faith and morals, there was one social tradition that deeply divided them: the consumption of alcohol. Alcohol was blamed by some for poor attendance and performance at work, for crime and antisocial behavior, and for domestic violence. Late-nineteenth and early-twentieth-century newspapers regularly contained accounts of crimes that were blamed on the consumption of alcohol, such as a case in 1911 when Fred Ball of Ozark apparently killed his wife after a day of drinking in Springfield. Arguably, the most publicized alcohol-related crime of the era occurred in St. Louis in 1895, when state senator Peter Morrissey of St. Louis was killed by his mistress, a well-known local prostitute named Maud Lewis, after a night of heavy drinking. Testimony at Lewis's trial revealed that Lewis, Morrissey, and two other couples had gone to Lewis's bawdy house after drinking for hours in a saloon run by Morrissey. They were joined in their revelry by a policeman who happened to be walking his beat when they arrived at the house. The policeman entered the well-known house of prostitution and drank with the intoxicated group before returning to his beat. Less than half an hour later, the senator was found shot to death. Although no one witnessed the shooting and Maud was too drunk to remember what had happened, she was convicted of second-degree murder.

Incidents such as these caused many Missourians, especially those active in evangelistic denominations such as the Baptists and Methodists, to oppose the sale of liquor. Those of the Catholic faith, especially those who were either immigrants or the children of immigrants, could not abide the movement to prohibit the sale and manufacture of liquor. In St. Louis, Catholics even opposed laws that tried to close taverns on Sundays, a position that caused people such as R. H. Jones of Kennett to assert, "With five saloons in town, it does seem everybody could get drunk often enough in the six working days of the week, without having to resort to Sunday." The Women's Christian Temperance Union, a Protestant organization, spearheaded the drive to rid the country of alcohol. In 1890, the General Conference of the Methodist Church, South, in Missouri, came out clearly against the liquor trade. In 1893, the Anti-Saloon League organized, and soon thereafter, the W.C.T.U. joined it to create a truly formidable force for Prohibition.

In Missouri, Mrs. Helen Harford took over for Mrs. Clara Cleghorn Hoffman as Missouri state organizer for the group. On one typical day for her, she gave a talk to women in the morning at the town of Union, four miles east of Mount Vernon; held a meeting in Mount Vernon in the afternoon; and delivered a major address in the evening. Receiving even more celebrity than either Hoffman or Harford was Carrie Nation, who lived in Holden and Belton, Missouri, from time to time. Nation lectured against the liquor trade, but more sensationally, she entered taverns carrying a hatchet that she used to smash bottles and barrels containing alcoholic beverages before the eyes of the consumers of the hated stuff.

The efforts of Carrie Nation and the W.C.T.U. notwithstanding, saloons and taverns were common places of recreation and relaxation in turn-of-the-century Missouri, especially in larger towns and cities and in communities that featured large German immigrant populations. Historian Susan Curtis, describing the town of Sedalia during the mid-1890s, writes that "the depression of 1893 had loosened Sedalians' attachment to Victorian prescriptions, and the people's inchoate dissatisfaction with self-control and repression was finding expression in new social relations and cultural interests." One of these new interests was ragtime music, popularized in Sedalia and Missouri by the "King of Ragtime," Scott Joplin. By 1899, when his famous "Maple Leaf Rag" was published, Joplin had moved beyond playing only in African American saloons and honky-tonks and was performing in front of white middle-class audiences. The result, Curtis writes, was that "Sedalians, like other Americans . . . faced economic and cultural challenges that pre-disposed them to the daring new African American music that offered emotional and cultural release."

A widely acceptable alternative to taverns and saloons as places of entertainment and relaxation was the city or community park. Historian Alan Havig has pointed out that "The founding of the Playground Association of America in 1906 signaled the maturing of a national movement to provide parks, playgrounds and community recreation centers for urban populations." The increased concentration of Missourians in towns and cities led to a growing recognition of a need to create outdoor public places for recreation and play. Although St. Louis already had Forest Park (laid out in 1875) and Tower Grove Park (donated to the city by Henry Shaw in 1867), the dawning of a new century called for new public spaces. One visionary who was asked to plan these new spaces was George Kessler, the well-known landscape architect and Progressive reformer who had come to St. Louis in 1902 to help plan the Louisiana Purchase Exposition.

Kessler and the St. Louis Civic Improvement League, which was organized in 1901, envisioned an extensive boulevard system that would connect the city's parks while encircling the city's population. The northern terminus of this system, according to historian Renee West, was to be the Chain of Rocks Park, which was established on 19.76 acres in 1893 and surrounded a waterworks built the previous year. The Chain of Rocks Park provided north St. Louisans with fountains and gardens, a pleasant reprieve from the city's grime and dirt. "It is a beautiful spot," a contemporary wrote. "If one stands on the bluff in Chain of Rocks Park, directly above the works, it presents a wonderful sight." The southern terminus was to be a park at Carondelet known as the Riverside Park.

Not only were new public spaces needed but also a need existed for new uses of those spaces. During the 1890s there emerged in Missouri, and the rest of the United States, a new phenomenon known as the "amusement park," which, as historian George Lipsitz points out, "emerged as a kind of liberated zone, a place reserved exclusively for pleasure, excitement, and risk." One of Missouri's earliest amusement parks was the Meramec Highlands, which opened as a 438-acre resort in Kirkwood in May 1895. At the Highlands, one could ride a steam-powered merry-go-round, enjoy a boat or horseback ride, or go dancing. Lipsitz argues, "In an age that doted on passive spectator sports and frowned on excessive physical exertion, the amusement park created a space for active recreation. Instead of watching a horse race, baseball game or boxing match, visitors to Meramec Highlands could ride horses and pedal bicycles, row boats, or swim in the Meramec River."

Another George Kessler–influenced park in Missouri was Boonville's Harley Park, established on eight acres at the west edge of town in 1887 and expanded to twenty acres in 1905. Although Kessler's work on the park came some years later, by 1910 Harley Park had become, as historian Robert L. Dyer has written, "a favorite spot for picnics, as well as fairs and circuses." Springfield had Doling Park, where one could walk on a white gravel path bordering a lake, rent a boat and fish, or ride a "chute-the-chutes" ride that consisted of a flat-bottomed boat gliding down a steep incline into the lake. Doling Park also featured the Giboney Cave, which could be toured by boat; a skating rink; a grandstand; and a much-used baseball diamond. Springfield's White City Park featured a roller coaster, which was a popular source of entertainment during the early 1900s.

Arguably, one of the most exciting new recreation sites in modernizing Missouri was the White River country in the southwest part of the state. Middle- and upper-class urbanites, yearning for escape from dirty, noisy cities, sought refuge on floating and fishing trips on the James and White Rivers. This trend was enhanced greatly with the 1913 construction of Powersite Dam across the White River, creating Lake Taneycomo. According to historian Linda Myers-Phinney, Lake Taneycomo soon became the "Playground of the Middle West."

Although the places Missouri families could go for entertainment were becoming more numerous during the early twentieth century, the size of the family was actually declining, continuing a trend that had been underway since the Civil War. In 1890 the average Missouri family size was 5.1 persons, with an average of 5.5 persons living in each dwelling in the state. Those numbers dropped to 4.4 persons per family in 1910, with 4.9 persons per dwelling. In addition to becoming smaller, Missouri families were also becoming more fragile. Urbanization and industrialization not only placed great strains on marriages but also provided marriage partners with perceived alternatives to a life of suffering with an abusive or neglectful spouse. In the city, one could at least hope to earn money to support oneself if that seemed a preferable alternative to marriage. The increase in the number of divorces in modernizing Missouri between 1877 and 1906 is striking. Between 1877 and 1886, there were 9,777 divorces granted in the state. Between 1887 and 1906, 34,425 divorces were granted. In 1890 the total number of divorced persons living in Missouri was 5,432. That number nearly tripled by 1910, to 15,578, although the increase in the number of adults older than fifteen did not even double. Not surprisingly, the smallest number of divorces occurred in rural counties such as Carter, Maries, Reynolds, and Ste. Genevieve. St. Louis was the leader in the number of divorces granted. More than two-thirds of the divorce petitions in Missouri were initiated by women.

Increasingly after the 1893 Panic, Missouri families were building new and more modern houses. By 1895, in fact, one could order a house plan directly from Sears, Roebuck and Company. Over the course of the next several decades, as many as fifteen different house types would be made available through Sears. The mail order business was greatly enhanced by the introduction of Rural Free Delivery (RFD) to Missouri in October 1896. The first experimental RFD routes in the state were in Randolph County, and although customers and carriers were slow in becoming accustomed to the new service, by the turn of the century rural and small-town Missourians had come to count on RFD as a way of lessening their isolation from the rest of the world and of allowing them to be consumers without ever having to leave their farms.

Turn-of-the-century Missouri provided its residents with a great number of opportunities that previous generations could only have dreamed of. But there were challenges as well. How would increased educational opportunities, new reading materials, new consumer products, and expanded and new entertainment opportunities affect Missourians? Answers to those questions awaited a new century and a new generation of Missourians.

CHAPTER VI

THE REFORM IMPULSE AND
ITS TENSIONS

Throughout the last decade of the nineteenth century, Missourians were buffeted by the complex changes that were transforming their lives and the lives of countless other Americans. Although the state remained largely rural and agricultural in character, it also underwent immense changes: the expansion of urban areas; the continued impact of industrialization, immigration, and demographic change; the increased consolidation of business into the hands of trusts and pools; and, finally, the often devastating effects of a cyclical and unpredictable economy.

While few Missourians opposed the basic idea of prosperity and economic growth, a growing number felt angry and victimized by changes that promised progress but delivered stagnation or decline. More and more they looked to their political leaders to direct the forces of change to enhance their economic status and physical well-being. The solution seemed to many to be for their government to take a firm regulatory stance against the negative forces of powerful monopolies, corrupt politicians, industrial polluters, extravagant governments, and many others. As a result, what began with the Populist movement during the early part of the decade eventually transformed itself into an early form of progressivism characterized by a somewhat amorphous political ideology that eventually gave rise in the early years of the twentieth century to what has been referred to by scholars as the "Missouri Idea."

Throughout the 1890s, many of Missouri's political leaders, such as Richard P. Bland, dedicated themselves to this growing reform impulse, while others merely felt compelled to accommodate themselves to it in order to maintain public support. As a result, politicians often found themselves walking a tightrope between this powerful, at times uncontrollable, impulse and their own particular goals for Missouri's economic growth and prosperity. Not all Missourians were overcome by a desire for reform. Many were essentially content with American society as it was. Many urban and rural residents were unmoved by the struggles waged by the Populists, the advocates of municipal ownership of public utilities, or those who campaigned for initiative and referendum. All of this ensured that Missouri's political scene in the late nineteenth century would continue to be a contested environment characterized by fragmentation and turbulence.

In January 1889 the newly elected Democratic candidate for governor, David Francis, had high hopes for a return to prosperity and stability following the politically and economically unstable period of the preceding two decades. Reconstruction, labor unrest, depression, and violence punctuated those years. In winning the gubernatorial election, Francis had ridden his party's pledge to bring order to Missouri. He and other politicians had successfully capitalized on Missourians' intense desire for efficient, inexpensive, and limited government. In his inaugural address to the state legislature and the people of Missouri, Francis stressed comforting and time-tested images that emphasized such themes as states' rights, the danger of centralized power, fiscal conservatism, and even the need for regulation of untamed corporations such as the railroads, banks, and insurance companies. All these concerns were dear to the hearts of his receptive constituency, which consisted of many rural and small-town residents, most of whom were working people, farmers, and small businessmen. Further, like many Missourians, the new governor was also concerned about social issues such as the "corrupting influence of the saloon on the morals of the community and the politics of the country." He pledged to check its growth and to confine the liquor business to "the narrowest possible limits." Yet Francis also made it clear that all of this regulation would be in the people's best interests and would not interfere with their personal freedoms or traditional democratic processes: "It has been well said that the only legitimate end of government is to protect the citizen in the enjoyment of life, liberty, and property. When it assumes other functions, it is usurpation and oppression." Here the governor was careful to reassure voters that government's limits would be "fixed and defined" by them, not by the politicians, because "an intelligent and self-governing people" wanted as few laws as possible. In other words, residents could rest easy—democracy was safe in Missouri because "the people" were in complete control of their government, not the reverse.

It is important to understand that Francis, essentially a businessman and a booster at heart, was part of a new breed of politician beginning to emerge throughout the state and nation in the late nineteenth century. In Missouri, most of the Civil War veterans who dominated the Democratic party in prior years were now either deceased or retired from politics. New leaders, such as Francis and William J. Stone, slowly emerged to fill their places. These newcomers represented modern Progressive ideals that included the promotion of business, organization, efficiency, expansion, and professionalism. Francis possessed a broad perspective, a competitive nature, and, like many Missourians, an intense desire to see his state develop and progress. Unfortunately, this outlook was at times incompatible with other demands for limited government and fiscal conservatism, as well as with the public's growing fear of corporate power. It was not that citizens in Missouri were opposed to the idea of big business, prosperity, or economic growth, but rather that many residents throughout the state were becoming concerned by what they considered growing corporate malfeasance and its apparent corrupting effect on their political institutions. Yet the governor, along with many other politicians and businessmen of the day, at times appeared to embrace the progress and wealth that these corporations represented without addressing some of the negative consequences of this growth. His enthusiasm and boosterism is revealed in an early address:

> The enactment of wise statutes and their impartial enforcement, by inducing the investment of capital and the immigration of good citizens, can materially accelerate the development of its [the State of Missouri] extensive and varied resources. . . . Affirmative and positive action is necessary if we would advance the interests of the people, and push Missouri forward to a higher place among the great states.

In other speeches, Francis exclaimed that the entire country was "throbbing with a new life. It is advancing with an increased strength, and with a quicker step." The governor emphasized that it was up to Missourians to take advantage of this new era of economic potential and not to fall behind in the race for growth and prosperity.

Francis lost little time in applying modern business methods in a popular effort to streamline some aspects of state government. In 1891 he pressed for the lowering of the state taxation rate from forty cents on one hundred dollars to thirty cents, a 25 percent reduction in state revenue, pleasing those individuals concerned about the growing expense of "big government." In addition, the governor was also concerned about the growing cost of the state's prisons, schools, and other institutions, and strongly urged those policy makers involved to economize. He also took steps to lower the costs of textbooks to ensure that their expense would no longer prove a burden on rural citizens. In one official statement, he reassured Missourians that it was "a well-settled principle of good government that no more money should be forced from a people in taxes, direct or indirect, than is necessary to accomplish the end sought."

Francis's devotion to antimonopoly principles was more dubious than was his commitment to pecuniary conservatism. Although he stated that there was a "danger in the centralizing tendencies of business," he was hesitant to support legislation that might alienate big business in the state unless he was obliged to do so by popular opinion. As will be illustrated later, David Francis throughout his term as governor attempted to walk the tightrope between his own desires for growth and development, and his constituency's growing demands to regulate that growth. At times efforts by Missouri's political and economic boosters to effect what they considered to be necessary Progressive change would be hamstrung by the powerful force of popular demands for regulation. This tension set the tone for the future administrations of William Stone and Lawrence "Lon" V. Stephens, who were caught within these same circumstances.

During the first half of the 1890s, two developments combined to reshape Missouri politics for years to come. One of these changes was the sudden division and restructuring of the Democratic party on the state and federal level over economic issues. Another critical transformation took the guise of a direct challenge to Democratic control of the state by Missouri farmers who involved themselves in the agrarian movement and the People's party. It was essential that Missouri Democrats overcome these dilemmas quickly and decisively if they hoped to maintain continued political supremacy over the state. Both developments worked in tandem to reshape Missouri's political landscape and to ensure that small-town and rural Missourians would continue to exercise a considerable degree of control over the character of state and local politics.

One important event that shaped the contours of Missouri politics in the late nineteenth century took the form of a political crisis occurring deep within the Democratic party on the national and state levels.

The origins of this dilemma were found in the enthusiastic support of many rural residents across the country for policies such as the Sherman Silver Purchase Act (1890) designed to increase the nation's supply of currency, create inflation, and ease the extreme financial pressure exerted on Americans. Many Americans hoped that artificially induced inflation would benefit farmers by increasing the prices they received for their produce. Conservative Democrats, referred to as Gold Democrats because of their devotion to the gold standard, and most Republicans had opposed the bill for many reasons, but especially because it required the U.S. government to buy large quantities of silver and issue certificates redeemable in silver or gold upon demand. These politicians were dedicated to high interest rates, a contracted, solid money supply based solely upon gold, and low prices for raw materials and manufactured goods.

Problems surrounding this complex issue began to surface during the early 1890s when the entire country entered a prolonged depression. Critics of the bill blamed the Sherman Silver Purchase Act for this economic downturn. In addition, these politicians charged that the U.S. Treasury was being depleted of its valuable gold reserve by flocks of U.S. and foreign speculators who were eagerly buying up large quantities of gold bullion. As a result, President Grover Cleveland, a Gold Democrat himself, and other outspoken members of Congress worked toward the eventual repeal of the act in 1893. The government then turned to eastern bankers for loans to replenish the dwindling gold reserve. The Treasury also offered bonds to investors for the same purpose. Both of these acts were viewed by many Americans as a sell-out to eastern businessmen and speculators. The U.S. government's first experiment with bimetallism was at an end and the country was again placed firmly on the gold standard.

The actions of Cleveland and the Gold Democrats infuriated many Missouri Democrats, especially those from the rural areas of the state. Many shared the opinion of Missouri Senator George Vest, who exclaimed that "we have had too much New York politics and I am tired of seeing the West and South subordinated." Rural and urban businessmen and farmers also shared these views. As a result, Missouri's Silverite Democrats, those party members in favor of inflationary measures, turned against Grover Cleveland and by 1896 had purged from the party many Gold Democrats, including David Francis. These politicians also used economic issues to propel themselves into state and local victories throughout the late 1890s by habitually resurrecting the "free silver" issue as a "bloody shirt" until it became hollow, antiquated, and then quietly forgotten by 1900. This train of events could have turned out quite differently if the Republican party had been stronger and able to take full advantage of Democratic disagreements, or if Gold Democrats had accounted for a greater percentage of the party within the state. As it turned out, disaster was largely averted and one force within the Democratic party eventually seized the day.

The second major political issue facing Missouri Democrats was the renewal of third-party threats, this time from the state's increasingly politicized farmers. Missouri farmers had suffered since the mid-1870s from low prices for their produce, high transportation costs, inflated interest rates, and overproduction. They had tried organizations and cooperatives, such as the Grange, to strike back at what often appeared to be insurmountable problems. Some had even turned to third parties, most notably the Greenbacker party, during the 1870s.

By the late 1880s a new wave of agrarian unrest moved across the state. Initially, it appeared primarily in two forms. The first was in the creation of local chapters of the National Farmers' Alliance and Cooperative Union of America. Organized in Texas in 1886, the alliance soon moved into other states and by 1888 claimed thirteen thousand members in thirty-eight Missouri counties. Another national farmers' movement, the National Agricultural Wheel, also began in 1886. An estimated fifty-eight thousand Missouri farmers had become "Wheelers" by 1888. Recognizing that Alliance and Wheel members shared common goals, and often common memberships, the two movements merged in 1889 to form the Farmers' and Laborers' Union of America. A Missouri chapter of this organization, commonly called the Missouri Alliance, was formed in Springfield in August of 1889.

Not surprisingly, Missouri Democrats feared that a third party of agrarians would siphon off votes that would normally go to them. As a result, they moved quickly to tame and subordinate protestors to the Democratic party. In 1889, Governor Francis made a special appeal to farmers in his inaugural address. Calling attention to the plight of farmers, he tried to blame Congress: "The widespread discontent which pervades the agriculturalists of the country is a natural result of the class legislation which has been enacted at Washington during the past thirty years." In addition, he emphasized that Congress was to blame for the "limited supply of money" and that state legislators were "powerless to provide a remedy."

As the 1890 election approached, Missouri Democrats moved to disarm the Missouri Alliance by distributing offices to some of its more visible and less radical leaders. Alliance president Henry W. Hickman was nominated and elected railroad commissioner on the Democratic ticket, while Lloyd E. Wolfe was nominated and elected state school superintendent. Uriel S. Hall, another Alliance member, was also given the honor of acting as floor leader at the Democratic Party Convention in 1890. Although there was no indication that these individuals had abandoned their commitment to the principles of the movement, many Alliance members interpreted their joining forces with the Democrats as an act of betrayal. As a result, dissatisfied Alliance chapters in twelve Missouri counties bolted from the organization and nominated their own candidates in local and county elections. Angry Alliance leaders quickly revoked their charters. The Democrats had succeeded in temporarily dividing and, more importantly, defusing the farmers' movement by pacifying some of its leaders with the attractive offer of political office.

However, the members of the Missouri Farmers Alliance quickly overcame this setback. In March 1892 they made the important decision to join a new national third party, known as the Populist or People's party. One disgruntled Alliance member bitterly commented on the reason:

> We have witnessed for more than a quarter of a century the struggles of the two great political parties for power and plunder, while grievous wrongs have been inflicted on the suffering people. We charge that the controlling influences dominating both these parties have permitted the existing dreadful conditions to develop without serious effort to . . . restrain them.

Farmers across the nation, dissatisfied with both the Democratic and Republican parties, joined the new organization in 1892 with hopes of electing their own representatives who would be sympathetic to their needs.

The fledgling Missouri People's party held its first convention in Sedalia in June 1892. Ninety-five delegates attended the first day, most of whom were farmers and members of the Missouri Alliance. Once there, they quickly hammered out a political platform that addressed their demands and reflected their ideology. Members composed a broad list of party objectives, hoping to attract a wide variety of potential supporters. At the top of their agenda were the silver issue and economic reform, followed by proposals for a reduction in the expense of state government, tax law revision, free school textbooks, and public road construction. In an attempt to attract urban laborers to the party, leaders also included in their demands the eight-hour workday, the abolition of child and convict labor, and laws that would restrict corporations from hiring professional strikebreakers such as the Pinkerton Detective Agency. A small effort was made to attract the support of women by taking a stand in favor of women's suffrage and equal pay for equal work laws. The Missouri Populists agreed to support James B. Weaver, the Populist candidate, in the presidential campaign and Leverett Leonard, a farmer from Saline County, as their candidate for Missouri governor. They also fielded a host of other candidates for local and state offices throughout Missouri.

However, most of Missouri's rural and small-town voters, even those who had enthusiastically voiced their approval of many of the Populist principles before the election, were apparently not prepared to support a third party. In the elections of 1892, the Populists failed to elect any candidates in Missouri, even when they fused with another political party. Weaver did receive 41,204 votes from Missouri, but the Democratic presidential candidate, Grover Cleveland, won 268,400 votes in the state. The Republican candidate, President Benjamin Harrison, was not far behind, receiving 227,646 Missouri votes in his bid for reelection. In the gubernatorial race, Leonard received 37,262 votes in losing to Silverite Democrat William Stone. Leonard polled more than a thousand votes in only five counties (Atchison, Bates, Greene, Jackson, and Jasper). He won in only two counties, Hickory and Stone. William Stone, a lawyer who had served as prosecuting attorney in Vernon County during the 1870s and as a U.S. congressman from southwest Missouri during the 1880s, had long been identified with agrarian interests. Stone defeated his Republican rival, Congressman William Warner, former mayor of Kansas City, by nearly thirty thousand votes, although Warner carried 44 of Missouri's 114 counties and the city of St. Louis. The Prohibitionist candidate for governor, John Sobieski, polled less than thirty-four hundred votes.

Several factors might account for the Populist party's lack of success at the polls. Perhaps Missouri voters were still too bound to sectionalism and the traditional two-party system to vote for a new third-party contender. Or perhaps the Missouri Populists failed because the

Democrats took on the silver issue and began to engage in class politics with the state's rural voters. To many citizens, this negated the utility of a third party, so that they could support their traditional party with a clear conscience. Further, Missouri's politically active farmers were unable to attract large numbers of urban working-class people to their cause. To many workers, a farmers' organization dedicated to agrarian issues such as silver and inflation held little attraction. Farmers wanted inflation, but urban workers would be hurt if prices increased without their wages keeping pace. Finally, People's party leaders, such as Leonard, were politically naive and inexperienced. They were unable to exploit fully the issues and to present a coherent, appealing message to convince voters to leave the Democratic and Republican parties. As a result, the majority of Missourians rejected the Populist platform and allowed the Democratic party, increasingly dominated by the pro-silver faction, to control the state. Yet the Populists, who had begun to stir the consciousness of many rural and small-town residents with their message of political and economic reform, remained a potential threat to the Democrats for the future. The stage was set for further struggles that lay ahead.

For their part, Missouri Republicans also did poorly in state and local elections in 1892, mirroring the party's lack of success nationwide. Democratic denunciation of the McKinley Tariff and of the so-called Billion Dollar Congress played well throughout the country, including in Missouri. Republicans did manage to send two representatives, Richard Bartholdt of the Tenth District and Charles F. Joy of the Eleventh District, to Congress. In spite of this, Missouri Republicans were disheartened by the 1892 elections, as a letter written by O. F. Smith, a Missouri Republican leader, to his friend L. Benekie in November 1892 indicates:

> I have no information from any of the other counties concerning the judicial race. In fact, since the general election returns have been coming in, I have been so *greatly astonished* that I made no effort to get *any news* from *any quarter.* I have nothing to surrender in political principles, but can gracefully bow to the *will of the majority.* . . . It will require *at least eight* and perhaps *twelve years* to rally the Republicans of Missouri back to the position they held before this defeat.

He continued with what appears to have been an obituary for the Missouri Republican party by lamenting that "they [the party] entered

their battle with good nerve and strong hope—they go out of it routed—
unexpectedly routed, not only in the state but in the nation." Smith
concluded his correspondence by informing his colleague that now was
the time for "a *long rest* from the unprofitable business of politics." The
Democrats, by adroitly manipulating issues such as the tariff, finance,
and reform of state government, emerged victorious in 1892 over the
Republican and Populist opposition. Missourians, given a choice, voted
Democratic.

Between 1895 and 1897, Missouri's Democratic party continued to
successfully exploit the silver issue, agrarian politics, and the promise
of reform to maintain their control over the state. Most importantly,
they continued to skillfully address the potential political threat posed
by the Missouri Alliance and the Populists by absorbing elements of
their platform as well as some of their leaders. As a result, mid-decade
was a pivotal period for Democratic party leaders in the state. During
this interval, they fully embraced the silver issue as well as many other
popular reforms.

Missouri's Democratic party leaders did not allot free silver a central
place in their platform by chance alone. The Panic of 1893 and President
Cleveland's seemingly regressive stance on economic issues had angered
and activated many of the state's rural residents by 1894. Following
the Missouri People's party failure in 1892, it fielded candidates for
state and local offices with some success in 1893. In 1894, under the
leadership of Orville D. Jones, Missouri Populists intensified their efforts
to convince rural Missourians to vote for a third party. Throughout
the year, leaders made speeches, conducted meetings, and staged rallies
and marches to persuade voters to their way of thinking. They were
aided in this objective by the People's party press, consisting of thirty-
nine newspapers in thirty-two counties, which attempted to explain the
Populist stance to rural residents. Their platform was once again devoted
to the support of the inflation of the country's monetary system, an
income tax, government ownership of the railroad industry, a reduction
in interest rates, and many other "reforms." As a result of the 1894
elections, the Populists elected two representatives to the state house of
representatives, two to the state senate, and twelve members to county
offices throughout Missouri. At times this was achieved by fusing with
local Democrats or Republicans sympathetic to the Populist cause.
The People's party's strongest support in 1894 came from residents

of counties such as Adair, Atchison, Bates, Camden, Dade, Douglas, Greene, Laclede, Polk, and Wright. But with only twelve elected officials from all of Missouri's counties, Populists had little success in 1894. Indeed, the year proved quite good for the Republican party, which captured ten of the state's fifteen congressional seats.

In 1896 the Democratic party, under the leadership of Governor Stone and other Silverite Democrats, further reduced the already shrinking support for Populism by adopting even more clearly the silver issue as the defining factor for party loyalty. With the silver issue now being taken up by the Democrats, many Populist leaders believed that most traditionally minded rural Missourians would again choose to vote for a Democratic candidate rather than for a third-party contender. They presumed that it would be better to throw their support to the Democratic party in the hope of being in a position to eventually shape policy. Not all Populists agreed that this was the best strategy. Many "middle-of-roaders" wanted to maintain their separate third-party status. However, the majority of Missouri Populists ultimately decided to support William Jennings Bryan for president. Although Bryan, a man sympathetic to the farmer's plight, was clearly the favorite in Missouri, the Republican contender, William McKinley, carried the day nationally.

The 1896 gubernatorial race was a much more complex and perplexing affair for all those involved. In 1896 the Missouri Democratic party followed the precedent of the national organization by officially dividing into two factions. Richard "Silver Dick" Bland and Governor Stone led the Silver Democrats. Bland, a popular and charismatic figure, was born in Hartford County, Kentucky, in 1835 and moved to Wayne County, Missouri, in 1855. After a brief teaching stint in Missouri, Bland moved to California and then Nevada, where he took up the practice of law and became acquainted with the debate over silver. Returning to Missouri in 1865, Bland eventually settled in Lebanon and was first elected to Congress in 1872. Once in Congress, Bland quickly embarked on the volatile terrain of monetary policy. He gained popularity with Missouri farmers as one of the foremost advocates of free silver and was labeled by others as a champion of the rights of the common man. Indeed, he was so popular among many at the national level that he was thought by some to be an ideal presidential candidate in 1896. This respected politician provided a critical link between the Missouri Democratic party and rural residents of the state and, along with other Silverite Democrats, gave the party its direction throughout the 1890s.

In August of 1896, this group, which consisted of the majority of Missouri Democrats, gathered in Jefferson City and nominated Lon Stephens, a lawyer from Boonville with experience in journalism and banking, for governor and August Bolte for lieutenant governor. The opposing contingent, calling themselves the National Democratic party (Gold Democrats), consisted of those members who ardently opposed all inflationary policies. They conducted their own convention in St. Louis in August 1896, during which they nominated J. McDonald Trimble, a longtime Audrain County lawyer who moved to Kansas City in the late 1880s, for governor and Alfred P. Osterman for lieutenant governor. This group also nominated John M. Palmer, a United States senator from Illinois, as their own presidential candidate. At the same time, other groups also named their contenders for the governor's seat. Missouri Republicans nominated Robert E. Lewis, while the Prohibition party, which met at Sedalia in May 1896, nominated Herman P. Faris. The People's party, which had fused with the Democrats in support of a presidential contender, originally declined to support the Democrats when it came to the state elections. To the chagrin of the Silver Democrats, Missouri farmers nominated Orville D. Jones, an Edina lawyer and former Greenback candidate for auditor and supreme court judge, for governor and James Hillis for lieutenant governor. At the last minute, for reasons that remain unclear, Jones suddenly withdrew from the race. One explanation may be that Missouri Silver Democrats had become more attractive to Populist leaders after having successfully driven the more conservative "gold" faction from the party, or it may have been due to their respect for Congressman Richard Bland and his battle for free silver. As the election approached, Democratic rhetoric made them and the Populists almost indistinguishable, even though the Democrats refused to embrace such radical People's party demands as the Subtreasury Plan, a proposal that would have enabled American farmers to obtain government loans at 2 percent interest, using their crops as collateral. Whatever the reasons, many leading Populists decided to vote for Stephens. A number of Missouri People's party members may have viewed this decision by their leaders as an act of betrayal and therefore refused to vote for any gubernatorial candidate. The important fact is that Stephens won the race for the governor's seat, overcoming his Republican opponent 351,062 votes to 307,729.

This election was essentially the last gasp of agrarian resistance in Missouri until the 1930s and the advent of the Southern Tenant Farmers Union. For their part, the Silver Democrats had made important gains throughout the state, while simultaneously driving out the more conservative Gold Democrats. Ironically, Stephens, considering all of the angry silverite posturing and class politics, was also a leader who, like his two predecessors, had a strong desire to develop his state and to make his tenure a "distinctly business administration." A "business administration" apparently appealed to many Missourians who were dedicated to fiscal conservatism, low taxes, and efficient government. However, Stephens quickly discovered that a number of Missourians were not satisfied with these promises. Many Missourians also increasingly demanded the regulation of big business.

Aside from exploiting popular issues such as free silver, Missouri Democrats also searched out new political allies to offset the potential threat of the Populists and to thwart Missouri Republicans, who consistently remained popular with Germans, recent Northern immigrants, and upcountry residents of the southwestern Ozarks region. Thus, many Democrats within the state found themselves turning more and more to African Americans, who as a group were in the process of relocating from the countryside to towns and cities throughout the state. Although Missouri blacks traditionally had been devoted to the Republican party since Reconstruction, they had, over time, become frustrated and disenchanted with the party in the state. The Republican party underwent a slow change from 1890 to 1900. The state's Radical Republicans, who in their own fashion had been devoted to black equality before the law since Reconstruction, were slowly replaced by more conservative politicians less concerned with the rights of blacks. In small towns and rural areas, especially in the Little Dixie and Bootheel regions, Missouri Republicans joined Democrats in using race politics to attract poor whites to their fold. Missouri blacks discovered that Republicans no longer wanted to risk being associated with blacks, and therefore were no longer committed to them. In the mid-1890s, Missouri Republicans failed to include black candidates or civil rights issues within their political campaigns. Moreover, Missouri's Republican politicians did not hold any statewide offices and thus could not engage in the customary practice of dispensing state and county patronage employment as rewards to faithful African Americans. For their part, Missouri's Republican party leaders hoped to separate their party from blacks in an effort to appeal to

Missouri's color-conscious voters, who associated blacks with ignorance, inferiority, and political corruption.

For many of Missouri's blacks, who had been consistently devoted to the GOP, this change appeared as an act of blatant political betrayal. Although many black voters remained loyal to the party, others, especially those residing in cities, found themselves drawn to the Democratic party, which ironically had traditionally been devoted to social and political marginalization of blacks. In 1890 James Milton Turner, one of Missouri's leading black political leaders, urged African Americans residing in the state to desert the party if the Republicans continued to ignore their needs. Near the close of the century, the political machines of James Pendergast in Kansas City and of Ed Butler and the Jefferson Club in St. Louis overcame race politics in order to take advantage of black disenchantment with their opponents. By 1898 these machines had successfully incorporated the majority of black city dwellers into the Democratic fold. In 1900 black voters helped elect James Reed as Kansas City's mayor, making him the city's second Democratic mayor in twelve years. In return, Reed gave city jobs to a significant number of blacks and publicly recognized the importance of black voters to the Democratic political cause. Unfortunately, Missouri blacks were not yet a permanent feature of a new Democratic order in the state. By mid-decade, blacks slowly began to return to the Republican party, especially in St. Louis, largely because of a rising tide of racism that overwhelmed Democratic party politics throughout the state during the early twentieth century. As detailed in chapter 7, the critical cement that held this new relationship together in St. Louis, an urban political machine, was slowly disassembled by political reformers who were intent on breaking its political hold over their city. As in Kansas City, the well-organized discipline of a political machine had temporarily submerged race politics and worked to incorporate blacks into the party in St. Louis. Without the machine, racism reappeared, putting an end to future cooperation between the two groups. Kansas City Democrats were more successful at retaining black support, although many blacks remained alienated from the political process and refused to participate at all. It should, perhaps, be pointed out that this courting of black votes in urban Missouri was in stark contrast to the political disfranchisement African Americans were experiencing in the solidly Democratic South. There, under one-party rule, Democrats felt no need to cater in any way to black voters; indeed, they felt no need even to acknowledge the right of blacks to vote.

From 1889 to 1896, the Democratic party in Missouri had successfully overcome the potential challenges posed by party division and the political revolt presented by the People's party. Although Missouri Populism lost its momentum following the 1896 political campaign, Missouri farmers and rural residents had succeeded in encouraging Democrats to incorporate some of their ideas into their platform by mid-decade. As the 1890s progressed, other Missourians, including some in large urban centers such as St. Louis but also others in smaller towns and cities such as Columbia and Boonville, began to redefine the terms of political debate. Consequently, Missouri's political landscape would be influenced by a growing chorus of voices urging urban reforms and the regulation of large corporations.

The economic crisis that struck the country after 1893 manifested itself in some places in chronic unemployment, declining wages, declining profits for many businessmen, and depressed prices for agricultural produce. Suffering the most were small farmers, urban laborers, and businessmen, but Missouri's consumers also experienced the weight of these hard times. During this national economic crisis, some Missourians became increasingly aware that new business practices and a new national market made them vulnerable in ways they had not been before. Many urban residents, small businessmen, and some politicians concluded that large corporations or "trusts" were prospering at the people's expense. This new consciousness first manifested itself as popular anger and frustration and was then transformed into political activism. This early stage of what would in later years become known as the Progressive movement has been termed by one historian, Steven J. Piott, as the "Anti-monopoly Persuasion." This emerging demand for reform and government regulation was a defining characteristic of Missouri's political landscape after 1896.

Although the upswell of antimonopoly sentiment did not reach full fruition until after 1896, its roots traced back to the early 1890s during the administration of Governor David Francis. Part of Francis's appeal rested on his promise to regulate trusts operating within the state. He boldly informed voters that these "monopolies and trusts . . . unchecked by any feeling of individual responsibility, moved only by love of gain" had eliminated "all healthy competition." He concluded by exclaiming that "monopolies are contrary to the genious [sic] of a free state, and should not be allowed."

In this address, Francis was appealing to a sentiment that many Missourians had been expressing—that the consolidation of big business often led to practices that were contrary to the needs and welfare of consumers. As early as the late 1880s, farmers and laborers had become concerned about the growing power of big business, its apparent proclivity to manipulate politics through corruption, and its tendency to abuse consumers with high prices and poor-quality goods and services. In the mid-1890s, Governor Stone told the legislature:

> For a number of years the state has been disgraced by an organized and salaried lobby maintained by special interests at the capitol during the sessions of the General Assembly for the purpose of influencing legislative action. It has come to pass that almost every important measure of legislation must undergo the scrutiny of the lobby before its fate can be determined. We are confronted by a question whether the people or the lobby shall rule Missouri. The public safety and the honor of the state are at stake.

And in his inaugural address, Governor Stephens asked the General Assembly to take action to "curb the insolence and check the oppression of the trusts." By 1901, journalists for the *Kansas City Star* angrily announced that "the trusts and monopolies find their opportunities in the necessities of the people." With the press and politicians recognizing problems, citizens began to expect government to find solutions. Despite most Missourians' commitment to limited government, these men and women, largely the residents of towns and cities, were apparently willing to concede that the state needed to increase its power over corporations. This popular reform momentum in Missouri encouraged Francis and his successors to formulate and pass antitrust legislation.

In the fall of 1889 Francis proposed an antitrust law; the law was passed by the Democrat-dominated state legislature. Secretary of State Alexander A. Lesueur, encouraged by popular agitation, began to put the new antitrust law into effect soon after its passage. The new legislation required every corporation operating within Missouri to sign an affidavit stating that it was not a member of any trust, pool, or other combination, or was not involved in other illegal activities such as price-fixing or agreements to artificially limit production in an attempt to raise prices. Lesueur and his staff contacted seventy-five hundred

Missouri companies, which included those manufacturing products such as sugar, cotton, lead, alcohol, linseed, and caskets, and other firms such as insurance companies. His office especially targeted corporations based in Missouri's two largest cities, Kansas City and St. Louis.

The corporations' responses to this new scrutiny were mixed. Most readily complied with what appeared to be only a minor requirement. However, at least two hundred Missouri companies refused to respond to the state's request and bitterly declared their resistance to the entire process. Subsequently, the names of these firms were turned over to Attorney General John M. Wood, who began legal proceedings against them.

The state's first case was against the Simmons Hardware Company, which was charged with illegally participating in a trust and failing to comply with the secretary of state's request for the proper documents. If the courts ruled against the company, its corporate charter could be revoked and it would no longer be permitted to conduct business in Missouri. Corporate lawyers argued late in 1889 that the new law was unconstitutional because it interfered with the rights of corporations, forced the officers of firms to testify against themselves, and gave power to the secretary of state to enforce the statute that should constitutionally be given to the judiciary of the state. On March 11, 1890, a sympathetic Missouri Supreme Court agreed with these arguments and ruled the law unconstitutional. Governor Francis's only response was that the outcome was "somewhat unfortunate." Missouri's first experiment in the regulation of big business had ended in complete failure.

In spite of this defeat, the crusade against monopoly in Missouri continued. In April 1891 the state responded with another antitrust law to replace the old one, but it suffered from the same limitations. First, companies were on their honor to provide the state with the appropriate corporate records and signed statements. Since no company would voluntarily hand over incriminating evidence that would link it to a trust, the state would therefore lack sufficient evidence to prosecute. In addition, the state failed to aggressively enforce even this weak law by conducting serious investigations or research into company practices. Thus, state government proved to be little threat to big business in Missouri. When a company refused to comply adequately, the courts, which appeared to many to have too large a measure of sympathy for the firms involved, merely inflicted a modest fine that the company promptly paid before going back to conducting business as usual.

The next chapter in the popular movement to regulate big business in Missouri occurred following the onset of the 1893 Panic, which created difficult times for many Missouri businessmen. This was especially the case for the state's insurance companies, which were required to settle an enormous number of expensive claims for an above-average number of fires and floods that had occurred the preceding year. In an attempt to compensate for these heavy losses, Missouri's insurance companies, which were organized into several large trusts, raised their premiums in some instances by 80 to 100 percent. Because the insurance industry was so thoroughly consolidated, there was no cheaper alternative available that consumers could turn to in Missouri or, for that matter, throughout the nation.

Some Missouri residents responded to this action in 1893 by angrily and correctly observing that the state's insurance companies participated in a trust and were gouging customers with high premiums. The editors of the *Mexico Intelligencer* accused several fire insurance firms of "robbery." One reader exclaimed, "In all ordinary lines of business, sharp competition has naturally reduced the profits of trade to a close margin. The insurance companies, however, by combination managed to increase their charges." Missourians were correct: competition was being subverted and consumers were the victims of a price-setting trust.

The responsible organization was the Kansas City Board of Fire Underwriters, of which most of the state's fire insurance firms were members. This board collectively established fire insurance rates statewide in order to effectively minimize competition. Vicious rivalries among companies had severely driven down rates in the past, thus jeopardizing the profitability of all those engaged in the insurance business. This, combined with huge payoffs to fire victims, encouraged the fire insurance industry to collectively organize and establish rates. While this strategy was beneficial for big business, it had unfortunate consequences for consumers, who, living in highly combustible homes and business places, were forced by necessity to carry fire insurance. Missourians found themselves victims in a no-win situation.

Divided and disputed jurisdictions, lack of vigorous enforcement, weak penalties, corruption, and general incompetence all combined to ensure that the state's antitrust legislation was effectively hamstrung. And despite their occasional rhetoric, Governors Francis and Stone oversaw generally procorporate administrations that apparently hindered attempts at regulation. However, the combined efforts of popular outcry and critical "muckraker" newspapers such as the *St. Louis Post-Dispatch* caused the state legislature to respond to the consumers' plight. In 1893 it passed a third antitrust law. Severely crippled by the efforts of corporate lobbyists and legislators sympathetic to the interests of big business, this law exempted from its provisions all firms based in communities possessing a population greater than one hundred thousand inhabitants. Since 75 percent of all fire insurance companies doing business in the state were headquartered in either Kansas City or St. Louis, which both had populations greater than one hundred thousand, the statute was useless from the outset in dealing with the insurance trust. Indeed, this law may have even further eliminated competition by targeting smaller companies based elsewhere throughout the state. Once again, many Missourians found themselves victims of economic expansion and consolidation.

It appeared that some Missouri politicians, despite their adeptness at employing antimonopoly rhetoric, were unwilling to regulate, coerce, or possibly discourage competition-threatening businesses from operating in their state. In the minds of many legislators, the corporations, trusts, and pools were merely essential elements of the modern way of doing business, which they had willingly embraced. To the big businessmen operating in the state such as those who were members of the Kansas City Board of Fire Underwriters, the trust was only one response to the disorder, inefficiency, and unprofitable nature of cutthroat competition in America. Both Governor Stone and his successor Lon V. Stephens recognized the important role these businesses played in their state's economic development. They and many of their colleagues slowly began to dissociate themselves from the earlier, more openly anticorporate stance of the silverite faction of the Democratic party. This new outlook was implied by Governor Stone in his final address to the legislature in January 1897:

> The state cannot afford to make war on any legitimate interest—for war means to tear down and destroy, not to create and build up. The property of corporations is the property of the citizen. It is entitled to the same measure of protection accorded the possessions of others, and should be required to bear only its just and equal proportion of the public burdens. Just laws for the government of corporations should exist, but no law which unfairly discriminates against them should be enacted.

Stone concluded by counseling moderation concerning the state's relationship to big businesses operating in Missouri. He insisted that the "spirit of resentment should never give direction to public policy." What the governor was really suggesting was that Missouri legislators should not create a hostile legal landscape that might discourage future investment in the state.

However, popular resentment against monopolies and demands for the regulation of big business did not readily dissipate. In August 1897, the people of Missouri found a new antimonopoly champion within the administration of Governor Lon Stephens. This antitrust crusader was newly elected Attorney General Edward C. Crow. Born in Holt County in 1861, Crow grew up in Carthage, where he graduated from high school. He earned a law degree from the St. Louis Law School and received appointment as Webb City attorney in 1893. He served as a judge of the 25th judicial circuit between 1894 and 1896. The five-feet-three-inch, 125-pound, forty-one-year-old Crow proved tenacious in defending the public interest. Believing that "every man who has to carry insurance in Missouri is a victim of a trust," Crow once again renewed the fight against the state's insurance companies. By September 1897, Attorney General Crow had filed suit against a long list of insurance companies operating within the state. In doing this, Crow was responding to popular complaints that were being broadcast from communities throughout Missouri, such as Mexico, Pineville, and Joplin, whose citizens were outraged at what they perceived as the intolerable conduct of large corporations operating in the state. As a result, many Missourians, together with a large number of muckraking newspapers, demanded an antimonopoly campaign. Crow responded by charging these companies with illegally combining and conspiring to fix premiums—acts that violated the state's existing antitrust law. In addition, Crow challenged the statute's special clause that had exempted firms based in large cities from antitrust prosecution. All of these actions were part of a newly invigorated Progressive upswell that had begun with angry citizens from cities, towns, and farms throughout Missouri.

The outcome of Crow's efforts was, to say the least, disappointing for many Missourians. In December 1897 the state supreme court upheld the constitutionality of the exemption clause. Yet, all was not lost. Governor Stephens had perceptively sensed the growing tide of opposition to trusts, as indicated by his inaugural address, and he quickly joined the antimonopoly crusade. Born in Boonville, Missouri, in 1858, Stephens was an energetic politician possessing a varied education and a wide variety of experience that included law, telegraphy, banking, writing, and service as editor of the *Boonville Advertiser.* In 1890 he was appointed state treasurer by Governor Francis. A few years later, in 1897, Stephens won the governor's seat himself by eloquently supporting the rising tide of free silver. Prior to his election, he had vocally supported Richard Bland and William Jennings Bryan, and he had written a short pamphlet entitled "Silver Nuggets," which discussed the free silver issue and won him popular support. Now Stephens turned his vast talents and energy toward the antimonopoly cause. In January 1899, Governor Lon Stephens made the following passionate address to the legislature:

> I believe if it is made illegal to combine to control rates in the country in towns like Springfield, Joplin, and St. Joseph, it should be illegal to do so in Kansas City and St. Louis. The law as it stands operates to give fire insurance corporations doing business in St. Louis and Kansas City a special exemption and privilege not given insurance companies doing business in Moberly, Hannibal, or elsewhere in the state. . . . Unequal, partial, and discriminatory legislation which secures rights to some favored class or classes and denies it to others is contrary to the spirit and safety of our institutions.

Here Stephens astutely broadened his constituency by attacking special privilege rather than trusts or even big business itself. The governor thereby carefully avoided engaging in open hostilities against corporations whose presence he realized was essential to the economic development of the state. By this act he conveniently climbed upon the antimonopoly bandwagon while theoretically retaining his pro-business stance. Stephens concluded by passionately recommending the repeal of the clause. The governor was convinced that "the same national characteristic which sustained Jackson in his overthrow of the old United States Bank can be relied upon to deal successfully with the modern trust."

Missouri's legislators, sensitive to the pulse of public opinion, finally responded with a piece of legislation known as the Farris Bill that became law on April 18, 1899. This new antitrust law, subsequently upheld by the Missouri Supreme Court, omitted the clause that had previously exempted trusts located in large cities from prosecution. Insurance trusts headquartered in both St. Louis and Kansas City were officially ordered to disband. Governor Stephens also discovered another convenient, although controversial, use for popular anticorporation sentiment. In 1899, the State of Missouri had achieved a significant deficit that might have caused legislators and taxpayers a certain degree of grief. To complicate matters, Stephens had promised Missourians that there would be no new taxes, and he had also guaranteed voters that he would cut state spending. Suddenly, Missouri politicians discovered themselves caught between fiscal realities and the expectations of thousands of rural and small-town residents. After giving the question a considerable degree of attention, the governor and his associates thought they had solved the state's fiscal dilemma. The answer was found within the current popular demand for the regulation of big business. Legislators were convinced that by taxing certain industries, the State of Missouri could generate the revenue it required while appealing to a politically popular cause. Subsequently, several large concerns, such as insurance companies, dramshops, and breweries, became targets for new or increased taxation by the state. Stephens and his supporters hoped to appeal not only to those individuals and groups dedicated to the antitrust campaign but also to the powerful Missouri temperance movement. In doing this, some Democrats attempted to move the party away from the silver issue, which was dying a quiet death by 1899, and to fill the vacuum with vigorous antimonopoly activity.

But a conflict over the establishment of a new franchise tax for corporations in the legislature in 1899 nurtured a growing fear among many Missouri citizens: the fear that corporate interests were corrupting the legislative process. Political corruption, of course, was not new to Missouri or America during this period. Richard McCormick, a scholar of progressivism, has written that during the 1890s Americans discovered that "business corrupts politics" through lobbying and blatant bribery. For some time, Missourians had looked on as railroad owners bribed their legislators, urban political bosses bought votes, and public utility companies manipulated city councils for their own benefit.

The debate on the franchise tax—a tax on corporations—began soon after it was proposed in the legislature early in 1899. The bill's sponsor predicted that the tax "would put into the State Treasury one million dollars each year, and relieve the overtaxed farmer of part of his heavy burden." However, this legislation may also have served a convenient political purpose. Missouri Democrats were increasingly coming under attack by Progressive journalists for failing to meet their popular mandates from the people, which included a vigorous antitrust stance. The proposed franchise tax provided a way to appease these critics and to direct attention away from the party.

Thus the state house of representatives quickly drafted a proposal to tax corporations operating within the state and forwarded it to the senate for consideration. Many in the senate, when faced with a concrete piece of legislation, suddenly became apprehensive at the prospect of anticorporate action and pushed the bill into committee, where it remained for more than a month. During this period, the Democratic party became bitterly divided over the issue of a franchise tax. A majority in the senate proved to be rigidly resistant to any such potentially radical fiscal reform. Democrats and Republicans came together in the senate to defeat the house proposal.

Subsequently, the state's muckraking press, disillusioned over the senate's opposition to the tax, responded angrily. The editor of the *St. Louis Post-Dispatch* lashed out at the Democrats in the senate in particular, calling the entire episode the "work of a lobby-ridden legislature." On May 28, the newspaper castigated those Democrats opposing the bill with the following words: "Never before in the state's history did corporate influence wield so potent a power . . . it demonstrates the inability or unwillingness of Democratic politicians to throw off the yoke of corporations and stand for the people. . . . The . . . legislative branch of . . . government is absolutely at the mercy of the lobby." He concluded by emphasizing that the "record of the session shows nothing done for the farmer, little for the laboring man, and everything for the corporation."

The press was convinced that railroad lobbyists such as John Carroll had intervened, pressuring their allies in the legislature to sabotage the tax on corporations, which would have had a negative impact on railroads operating in Missouri. As a result, citizens throughout the state had some cause to believe that in some instances political power rested not with the people and their representatives, but with corporations such as the Missouri Pacific Railroad. It was rumored that even the governor, while remaining largely silent on the entire issue, had met regularly with railroad representatives throughout the entire affair. This scandalous event no doubt convinced many Missourians that big business illegally gained influence over the legislature and occasionally subverted the democratic process.

Some Missourians sought a solution to the growing problem of government corruption and misgovernment through the initiative and referendum. Initiative describes the process by which citizens directly formulate legislation that best serves their needs and ideals; referendum is the process by which voters approve or reject the proposed legislation. These tools could theoretically bypass the legislature and place the advantage clearly with the majority of people. These mechanisms were not new. Populists, who had long believed that the answer to their problems lay outside the traditional two-party system, had proposed adoption of the initiative and referendum. The principle behind these reforms also harkened back to an earlier period when small communities made face-to-face relationships possible and town meetings allowed this pattern of direct democracy to prevail. This more traditional political culture had long ago given way to a less direct, less personal system.

Although the principles behind the initiative and referendum were not new, in 1899 a group of idealistic St. Louis citizens created an organization called the Direct Legislation League of Missouri. President Silas L. Moser's goal was to place this concept before the state legislature for its consideration during the approaching 1899 session. The proposal incorporated the simple principle that the signatures of 5 percent of the voters of the state would be required to get an important issue before the people. Not all legislation would be open to this process; existing laws relating to "public peace, health, or safety" and those for the support of the "state government and existing public institutions" were exempt. Governor Stephens enthusiastically supported the issue, as the following passage from an 1899 address reveals:

> Such a method of legislation would tend largely to limit the evil practices of boodlers and bribe-givers. They would hesitate to spend their money corrupting the representatives of the people if they knew that any law which they might procure to be enacted could not become operative until the people themselves had ratified it. It is at least doubtful whether the system is not a necessity to the continued existence of our free institutions. The tendency of the times is toward a concentration of both all wealth and all power in the hands of a favored oligarchy. To prevent this, the people themselves must hold the reins of government.

Stephens's speech illustrates the power of Missourians' increasing distrust of both government and big business. In spite of the governor's support, the amendment failed to pass in the house and never reached the senate.

The energetic members of the Direct Legislation League were not discouraged by this disappointing failure. They redoubled their efforts, hoping to present the issues to the legislature in 1901. This time Moser found allies for his cause in the State Federation of Labor, which enthusiastically supported the league's drive for direct legislation. Labor leaders hoped to use the new legal process to obtain pro-labor legislation, such as the eight-hour day. This time the house, sensing the increasing popularity of the initiative and referendum, passed the bill by a vote of 79 to 35. However, the legislation experienced strong opposition in the senate from a more conservative clique of senators referred to by many critics as the "Big Four." This pro-corporate group consisted of John Morton from Richmond, who represented the 8th district, James Orchard from West Plains, who represented the 22d district, John Whaley from Osceola, who represented the 16th district, and Frank Farris from Steelville, who represented the 24th district. These senators did not support this kind of radical reform and successfully worked toward the bill's ultimate defeat. Some concerned Missourians were convinced that once again the direct legislation cause had been effectively barred by a legislature that had been corrupted by big business. For the time being the movement stalled, but it would be taken up again in the next decade by the Folk Progressives.

As Missourians entered the twentieth century, they found themselves caught within a complex and often turbulent political landscape. Throughout the decade of the 1890s, different groups attempted to use the political system to impose their version of order onto a society and economy that they thought flawed. This movement, although far from unified, was driven by an intense desire to take back power from business and restore it to producers and consumers, who believed they were increasingly being victimized by the activities of large trusts. This early phase of the Progressive movement witnessed farmers, politicians, and urban workers struggling in their own ways to correct what they believed to be the worst aspects of modern society. In St. Louis, for example, a group of women calling themselves the Wednesday Club of St. Louis Women established a crusade against polluted air in their city and sought environmental regulations directed against those companies emitting "dense black or thick grey smoke." It must be understood, however, that although these types of reform movements appear to have dominated the political discourse of the period, not all Missourians were sympathetic to all of these efforts. This explains the ultimate failure of the Populist cause and the lack of success by those fighting for direct democracy. Apparently a great many people did not perceive turn-of-the-century Missouri as a disorderly society desperately in need of repair. The men and women seeking reform were seldom content with the outcome of their efforts. For instance, Missouri farmers ultimately failed to bring about the lasting changes they had sought. Yet Missouri agriculturists who joined the Missouri Farmers Alliance and the Populist party did assist in shaping some of the terms of political debate.

This early phase of sporadic reform was finally punctuated by the popular movement to gain the adoption of initiative and referendum, acts that many Missourians believed would restore popular control over a state government that appeared to be saturated with corruption. The period of the 1890s marks only the beginning of the Progressive movement in the state. After 1900, Missourians experienced the maturation of a new complex impulse known as the Missouri Idea and the flowering of the Progressive reform movement.

CHAPTER VII

JOSEPH FOLK, THE MISSOURI IDEA,
AND PROGRESSIVISM

It is Joseph W. Folk's name that is most clearly associated with
the Progressive movement in Missouri. Progressivism, with its ideal
of moral reform, made a sweeping, nationwide impact in the early
twentieth century. The "Missouri Idea," based in large part on moral
guidelines for officeholders and expressed most prominently by Folk,
became widely influential within the Progressive movement. Through
his identification with progressivism and the Missouri Idea, Folk not
only won the governor's office in Jefferson City but also became a
nationally known figure, even attracting fleeting mention as a possible
candidate for the presidency.

In Missouri, the St. Louis Transit Strike in 1900 provided the first
broad public awareness of Folk, although those familiar with politics
knew him as early as 1898, when he served as president of a Democratic
political organization, the Jefferson Club. Folk migrated to St. Louis
just seven years before the strike. Four years after it, voters sent him to
Jefferson City as governor of the state. Folk never won another political
office, although he remained a significant public figure for the next
fourteen years, running for a seat in the United States Senate in 1908
and in 1918.

The consolidation of St. Louis's street railways during 1899 set the
stage for the strike of the Amalgamated Association of Street Railway
Employees of America, Local 131. The state legislature passed a law in
that year allowing one company to acquire other companies. By January
1900, the St. Louis Transit Company had assumed control of all the
St. Louis street railways except the Suburban Street Railway Company,
and had set aside $4 million for the purchase of that line.

Rail company consolidation prompted labor organization. Railway officials resisted unionization, discharging union sympathizers. On
March 7, 1900, the union demanded recognition, reinstatement of

discharged supporters, a ten-hour workday, wages of twenty cents an hour, an end to split shifts, and the right to discuss future grievances with company directors. Folk and another lawyer represented the union. On March 10, the president of the St. Louis Transit Company, Edwards Whitaker, accepted most of the union's demands. Union officials thanked Folk for his efforts, and local newspapers reported the story. Folk's work for the union seemed to end with that conclusion. But when the union made similar demands of the Suburban Railway Company, that company's directors refused to agree to the union's terms. Ironically, the union struck the Suburban Company rather than St. Louis Transit, the catalyst for union organization.

The strike began on April 29, and soon after Harry B. Hawes, president of the police board and president of the Jefferson Club in 1899, ordered policemen to protect company property and allowed nonstriking workers to arm themselves. The strike proved ineffective, as about half of the employees continued to work. Then on May 8 more than three thousand St. Louis Transit Company employees struck. Samuel Lee, a national union official, claimed that the company had failed to comply with its earlier agreement: it had not reinstated fired workers, it had violated the ten-hour work rule, and it had discriminated against union members. A week after this larger work stoppage, union leaders and officials of the Suburban Railway Company accepted arbitration of their dispute.

No settlement seemed close in the St. Louis Transit strike. The union gave up on its demand for a closed shop, which would have meant that only union members could work for the company, but it held firm on the question of worker reinstatement. The company had hired some five hundred workers from eastern cities with the promise of permanent employment, and it refused to fire them in order to reinstate those workers who had struck. Armed and protected by guards, the new workers ran the cars. As no headway was made, violence increased. Union members and their surrogates blocked and blew up tracks. They cut electric lines and used other means to reduce efficiency. Public opinion was split, with some seven hundred merchants signing a document against "tyrannical trusts." By May 18 only 239 of an estimated 800 cars were in service.

During the effort to stop movement on the lines, strikers stopped cars under contract with the federal government to carry mail, causing federal judge Elmer B. Adams to issue an injunction against the union. The judge also authorized an increase in the number of deputy marshals and even allowed for the creation of a citizens's posse to aid the police. On May 29, a confrontation between armed Transit Company workers and strike sympathizers in south St. Louis produced some shooting deaths. Harry Hawes ordered Sheriff John H. Pohlman to create a posse. Eventually Pohlman recruited some twenty-five hundred citizens into service. Colonel John H. Cavender assumed leadership of the posse and divided it into twenty military units. A number of Jefferson Club members served, including Joseph W. Folk, who no doubt guarded Transit Company property, the chief function of the posse.

According to Folk's biographer, Louis G. Geiger, no evidence links Folk to any of the physical conflicts of the strike, including the most violent, a June 10 clash between marching strikers and the posse. Three men died and fourteen received wounds in the altercation. Samuel Gompers, president of the American Federation of Labor, came to St. Louis to negotiate an end to the strike and failed. After that clash and the failure of Gompers to make any headway, negotiations between the union and company officials resumed, as an end to the strike, according to Geiger, became "a sort of civic project." Former governor William J. Stone, at the time a lawyer practicing in St. Louis, asked Folk to again act as counsel for the union. Folk accepted the challenge, and with the aid of the highly regarded minister of the Second Baptist Church, Willard W. Boyd, he helped reach a settlement on July 2. By then fifteen men had died as a result of the strike and about $3.5 million worth of wages and property had been lost.

In the settlement, the company promised to allow employees to join the union and to dismiss executives who participated in antiunion activities. When vacancies became available in the workforce, the company said it would hire those who had worked for the company before, if they had no record of violent acts during the strike. The company refused to recognize the union as the sole bargaining agent for workers and rejected a provision for a union shop. On July 9, union members walked out again, because the company reneged on its promise to hire union members when vacancies occurred. The walk-out ended in mid-September with the union defeated on all of the crucial issues.

The strike had numerous consequences. It demonstrated worker solidarity and a sense of community consciousness across class lines. Some seven hundred St. Louis merchants, after all, went on record in support of the strike, and a broad cross section of the community boycotted the company during the strike. In addition, the Missouri legislature passed a franchise tax law in 1901 to make companies pay for the privilege of doing business in the state. Finally, the strike launched the political career of Joseph W. Folk.

Folk embodied a number of characteristics of the Progressive movement. Born in 1869, the seventh of ten children, to a middle-class Tennessee family, Folk grew up in a strongly religious Baptist atmosphere. His father had graduated from Wake Forest College in 1849, taught in rural schools, and read law, beginning a practice in Brownsville, Tennessee, in 1865. His father married the lovely Cornelia Estes, the daughter of a wealthy Brownsville planter, who had graduated from the Brownsville Female Academy. Only seventeen when she married, Cornelia raised eight of her ten children to adulthood. All of them received college or professional training; grew up attending church, Sunday school, and Wednesday night prayer meeting; heard grace before meals; and participated in daily Bible readings. Neither dancing nor card playing entertained the Folk household. In 1899, Folk's father received ordination as a Baptist minister. Earlier he had been a lawyer for the Louisville and Nashville Railroad Company, had owned the Brownsville gas plant that provided lighting to the town, and had been given the title of judge by admiring residents of his chosen home.

Christened Joel after an Estes uncle, the young Folk graduated from Brownsville Academy in 1885 and worked in a variety of businesses before becoming ill in Memphis in 1887. He returned home to recover and began reading law with his cousin, J. W. E. Moore. During that year, he changed his name to Joseph for some unknown reason. In 1888, he enrolled in the Vanderbilt University law school, earning a degree in 1890. He joined Moore in practicing law for a year before hanging out his own shingle. While in Brownsville, Folk entered politics and won local respect. In 1893 he decided to try his luck in a big practice, accepting the invitation of his St. Louis uncle, Frank Estes, to join his firm. A year later, Folk joined other "young Democratic businessmen and lawyers in forming the Jefferson Club." The Jefferson Club worked in opposition to Edward Butler's Indians, the dominant Democratic force in the city. Folk served as the club's campaign manager during the election in 1896. He became an ardent follower of William Jennings Bryan and an advocate of the doctrine of free silver. Jefferson Club members elected him president of the organization in 1898.

Beyond adhering to the same principles as Bryan, Folk left no record of his stance on key public issues during the 1890s. Louis Geiger called him a professional man and despite his Bryan leaning, "essentially a city man." Although reared a Baptist, he did not join the church until he was in his mid-twenties, and then he maintained a "casual" relationship to it. Nevertheless, his middle-class background, his grounding in Protestant religious orthodoxy, and his educational and professional status placed him in the mainstream of progressivism. Folk's opposition to the corruption and political malfeasance of the Butler machine also fit the pattern.

While the ideological features of the Progressive movement have occasioned much debate, Mary R. Beard summarized the basic ideas behind the movement in her 1945 book, *Woman As Force in History: A Study in Traditions and Realities.* The wife of Progressive historian Charles A. Beard, Mary Beard coauthored books with her husband and shared his belief in progress. She defined the idea of progress in these terms:

> In its composite formulation it embraces a conception of history as the struggle of human beings for individual and social perfection—for the good, the true, and the beautiful—against ignorance, disease, the harshness of physical nature, the forces of barbarism in individuals and in society. . . . Inherent in the idea is the social principle. That is to say, the civilization of men and women occurs in society, and all the agencies used in the process— language, ideas, knowledge, institutions, property, arts, and inventions—are social products, the work of men and women indissolubly united by the very nature of life, in a struggle for a decent and wholesome existence against the forces of barbarism and pessimism wrestling for the possession of the human spirit.

More recently, Robert M. Crunden in his *Ministers of Reform: The Progressive Achievement in American Civilization, 1889–1920* rightly emphasizes progressivism as

> a climate of creativity within which writers, artists, politicians, and thinkers functioned. . . . In general [progressives] shared moral values and agreed that America needed a spiritual reformation to fulfill God's plan for democracy in the New World. . . . Born between 1854 and 1874, the first generation of creative progressives absorbed the severe, Protestant moral values of their

parents. . . . [T]hey grew up in a world where the ministry no longer seemed
intellectually respectable and alternatives were few. Educated men and
women demanded useful careers that satisfied demanding consciences. They
groped toward new professions such as social work, journalism, academia,
the law, and politics. In each of these careers, they could become preachers
urging moral reform on institutions as well as on individuals.

Crunden argued that because of its broad appeal, progressivism
"often seems amorphous, inchoate, and difficult to define. The subject
is not all that complicated. Protestantism provided the chief thrust and
defined the perimeters of discourse, but the civil religion of American
mission soon transcended its origins and became a complex of secular
democratic values." Progressives viewed the state as an "educational
and ethical agency whose positive aid is an indispensable condition of
human progress." Thus, efforts to carefully draw lines between populism,
progressivism, and socialism lead to more confusion than clarity. "Most
of the leaders in these movements shared similar values, read similar
books, and even seemed to be the same people at different times or in
different circumstances." Folk's first political hero, William Jennings
Bryan, whose career spanned both the Progressive and Populist movements, fit Crunden's description well. Finally, Progressives sought for the
long term "an educated democracy that would create laws that would,
in turn, produce a moral democracy."

Folk's actions and words place him firmly in Crunden's configura-
tion. Two years after he left the office of governor, he continued to preach
and instruct. In a 1910 speech in Kansas City, he stressed equal rights
for all in what a newspaper reporter described as "more of a lecture than
a political speech." The reporter went on to say that Folk "insisted on
his old-time plea for principles above men, morals above money," and
progress over decay. By the time of Folk's speech, Progressives in Missouri
had enacted a number of Populist proposals into law, including the
initiative and referendum and the direct primary, illustrating Crunden's
point about the similarities in the two movements. Both sought to rid
society of monopoly, special privilege, and corruption.

While hindsight makes clear the current of reform that led to
progressivism, those engaged in the heat of politics sometimes failed
to see the connections. For example, in 1900, Alexander M. Dockery
became a leading contender for the Democratic nomination for governor.
Writing in August, the Populist editor of the *People's Record,* published

in Harrisonville, commented: "Populists, have you forgotten that you were inveigled into supporting Stephens & Co., and how you got left, and are you going to support the combination of Stephens, Dockery, . . . and the whole tribe of egg suckers that have bled the people of Missouri so long? Populists remember that the Democratic party forgot to put in their platform an income tax plank, no reference to referendum and have relegated the money question into a secondary place."

Earlier, the *Calumet Banner,* published in Clarksville, accused Dockery of opportunism. As a congressman, he jumped "on the silver wagon only when forced" and became an instant expansionist after having opposed expansion in Congress. The editor asserted, "The strait-jacket, free silver, anti-imperialist element of the Missouri Democracy, which loves principles more than men, will not accept a man whose record on these issues is not absolutely straight." In another place, the *Banner* ridiculed the idea that because Colonel Mose Wetmore, who had been accused of carrying out assignations with a number of women, supported Dockery, others should. "There can be no more potent reason why Dockery should not be governor than he is supported by such a conscienceless reprobate as Mose Wetmore. Mother's of Missouri! are you going to submit to the insult that a man should be governor because he has the support of an old He-Devil who goes out destroying the virtues of your daughters?" Another newspaper called Dockery a "notorious corruptionist" who took his orders from the Rock Island Railroad while in Congress. Despite such opposition, Dockery and the Democrats dominated the election. Missouri's voters returned Attorney General Edward C. Crow to office for a second term, gave Bryan the state's electoral votes by more than a 35,000 vote majority, and placed Democrats in thirteen of Missouri's fifteen U.S. representative seats.

Dockery, who was born in Daviess County in 1845, attended public school there before enrolling in Macon Academy and the St. Louis Medical College. From 1866 to 1874 he practiced medicine in Chillicothe, then he moved to Gallatin to accept a position as a bank cashier. Voters elected him to Congress in 1882 and sent him back at each election until 1898, when he started his pursuit for the nomination to run for governor. As a congressman, Dockery earned a reputation for government frugality, and as governor he added to that reputation, as well as establishing a state labor mediation board, state factory inspections, and the beginning of a juvenile court system. However, Dockery disagreed with Attorney General Crow's pursuit of trusts and employed Judge William M. Williams as a "special legal advisor" during his first year as governor. J. McAuliffe, a *Post-Dispatch* reporter, called Crow a "piercing thorn in the side of the Dockery administration."

Marching to his own drummer, Crow continued his prosecution of antitrust violators, providing a link with the progressivism that would follow. After establishing his antitrust credentials during the Stephens administration by contesting the insurance companies, Crow challenged the meat trust in 1902. He asked the state supreme court to require packing interests to appear for questioning about price-fixing. Chief Justice Gavon B. Burgess set May 6 for the hearing. A number of retailers complied, but the major packinghouses sent their lawyers to argue that the antitrust law violated the constitution. Butchers and store owners testified that the "Big Four," Armour, Swift, Cudahy, and Morris, set prices and forced their salesmen to maintain them. They also said that the packers sold them diseased cattle and spoiled meat. The supreme court denied the claim that the law failed to apply and appointed I. H. Kinley to investigate Crow's findings. Kinley verified the charges, and on March 20, 1903, the state fined the Armour, Hammond, Cudahy, Swift, Schwarzschild, and Sulzberger packing companies $5,000 apiece, leaving the meat trust intact and blunting the aggressive campaign of Crow. Those citizens in Sedalia, St. Louis, and Kansas City who had supported the effort to fight the trust by boycotting the packing companies saw their efforts frustrated by the courts.

By the time of the decision on the meat trust, the cases concerning political corruption, in which Boss Ed Butler and Circuit Attorney Joseph Folk were prominent, had captured the state's and the nation's attention. Born in Ireland in 1838, Butler arrived in New York at the age of twelve and learned the trade of blacksmithing. He moved to St. Louis before the Civil War, and within two years owned a black-smith's shop. He saved his money, invested successfully in St. Louis real estate and securities, and gained great wealth. During the 1870s he became politically active as a behind-the-scenes supporter of Democratic candidates for city offices. Butler developed a political machine, which was dependent upon his taking care of his followers, keeping his word, and using his wealth to achieve access to decision makers.

When St. Louis adopted a new charter in 1876, city government became more susceptible to corrupt influences. The charter created a two-house chamber: an upper house or council, composed of thirteen members elected at large for four-year terms, and a lower house, or house of delegates, composed of one member from each ward elected for a two-year term. The Assembly fixed tax rates, granted franchises, and approved all propositions for public improvements. A mayor served as chief executive with veto power over Assembly actions, but with limited control over the administration of city government because voters elected most of the administrative officers, and the six officers appointed by the mayor could not be dismissed without Assembly approval. Mayors served four-year terms. The state controlled elections, the city police, and city tax collectors. Such divided power with its accompanying divided responsibility for actions opened the city to influence peddling and corruption. Butler took advantage of every opening, serving as a liaison between those who needed something from government and officeholders. Nominally a Democrat, Butler worked with officeholders of both parties.

In 1900, the two centers of power within the St. Louis Democratic party converged. The Butler machine, with its repeat voters, called "Indians," could pack ballot boxes across the city. The Jefferson Club, originally created to oppose Butler, under the leadership of Harry Hawes made a deal with the boss in order to acquire some power. In his dual roles as president of the Jefferson Club and as president of the police board, Hawes enrolled the entire police force into Jefferson Club membership, greatly increasing the club's numbers and its treasury. Hawes even created a dozen other clubs outside the city, and the Jefferson Club reached the zenith of its influence between 1899 and 1902.

In his biography of Folk, Louis Geiger quoted the important writer and magazine publisher William Marion Reedy, who analyzed Hawes's success in a 1901 *Mirror* article: "The heart of his strength in the Jefferson Club is the crowd of young men of education and professional standing and southern sympathies and distinctive gentle manliness, as opposed to the crap-game, bar-tending, touting, sporting characters that heretofore have had such sway in politics. He has them put a respectable front. He pushes them forward. And at the same time Hawes takes especial pains to ingratiate himself with the elements that came up from the groggeries." The combination of the respectable, the old-line Democrats, and the police department represented sufficient power for Butler to acknowledge.

Before the 1900 elections, Butler and Hawes met to create a slate of Democratic candidates for the November poll and the April 1901 mayoral contest. Butler had one overriding desire: to make his son James J. Butler a member of the United States House of Representatives. Born in 1862, the younger Butler earned a law degree from St. Louis University and by 1900 had served as city attorney of St. Louis for eight years. Both factions wanted a reform ticket to oust Republican mayor Henry Ziegenhein and a Republican-controlled Assembly that in complicated maneuvers in 1896 and 1897 Butler had helped elect. Critics styled Ziegenhein the "one candlepower mayor." A grand jury report summarized the quality of members of the house of delegates as "utterly illiterate and lacking in ordinary intelligence, unable to give a better reason for favoring or opposing a measure than a desire to act with the majority. In some no trace of mentality or morality could be found; in others a low order of training appeared united with base cunning, groveling instincts, and sordid desires." With the World's Fair looming on the horizon and with the city reaching what one commentator described as a "shameful condition . . . where there is no money to pay anything except 'official salaries'—where the garbage rots in the streets and the dead cats and dogs are not removed because the defunct dog outsmells the dead cat and the garbage outsmells the dog, and therefore what is the use of bothering about?" a change seemed appropriate. Hawes and Butler backed Folk for circuit attorney, James Butler for Congress, and the wealthy Rolla Wells for mayor.

Hawes's police stood by while Butler's Indians voted as many times as needed to put the ticket over the top. Folk and Butler won in November, and Rolla Wells won in April. The Democrats also captured both houses of the Assembly. Because of voting fraud, the U.S. House of Representatives refused to seat Butler. Of course, Folk won his office with the same repeat votes cast for the other Democratic candidates. At a victory gathering attended by more than twenty thousand people, Wells and Hawes both spoke, while Edward Butler and his son sat in places of honor with a number of prominent businessmen, including Charles H. Turner, the president of the Suburban Railway. William Marion Reedy labeled the group the "local nobility," and Alexander S. McConachie, a historian, called them "The Big Cinch." McConachie credited William Marion Reedy with a 1901 article in the *Iconoclast,* a little magazine of the period, that criticized the "local nobility" composed of James

Campbell, Ed Butler, Thomas West, C. C. Maffitt, Edwards Whitaker, Julius Walsh, D. R. Francis, and John Scullin. The article concluded that they controlled "everything worth owning, banks, transit companies, gas, telephone, electric franchises," buying aldermen "like cattle" and placing the city "at their mercy." And all of their power and wealth rested upon fraud and injustice. Not long after the November election, Boss Butler met with Folk and asked him to appoint two Butler men as assistant circuit attorneys. Folk rejected Butler's nominees, saying, "As circuit attorney I am neither Democrat nor Republican." Then on January 2, 1901, Folk announced that he would call a grand jury to investigate charges of election fraud. Democratic leaders suggested he confine himself to Republican malfeasance, but Folk pursued Democrats as well as Republicans, and did so just as voters prepared for the April election. The grand jury brought indictments against seventeen Democrats and fifteen Republicans for violating election laws in the November election. By December, the Hawes-Butler coalition had broken down, and Folk found himself outside both factions.

Next, Folk focused upon corruption in the municipal Assembly. The corruption itself was nothing new—newspaper coverage of St. Louis's shady local politics predated the muckraking of *McClure's* and the *Atlantic* by two decades, as historian James Neal Primm pointed out in his study of St. Louis. The *Post-Dispatch* during the 1880s continually harassed the "ruling class." Articles about buying political preferment through bribes of assemblymen frequently appeared in the paper. Called the "combine" and run by Boss Butler, the operation allowed those seeking such privileges as municipal franchises to buy them by paying assemblymen. Butler negotiated the prices, collected the money, distributed payments to the right politicians, and kept a portion of the money for his services. The process became so refined that prices became standardized. According to one authority, if action slowed, a member of the Assembly would introduce a measure injurious to some interest so that those affected would pay to have the legislation killed.

In 1902, Folk revealed the details of a 1900 franchise deal involving the St. Louis and Suburban Railway Company. When approached to handle the transaction, Butler requested $145,000. Charles H. Turner, president of the railway, decided to go directly to the Assembly. He enlisted Philip Stock as his go-between. Stock saved Turner $10,000 by agreeing to pay house leaders $75,000 and council leaders $60,000.

Neither side trusted the other. Stock refused to pay the money until the legislation passed; the "combine" refused to act until Stock paid it the money. Stock put the money into two bank deposit boxes, keeping one set of keys and giving representatives of the "combine" another set. The council passed the necessary bill, but before the house of delegates acted, some concerned citizens secured an injunction against the expansion. Stock refused to pay the "combine." After months of argument, James M. Galvin, a reporter for the *St. Louis Star,* heard about the deal and the controversy. His story appeared in the January 21, 1902, edition of the paper. When reporters asked Butler about the case, the boss told them that if he had handled the proposition, "There wouldn't have been any safe deposit boxes in it. . . . [W]hen I get my fee the delivery of the goods is certain and expeditious." Folk read the story in the *Star* and discussed it with Galvin. The circuit attorney summoned more than one hundred people to appear before a grand jury, but failed to get the facts he needed. Next, he brazenly called Turner and Stock into his office and threatened to send them to prison if they did not testify before the grand jury within forty-eight hours. Frightened, and given immunity, they appeared and confessed. Folk secured thirteen convictions in lower courts for corruption, but the state supreme court reversed all of them on technicalities.

His investigation of the Suburban led Folk to Robert M. Snyder's effort to consolidate St. Louis's streetcar lines in 1898. A Kansas City banker and owner of Hahatonka castle in the Ozarks, Snyder established the Central Traction Company in St. Louis. To secure his monopoly, he needed a citywide franchise. Snyder soon learned that presidents of the independent lines had a deal with Butler to protect them against the sort of legislation the Kansas Citian desired. The Boss paid seven of the thirteen council members $5,000 per year to vote against any measure of consolidation. They received $300 per year as their compensation for serving on the council, so their loyalty to Butler superseded their commitment to the public interest. Through Butler the railway presidents paid another council member, Frederick Uthoff, $25,000 to keep the others on the take in line. Snyder outbid the independents. Uthoff sold out to Snyder for $50,000, but righteously, he returned the $25,000 that the independents had paid him. Snyder next bought sufficient members of both houses to pass his franchise. His investment totaled $250,000, with payments of $3,000 to twenty-five members of the house of delegates and between $10,000 and $17,000 to seven council members. Mayor Ziegenhein refused to go along, but the Assembly passed the measure over his veto on April 12, 1898. Snyder agreed to pay the city $1 million a year for fifty years for the franchise. At that point, the independents pooled their resources and purchased the franchise from Snyder for $1.25 million. Snyder moved to New York with a nifty profit of $1 million.

Snyder's residency in New York made him indictable in 1902. All of the other people involved in the corruption escaped prosecution because bribery had a three-year statute of limitations for those who did not become fugitives from justice. Although the *Post-Dispatch* had published details of the Snyder franchise deal in 1898, it took the grand jury testimony of George J. Kobush, president of the St. Louis Street Car Company, to make the case against Snyder. Kobush testified under the threat of being tried for perjury. The police issued a warrant for Snyder's arrest on February 15, 1902.

The Snyder trial occurred in October, with Uthoff admitting that Snyder had bribed him. Perhaps Uthoff still smarted from the fact that he had returned Snyder's original bribe of $50,000 and had demanded $100,000 from him. Before Snyder could respond, the Assembly passed the franchise. Snyder pocketed the $45,000 and gave Uthoff $5,000 as a consulting fee. A jury found Snyder guilty after deliberating for only an hour. Snyder's lawyer in his closing argument called bribery a "conventional offense, a mere perversion of justice." Folk jumped on that statement, calling bribery "treason, and the givers and takers of bribes . . . traitors to the peace." The jury sentenced Snyder to five years in prison. Snyder's lawyers appealed the case to the Missouri Supreme Court. The court ruled that the statute of limitations applied to Snyder also, since he maintained a residence in Kansas City during the entire time, and he had returned to Missouri frequently without being arrested.

Meanwhile, Folk and the grand jury investigated corruption in the granting of contracts for lighting the city and for collecting and treating its garbage. Testimony revealed that while holding the office of city collector, former mayor Ziegenhein illegally loaned city money to private individuals and collected the interest on the loans for his personal use. The statute of limitations protected Ziegenhein from prosecution. The lighting case involved James Campbell, a prominent self-made businessman, and the granting of a ten-year contract to his Welsbach

Company in 1899. The bribe amounted to $75,000. According to one witness, James Campbell had personally handed $47,000 to Boss Butler, but Butler refused to comment and Charles Kelly, speaker of the house of delegates, who received the money, awaited the statute of limitations to save him as he remained in Europe. Ironically, Kelly's decision to flee made him vulnerable to prosecution, but Butler and Campbell could not be touched. The garbage contract proved to be a different matter.

Ed Butler owned a large quantity of St. Louis Sanitary Company stock. He tried to bribe two physicians on the Board of Health with $2,500 each to award the garbage contract to his company. Even though the doctors refused the bribe, the police arrested Butler on March 14, 1902, for offering it. Since Butler epitomized the corruption in the city, his arrest caused quite a stir and made clear Folk's commitment to rid the government of dishonesty. The grand jury report of April 5, 1902, revealed the scope of the corruption. It asserted that "all franchises for the past ten years, with few exceptions, had been secured fraudulently."

Butler's lawyers persuaded a judge to move the trial to Columbia on a change of venue. When the trial began on October 13, 1902, six lawyers sat at the defense table: Charles P. Johnson, Chester H. Krum, and Thomas J. Rowe from St. Louis; North Todd Gentry and William W. Williams from Columbia, and Alexander Waller from Moberly. The courtroom filled with spectators. Rolla Wells and a contingent from the municipal Assembly attended, as did Lincoln Steffens, editor of *McClure's* and coauthor with former *Post-Dispatch* editor Claude Wetmore of "Tweed Days in St. Louis," which appeared in the magazine the same month as the trial. Credited by many as being the first "muckraking" article," "Tweed Days" really just added to the national publicity that Folk's efforts to eradicate corruption had received. On October 9, a few days before the trial, another national magazine, the *Independent,* had published a five-page account of Folk's activities. And as noted earlier, the *Post-Dispatch* had carried articles in the style of "muckraking" or investigative reporting throughout the 1890s. Louis Geiger maintained that by the time "Tweed Days" appeared Folk had achieved national recognition, in part because of self-promotion, and that Folk's fame made the article important, not vice versa. Months before the magazine articles appeared, the municipal Assembly had refused to appropriate more funds for Folk's office and the *Post-Dispatch* had appealed frequently for private contributions. Mayor Wells found some money in a contingency fund, but after the grand jury indictments in April 1902, Folk could expect no more support from his former colleagues in the Democratic party.

It took only an hour and ten minutes to select a jury in Columbia. The jurors, mostly farmers, heard Folk's case in only two days. Despite Butler's showing up in a broad hat and farmer clothes and his attorneys making constant reference to his advanced age, the jury found him guilty and sentenced him to three years in prison.

Butler's conviction made little difference in the November elections. With Folk on the sidelines, Hawes and Butler reconciled again, producing another Democratic victory. Mayor Rolla Wells, upright and virtuous, nevertheless appeared at a number of rallies with Boss Butler prominently in attendance. By the end of 1902, Folk had gained thirteen convictions, losing only his case against Henry Nicolaus, president of the Brewer's Association. A bank director who was involved in the Suburban Railway expansion case, Nicolaus escaped conviction when Charles Turner changed his testimony about the defendant's involvement. All told, the grand jury had brought sixty-one bribery indictments and forty-three perjury indictments involving twenty-four people. Folk sent eight members of the house of delegates to prison. However, no major figure went to jail, and in 1903 the Missouri Supreme Court set aside Butler's conviction on the grounds that the Board of Health had no constitutional power to grant contracts on garbage removal, even though it had been doing so for twelve years.

Folk brought Butler to trial again in July of 1903. A change of venue placed the trial in Fulton. The indictment charged Butler with fixing the 1899 lighting contract by bribing Charles Kelly, the speaker of the house of delegates. The Fulton jury acquitted him. Folk indicted Butler a third time in 1904 for making Kelly a fugitive, but the circuit attorney also lost that case. Although Folk failed to send Butler to jail, he succeeded in reducing the Boss's influence to only two of the city's twenty-six wards. Butler died in 1911.

Besides trying Butler in 1903, Folk aided in bringing Lieutenant Governor John Adams Lee to justice. *Post-Dispatch* reporter J. J. Mc-Auliffe came to Folk with evidence that Daniel Kelley, a lobbyist for the Royal Baking Company, had given Lee $7,500 to bribe six state senators. Kelley wanted to ensure that a law that gave his company a monopoly in Missouri remained on the books. The bribe occurred in 1901. Lee gave each senator $1,000 for his vote and kept $1,500 as his fee. Folk took the evidence about Lee to Attorney General Crow. When Crow called the lieutenant governor to his office for an interview, Lee broke down and disclosed all of the details of the transaction. Lee resigned his office, but not before a long line of Missouri Democrats had been called before a Cole County grand jury to answer questions about the Royal Baking Company case and a case involving statewide purchases of textbooks. None of those indicted went to jail, but a number decided to retire from politics. Everyone knew of Folk's role in the Lee resignation; his involvement, added to his actions against Butler, left Folk with little standing among Democratic party regulars.

As historian James Neal Primm has pointed out, the cases involving political corruption made Folk's reputation, but the circuit attorney's progressivism went deeper. Folk crusaded against what he considered immoral activities. He attacked gambling in the city, revealed the existence of graft in the police department, and shut down questionable investment schemes. Critics called him "Holy Joe," and not without reason. He certainly fit the idea of politician as crusader for the moral improvement of society.

The public responded with support. Private contributions helped fund Folk's office during 1902. A group of thirteen hundred wholesale merchants in St. Louis signed a document approving of his actions. One committee of citizens offered him a $15,000 house, which he declined. Letters came from President Theodore Roosevelt and other national leaders of both parties praising his good work. His Missouri Idea of aggressive honesty against corruption in public office struck a resonant note. Geiger wrote that by the spring of 1903, "Folk had become Missouri's first citizen." Many spoke of him as a logical choice for governor; some mentioned him as a distinct possibility for the presidency. According to Primm, the latter mention caused his budding relationship with Theodore Roosevelt, the incumbent, to cool.

Harry Hawes, James A. Reed, and James B. Gantt created a strategy during 1903 to deny Folk the nomination for governor. Hawes would control the St. Louis delegation; Reed, a James Pendergast machine politician and Kansas City's mayor, would take care of Jackson County and the western part of the state; and Gantt, a state supreme court justice who wanted the nomination, would pick up some rural delegates and wait for a deadlocked convention, to become the compromise candidate. Geiger called the contest for the nomination the most bitter political contest in Missouri since Thomas Hart Benton's fight to retain his senate seat in 1850.

Hawes carried St. Louis by a large margin and won every contested ward, but not without cheating. Even the wealthy West End participated in voter fraud. Thugs kept Norman J. Colman, Folk's good friend, from voting at all. David R. Francis's burly sons had to fight their way to the polls because they refused to tell some other thugs how they planned to vote. Ironically, they both supported Hawes. Police stationed at West End polling places where these incidents took place did nothing. A grand jury investigation of election fraud led to indictments of seventeen policemen, and Governor Dockery, who had opposed Folk's candidacy, was charged with standing by while the police publicly served Hawes's political interests.

The Hawes group's strategy failed. Gantt dropped out of contention early, and Hawes and Reed soon followed. Hawes finally recognized that he no longer opposed a man but a movement. He called Folk an ideal rather than a person. In rural Missouri, Folk took ten of eleven county delegations on May 7, including populous Greene County. When the convention met, Folk claimed 473 delegates to Hawes's 111, Reed's 41, and 14 uninstructed.

With his nomination assured, Folk wrote a platform that suited his philosophy. At center stage was the Missouri Idea: that citizenship in a democracy required a "civic obligation to enforce the performance of every public trust; bribery is treason, and the givers and takers of bribes are traitors of peace; laws are made to be enforced, not to be ignored; that officials should no more embezzle public power entrusted to them than public money in their custody." In addition, the platform called for a statewide direct primary law, the end of corporate privilege, equal treatment of the interests of labor and capital, municipal home rule for large cities, the removal of police forces from politics, and the right of municipalities to own their utilities.

While Folk won the nomination and wrote a Progressive platform, he failed to develop a political organization. Party regulars chose the other nominees for statewide office and during the campaign they pretty well ignored their candidate for governor. At the state convention to choose delegates to the presidential nominating convention in Joplin, Folk forces exerted little influence. Geiger called them "a minority and badly led." Voters gave Folk a remarkable personal victory. No other

Democrat won a major office, and he outpolled Theodore Roosevelt's vote 326,652 to 321,449. By voting for Folk and Roosevelt, Missourians showed their disdain for politics as usual. They voted for a gubernatorial candidate who received practically no support from his party, and for the first time since 1868, they gave a majority of their electoral votes to a Republican candidate for the presidency. Folk defeated his Republican opponent by more than thirty thousand votes. Republicans gained control of the legislature and won nine of sixteen congressional races. William Warner became the first Republican senator from Missouri in thirty-four years. Besides representing a widespread splitting of ballots, the election revealed a failure of both parties to get out the vote. Forty thousand fewer voters cast ballots in 1904 than in 1900; each party received about twenty thousand fewer votes.

Nevertheless, Republican strength represented the influence of Theodore Roosevelt, although party regulars failed to adequately gauge the power of Progressive ideas. They nominated conservative Cyrus P. Walbridge from St. Louis as their candidate for governor. Walbridge had been mayor of St. Louis and served as the president of the Bell Telephone Company in the city. The Republican platform contained some Progressive principles without making specific promises. It condemned "bribe-givers and bribe-takers alike" and advocated "strict enforcement of the laws forbidding rail-road passes to public officials." The platform promised better roads for Missourians and support for home rule for municipalities. As David March noted, "Although some Republicans who had praised Folk before his nomination for governor attacked him during the campaign, many others refused to back Walbridge and openly urged the people to vote for both Roosevelt and Folk."

Missouri voters, presented with the opportunity to approve of an initiative and referendum proposal, also became the first in the country to reject procedures for direct government. Failure to secure legislative approval for initiative and referendum in 1901 produced a broad educational campaign over the next three years and placement of the proposition on the ballot in 1904. The State Federation of Labor, the Prohibition party, the Socialist party, and the Public Ownership party had worked together on behalf of the measure. The Democrats had included the item in their 1904 platform, even though their version called for larger percentages of voters to initiate and to approve legislation than those advocated by the Direct Legislation League, the major promoter of the idea. The initiative and referendum amendment lost by 53,540 votes. Apparently, urban reformers supporting direct legislation failed to convince small-town and rural voters of the benefits of their plan. Folk's support for a direct government amendment led to its placement on the ballot again in 1908, when Missouri voters approved it by a majority of 30,325. It won because of urban voters who favored it by more than 60 percent; rural voters gave it only a 45 percent rate of approval.

During his first two years in office, Folk concentrated on enforcing existing laws. He eliminated what reformers considered societal evils: gambling, including horse racing, and Sunday drinking in saloons. In his appointments, he purged state government of Dockery people, replacing them with "zealous and young" people like himself. He neglected using his power of appointment to build an organization. For example, he made Matthew Hall warden of the state penitentiary, a position that held great possibilities for patronage, instead of a candidate supported by former governor Lon V. Stephens. As a result, he lost the support of the still politically powerful Stephens. Working with the Republican majority in the legislature, Folk did secure legislation reducing railroad freight rates by 15 to 40 percent and more than a dozen other acts of railroad regulation. In addition, the legislature passed a compulsory school attendance law and did away with the school textbook commission. With his support, the state established teacher training schools in Maryville and Springfield.

Folk showed his moral fiber by speaking out against the lynching of black citizens in Belmont in 1905 and Springfield in 1906. His gubernatorial term came during increasing racial tensions in the nation and the state. In 1903, Democratic legislators tried to pass a segregation law to separate the races on Missouri's trains. The effort failed because of the strength of black voters, primarily in St. Louis. In the Bootheel region in 1902, white railroad workers in Marston forced a new black crew to leave their work under the threat of violence, and in New Madrid County in 1905 "a gang fired 500 shots into the home of a mill owner who had imported blacks to a traditionally white-only area." In 1910 and 1911, with the influx of more blacks into the Bootheel to work the land reclaimed from the swamps, further violence erupted.

In May of 1910, a black quarreled with a New Madrid city marshal, who jailed him. In the words of historian David Thelen, "The next morning residents found the black stranger hanging dead from a pecan tree."

That same summer in Charleston two "itinerant" blacks accused of robbing and murdering a white farmer named William Fox were seized from jail by a mob estimated to be a thousand strong. Members of the mob hanged one of the men on the courthouse square and took the other to the black housing section of Charleston and hanged him from a railroad crossing sign. At the behest of Governor Herbert Hadley, the prosecuting attorney, J. M. Haw, got a grand jury to indict four whites, but a local judge gave a "directed verdict of not guilty," and they went free.

In 1911, terrorism came to the Pemiscot County community of Caruthersville. During the first nine months of 1911 the county had a murder each month. The law seemed ineffective as law officers caught and punished only a single individual for the crimes. In October, officers avoided one lynching by moving out of town a black who had stabbed two whites in a brawl outside a saloon. On October 10, separate incidents produced two arrests of blacks. A white woman charged that Ben Woods had "pestered her." That evening police took into custody A. B. Richardson on a complaint of stealing. A lynch mob of three hundred took the prisoners from jail. While they clubbed Woods, Richardson began insulting them. The mob turned on Richardson, beating him to death on their way to disposing of the body in the Mississippi River. Woods escaped with only a beating. The mob moved on to burn a black boardinghouse. Blacks fled from Pemiscot County in droves in the wake of this violence. A coroner's jury reported Richardson's death as occurring from "causes unknown."

In the Springfield tragedy, whites killed three blacks. Folk sent state troops to stop the violence, offered rewards for information leading to the capture of the ringleaders, and provided an assistant attorney general to aid the county prosecutor in a grand jury investigation. Unlike in most lynchings, officials brought three people to trial. The result of the trial, however, followed a familiar pattern: all three defendants went free.

Folk's various accomplishments did nothing to heal the wounds within the Democratic party. Hawes, Dockery, William J. Stone, and Rolla Wells continued to oppose him, and David R. Francis brought his supporters into the anti-Folk coalition. In 1906, when William Jennings Bryan came to St. Louis as a part of his effort to gain the nomination for president again, the regular Democrats excluded Folk from participating in the event. Despite his lack of acceptance by traditional party leaders, Folk dominated the party platform in 1906, and the party's success in the election indicated popular endorsement of his administration and the willingness of those who opposed him to temporarily put their differences on hold in order to prevail in the election. The Republicans carried both St. Louis and Kansas City, but rural voters provided sufficient margin to elect four Democrats to statewide offices and to take control of the state legislature. The number of Democrats in the U.S. House of Representatives increased from seven to twelve.

When the legislature assembled, Folk presented it a long list of Progressive measures to enact. The governor requested a larger role for government in the economy, including more regulation and taxation of corporations and a stricter child labor law. He asked the legislature to outlaw holding companies, to appropriate funds for road building, to allow municipalities to own utilities, and to improve public education. Expressing a belief that individuals deserved a greater voice in government, Folk requested direct primaries for nominating candidates, and in anticipation of direct election of U.S. senators, he asked that voters be allowed to state their preferences for senatorial candidates. Other requests included home rule for municipalities and registration of voters in towns with populations larger than ten thousand. He wanted the police in Kansas City, St. Joseph, and St. Louis controlled by city administrations instead of by the state.

Folk won passage of most of his legislative agenda, despite being a lame-duck governor and being opposed by political leaders who anticipated his campaign for William J. Stone's senatorial seat in 1908. He had worked diligently among legislators to win support for his measures, and the legislature responded. It passed more than twenty laws regulating railroads and insurance companies. Folk signed four measures that thoroughly revised the state's antitrust laws. Another act established a state banking department. Other measures made it illegal to sell adulterated food or drugs, regulated lobbying, lengthened the school year from six to eight months, limited the work of telegraph operators and train dispatchers to eight hours per day, and provided for the inspection of mines. Fourteen laws dealt with highways, including legislation to create the offices of state and county highway engineers. Folk overcame political odds to accomplish so much, but his success also suggested that he rode a wave of reform that permeated Missouri and the nation.

Republican Herbert W. Hadley served as attorney general during the Folk administration and promoted Progressive reform in that office just as ably as Folk pursued it as governor. Born in Olathe, Kansas, on February 2, 1872, Hadley earned a bachelor of arts degree from the University of Kansas at age twenty and a degree in law from the Union Law School, later Northwestern University's school of law, in Illinois in 1894. He established his legal practice in Kansas City. Hadley achieved a citywide reputation as assistant city counselor in lawsuits brought by pedestrians against the city because of faulty plank sidewalks. In 1900 he won the office of prosecuting attorney in Jackson County. Two years later he lost a bid for reelection. But in 1904, Hadley won the Republican nomination for attorney general and joined Folk in Jefferson City after the election.

During four years as attorney general, Hadley brought suits against Standard Oil of New Jersey, International Harvester, and a group of monopolistic lumber companies. In other actions, he defended consumers against insurance companies and railroads that exploited the state's citizens. His hard work on behalf of Missourians positioned him for the governor's race in 1908. Only months after becoming attorney general, Hadley had begun hearings into the charge that Standard Oil of New Jersey monopolized petroleum sales in Missouri through three subsidiaries: Standard Oil of Indiana, the Republic Oil Company, and the Waters-Pierce Oil Company. Each subsidiary operated in its own region. The same auditor worked for all three companies, and all three companies maintained the same office at 26 Broadway, New York City. Testimony revealed that major Missouri railroads had agreed not to transport the products of Standard's competitors. Hadley asked the Missouri Supreme Court to cancel these companies' charters and to prohibit them from conducting business in the state. The attorney general knew that to succeed he must show that Standard Oil of New Jersey owned the companies. He sought to force company executives to admit this fact. Hadley moved his proceedings to a New York courtroom and tried unsuccessfully to get John D. Rockefeller, the owner of Standard Oil, on the stand. According to David Thelen, Rockefeller disguised himself and fled the country.

The persistent prosecutor achieved more success with other officials. The United States Supreme Court aided him when it ruled that corporate officials could not claim immunity from self-incrimination when a corporation committed a crime. The Missouri Supreme Court ordered key Standard official Henry H. Rogers to answer Hadley's questions. Earlier, Rogers had expressed only contempt for Hadley and Missouri's supreme court. With the ruling by the U.S. Supreme Court, Rogers changed his tune and admitted that Standard Oil of New Jersey owned the other companies.

Other states and the federal government followed Hadley's lead against Standard Oil. Although Hadley had gained Rogers's testimony in March of 1906, the case dragged on until 1909 in state courts and until 1912 in federal courts. Despite the delay, Standard Oil lost the case. Hadley's success meant that independent oil companies now competed in Missouri, and the price of oil declined by about one-third. In addition, the Missouri legislature on March 19, 1907, amended its antitrust law to make violations a felony. Violators could go to prison for up to five years.

About the same time, the Missouri House of Representatives reacted to farmers' complaints about noncompetitive farm machinery prices by asking Hadley to investigate the matter. The attorney general found that Cyrus McCormick had eliminated competition by creating the International Harvester holding company through a 1902 agreement with the five major farm machinery manufacturers. Hadley sued International Harvester in November 1907. His successor as attorney general, Elliot Major, continued the suit and won the case in 1911. The Missouri Supreme Court fined Harvester $50,000, but later reduced the levy to $25,000. The court ruled further that if Harvester reorganized, paid the fine, and agreed to obey Missouri law in the future, it could continue to do business in the state.

Lumber companies and insurance companies also attracted Hadley's attention. In 1906 he heard complaints that insurance companies fixed rates arbitrarily with little regard for the risks involved. Edward Crow had won an antitrust suit against some of the same companies in 1899, but by the time Hadley became attorney general, the companies had returned to their earlier practices. Hadley negotiated a settlement with the companies rather than bringing suit. The companies agreed to establish new rates on property based on a standardized base that included risks. Rates dropped on St. Louis property by as much as 40 percent, and they declined across the state by about 10 percent. In 1908 Hadley found that an association of lumber companies set prices and restricted production in order to ensure higher profits. He brought suit against the association. The companies stopped these practices long before the Missouri Supreme Court finally decided in favor of the state in 1914.

Hadley conducted an extended battle with Missouri railroads. In 1905 the legislature passed a maximum rate law to reduce freight rates by an average of 25 percent. The railroads questioned the constitutionality of the law in the federal district court of Kansas City. While the case proceeded, Hadley and Folk cooperated to strengthen the 1905 law and to add a provision that lowered passenger rates on trains from three cents per mile to two cents per mile. The legislature passed the new laws in 1907.

Anticipating that the railroads would try to prevent implementation of the laws in federal court, Hadley asked state courts in Kansas City and St. Louis to enjoin the railroads from disobeying the laws. He also warned the railroads that if they tried to avoid the reduction of passenger rates, he would ask the Missouri Supreme Court to annul their right to operate in Missouri. The attorney general threatened to force the trains to lock their doors when they crossed the state line and promised to post guards on the trains when they crossed Missouri to ensure the doors remained closed. Station agents or conductors who charged more than the two cents per mile would be arrested. The railroads heeded Hadley's threat but continued to question the law's constitutionality. They lost their case in the U.S. Supreme Court in 1913.

Hadley's actions as attorney general complemented Folk's efforts as governor to bring progressivism to Missouri. By 1908, however, Hadley and Folk diverged on the role of corporations in American society. Hadley had decided that it made more sense to regulate corporations than to break them up. Folk, however, continued to see matters in black and white. If corporations violated laws, they must be brought to justice. In accepting regulation over dissolution of corporations, Hadley followed the leadership of the national Republican party and influenced leaders in other states to move in that direction, since he had provided leadership in attacking corporate power on the state level earlier. Hadley was a Republican without Folk's moralistic approach to secular society. According to David Thelen, he "believed that disputes should be settled by independent tribunals on the basis of unassailable expertise, and this made regulation appealing." Hadley drew upon Republican doctrine that individual ambition should be unleashed through the promotion of competition and growth, and he combined that with the "belief that the community ought to use strong governmental sanctions against malefactors." Hadley did not carry the traditional Democratic fear of strong government, but instead reflected the approach of Theodore Roosevelt and what eventually came to be called "New Nationalism."

In 1907, Hadley called the first meeting of attorney generals to discuss what to do about corporate power. Their resolutions advocated "the dissolution of trusts and the imprisonment of guilty corporate directors." When the group met a year later, Hadley gave an opening address that expressed dissatisfaction with trust busting and suggested the inevitability of combinations. He argued that it made more practical sense to regulate large enterprises than to attempt to dissolve them.

The Panic of 1907 had caused Hadley to rethink his position. His negotiations with the insurance companies evidenced the change in his thinking. In 1908, Hadley decided against continuing cases against beef and lumber monopolies, two interests that had modified their conduct because of his actions, observing, "It would be better to permit these evils to go uncorrected and unpunished for a while than to undertake the work of their correction under [economic] circumstances which would result in a more serious injury to the public and the business world."

Folk's moral approach led to a different conclusion. Folk said, "The man who says that the depression in the industrial world is caused by punishing crooks argues that there can be no such thing as honest prosperity. . . . If the country had to choose between great prosperity coupled with crookedness, and less prosperity and more honesty, it would undoubtedly take the latter." Folk's continued adherence to a carefully defined sense of right and wrong placed him under the Robert Crunden definition of a "Minister of Reform."

In 1908 Folk tried to replace fellow Democrat William J. Stone in the United States Senate. Folk's effort appeared doomed from the beginning because he failed to pay attention to political organization. He believed that his ideas and accomplishments should be sufficient to secure office. Hadley once observed to writer Mark Sullivan that Folk failed to bind "men to him personally." The absence of organization appeared when four Folk men vied for the gubernatorial nomination, while his opponents within the Democratic party, Stone, Harry Hawes, and David R. Francis, all supported the eventual winner, longtime party regular William S. Cowherd.

During the campaign, Folk appealed to independents as well as Democrats in some 300 speeches that emphasized his record of reform. Stone gave about 250 speeches, emphasizing national issues and party regularity while acknowledging the record of accomplishment made by Folk that the party had inscribed in its platform. For the first time the candidates traveled to outstate Missouri by automobile. Folk sometimes went from town to town in a caravan of as many as twenty cars, attracting a good deal of attention because few rural Missourians saw many cars. Folk received a majority of the vote in fifty-seven counties; Stone won in forty-seven, but he defeated Folk by more than 23,000 votes in Kansas City and St. Louis. The final tally gave Stone the nomination by a vote of 159,512 to 144,718.

Hadley faced no opponent for the Republican nomination for governor. He and his party fashioned a Progressive platform that included enforcement of all liquor laws; primary nominating elections, including senatorial preferential primaries; a host of railroad and other business regulatory proposals; improved judiciary procedures; state financing of roads; increased support for schools; new pure food and drug laws; conservation of natural resources; and measures to improve working conditions for laborers. Hadley rightly took credit for a number of initiatives developed during the Folk administration, and the Republicans succeeded in styling themselves as more Progressive than the Cowherd-led Democratic party.

Hadley defeated Cowherd by more than fifteen thousand votes, becoming the only Republican to win statewide office in 1908 and the first Republican governor since the 1870s. He received more votes than any of his predecessors for political office. For the second time in a row, the Republican candidate for president carried Missouri, as William Howard Taft defeated William Jennings Bryan by a slim 449 votes. Splitting their tickets, Missouri voters endorsed Progressive ideas by voting for Hadley. They also elected ten Democrats and six Republicans to seats in the U.S. House of Representatives. Republicans won a slight majority in the Missouri House of Representatives, but Democrats held a more than two-to-one majority in the Missouri Senate. That circumstance prevailed for the first two years of Hadley's administration, and during his last two years, Democrats controlled both houses of the General Assembly.

The new governor had little choice but to appeal to Progressives of both parties, and he succeeded. The General Assembly passed laws to make the state more responsible for the health and welfare of its citizens. It created a state dairy commissioner and a game and fish commissioner, and it initiated procedures to preserve wildlife. The legislature established a bureau of vital statistics; passed laws encouraging cities and towns to improve sewers, streets, and parks; and provided for a court of appeals in Springfield, an industrial home for delinquent African American girls in Tipton, and legislation to improve the juvenile court system. Other legislation established a state waterways commission and a poultry experiment station at Mountain Grove.

Equally important, Hadley emphasized growth and development. He called for massive state highway building and river improvements as stimulants to economic advance and as competition to railroads. As David Thelen has observed, "The idea that improved transportation would encourage economic growth became the theme of his governorship." Regulation replaced destruction of corporate power. Persuading corporations to work with the state became a part of the governor's effort to improve conditions. Hadley believed he could stimulate investment and protect consumers at the same time. For example, he asked for a public service commission that would "give to the owners of . . . [railroads and other enterprises] a reasonable return" on investments and "regulate the charges and the conduct of business enterprises to which the public must resort." In fine Progressive fashion, Hadley wanted experts to decide reasonable returns to investors and the state to protect citizens from exploitation.

Increased government activity required more revenue. The state ran a deficit of about $1.5 million during the period from 1907 to 1909; Hadley projected an even larger deficit of $3.5 million during the next biennium. The governor made no apology for larger government. In his inaugural address he noted just how much the role of government had changed in Missouri over the previous three decades:

In 1875, when our present constitution was adopted and our present revenue system devised, the theory that the government that governs least was the controlling thought in public affairs. Today all political parties apparently act upon the theory that it is the duty of government to exercise its authority when there is any justification therefor. It is unnecessary that I should even refer to the increased number of instances in which it has been not only advisable, but necessary for the people of the State to exercise, in their governmental capacity, an authority and supervision that a third of a century ago would have been unjustified and unnecessary.

Changed circumstances required new money. Hadley recommended taxing inheritances that exceeded $10,000. He wanted taxes placed on corporate stocks and on liquor. He sought to raise revenue by charging inspection fees on petroleum products and advocated that market value of real and personal property be the basis for taxation. The legislature responded by placing fees on petroleum inspections and by taxing the manufacturers and wholesale distributors of liquor, but it refused to go along with Hadley's other requests.

As governor, Hadley made administrative decisions that aided social welfare. Conditions in the Missouri State Penitentiary attracted his attention. The largest prison in the world, it provided inmates with few amenities. He had showers installed, improved the food, and instituted a program of teaching job skills. Hadley ended the practice of flogging prisoners and making them go from one place to another by marching in lockstep. These changes resulted in cutting discipline cases in half.

Despite his hard work, Hadley left the governor's mansion with his goals of improving education and social services unfulfilled. In his final message to the legislature in 1913, he provided a succinct and comprehensive statement of his view of government's role in society:

> While the practice of economy in the conduct of public affairs is a policy which is absolutely necessary, yet, upon the other hand, the concern of those in charge of public affairs should be not to see how little money can be spent, but what expenditures are necessary in order to make the State government mean as much as possible to the people. . . . You can do much towards preventing discrimination, overthrowing privilege, correcting injustice and creating conditions which will tend to produce an equality of opportunity and achievement. What you can do you should do to bring about a larger measure of social and industrial justice, and a physical well-being and prosperity which must be the basis of substantial progress towards a better condition of life, higher ideals and a higher standard of citizenship.

In Hadley's view, neither the Missouri legislature nor the administration of William Howard Taft had gone far enough in realizing Progressive goals. As the presidential election of 1912 approached,

Hadley tried to move Taft in the direction of Progressive ideas. Taft made too little progress, and Theodore Roosevelt proposed a program that mirrored Hadley's politics. Hadley along with seven other Republican governors called upon Roosevelt to seek the Republican nomination for president. Hadley hoped to have Missouri Republicans decide on their candidate through a preferential primary, believing that Roosevelt would win and that a split in the party could be avoided. That effort failed, and the delegate selection process produced dissension, including fistfights between Taft and Roosevelt supporters. At the state convention Roosevelt carried the day by a two-to-one margin, but the process had produced a serious split in the party.

Hadley attended the national Republican convention in Chicago. At one point he asked that Roosevelt delegates be seated instead of Taft delegates, stating his position so eloquently that the next day a Hadley demonstration of more than twenty minutes "frightened both Roosevelt and Taft leaders," according to Thelen. When Roosevelt delegates walked out of the convention, Hadley stayed with Taft, knowing that splitting the party would mean Republican defeat in Missouri. Hadley extracted a promise from Taft to support popular primaries to nominate future presidential candidates and gave him a weak endorsement in October, but to no avail. A divided Republican party could not carry Missouri. Always a more practical politician than Folk, a reformer but not of the Crunden mold, Hadley retired from politics.

Meanwhile, Folk's career encountered its own difficulties. As Hadley understood and as Louis Geiger emphasized, Folk failed to create a personal political following, either because he seemed too aloof or because he devoted too little attention to the process. Another opportunity to win a U.S. Senate seat existed in 1910, but the crusader had little support. Such important former Folk supporters as Lon V. Stephens and Kansas City's Joseph Shannon now expressed hostility toward him. The Jefferson Club had lost influence in St. Louis, and Folk had little support in Kansas City, where James A. Reed represented an emerging political machine led by James Pendergast. Folk, who may have been looking toward the 1912 presidential nomination instead of focusing on a nomination for the Senate, had little money behind him. Reed won the nomination over David R. Francis and Folk.

The Republican party nominated John C. McKinley of Unionville as their candidate for the Senate. McKinley served as lieutenant governor during Folk's term as governor. When Stone won a U.S. Senate seat in 1908, McKinley had been the Republican opponent. With the Democrats in charge of the General Assembly, Reed won the Senate seat in 1910, replacing William Warner, a St. Louis Republican, whom the Republican-controlled General Assembly had sent to Washington in 1905.

Whatever Folk had hoped in 1910, in early 1911 his chances of becoming the Democratic candidate for president seemed slim. During January and February of 1911, the *Post-Dispatch* ran a series of candidate profiles. The paper omitted Folk from its list while including Thomas Marshall of Indiana, Judson Harmon of Ohio, and Representative James Beauchamp Clark of Missouri. Then William Jennings Bryan began touting Folk as a candidate during the summer of 1911. Bryan and Folk shared a general Progressive creed and refused to adhere to notions of promotion to offices because of some order imposed by their political party. In addition, Bryan distrusted Champ Clark's commitment to progressivism and liked Folk's position on the "liquor question." While not a Prohibitionist, Folk supported strict enforcement of all liquor laws. Described as a "wet," Clark strongly opposed Prohibition. By late summer, Bryan had proclaimed for Folk. But Folk's candidacy went nowhere. He could not depend on Missouri Democrats to provide him continued support. Initially, the Missouri Democratic party had given Folk its endorsement as its favorite son, but it soon reversed itself, giving the nod to Clark. By January, Bryan had abandoned Folk. Folk formally withdrew from consideration on February 10. In the presidential primary in Missouri, Clark easily carried the day.

Born in Lawrenceburg, Kentucky, on March 7, 1850, Champ Clark received a basic education and began teaching at the age of fourteen in order to gain more knowledge. Later he attended Transylvania University until an exchange of pistol shots with another student led to his expulsion. He then enrolled in Bethany College in West Virginia, graduating with high honors. Clark briefly held the presidency of Marshall College, another West Virginia school, and then entered the Cincinnati Law School. After graduation he moved to Wichita, but opportunities seemed too few in the Kansas town. He traveled east to Louisiana, Missouri, in 1875, taught school, practiced law, and edited the *Louisiana Daily News*. In 1880 Clark moved to Bowling Green, Missouri, his home until his death.

In 1888, voters sent him to the Missouri House of Representatives. In a brief four years, he earned a reputation as a serious legislator. Clark authored twenty-two pieces of Progressive legislation in only one term. In 1892 he won a seat in the U.S. House of Representatives. He retained his seat in Congress in each subsequent election except for the period from 1895 to 1897. In 1907, Democratic House members elected Clark minority leader. In the so-called revolution of 1910–1911, he led in the fight to change House rules that ended the authoritarian speakership of Republican Joseph Cannon. Democrats won a majority of seats in the House in the 1910 election, and Clark assumed the speakership when Congress met in January of 1911.

When the Democratic presidential nominating convention convened in Baltimore, Clark appeared to be the front-runner. Senator James Reed placed Clark's name in nomination, and during the early balloting, the Missourian received more votes than any other candidate but not the two-thirds required for victory. Woodrow Wilson, former president of Princeton and Progressive governor of New Jersey, always came in second. On the tenth ballot, Charles F. Murphy, who led New York's Tammany Hall political machine, announced a shift of his delegation's ninety votes to Clark from Ohio governor Judson Harmon. That gave Clark a majority of the delegates. His supporters assumed that the convention would quickly nominate him. On the thirteenth ballot, however, William Jennings Bryan accused Clark of making a deal with Wall Street and proclaimed that he could not support the Missourian so long as New York voted for him. He switched his support to Wilson. David March, an astute student of Missouri politics, wrote that Bryan's defection did not cause Clark's defeat. Clark lost because delegates committed to Wilson and to Oscar W. Underwood refused to leave their candidates on the eleventh and twelfth ballots. March summarized, "It was the work of the Wilson leaders among the boss-controlled delegations and the Underwood men that gave the New Jersey governor the eventual victory." Victory finally came on the forty-sixth ballot. A party man, Clark returned to Missouri to campaign for his party's nominee.

On the state level, William S. Cowherd, who had lost to Hadley in 1908, challenged Elliot Woolfolk Major of Bowling Green for the Democratic nomination for governor. Cowherd represented old-line party Democrats, although David R. Francis supported Major. Despite

Francis's endorsement, Folk and other Progressives claimed Major. Born on October 20, 1864, Major read law in the offices of Champ Clark and became a lawyer at the age of twenty-one. In 1896 he won a seat in the Missouri Senate, where he served one term. He lost the race for attorney general in 1904. Nominated for attorney general four years later, he won this time, and over the course of his term he ardently prosecuted the cases against Standard Oil, International Harvester, and the lumber companies originally brought by Hadley. As attorney general, Major argued more than fifty cases before the United States Supreme Court and more than forty cases in lower courts. He won the 1912 gubernatorial primary by attracting large majorities in the rural areas of Missouri, while Cowherd carried both St. Louis and Kansas City. In Missouri, rural voters supported Progressive politicians. Major's prospects for becoming governor looked good, since the state Republican party had divided just as the national party had done. John McKinley of Unionville, who had been elected lieutenant governor in 1904 but who had lost both the 1908 and 1910 races for the U.S. Senate, won the nomination of the regular Republicans. Albert D. Nortoni ran as the candidate of the Progressive party. Major carried the state with a total vote of 337,019 to McKinley's 217,819 and Nortoni's 109,146. He received approximately 10,000 more votes than all of his competitors combined. While Woodrow Wilson also carried Missouri, his 330,746 votes failed to match the 332,192 garnered by his two opponents. Taft received 207,821 votes, and Roosevelt took 124,371. Democrats also won fourteen of sixteen seats allotted Missouri in the U.S. House of Representatives.

Eugene V. Debs, the Socialist party candidate for president, garnered only 28,466 votes in Missouri. But by 1912 two nationally significant Socialists had settled in the state: Kate and Frank P. O'Hare. After the national Socialist party formed in 1901, St. Louis had served as its national headquarters. Frank O'Hare had been born in St. Louis, and he and his wife returned to the city in 1911, taking over the *National Rip-Saw* magazine. They brought new life to the publication and made it nationally significant. Both Kate and Frank toured the nation spreading the Socialist gospel.

Two men stood out as leading Socialists in Missouri, Gottlieb A. Hoehn of St. Louis and E. T. Behrens of Sedalia. Behrens served as president of the State Federation of Labor from 1901 to 1905 and ran on the Socialist ticket for governor in 1904, one of many offices that he stood for during his active career. Hoehn published and edited *St. Louis Labor,* an influential Socialist newspaper. A founder of the Social Democratic party and a member of the first National Committee of the Socialist party, Hoehn played a significant role in the ranks of organized labor in Missouri. During the 1910s, Socialists held high office in the Missouri Federation of Labor and the St. Louis Central Trades and Labor Union. According to Gary Fink, Socialists firmly controlled the Springfield Trades and Labor Assembly and exerted significant influence in the machinist, cigar makers, miners, brewers, carpenters, and bakers unions.

Even the Bootheel had Socialist adherents. David Thelen noted that Socialist candidates for president garnered the following number of votes in the six counties that composed the region: 207 votes in 1904, 1,291 or 5.5 percent of the vote in 1908, and 3,240 or 12.9 percent of the vote in 1912. Thelen's analysis attributed the strength of socialism in the Bootheel to the disruptions caused by rapid social change in the region resulting from the drainage of the swamps there. In 1916, support for Debs in the presidential race declined by more than 66 percent in the Bootheel and by 50 percent across the state.

Major's inauguration as governor took place in a temporary state-house. At 8 P.M. on February 5, 1911, lightning struck the old frame structure, and it erupted into flames. Trains loaded with fire-fighting equipment came from Sedalia and requests went to other towns, but the capitol building could not be saved. Luckily, an absence of wind kept the fire from spreading to other sections of Jefferson City. Governor Hadley, Senator Reed, and many legislators helped fight the blaze. Officials enlisted penitentiary inmates to combat the fire and to carry important documents out of the building. While some valuable papers burned, Secretary of State Cornelius Roach and volunteers saved the state's original land grants. Before eight weeks elapsed, the General Assembly acted on Governor Hadley's suggestion to propose the issuance of some $3.5 million in bonds for the construction of a new capitol. Voters approved the bond issue in August. Completed in 1917, the lovely structure built of Jasper and Greene County stone sits on a high Missouri River bluff. The four-person commission in charge of construction wisely filled the building with lovely paintings and murals by well-known artists.

As governor, Major continued the Progressive push of his prede-cessors. In 1913 he signed legislation establishing the Missouri Public Service Commission, which assumed control of the state's utilities. He also secured passage of the first comprehensive securities act, which tightened and clarified the responsibility for supervising corporations within the state. In 1915, legislation was passed to establish state control of building and loan associations; other measures placed Missouri's banking laws in compliance with the new Federal Reserve System. Penal reform concerned Major. The state established the first Board of Pardons and Paroles in 1913. Three years later, Major ordered the end to the system of contracting the labor of prison inmates. Major addressed the problems of sightless Missourians by creating a commission, and in 1916 the state began providing pensions for the visually impaired. In addition, Major worked to get support for the public school system, better financing of roads, a workmen's compensation act, and improvement of criminal court procedures.

When Major left office in 1917, the state had taken increased responsibility for health, the environment, transportation, education, and penal institutions. Major and Hadley established the foundation for modern Missouri government. In doing so, Major like Hadley before him moved from breaking up concentrations of business power to regulating them. Both thought economic growth would lead to society's improvement. Major's call to "Pull Missouri Out of the Mud," a request for volunteers to spend two days working on Missouri's roads, attracted a quarter of a million people to donate their labor in 1913. As historian David Thelen maintained, " 'Civic pride' had come . . . to mean economic growth." Hadley's and Major's attempts to raise revenue to finance modern government met with less success. The money raised by Governor Major's modest income tax and by Hadley's inheritance tax and corporate franchise tax failed to meet the costs of new governmental initiatives. When Major left office the state debt stood at $2.5 million, all of it accumulated during his administration. Major offered no apology. In his last words to the legislature, he asserted, "You can not conduct your institutions properly with our small revenue, and at the same time carry a large balance in the general revenue fund. In other words, you can not eat your cake and have it, too."

Ironically, the years of Progressive reform coincided with the rise of the most powerful political machine in Missouri history. James Pendergast started the machine in Kansas City's West Bottoms, the area of the city that housed the stockyards, packing plants, iron foundries, and cheap housing. He had come to Kansas City from St. Joseph in 1876 at twenty years of age. Pendergast worked in a packinghouse and as an iron worker, saving his money and awaiting a break. It came when he bet on a horse named Climax in 1881. With his winnings, Pendergast purchased a hotel and saloon in the Bottoms. He succeeded in business, eventually buying taverns on Main Street and on Ninth Street.

During the 1880s, Pendergast became active in ward politics. Re-organization of the city's wards placed most of the West Bottoms in the First Ward in 1886. Ed Kelly and John Grady vied for Democratic control of the ward, and Pendergast stayed on good terms with both factions. In 1892 he received the Democratic nomination for alderman of the First Ward and easily defeated his Republican opponent. He won successive elections to the post until his retirement from politics in 1910, when voters chose his brother Tom to succeed him. As early as 1894, James Pendergast had established himself as an important figure in city politics, when voters in his ward returned him to office in a Republican landslide. Only Pendergast and a fellow northside Democrat retained their seats. The Republicans won the remaining twenty-three.

According to Lyle W. Dorsett, who has written the most knowingly about the machine, Kansas City pundits recognized Pendergast's influence as early as 1898, when the *Kansas City Star* cited him as "A New Democratic Boss." Four years later, the *Star* credited Pendergast with controlling the entire Democratic vote in the city. Machine politician James Reed had been elected prosecuting attorney in 1898 and mayor in 1900. Dorsett claimed that Pendergast controlled more than "a hundred jobs on the police force, a goodly number in the fire department, and could get his backers at one of the city's large breweries and in the Metropolitan Street Railway Company." Tom Pendergast served the city as superintendent of streets, "where there were over 200 more jobs waiting for the proper applicants." Pendergast knew that patronage served as the glue of politics; he had plenty of glue.

Pendergast built his Machine to serve the needs of his constituents in the West Bottoms. The poor of the district could depend on Jim to provide a loan, food, fuel, or clothing. If a First Ward resident needed something done by the city, he went to councilman Jim, who quickly interceded. A precinct captain met new residents of the ward with assurances that if they had a problem, they should just let the ward heeler know. A newspaper account in 1892 described a crowd at a rally for Jim as composed of "hard-handed men . . . in oily blue jumpers . . .

with packinghouse mud on their boots, switchmen, freight handlers, engineers. . . . There were not many silk hats in the crowd." Tom learned from Jim. In 1903, Tom gave Christmas dinners to 120 prisoners in the Jackson County jail.

Voters knew that the Pendergasts did. not just buy votes. They showed that they had genuine concern for their constituents. During the flood of 1903, for example, Jim spent his own money to help those who experienced damage. With his saloon under the siege of flood waters, he provided furniture, food, and other necessities to flood victims. When asked by a newspaper man about his efforts during the flood, Pendergast replied, "It was my own money I spent, and the public is not interested in how I spend my money."

In extending their umbrella over the First Ward, the Pendergasts took in all ethnic groups, not just their Irish American counterparts. Italian leaders spoke in their native tongue in support of Pendergast candidates; the German American Heim brewing family provided free beer for Pendergast political rallies; even a black Republican newspaper endorsed the Machine in 1908. The Pendergasts took care of their district, and district voters cast their ballots for Machine candidates. Voting fraud did not occur in the First Ward. Jim put it simply. He once told a reporter, "I never needed a crooked vote. All I want is a chance for my friends to get to the polls." Further, the Pendergasts knew Kansas City politics as few others did and often supported the same political and social reforms as the zealous William Rockhill Nelson and his *Kansas City Star.* As saloon keepers they opposed Prohibition, and as party politicians they fought efforts to destroy patronage opportunities.

Despite their power, the Pendergasts frequently shared power with another group of Democrats led by Joseph Shannon. The two groups competed in the primaries, and most often joined forces in the general election, splitting patronage positions on a fifty-fifty basis. That condition continued until the death of James Pendergast in 1911.

Tom liked wielding political power but took little pleasure from holding political office. He served as an alderman for the years 1910 to 1915, but never again ran for elective office. He preferred to work from a cubbyhole office in his Jefferson Hotel. Tom Pendergast, some sixteen years the junior of Jim, had an eye for the business side of politics. He capitalized on the concept of "to the victor belongs the spoils." He acquired more saloons, sold his wholesale liquor more widely, particularly after brother Mike became the Jackson County liquor license inspector, and entered the building industry. He owned the Ready-Mix Concrete Company, a truly important business in rapidly expanding Kansas City. One of the first companies to mix concrete at a plant and deliver by truck to the job, Pendergast's company produced a quality product for a good price. He joined W. A. Ross in a building contracting company and involved himself in the Midwest Paving Company, the Kansas City Concrete Pipe Company, and others. Tom Pendergast became rich.

But people remembered him for his presence, his ability to listen and make people feel comfortable, and his generosity. Relatively short at only 5 feet 9 inches, he had a massive head that seemed to go right into his broad, thick shoulders. He had huge fists that contemporaries said could drop a man with a single blow. His pleasant manner with people reduced his threatening appearance, but not altogether. He relayed a clear notion of being in charge.

The generosity came from empathy toward those with problems and the belief that if a political leader helped someone, the person helped would return the aid in the polling booth. For Tom, politics demanded work 365 days a year. He arranged jobs for thousands. During the 1918–1919 flu epidemic, "Tom Pendergast, at great personal risk, . . . made a personal survey, house to house, to see who needed help." During the cold of winter, Pendergast trucks arrived in the West Bottoms loaded with clothing that anyone in need could get simply by showing up. Pendergast supplied about three thousand free Christmas dinners every year. He stated his philosophy succinctly, "When a man's in need we don't ask whether he's a Republican or Democrat. . . . We function as nearly as we can 100 percent by making people feel kindly toward us."

Pendergast did not hold complete control of Kansas City politics until after the city's governing charter was revised to a city manager form of government in 1924, and it was not until the 1930s that he became a dominant power in the state. But even in the election of 1916, the Machine aided in a statewide Democratic victory that extended Progressive measures a bit further before the nation's entry into World War I pushed domestic reform out of the picture.

In 1916, Missouri Democrats nominated a St. Louis businessman without previous elective office experience as their candidate for governor. Frederick D. Gardner had come to St. Louis as a seventeen-year-old in

1886 and began working in an establishment that manufactured coffins. Born in Hickman, Kentucky, on November 6, 1869, Gardner went to Tennessee in 1878 when his mother died from yellow fever and his father took the family back to his home in Weakley County. Possessing only a public school education when he arrived in St. Louis, Gardner nevertheless succeeded in his work, and he owned the St. Louis Coffin Company at the time he was nominated for governor. A businessman all of his life, Gardner promised to bring business practices to government. During the campaign he blunted a key Republican issue, the $2.5 million state debt, by promising to address that problem promptly.

The results of the election revealed a Democratic sweep of offices, but Gardner defeated Henry Lamm of Sedalia by only 2,263 votes and Woodrow Wilson carried the state against his strong challenger Charles Evans Hughes with only 50.6 percent of the vote. James Reed won a second term in the U.S. Senate by 24,456 votes over his Republican opponent, Walter S. Dickey. Democrats took fourteen congressional seats and obtained majorities in both houses of the General Assembly. George Hackman of Warrenton, who won the auditor's race, was the only Republican to win a statewide office.

Gardner moved quickly to put the state on a sound financial basis. In his inaugural address he advocated new taxes and a reorganization of state funding. He pointed out that "Our general revenue fund costs the people of Missouri about $1.70 per capita. In Illinois the per capita tax . . . is $5.03." While Missouri did not need to raise that much money, the new governor said the public schools needed an additional $1.5 million; to balance the budget required $1.8 million; and it would take another $750,000 to reform the penal system.

To raise funds, Gardner asked for a 2.5 percent increase in inheritance taxes, an increase in corporate taxes, and a state income tax based on 10 percent of the federal income tax. He also asked the General Assembly to create a state tax commission, a state highway commission, and a central pardons and parole board. He secured them all. Gardner fought for a balanced budget so relentlessly that he vetoed measures that would have provided pensions for the blind and would have established a home for destitute children because the legislature appropriated no money to pay the costs. He supported the concepts but refused to go into debt to finance them. He signed legislation to establish the state park system, financed by hunting and fishing fees, and he urged that the penal system support itself by putting inmates to work in meaningful ways run by the state. Educational opportunities in the penal system are a legacy of the Gardner administration.

David March described Gardner as a "progressive-minded governor who kept a good eye on the balance sheet." March concluded, "In sum, without curtailing the services of the state to the people, Governor Gardner, by prudent management and increased revenues was able to pay off the debt his administration had inherited and to leave office with 'overflowing treasury.' "

Of the chief figures associated with the Progressive movement in Missouri, only Folk clearly fits the Crunden description. Attorney General Crow saw corruption and attacked it as a legal problem, not a crusade. Hadley believed in reform and a changed role for government, but he also understood and practiced traditional party politics. Major did the same. Less certainly in the line of even the progressivism of Hadley or Major, Gardner did not have the luxury, as they did, to focus most of his attention on reform. He faced the enormous burden of leading the state during World War I.

CHAPTER VIII

MISSOURI GOES TO WAR

When war erupted in Europe in August of 1914, Missourians faced difficult times. Out of a population of more than 3 million, German-born Missourians numbered at least 80,000 and an additional 280,000 had German-born parents. First- and second-generation German immigrants constituted 11.7 percent of the state's population. Missouri had six German-language daily newspapers and eighteen weeklies. The state's 100,000 Irish Americans further swelled the ranks of those who had little use for the cause of England and France. In 1910, however, only 7 percent of the population claimed foreign birth and more than 67 percent had been born in Missouri. The state's population remained primarily rural, with more than 57 percent living in places of 2,500 or fewer residents and more than 40 percent making their living from farming. The diversity of the population was one of the main reasons why President Woodrow Wilson's proclamation of neutrality initially met with widespread approval in the state. The *Bethany Democrat* reprinted Wilson's address proclaiming neutrality and endorsed the policy, stating: "Every man who really loves America will act and speak in the true spirit of neutrality, which is, the spirit of impartiality and fairness and of friendliness to all concerned."

The large German American community sought to ensure absolute neutrality. German Americans had a history of organization for political influence through the German-American Alliance, which had strong support in St. Louis. Before 1914, opposition to the prohibition of alcohol had occupied the Alliance. Even though eighty-one Missouri counties had adopted Prohibition, the Alliance had helped defeat statewide adoption. In 1917 Missouri still had 3,504 licensed saloons in the urban counties of Jackson, Buchanan, St. Charles, Greene, and St. Louis, with more than 2,100 of them in St. Louis City. Rural counties with large German populations such as Osage, Warren, Jefferson, Perry, Gasconade, and Franklin remained wet by refusing to adopt Prohibition through local option.

Alliance leaders had experienced such success in their fight against Prohibition that they believed they could shift quickly in 1914 to lobbying for a neutral position of an embargo on all trade with the belligerents. (In reality, such a policy favored the Central powers, since Britain's superiority at sea meant that the Allies could control trade, a major advantage in a war of attrition.) Alliance leaders based their confidence on the "very size and stability of the St. Louis German-American community prior to the war, as well as the social and political acceptance that German-American institutions had found in the native American press and among political officeholders." According to David Detjen, the Alliance's historian, its leaders believed they could make the shift from anti-Prohibition to foreign-policy lobbying without fear of reprisal because their experiences of participating in German cultural activities and preserving their German heritage in the past had not precluded their acceptance as people loyal to their adopted country. This belief led the group into thinking that sympathizing with the German war cause would not cause them difficulties.

The Alliance led in organizing a response to anti-German editorials that appeared in the *St. Louis Post-Dispatch,* the *Republic,* and the *Star* in the fall of 1914. Several thousand Germans met and called for balanced treatment of Germany, and, soon after, representatives of German societies pledged to raise $100,000 for the widows and orphans of German soldiers. The fund did not reach that figure until a year later.

Meanwhile, St. Louis Germans along with St. Louisans of Irish descent combined to form the Neutrality League, the chief anti-British organization in the state, in December of 1914. The league argued for an embargo of all goods to belligerents as the only truly neutral policy for the United States. St. Louis historian James Neal Primm described the highlight of the league's efforts as coming on January 10, 1915, when "a League-sponsored demonstration against arms shipment attracted 12,000 people. Speakers attacked Britain as the 'bully of the World;' the crowd roared in song as the band played *Deutschland Uber Alles;* and hawkers sold German, Irish, and American flags." Seven months later, not more than 350 people attended a league function at the Delmar Garden Theatre. The *Globe-Democrat* explained the low attendance as the result of "the growing feeling that our international relations are so delicate that it is the duty of American citizens to cease their boat rocking."

While the Wilson administration advocated neutrality, its policies during 1914 and 1915 favored England and France as the United States sought to make it possible for belligerents to acquire American manufactured goods and agricultural products. Long soup lines in St. Louis and Kansas City and agricultural products piling up on shipping docks during the winter of 1914–1915 indicated what the disruption of trade had done to the Missouri economy. In St. Louis, the Provident Association, a charity organization, by itself provided aid to about fifty thousand people in January and February 1915.

In late 1914, Congress moved to facilitate trade by providing ships to carry the goods. It took until August of 1916 for the government to succeed in establishing the United Shipping Board, primarily because of Republican opposition. Joshua Alexander, a congressman from Missouri, introduced the initial legislation in the House of Representatives, and Missourian William J. Stone, the chairman of the Senate Foreign Relations Committee, shepherded the legislation through that chamber. Only the two Republican members of the Missouri congressional delegation, Leonides C. Dyer and Jacob E. Meeker, voted no.

Meanwhile, it became obvious that England and France would need loans in order to purchase American goods. Despite organized opposition from the German-American Alliance and the warning by Senator Stone that loans would give the lenders a vital interest in the outcome of the war, the United States allowed private banks to extend credit to belligerents. Nine St. Louis banks cooperated to provide England and France with $2.7 million in credits on October 2, 1915. To offset criticism of their action by those opposed to favoritism to the Allies, the bankers announced that German bonds were available for purchase as well. Kansas City bankers refused to go along with the loans, citing trade violations against U.S. neutrality by the British as the reason for denial. The result of the loan policy showed who received most favor. When the United States entered the war in 1917, the Allies owed U.S. bankers $2.3 billion. Germany owed them $27 million.

As historian David March has pointed out, all segments of the Missouri economy benefited from trade with belligerents: "the economic welfare of the state was tied closely to Allied war purchases. The question of loans was one which directly affected not only bankers and munition makers, but also farmers, miners, packers, and the manufacturers of numerous articles." Dependence on trade, however, did not keep many

Missourians from protesting against England's violations of American neutrality during the first year of the war. Protestors included a wider spectrum than the German-American Alliance and the Neutrality League.

In the spring of 1915, German war efforts made English violations of neutrality less important to many former critics. On May 7, German torpedoes sank the British ship *Lusitania.* One hundred and twenty-eight Americans lost their lives aboard the ship. The *Lawrence Chieftain,* published in Mount Vernon, expressed what was probably a view of the incident held by many Missourians. The editor approved of the State Department policy of discouraging travel, and yet Americans continued to travel to "dear old Hingland [*sic*]." He concluded: "While such warfare seems a step back into barbarism, when women and children were slaughtered with the men, it is pretty hard to arouse a great deal of sympathy over the fate of those rovers who can't be satisfied with the best country on earth—the United States. There will be no war with Germany over their fate."

Other Missourians took the *Lusitania* disaster as reason to question U.S. defense policy. John C. Crighton, who wrote a book on newspaper reaction to World War I in Missouri, noted that the *Lusitania* sinking produced widespread print media support for increased preparedness. The *St. Louis Post-Dispatch* and the *St. Louis Republic,* newspapers in Carthage, Chillicothe, and Columbia, and farm papers such as the *Missouri Farmer, Journal of Agriculture,* and the *Star Farmer* asked for greater commitment to the military. In a poll of Democratic editors conducted by the *St. Louis Republic* in September 1915, forty of fifty-nine respondents favored enhanced defense of the country. Only five opposed better defense; five more expressed weak approval; six remained neutral on the question; and three supported the same level of defense.

By the time the *Republic* released its poll, Missourians in St. Louis and Kansas City had established branches of the Navy League and of the National Security League. St. Joseph citizens also had a branch of the Security League. Prominent St. Louisan Albert Bond Lambert served as president of the Navy League in that city, while lumberman and civic leader Robert Alexander Long led the league in Kansas City. The Navy and Security Leagues advertised the need for enhanced military defense through parades, banquets, speeches, and other promotions.

In early December 1915, President Wilson asked Congress to increase the army from 108,000 to 142,000 troops, and he requested the creation of a reserve force of 400,000. In addition, he called for a larger navy to be built over five years that would include ten battleships, sixteen cruisers, fifty destroyers, and support ships needed for "a balanced and efficient sea force."

On February 16, 1916, Wilson came to Kansas City to sell his program. More than eighteen thousand people in the Convention Hall heard his argument, while a huge crowd stood outside the hall, giving the president vocal support. The president's St. Louis appearance occurred at 10:30 in the morning. A crowd too large for the coliseum gave its strong support of his preparedness measures. Only a Socialist handbill condemning Wilson's proposals as an extension of "Old World militarism" revealed opposition to the president's proposals during his appearances in Missouri.

Beneath the surface, however, a variety of interests opposed increased preparedness. The Neutrality League, of course, found in the proposals another example of the administration abandoning genuine neutrality. Organized labor blamed the war on autocratic governments, armament manufacturers, and capitalists. Labor feared that increasing the military would produce U.S. involvement. Labor unrest marked 1916 in Missouri as industrial workers found their position in the economy eroding. Their wages had increased by 16 percent, but food prices had increased by 33 percent. Socialists opposed the war and any growth of the U.S. military. The Missouri State Grange, an organization of farmers, also opposed increased armaments because such a course, they thought, favored munitions makers and the eastern establishment.

Wilson also received criticism from those who thought he did too little to prepare the nation for possible war. Republican presidential candidate Theodore Roosevelt attacked him vehemently for his lack of leadership. A weekly Edina, Missouri, newspaper captured the debate when the editor wrote that opinion ranged from "those who advocate the greatest army and navy in the world down to the man who is so craven and cowardly he would not fight a jack rabbit to save his birthright." Germany's use of submarines and Wilson's requirements that Germany forgo the practice in the year after the sinking of the *Lusitania* provided the context for the debate. Perhaps most Missourians agreed with the editor of the *Knox County Democrat* when he observed in early February of 1916, "The American people do not want war, but there may come a time when it will be impossible for us to prevent war. If such a time comes we should be prepared to meet it, and to meet it in a manner that will effectively expel the invader from our shores and insure us against future invasions."

After much debate during the session of 1916, Congress passed legislation that doubled the size of the regular army, increased the National Guard to 475,000 over a five-year period, and provided "one of the greatest naval authorizations in American history." Missouri's U.S. Senators Stone and James A. Reed and ten of Missouri's sixteen House members voted for preparedness. The other six House members abstained on the naval package, while all fourteen Democratic members of the House from Missouri supported the expansion of the army. Wilson signed the legislation, although the National Security League recommended that he veto the measure because it did too little.

Debate over preparedness took place in the midst of the 1916 election campaign. David March summarized Missouri's importance to the incumbent president in these words: "Wilson and his political advisers saw Missouri as a key state in their plan to rely on the West and the South for victory. It was a border state linking East and West as well as North and South, and only one state west of the Mississippi and five in the nation had more electoral votes."

The Democratic National Committee showed the significance of Missouri by selecting St. Louis as the site of its presidential nominating convention. Meeting in June, the party hammered out a peace plank, using the phrase, "He [Wilson] kept us out of war." The same platform claimed that the nation needed a military force sufficiently strong to defend the interests of the country around the world, and condemned those who would place the interests of a foreign power over the interests of the United States and those who would divide the American people. Missouri Senator Stone presided over the platform committee.

Initially, it appeared that Wilson would lose the German American and Irish American vote in Missouri. But as the campaign wore on, Theodore Roosevelt became increasingly jingoistic, attacking Wilson for not being more aggressive in upholding U.S. rights in such crises as the sinking of the *Lusitania,* and Republican presidential candidate Charles Evans Hughes endorsed Roosevelt's comments. Wilson came to look ever more moderate. Missouri Senators Stone and Reed worked assiduously to persuade Irish and German Missourians of Wilson's moderation in an effort to counter the formation of a German American anti-Wilson bloc vote. Stone met with New York, Chicago, and St. Louis German American leaders during the fall of 1916, emphasizing that Wilson's policies maintained the peace whereas Hughes, because of the militantly anti-German men around him, would produce war.

On October 11, in his reelection campaign against Walter S. Dickey, Reed gave a speech to a large St. Louis German American audience. The colorful senator said that Wilson's policies toward Germany must be about right. Some supported his opponent because Wilson had mistreated Germany; others thought Hughes should be elected because the president had been too gentle with Germany. Further, Reed noted that both Britain and Germany had violated American neutrality, but German violations had taken U.S. lives and British violations had only interfered with commerce. Thus, Wilson had little choice but to remonstrate against Germany. Reed enumerated every ship Germany had torpedoed and pointed out that the German government itself had recognized that its acts violated neutrality. Finally, he warned that the election of Hughes would result in a declaration of war against Germany and that the American people would get just what they deserved because the Republican candidate had made his position clear during the campaign.

With this support and the bungling of his opponent, Wilson defeated Hughes, but with little margin to spare. In Missouri, the president ran ahead of congressmen Dorsey W. Shackleford, Walter L. Hensley, and Perl D. Decker, all Democrats who had opposed some phase of his foreign policy. He outdistanced Shackleford by more than 200 votes; Hensley by 118 votes; and Decker by 616 votes. He ran better in German wards in St. Louis than he had in 1912, and he ran only slightly behind his 1912 totals in rural counties with large German populations. The president carried Missouri by 27,849 votes, compiling a total that surpassed his 1912 vote by 66,270. He carried sixty-eight counties and won 50.6 percent of the total vote. In the cities, even the Socialists and organized labor supported the Democratic ticket. In rural Missouri, farm prosperity aided the Wilson cause. Of course, the theme that Wilson represented peace, and the fact that during the congressional session of 1916 the Democrat-dominated Congress had passed a host of progressive legislation, including the eight-hour day for railroad employees, rural credits, a child labor law, and workmen's compensation for federal employees, all helped the president win the crucial state of Missouri.

Wilson continued to pursue peace after his reelection. On December 18, 1916, he asked the belligerents to state their terms for peace. And on January 22, 1917, the president disclosed an outline of what he thought the terms of peace ought to be. He called for a peace without victory, a peace between equals, as the first step in creating a cooperative world. Wilson sought a world in which governments would exist by the consent of the governed and freedom of the seas would be the rule. He wanted a world without stockpiles of armaments and in which people could experience complete security, freedom of worship, and economic and social development. He said the United States would cooperate with other nations to make that vision a reality. Stone, Missouri's senior senator, embraced Wilson's vision with enthusiasm.

According to the *New York Times,* James A. Reed was the only Democratic senator to oppose the direction outlined by the president. Reed particularly "objected to the proposal to join a League to Enforce Peace." He said, "I will never give my consent to an international army big enough to conquer the United States when there are ninety-nine chances out of a hundred that the world court and the army will be picked by the monarchs of Europe." But before the nation had sufficient time to fully discuss these ideas, Germany declared that it would begin unrestricted submarine warfare, thus abrogating the *Sussex* pledge made in 1916 and making a break in diplomatic relations between the United States and Germany certain. Germany's announcement came on January 31. On February 3, Wilson broke diplomatic relations with Germany.

This turn of events created a crisis in the political life of Senator Stone. During Wilson's tenure as president, Stone had been his chief spokesman on foreign policy in the Senate. Only on the question of American citizens traveling aboard armed vessels had the two disagreed. Thus, Stone had tried to get Wilson to modify his course in the *Sussex* crises. But Wilson refused, and now the Missourian's foreboding that the president's stand would lead inevitably to war seemed on its way to becoming true.

When the president and Stone met on February 2, the senator tried to persuade the president not to break relations with Germany. He proposed that Wilson rally all neutral nations for peace; that Wilson tell the belligerents that he would arbitrate a peace based upon his statement of January 22; that if they refused to come to the table, he would institute a total embargo on trade; and if one side accepted the terms of peace, he would provide full economic aid to them and continue to embargo the other. What Stone proposed was a combination of the policies of Presidents Thomas Jefferson and James Madison during the years before the War of 1812. The *Boonville Weekly Advertiser* took a similar position when an editorial asserted that the president could "bring the crazy Europeans to their senses in less than six months by placing an embargo on all American food stuffs." Wilson thought the ideas had little value.

According to Ruth Warner Towne, Stone's biographer, the senator and president started from far different premises. Stone considered the outcome of the war of little moment. If anything, he thought an Allied victory might injure the United States more than a German victory because of future economic competition. Wilson believed differently. He saw a German victory as perpetuating militarism, autocracy, and disregard for international law, thus posing a serious threat to world order.

Most Missourians and most Americans thought the president's course the appropriate response to the German action. On February 9 the *Boonville Weekly Advertiser* editorialized: "The lines in America are obliterated now. We are all Democrats, all Republicans, all Americans. Let us stand shoulder to shoulder in defense of our country. If there are any traitors among us weed them out and send them where they belong." Days later the *Bethany Republican* observed, "President Wilson has the backing of about every American in this Germany mix-up. We will admit that the matter has not been handled just as it seems to us it should have been but what has been done, has been done, and it is our duty as American citizens to stand back of the president until the turbulent atmosphere clears." Almost all of the metropolitan newspapers agreed with the president's decision to break relationships with Germany.

The *Kansas City Journal* stood alone as a major Missouri newspaper registering disagreement. Even the *Westliche Post* said it would support the president, although it hated the turn of events. The *Post, Amerika, Labor,* and Sedalia's *Railway Federationist* feared that big business wanted war and advocated that any declaration of war should be submitted to the people, but few Missourians supported that idea. Walter L. Hensley, a U.S. congressman from Farmington, Missouri, appeared to be the only supporter of the referendum idea among Missouri officials. The Missouri General Assembly passed a resolution on February 5 giving the president full support "regardless of cost or sacrifice."

The threat of unleashed submarine warfare kept many ships at home and produced clogged rail lines and a greatly reduced market for goods, particularly after German submarines sank two American ships soon after the new policy was announced. Many called for the arming of U.S. merchant ships so they could defend themselves from submarine attack. On the morning of February 26, Wilson informed Stone that he would ask Congress to authorize the arming of merchant ships that afternoon. Stone told the president such a step would be a "serious blunder," would result in war, "and . . . was in direct conflict with the plain letter of the Constitution." Stone voted against the bill in committee and spoke for more than three hours on the Senate floor explaining his position. Democratic House members Dorsey Shackleford from Jefferson City and Perl Decker from Joplin voted against the bill in the House, the only two to do so in Missouri's sixteen-member delegation.

C. J. Walden, editor of the *Boonville Weekly Advertiser,* lambasted Stone for his stand in these words: "Stone must have felt very strange and uncomfortable, when he awoke the other morning and found he had been snoozing in the same trundle bed with [Robert] La Follette, [Albert] Cummings, [William] Kirby, and that long-haired guinea, Sister [James] Vardeman. This bunch of Allies must make the angels blush." Springfield clergymen called Stone, Shackleford, and Decker "pussy foot statesmen." The Missouri House of Representatives unanimously passed a resolution reprimanding Stone, Decker, and Shackleford for their action. Some small-town newspapers voiced support for Stone. The *Warrensburg Star-Journal* believed Stone's position represented the view of three-fourths of the residents of Johnson County, perhaps because the newspaper shared the senator's stance. The congressional session ended before final action on the bill could occur, but the president armed merchant ships under the aegis of an old law.

Release of the Zimmermann note on February 28, during the debate over the armed ship bill, charged the discussions with strong emotion and led to those in opposition to the president, such as Stone, being called traitors and cowards. The Zimmermann telegram, intercepted by Britain and given to U.S. Ambassador Walter Hines Page, was an offer from Germany to Mexico: if the United States went to war with

Germany and Mexico joined the Central Powers, Mexico would receive plenty of financial support, and, with victory, the return of Texas, New Mexico, and Arizona territories formerly controlled by Mexico. Senator Stone called the note a forgery and accused Page and Robert Lansing, the secretary of state, of being duped by the British and Anglophiles bent on misleading Wilson into war. Almost before Stone got those words out of his mouth, German Foreign Secretary Alfred Zimmermann proudly acknowledged authorship of the telegram.

The sinking of more ships (three went down on March 18) made it clear that armed neutrality would not end conflict. President Wilson moved up a call for a special session of Congress from April 16 to April 2. The two and a half years of struggle with neutrality had ended. President Wilson asked for a declaration of war against Germany. Stone could not bring himself to support his president. He and five other senators voted no. In the House of Representatives, Perl Decker, Dorsey Shackleford, Walter Hensley, and William L. Igoe of St. Louis joined forty-six others in a no vote. Stone came in for special criticism because of his position as a leader in foreign policy. On April 13, the *Boonville Weekly Advertiser* thought that "Ninety-five percent of Missouri's citizenship was humiliated at the conduct of Senator Stone. Hardly a newspaper of note endorsed his action, and cries of shame came from every section of the state and country. If it were possible to recall him, he would not last a month longer."

Both Stone and Shackleford represented the old silver wing of the Democratic party and distrusted eastern money and industry. Shackleford had advocated a munitions embargo of the belligerents in 1915 and 1916 and had opposed American citizens riding on armed ships. Although both represented areas with significant German American populations, they subscribed to traditional isolationism rather than to pro-German views. Stone distrusted England and its intentions, and according to Ruth Towne "accepted the same economic determinism held by socialists and the [George] Norris-La Follette wing of American progressivism." Apparently, Decker, Hensley, and Igoe held similar views. St. Louisan Igoe simply said, "I know the people of my district do not want to go to war."

Once the war came, Senator Stone gave it his full support and urged all Missourians to close ranks. He knew that only a quick victory could bring peace again. He supported conscription, unlike his fellow senator

James Reed, and all of the other major presidential recommendations. His service to the president and the country ended, however, long before peace came. Stone suffered a series of strokes and died on Sunday, April 14, 1918.

Like Stone, other individuals and groups who had opposed the direction of U.S. foreign policy now supported the war. John Crighton concluded that, "When war seemed unavoidable in April 1917, there was no serious division of opinion" [in Missouri]. Gary Fink, who recorded the Missouri labor movement's changing responses to international affairs, wrote that after the United States entered the war the attitude of Missouri labor leaders "changed dramatically." Those leaders, "while retaining some skepticism, . . . rationalized their support of the war in the moralistic and idealistic terms that had been articulated by Woodrow Wilson."

Even before the declaration of war against Germany created widespread expressions of patriotism, the *Bethany Republican* of March 28, 1917, noted that some towns had organized patriotic days. Bethany's mayor had not chosen a date, but the newspaper assured its readers, "There is little foreign sentiment in this section of the country, and our patriotism don't [*sic*] need much boosting, but when the time comes to *Do Things,* take it from us, the mayor will set the patriotic ball rolling." The paper urged its readers to raise their flags "to show that we are with the President in whatever he may choose to preserve the dignity and honor of our country." State Superintendent of Schools Uel Lamkin also sought to stimulate patriotism before the declaration of war. He called upon each county superintendent of schools to display the American flag in each school in the state beginning April 2, 1917.

Governor Frederick Gardner anticipated the declaration of war as well. A huge "loyalty" crowd assembled in the St. Louis Coliseum during the evening of April 5. Gardner "read a series of resolutions proclaiming the determination of St. Louis citizens to stand with the President of the United States in his every effort to safeguard the nation's honor and favoring 'immediate and compulsory universal military service and adequate means to secure, when the war shall end, lasting world peace.' " The crowd shouted their assent to these ideas. The governor then made his view of support for the war clear: "This is no time for slackers, copperheads, or soft pedalists. If there are any such among us, it is our duty to drive them out and brand them as traitors." These comments and expressions predated any effort on the part of the federal government to orchestrate patriotic fervor.

The declaration of war on April 6 produced a statewide demonstration of patriotism. In Boonville, a city of five thousand, an estimated seven thousand people participated in a war rally. The parade included marching schoolchildren, fifty automobiles, and four bands, one of which was composed of black residents; Boonville businesses shut their doors from two until four o'clock. Such an expression of support appeared necessary to the editor of the *Boonville Advertiser*, who warned of difficult times ahead. In mid-May he told his readers that the war would last a year or more and lamented that Wilson's full preparedness program had not been enacted. He advocated unstinting support of the president.

In southwest Missouri, Mount Vernon's *Lawrence Chieftain* called for "Unadulterated loyalty to the Stars and Stripes . . . by every person in the United States. . . . No patience should be shown toward any person who is lukewarm in his allegiance to this government. . . . However, the American-born American should not go out of his way to taunt any foreign-born American who is loyal to this government." The *Chieftain* editor expressed understanding for German-born citizens, "who would not be human if . . . [they] did not feel saddened at the prospect of bloody strife between the citizens of this country and . . . [their] blood brethern [*sic*] across the great waters." Under a picture of the American flag that appeared on the front page, the editor emblazoned, "My Country! In her intercourse with other nations may she always be in the right: but right or wrong, My Country."

Malta Bend became the first town in Saline County to display its patriotism. In a purely spontaneous action, townspeople raised a huge flag on a seventy-foot flagpole they had erected on a prominent spot near the center of town. Business owners decorated their stores, and citizens placed miniature flags in their lapels. A parade of automobiles, all elaborately decorated with stars and stripes, completed the celebration.

In southeast Missouri, celebrations took place in Kennett and Poplar Bluff. At the Kennett meeting an estimated six thousand participated. In Poplar Bluff an even larger crowd that ranged from schoolchildren to factory employees joined to display their patriotism. Practically every business and factory closed for two hours.

In Kirksville, some twenty-five hundred people took part in a loyalty parade, including students from the teachers college and osteopathy school. Another northeast Missouri community, Edina, apparently held no patriotic gathering, but the local newspaper saw the war as "thrust upon us by a bold, aggressive foreign power who has ignored our rights on land and sea. Every red-blooded American should rise to resent their [*sic*] conduct. This is no time for arguments or criticisms. The time is ripe for decisive, forceful, concerted action."

Across the state, Bethany's mayor, William Roleke, proclaimed Saturday, April 7, as patriotic day. Members of the Methodist aid society in Bethany pledged to give up serving refreshments during the war. "Each member will patriotically put into their [*sic*] treasury such amounts as she would use in entertaining and this fund will be used as war conditions demand."

And war conditions demanded much. For one thing, America's new allies needed to be fed. Paul Vincent, an authority on wartime conditions in Europe, called the food supply in Britain "precariously close to starvation" levels. As early as 1916, "Playgrounds, parks, golf courses, and suburban yards were broken up in the interest of food cultivation." England tried voluntary rationing, but increased submarine sinkings forced the British government to accept the necessity of controlled rationing in the spring of 1917. By April, sugar supplies had been depleted to only a four-day supply, and while rationing had allowed Britain to avoid starvation, "hunger remained an acute fact of life in wartime England."

Missouri farmers certainly knew of these conditions. They had reaped rich rewards from food demands in Europe for the last two years. Indeed, writing in February 1916, more than a year before the declaration of war, the *Knox County Democrat* editor expressed the belief that farm prosperity would continue no matter what happened. "Upon him [the farmer] will devolve the vast amount of supplies demanded by the world when this war ends. His will be the burden of feeding the millions of mouths that will be hungering for the products of the farm. And his will be the pockets that will sag with the weight of the gold that pays for these supplies."

An increased demand for Missouri agricultural products perhaps spurred further interest in scientific agriculture. The College of Agriculture of the University of Missouri produced an average of only two graduates per year between 1895 and 1900, and from 1900 to 1907 average enrollment stood at 166. In 1915 the school enrolled more than

1,000 students. In that year, the school established a department of agricultural engineering, and by that time the department of animal husbandry had been in the college for a decade. Making agriculture a required subject in elementary schools in 1900 no doubt gave this formalization of agricultural training some impetus as well.

Five years before the war began, the first county agent in Missouri began working in Cape Girardeau County. The United States Department of Agriculture and the College of Agriculture cooperated to start the program. On August 1, 1912, the College of Agriculture appointed C. M. McWilliams to advise the farmers in the Cape Girardeau area. A few days later, the Sedalia Boosters' Club employed Samuel Martin Jordan as "County Farm Advisor." The pattern of local farmers cooperating with the College of Agriculture and the U.S. Department of Agriculture to promote "scientific" farming resulted in the creation of the Farm Bureau Federation. In 1913, Buchanan, Johnson, Audrain, Dade, Jackson, Marion, Scott, and Cooper Counties joined Cape Girardeau and Pettis Counties in employing farm advisers or extension agents. Greene, St. Francois, and Saline Counties acquired county agents in 1914, and Carroll, Butler, Knox, and St. Charles Counties joined their ranks the next year.

Passage of the Smith-Lever Act in May 1914, which provided federal financial support for agricultural extension efforts, aided the movement. In 1915 the various county organizations formed the State Farm Bureau Federation, the first statewide organization of county farm bureaus. The organization's historian, Vera B. Schuttler, acknowledged that the Farm Bureau originated to support the extension movement, but she viewed the movement as a genuinely cooperative effort between farmers, businesses, and academic interests. She maintained that no one who knew such founders as Horace Windsor, R. W. Brown, J. W. Head, S. S. Connet, and C. C. Schuttler, farmers all, could argue that any group could manipulate them.

Evidence that local farmers welcomed extension efforts abounds. In Lawrence County the College of Agriculture offered short courses three years in a row beginning in 1912. Demand for the courses caused the editor of the *Lawrence Chieftain* in 1915 to wonder whether a date for a course could be obtained, since all of the dates to September 1 had been booked. Communities desiring such courses paid the hotel bill and traveling expenses of the instructors, while the College of Agriculture provided the instruction.

Lawrence County exhibited a history of progressivism. In 1914, residents around Walker, five miles from Mount Vernon, created a chapter of the Grange, with a membership of twenty-five. By fall it boasted seventy-five members. The group outgrew its one-room school building and built a new one for $1,500. Citizens held their Sunday school meetings there, and graduates of the University of Missouri conducted home economics classes in the new building. Residents raised the money for the structure by holding ice cream socials. In 1915, local citizens had begun a drive to build a modern high school.

In 1914, Greene County hired A. A. Cockefair as its extension agent with a three-year contract. After the three years, county administrators sought assurance that farmers wanted the program continued. Farmers attended a meeting, offered no complaints about the program, and agreed to provide $800 toward Cockefair's salary. In May 1917, 150 Chariton County farmers entered into a contract with Samuel Jordan, who had served as Pettis County's first agent, to pay him $5,660 a year for a term of three years, eloquent testimony about what those farmers thought about "scientific" agriculture. In Lamine Township of Cooper County, "progressive farmer" John H. Turley organized a Farmer's Club with fifty members. In northwest Missouri, more than 100 farmers attended a plowing demonstration put on by an implement dealer to showcase a new tractor in the spring of 1917.

Besides the county farm bureaus, Missouri farmers created another organization based on some 340 local farm clubs. In August of 1917, representatives of the clubs formed the Missouri Farmer's Association. The first of these clubs had been organized in Chariton County in 1914. William Hirth, publisher of the Association's official organ, the *Missouri Farmer,* also served as its president for many years. A longtime believer in farmers organizing, Hirth had been invited to the meeting in 1915 that led to the formation of the State Farm Bureau Federation. He could not attend, but he sent a telegram saying that he was "there in spirit." He went on: "Upon the fight that you and others like you are waging depends the future of agriculture. In it is involved not merely the happiness and prosperity of the farmers but of the entire nation. Despite the knockers, we must push on."

In addition, by 1916 more than eleven thousand Missouri children between the ages of ten and eighteen had become participants in a variety of agricultural clubs. In garden and canning clubs they learned to raise and preserve vegetables. Poultry, sheep, and cattle clubs taught them how to care for livestock. Before the war, in Harrison County the Women's Association sponsored a children's vegetable garden competition for children under fifteen. The rules required the children to do all of the work and cultivate a plot twelve feet square. For the best overall garden, the winner received a prize of three dollars; for the best one-half bushel of potatoes, two dollars; for the best one-half bushel of onions, two dollars. Additional prizes were given for the largest potato, the largest cabbage, and the largest onion. The association also held a contest for the best pair of chickens raised by a Harrison County girl or boy under age fourteen. Winners of the competitions gained entrance to the county fair contests in the fall.

In short, the ground had been well prepared in Missouri for one of the most important aspects of the U.S. war effort: the production and preservation of food. Just after the declaration of war Frederick B. Mumford, dean of the College of Agriculture, urged Missouri farmers to "aid the U.S. with larger crops." Within a matter of days, Governor Gardner appointed Mumford chairman of the Missouri Council of Defense, the organization given responsibility for organizing Missouri's entire war effort.

Notification to create state councils came from Secretary of War Newton D. Baker in a letter dated April 9, 1917. Three days later, Gardner issued a call for an April 23 meeting in Jefferson City. Gardner extended his invitation to "the mayor and chief executive of every village, town, and city"; to representatives of financial institutions and commercial enterprises; and to representatives of agricultural associations and clubs to meet with him and the State Board of Agriculture. He charged the group with figuring out how to get maximum food production in Missouri. The *Lawrence Chieftain,* which reported Gardner's call, editorialized: "Do you know that the young man on the farm, who uses his full energies to raise a big crop of food is doing just as much for his country as the town boy who takes his gun and goes to the front?"

Some five hundred people attended Gardner's meeting. He told his audience that "the burden of war will be placed on the shoulders of the farmers." Later, Mrs. Gardner took some of those attending the meeting behind the Governor's Mansion "and with hoe in hand, demonstrated how the first family planned to feed itself by cultivating a garden."

Even before the governor's meeting, the state school superintendent, Uel Lamkin, proposed that all boys age fourteen and older should be excused from school attendance if they worked on farms. Seven senior boys from Lawrence County took immediate advantage of leaving school to work on farms. Greene County's superintendent advised all teachers of rural schools to allow boys to take early examinations to free them to do spring farm work. By May, the State Board of Education had granted girls the same privilege of getting credit for school by working on farms, and the *Lawrence Chieftain* reported that "about 92 percent of the seventh and eighth grade pupils are helping in the production of food supplies." Administrators at the State Normal School in Cape Girardeau offered to make the same deal with its students, and nine men and one woman accepted the challenge of exchanging books for hoes.

Others quickly joined the war effort. C. H. Wortz, owner of biscuit plants in St. Joseph, Missouri, and Fort Smith, Arkansas, offered them to the government for any use it desired. F. E. Lewis said he would donate all or part of 120 acres of Howell County land to the government or to any individual who agreed to use the land to produce food for the war. Even the warden of the state penitentiary found something to contribute to the cause. He volunteered the state's inmates to work 90 acres of bottomland along the Missouri River in the interest of increasing the food supply.

Further support came from civic groups. In Dunklin County, the Kennett Commercial Club endorsed an appeal from President Wilson for Americans to produce more food. The *Dunklin Democrat* of May 4 reported that representatives from the University of Missouri College of Agriculture had arranged meetings with farmers across the county, asking them to increase production, ensuring that they had sufficient seed, and providing guidance on how to raise a huge harvest. According to the *Democrat*, "farmers are organizing in every school district in the United States."

The College of Agriculture assumed responsibility for arranging meetings of Missouri farmers. The college used telephones as well as postal circulars to notify farmers to meet in local school buildings. In Knox County, farm agent F. E. Lonmire presided over a countywide meeting of farm delegates representing the various school district meetings. The group discussed how to secure more seeds, particularly soybeans. The delegates also passed a resolution asking the federal government to prohibit the use of all food grains in the manufacture of liquor for the duration of the war. They ended by pledging to increase production and to support efforts to preserve food, and by requesting minimum prices for their products.

In Lawrence County the Bankers' Association resolved to help farmers "in every legitimate way to buy seed, fertilizer, live stock, and feed, to enable them to raise all kinds of food for man and beast." The association promised financial aid "to the best of our ability" and urged a spirit of cooperation between farmers and bankers "in the great crisis to the end that we may all do our part." In addition, the Federated Farm Clubs and the Aurora Federal Farm Loan Association jointly endorsed the creation of farm clubs in every school district in the county.

This outpouring of support for the war effort in Missouri suggests how well Herbert Hoover read the national character. In meeting the challenge of supplying food to the Allies, Hoover chose a philosophy of voluntarism. Appointed as head of the United States Food Administration after his successful work in feeding war-torn Belgium, Hoover adopted a program of voluntarism because, "Above all, we knew that, although Americans can be led to make great sacrifices, they do not like to be driven." He also chose a policy of decentralization. "With a country so great and so diverse and so used to local government, and with a problem which needed local co-operation, we decided on intense decentralization." Hoover understood from his Belgium experience that public relations would be essential in mobilizing the population and in linking Washington with the vast hinterland.

As chairman of the Missouri Council of Defense and later as federal food administrator for Missouri, Frederick B. Mumford followed the philosophy of voluntarism, decentralization, and publicity. His appointment as food administrator on October 9, 1917, simply formalized in that sphere what he had been doing since his appointment to head the Council of Defense on April 24, 1917. A longtime professor and administrator in the College of Agriculture, Mumford had been the first chair of the school's department of animal husbandry, organized in 1904. His appointment as chair of the Missouri Council of Defense indicated his statewide reputation and the significance of agricultural production in the war effort.

Mumford took voluntarism to its logical conclusions by enlisting patriotic citizens to work at every level of government from township to state. When the council ended its operation on January 31, 1919, some twelve thousand Missourians had volunteered in the mobilization effort. Missouri's Council of Defense organized faster than others, and Mumford's plan to create subcouncils at below the county level became a model for other states. Every Missouri county and the city of St. Louis had a county organization; in contrast, Iowa, despite the efforts of Food Administrator J. F. Deems, succeeded in establishing committees in only about half of its counties. Pennsylvania's Food Administration achieved greater success. There, civilian voluntarism "was carried to the last extreme." Only clerical assistants received compensation for their work. Pennsylvania organized at least down to the county level.

From top to bottom, voluntarism meant securing people in positions who would influence others to join the ranks. In the fall of 1917, Hoover wrote to Mumford asking for the names of people who might give service to the Food Administration. He listed lawyers, bankers, merchants, engineers, "who might upon short notice be able to devote considerable time to national service." By then, Missouri had county organizations in place in all 114 counties and the city of St. Louis, and township-level committees functioned in 67 counties. In all, more than 8,500 Missourians had volunteered for the civilian war effort.

Dependence on voluntarism rather than coercion required persuasion. On the national level the Committee on Public Information became the chief vehicle of persuasion. Led by former Missourian George Creel, the committee represented, in large part, the philosophy of Arthur Bullard. In March 1917 Bullard had published *Mobilizing America.* Bullard argued for the need to electrify public opinion as a major step in creating a spirit in America essential to fighting a war. Bullard, at the request of President Wilson and Colonel Edward House, helped Creel organize the committee. Staffed by liberal reformers, the committee tried to extend concepts of reform with their view of American democracy or Americanism "as the common denominator, the ideological cement, a secular religion, to unify an increasingly pluralistic society." Its chief critics during 1917 claimed that it failed to be sufficiently patriotic. They thought Creel guilty of "treasonable moderation."

In all of its work the Missouri Council of Defense took seriously its responsibility for mobilizing public opinion. It sponsored ninety-two pamphlets from agencies devoted to the state's agriculture alone. Topics included "The New Patriotism," "Swat the Rooster and Hints on Marketing Eggs," "Farming on a War Basis," "Hogging Down Corn," and "Handling Barnyard Manure." As these latter titles indicate, forty-three of the pamphlets came from the College of Agriculture Extension Service. Mumford used the service, the College of Agriculture Farmer's Institutes that had been inaugurated in 1890, the United States Department of Agriculture, and funds appropriated by Congress to reach "food producers in practically every county of the state." The number of county agriculture agents increased from seventeen when the war began to forty-two, and twenty-seven women became home demonstration agents. In May 1917, the College of Agriculture had more than thirty men in the field organizing farm bureaus, the first step in securing an agricultural agent. As Mumford boasted, "Altogether the College of Agriculture, through its extension service by co-operation with the United States Department of Agriculture, was able to place in the field 118 men and women, who gave their time exclusively to help farmers and housekeepers to meet the needs of the war."

For all those concerned with winning the war in 1917, increased food production became the chief priority. Hoover's Food Administration set a goal for Missouri farmers to produce at least 5 percent more wheat and 50 percent more pork in 1917. Farmers responded by increasing wheat acreage by 20 percent and total yield by more than 20 million bushels. Pork production increased by at least 20 percent, but as Mumford pointed out, record keeping in the hog industry left much to be desired. Conditions kept corn yields down. Despite the fact that in practically every corn-growing county the county Council of Defense appointed a seed corn chairman to distribute seed and that early planting promised a huge yield, drought interceded to create near failure.

To aid in harvesting the larger planting of wheat, the council created in "practically every town of any size, a volunteer movement," whereby townspeople went into the countryside to assist. Most of the volunteers shocked wheat, but a few helped with the threshing. The council appointed more than two hundred farm help directors to oversee the voluntary harvest workers. Missouri farmers lost no grain because of a lack of harvest aid. By April 1918 the council had compiled a list of owners of threshing machines across the state, and more than five thousand machine owners had signed pledges to eliminate waste at threshing time and to have their machines in first-class condition for the harvest.

Perhaps following the pattern established by the women of Harrison County, the council encouraged youngsters to plant gardens. It sought to form garden clubs in every town in Missouri. The clubs enlisted boys and girls to use vacant land in the towns to raise food for the war. The council also encouraged formation of poultry, pig, canning, sewing, and bread-baking clubs for children. In 1918, garden clubs claimed almost nine thousand youngsters as members. Baking clubs had the fewest members, with only 739 members enrolled. To save grain without reducing the supply of eggs or chickens, the council sponsored a "culling campaign." In forty-five counties with some seven thousand flocks of chickens, officials identified and disposed of "slacker hens," saving an estimated $175,000 in grain. To improve wheat production, a wheat campaign began in the summer of 1918. Agents treated all wheat seed to prevent smut. "As a result of this campaign, practically every county in the state sowed more smut-free wheat than has ever been sown in the history of the state." In addition, total wheat acreage at harvest time in 1919 stood at 4,243,000, an increase of almost 2 million acres over the 1918 harvest. The Missouri Council of Defense's campaign to encourage the building of silos involved thirty-five county councils.

The state council addressed marketing questions as well as production issues. The composition of the council's marketing committee suggested the cooperative nature of farm groups. C. O. Raine, master of the State Grange; E. W. Solomon, president of the Missouri State Farmers' Union; C. W. Schmutz, president of the Missouri State Farmer's Association; Professor A. J. Meyer, director of the Missouri College of Agriculture's Agricultural Extension; and Jewell Mayes, secretary of the State Board of Agriculture composed the committee membership. The Missouri committee reflected the commitment of the new United States Food Administration to increase supplies through voluntarism while controlling prices and avoiding black markets. Through voluntary marketing and consumer committees, Hoover's Food Administration set wheat prices at $2.20 a bushel and hog prices at first $15.50 and later $17.50 per hundred weight as a part of the overall policy.

In October 1917, Mumford officially took over wartime food activities in Missouri, after Congress passed legislation authorizing the U.S. Food Administration, an agency created in May by executive order. Mumford simply used the structure and many of the same people that he had brought together under the Council of Defense. County chairs of the council became county food administrators. By uniting the Missouri Council of Defense, the Missouri Food Administration, and the College of Agriculture with its extension work, Mumford created an organization "not surpassed by any other state." He also enlisted the services of the chair of the Women's Committee of the Council of Defense for the Food Administration. By March 1918 only two Missouri counties failed to have county food administrators. Chairs in the other 112 counties had appointed some 461 deputies and assistants, and Mumford had appointed women food chairs in 88 counties.

From the beginning of the war, Missouri women volunteered in large numbers. Mrs. Philip N. Moore, a member of the National Woman's Committee, called a meeting of the presidents of significant women's organizations in Missouri. Thirty-seven representatives met and elected Mrs. B. F. Bush as permanent chair and Miss Elizabeth Cueny as executive secretary. Subdivisions of the statewide committee included organization, finance, registration, courses of instruction, health and recreation, food production, food administration, Americanization, speakers, patriotic education, women in industry, liberty loan, Red Cross, child welfare, maintenance of existing social agencies, eleemosynary and punitive institutions, community singing, and publicity. The committee divided the state into eleven districts and chose a vice-chair for each. The vice-chairs then extended the organization to the county and town levels. The women established cooperating groups in more than 700 towns, 237 townships, and 137 school districts. Of the various counties, only Osage remained outside the women's structure. When the Children's Bureau of the U.S. Department of Labor created a program to weigh and measure every child in the nation under the age of five, the National Woman's Committee took on the task. In Missouri, unlike many other states, the women did the work without financial support, on a purely voluntary basis.

To recruit women for the labor force in the wake of wartime demands on men, Governor Gardner asked women to register for service. On July 28, 1917, more than 118,000 Missouri women signed up to take intensive courses in stenography, accounting, bookkeeping, telegraphy, filing, salesmanship, and office machine use. Another 12,000 registered later. Women assumed men's positions when the war created labor shortages. In the fall of 1917, the *Lawrence Chieftain* reported that twenty women and girls had replaced men in the shops of the Chicago, Burlington and Quincy Railroad in St. Joseph. "The women all wear overalls and jumpers." In St. Louis the Laclede Gas Company trained women as meter readers to take the place of departing men. In Springfield "thirty-five young business women" began drilling under the supervision of coach A. W. Briggs. They sought to get into physical condition to be ready to fill demanding positions held by men, who would eventually serve in the war. Despite this response, Gardner waited until September 1917 to appoint Bush, the state Women's Committee chair, to the Missouri Council of Defense. Bush's counterparts on county and township women's committees also became members of their councils of defense.

As the war progressed, Missouri women made a number of other contributions to the effort. They made "grab bags" for servicemen that contained toilet necessities, cigarettes, postcards, and other useful items. In many counties women gave servicemen going-away dinners, and St. Louis women entertained servicemen at Jefferson Barracks twice a week during the war. Some spent their Saturday afternoons at the barracks mending the clothing and darning the socks of soldiers. Women created their own speakers bureau, held classes on Americanization in thirteen counties and all the major cities, wrote a children's book entitled *The Mother Goose Rhymes in War Times,* and created pageants called "The Bugle Calls the Children" and "The Progress of Liberty." They produced the pageants in sixteen towns to audiences of twelve thousand and raised more than $3,000 for the Red Cross. In the difficult laundry strike in Kansas City that involved women workers and led to a general strike in 1918, members of the woman's committee served as mediators. On July 28, 1917, more than three hundred thousand Missouri women also signed Hoover Food Pledges, and in November the number of Missourians signing reached one million, making Missouri first among all the states in proportion to its population in committing to participate in the conservation effort.

Women signing food pledges to conserve food played a crucial role in Hoover's approach to the problem of feeding the Allies. At least in the short run, the United States could not increase production to meet the needs, so reducing U.S. consumption became essential. No other group could contribute more to the conservation of food than women because they were the country's principal cooks. Before fast-food restaurants captured American appetites, women in their home kitchens prepared at least 80 percent of the food consumed. Furthermore, to make voluntarism work, Hoover sought to create a spirit of self-denial, of self-sacrifice, within the population. Enlisting the women to conserve food voluntarily met all of the Food Administration's needs.

When the July 1917 pledge sign-up failed to produce the desired results, the Food Administration planned a broad appeal for the week of October 28–November 4, 1917. Don Farnsworth headed the national effort. In October he came to Missouri and met with representatives from all of Missouri's counties and many of its towns and cities to organize the pledge campaign. The campaign asked ministers and teachers to support the pledge effort. Frederick Mumford wrote to twenty-five hundred ministers asking them to preach about the pledge drive and to "take signatures" after their sermons. Uel Lamkin wrote a letter to nine thousand of the state's teachers asking them "to secure signatures of students." His appeal began by assuming that "every teacher in the state wants to do everything possible to win the war." He thought that they could contribute no greater service than "in doing your part in the *family food registration campaign.*" Directions on what the teachers could do would come from the county campaign committees, but Lamkin urged the teachers to use the whole week. "On school days work before and after school and on Saturday, the 3rd of November, meet your children, check up and finish your allotted work." Lamkin's entreaty represented nothing unique. Across the country teachers supported the war. Schools became "engines of patriotism," and teachers were "eager to give such service."

At the beginning of campaign week, William Saunders, the head of the effort in Missouri, complained that the Washington office had failed to mail enrollment blanks on time, but Saunders took some consolation from the efforts of ministers who complied with Mumford's request. He also praised the Speakers' Bureau of the Missouri Council of Defense for its support of the pledge drive.

Preliminary reports on November 6 encouraged Saunders. "Considering the large German population in the state and the enormous difficulty in making headway among them in some populous counties, this is a magnificent showing in support of the Hoover policies for food conservation and insures the government very strong backing in anything it may undertake along these lines in the future in this state."

He noted that 525,861 people enrolled, including students. A few days later the final results showed that more than 700,000 had signed pledges. According to Saunders, St. Louis signings made a big difference in the enrollment. The city's Council of Defense persuaded officials to use patrolmen to solicit enrollments. Saunders thought St. Louis had a chance to become the nation's number one city and promised to contact police officials in Kansas City to employ the "police plan" in that city.

Those who signed circulars made the following commitment: "I pledge myself to use the practical means within my power to aid the Food Administration in its effort to conserve the food supplies of the country, and, as evidence of my support, I wish to be enrolled with yourselves as a volunteer member of the Food Administration." Those who signed received two cards to display. One identified them as United States Food Administration members and was to be placed in the front window of their homes. The other listed the suggested weekly allowance of foods for each person and was to be placed in the kitchen.

According to the recommendations, a person could eat as much fish, poultry, and game "as necessary." Officials limited consumption of beef, veal, lamb, mutton, and pork to two and one-half pounds per week, and within that quota, discouraged people from eating pork and encouraged them to eat mutton. The card recommended no more than one-half pound of butter and no more cooking fats than necessary. It carried the reminder that pasta contained wheat flour and recommended that people consume no more than one-half pound of wheat flour in their cooking, i.e., macaroni, gravies, sauces, and breadings. You could have three pounds of "War Bread" per week. The bread could contain no more than 80 percent wheat flour. Nonwheat cereals, vegetables and fruits, and cheese could be consumed in quantities of "as much as necessary." Sugar carried a limitation of three-fourths of a pound per person per week. The Food Administration placed no limit on children's consumption of milk, but limited cream usage to "Only as much as necessary." By signing the kitchen card, one promised "the United States Food Administration to ration my household according to the regulations set forth in this card." On May 15, 1918, T. D. Stanford took charge of a sugar-rationing program that limited supplies to retailers, bakers, and public eating places, in addition to food manufacturers. Rationing affected the major metropolitan areas of St. Louis and St. Louis County, Kansas City and Jackson County, and St. Joseph and its environs.

While encouraging conservation, the St. Louis Food Administration warned against hoarding food:

> Any person in the United States who buys *More Foodstuffs* than he customarily keeps at home in peace times is defeating the *Food Administration* in its purpose to secure a just distribution of food and in its great endeavors to reduce prices. The hoarding of food in households is not only unnecessary, as the Government is protecting the food supply of our people, but it is selfish and is a cause of high prices.
>
> Hoarding always throws a sudden strain on the railway system, and, because of our military demands, it is with extreme difficulty we can now move the vitally necessary food to markets.
>
> Their [*sic*] is much insidious propaganda in the country against food savings and increased production. *ALL OPPOSITION TO PRODUCTION AND SAVINGS IS DIRECT ASSISTANCE TO THE ENEMY.*

W. P. Gephart headed the Food Administration in St. Louis, and by November 1, 1918, he oversaw a total of more than four thousand people, only eighteen of whom received any compensation.

Obviously, those mobilizing the society for war willingly used established authority—ministers, teachers, and police—and propaganda to advance their cause. A plan of the state Woman's Committee urged county food chairs to create displays in businesses. Bush believed businesses would readily volunteer their windows because they would be credited with patriotic service and would reap large publicity value from the display. She recommended that the county chairs get the cooperation of any available home economics agents, teachers of home economics in the schools, and high school home economics classes to create the displays. Displays should be changed each week. She suggested that the first one should illustrate how to save sugar by using syrup; additional ones included "Corn Breads," "Soy Beans Instead of Meat," "Liberty Bread," and "Eat More Potatoes."

Food pledges and store-window displays just scratched the surface of the ways Missourians sold the war. The Missouri Council of Defense and the Missouri Woman's Committee both employed speakers bureaus. Speakers spread the message of patriotism and aided in fund drives and money-raising efforts of the Red Cross, YMCA, Knights of Columbus, Salvation Army, Jewish Relief Society, Friends of German Democracy, and other organizations. Audiences included chambers of commerce, clubs, churches, schools, fraternities, county institutes, labor unions, chautauquas, factory patriotic clubs, and any other organization that might aid the prosecution of the war. The council's speakers included some four thousand "Four Minute" men and women, who not only spoke to varied audiences, including those attending movies and theaters, but also created a four-minute chorus to sing the message of patriotism.

In a world without radio or television, all of those involved with selling the war knew the importance of newspapers. The Missouri Council of Defense published its own paper from June 1917 until December 1918. Called *Missouri On Guard,* it went to all members of the Council of Defense network, state officials, and libraries, for a total of more than twelve thousand free copies per issue. But to reach a broader audience, Mumford depended on independent newspapers, and the press willingly spread his messages; even "the country newspapers made a notable response." The weeklies used plate matter, material sent to the publishers by the council, in aiding the food pledge campaign and other conservation efforts. In the winter of 1918, the Missouri Food Administration flooded the papers with material to promote food conservation. Articles written by the agency under such titles as "Join the Wheat Saver's League," "Our Hour of Trial,"and "Are You Doing Your Share" circulated. "Join the Wheat Saver's League" suggests the thrust of these pieces:

> Every person in Missouri is requested by F. B. Mumford, state food administrator, to join the National Wheat Saver's League. There is no card to sign, and there are no dues to pay. But membership in the league, the state food administrator points out, will be an honor today and a pride in the years to come.
>
> Each member has an agreement with himself, or with some members of the family, that he will save a bushel of wheat between now and next summer. He will do this by the faithful observance of the Food Administration's Wheatless Days and Wheatless Meals, and by such other saving of wheat as his own ingenuity will invent.
>
> Women are especially desired as members of the league on account of their ability to make appetizing menus without using wheat.

In "Our Hour of Trial," Mumford used the stick rather than the carrot: "If we are selfish or even careless, we are disloyal; we are the enemy at home! Food Will Win The War! Whose food, German or American? The world awaits your answer. We must save, serve, and sacrifice." And in "Are you Doing Your Share," Mumford reiterated the theme that food would win the war. If the United States failed to produce adequate food supplies, "this terrible sacrifice of blood and money will be in vain, and the cause of democracy will be defeated, unless every person, in every home, every day, guards the *Nation's* supply of *Wheat, Beef, Pork, Fats and Sugar.*"

Mumford drove home this message over and over again. On one occasion, he specified that the Allies needed seventy-five million bushels of wheat, so Mondays and Wednesdays must be wheatless days in Missouri. Farmers should ship their wheat quickly. They would secure no advantage from holding wheat, because the government would retain the $2.20 per bushel price. To prevent the possibility of hoarding, Mumford announced that millers and dealers could not sell more than a one-half barrel of flour at a time to rural people and no more than one-quarter barrel to urban dwellers. Further, a dealer could make no more profit than seventy-five cents per barrel. Limitations on the amount of bread that a restaurant could serve with each meal, whether the bread could be toasted, and the requirement that one could purchase a pound of wheat only if he purchased a pound of another cereal formed the contents of other announcements by the council. Other circulars announced the need to conserve meat and sugar and suggested substitutes for those being conserved. Mumford warned against hoarding of food, calling it a moral crime. Only repeated violations, however, would lead to legal charges, otherwise both purchaser and seller would have to appear before the county food administrator. At the peak of its efforts, the Missouri Food Administration and the Council of Defense supplied their material to more than four hundred weekly newspapers.

While many newspapers used Mumford's plate matter, the *Gilman City Guide* refused to do so. Its publisher nevertheless supported the war and printed a variety of forms, including sugar coupons that allowed those signing them to get extra sugar for canning. Loren Reid captured Gilman City's attitude toward the war in this passage about sugar: "Although sugar was a scarce commodity, it did not occur to anyone to fudge or cheat. Slick's cafe had a big sign back of the counter: 'Use less sugar. Stir like Hell. We Don't Mind the Noise.'" A youth during the war, Reid described the way he and another youngster "patrolled the back alleys and thus got copper, brass, zinc, and lead for the nation's smelter. We gathered peach stones, which were collected by the ton throughout the country and used for making charcoal for gas masks. Coconut shells were also good, but coconuts were seldom seen in Gilman City, and we would hardly have recognized one even if we had seen it." Reid may have been responding to a Council of Defense circular. Mumford requested that "All pits and shells saved should be dried and turned into the nearest Red Cross stations." The council arranged for some three hundred collection depots. Girl scouts entered the campaign, and "two little girls from one troop brought in 1,600 pits each, while another pair contributed 2,000 each."

As evidenced by the girl scouts, appeals to the public produced results. In the first year of the war, Missouri's farmers responded to higher prices and requests to produce more by harvesting so much grain that the state moved from fourteenth in the nation to fifth. The State Board of Agriculture estimated the 1917 oat yield at double the average state yield for a fifteen-year period. According to Mumford, the request for farmers to sell their wheat during the spring of 1918 resulted in wheat deliveries 50 percent greater than the wheat marketed the week before the appeal. Mumford wanted "every surplus bushel" marketed. "No Missouri farmer can afford to hold his wheat and run the risk of being called a slacker," he warned.

Urgings to save wheat caused the Red Cross auxiliary in Blackburn to cancel the annual ice cream and strawberry shortcake festival. In the summer of 1918, many Missourians agreed not to use any more wheat until the next harvest. Reports from across the state indicated that wheat flour consumption declined by 50 to 75 percent. Retailers in Lawrence County sold an average of three pounds of corn meal for every pound of wheat flour, with "consumers . . . showing a splendid spirit of co-operation." R. H. Bryan, food administrator for Osage County, wrote that even that heavily German county had pledged itself not to use wheat until the harvest. That same spring, when the council reported a shortage of strawberry pickers near Sarcoxie, twenty-five women students from the University of Missouri volunteered to help out. After the harvest, Sarcoxie residents held a celebration to honor the young women.

On the whole, retailers, bakers, and millers compiled a remarkable record of cooperation with the Food Administration in Missouri. During 1918, Mumford received reports of only nineteen violations of the administration's wheat guidelines. Four grocers in St. Joseph sold the wrong wheat substitutes, and Mumford closed them for a day. A baker in Warrenton used an inadequate amount of grain other than wheat in his bread and received a two-day suspension of business. In Sedalia, grocer Maurice Magariel sold two hundred pounds of flour without selling substitutes. Mumford ordered him closed for a week. Eight bakeries in Kansas City, one in St. Joseph, one in Novinger, as well as grocers in Neosho, Springfield, Hilo in Douglas County, and a miller in Dent County, committed similar offenses. County food administrators or Mumford penalized them with closure or by requiring them to pay profits gained from their illegal actions to the Red Cross. For example, the eight bakers in Kansas City gave the Red Cross $425 "in lieu of further prosecution." Harry Kempster, food administrator for egg production, received only two reports of producers failing to candle eggs.

In the fall of 1918, Hoover wrote to General Enoch Crowder, a Missourian in charge of the draft during World War I, about the success of the food program:

> The American Food Administration today constitutes not only the basis of supply for Allied Civilians, but is in many fundamentals a complete extension of the Quartermaster General's departments of all four western armies. We are either directly purchasing by this Administration or supervising the purchase of upwards of five hundred million dollars worth of food stuffs per month. And not only is it necessary to purchase and collect this quantity of food but as no such supply exists, except by self-denial of the American people, it is necessary to stimulate and guide this fundamental provision of food.

In his memoirs, Hoover recalled that voluntarism worked too well: "In one emergency I asked for a special saving of fats and butter. The people saved so much that the trades were demoralized, we flooded the Allies, and I had to retreat."

To finance the war, the federal government decided to raise taxes for about a third of the cost and to depend on loans for the remainder. All together the government floated five loans from May 14, 1917, through April 21, 1919. Each drive lasted about a month, and each occurred in the spring and fall: two in 1917; two in 1918; and the last from April 21 to May 10, 1919.

As those conducting the drives gained experience, they became more successful. Each drive depended on patriotism, intimidation, and voluntarism for success. Profit played no role. Congress allowed no commissions to those who sold bonds and provided only one-tenth of

1 percent of the amount of the bonds sold for all expenses. The system of marketing the bonds depended upon volunteers selling the bonds to their neighbors. The process began with the federal treasury allotting bonds to the twelve federal reserve districts according to each district's bank resources. Each federal reserve bank then appointed a committee to distribute its allocation to the states in its district. A state committee then allocated bonds to the counties, and county chairs apportioned its bonds to townships and towns. During the fourth loan drive in Missouri some local committees prescribed what each family should buy. In Boone County, for example, Hartley H. Banks chaired the fourth loan drive and issued an assessment card indicating the amount of bonds the committee expected each family to purchase. In some places, Missourians were warned that those not subscribing the full amount of assessment would have to appear before a local quota committee to explain why the amount was not purchased. Thus, a fine line divided patriotism from intimidation. The secretary of the treasury enlisted the services of fraternal organizations to sell bonds and urged men in the armed services to write at least one friend or family member to buy bonds and to help sell them. Local newspapers published lists of those who purchased bonds in the various drives and of those who did not purchase them. The *Knox County Democrat* commented that it would publish the names of the "slackers" who did not give because the list was shorter. Secretary William G. McAdoo's request worked with the Odd Fellows of Bethany. In the first loan drive, the lodge subscribed $1,000.

No doubt a wide variety of motivations influenced those who bought bonds. The fact remains that Missourians subscribed more than their quotas in every bond drive. Not surprisingly, those with the most money often bought the most bonds, and those involved with the Council of Defense supported the drives with their money and time. In the second loan drive, for example, the St. Louis Woman's Committee led by Mrs. John H. Holliday worked in close harmony with state chair Mrs. B. F. Bush and Mrs. Ernest Stix of the St. Louis Equal Suffrage League to canvass the city. In addition, "Four Minute Women Speakers" appeared in motion-picture houses to sell the bonds. Of course, they coordinated their efforts with male organizations. Such work sold $74 million worth of bonds in the city. In the third drive, the city of St. Louis became the first city in the country with a population of more than five hundred thousand to oversubscribe its quota. When officials completed the tally of the five loan drives and contributions to the Red Cross, YMCA, and other wartime fund-raising efforts, St. Louis raised a total of $258,745,410.

In the Third Liberty Loan drive, all of Missouri's counties subscribed more than their quotas. In the Fourth Liberty Loan drive, officials set per capita quotas at $50. St. Louis subscribed an average of $115 per person; Kansas City subscribed an average of $90 per person. Those levels of support made up for an average of $30 per capita in the rest of the state. In that drive twenty-seven counties failed to reach their quotas, but twenty of those subscribed more than 90 percent of their allocation. Twelve counties subscribed more than 125 percent of their quotas, including the rural counties of Atchison, Dent, Grundy, Howard, Lincoln, Miller, and Shannon. Shannon, one of the poorest and least populated counties in the state, subscribed 150 percent of its quota.

Each bond drive challenged the war workers. In the third bond drive in Dunklin County, citizens failed to meet their quota despite county bankers agreeing to subscribe for as much in Liberty bonds as 6 percent of their resources. The bankers then sold the bonds to citizens in easily purchased denominations. Kennett volunteers encouraged children to save their money and support the war by buying thrift stamps, which sold for twenty-five cents apiece. They accrued interest and could be redeemed for $5 after five years. School-children held competitions to see which group could sell the most stamps, with prizes going to the winners. Despite the effort, only 534 subscribers purchased $118,550 in Liberty bonds; the quota stood at $225,000. Similarly, the second bond drive failed to reach its quota in Knox County by $100,000. In the third drive, however, Knox Countians oversubscribed by more than $112,000, only to fall short again in the fourth bond drive by $100,000. Phelps County failed to reach its quota in the first two drives, but surpassed its quota in the last two.

In southwest Missouri's Lawrence County, citizens exceeded their $217,000 quota in the first drive by raising more than $320,000. In central Missouri, 2,898 subscribers went over the quota in the third bond drive by almost $200,000. According to the *Boonville Weekly Advertiser,* Boonville led all the districts in the Eighth Federal Reserve District in percentage of subscriptions, and "Missouri . . . made the best record of any state in the Union as to the per capita distributions." In the second bond drive, the *Bethany Republican* reported an oversubscription of more than $25,000 for Harrison County, although county residents had failed to meet their quota in the first drive. During the second drive, the paper had printed pleas from Senator Stone and Agriculture Secretary David F. Houston, a Missourian, to buy bonds. And with Missourians oversubscribing each of their bond quotas, those eager to mobilize the state for the war effort succeeded.

Despite the view of one interpreter of World War I in Missouri, few organizations elicited as much enthusiastic support during the war as did the Red Cross. In celebration of the Fourth of July in 1917 and to raise funds for the Red Cross, Nelson Leonard hosted between two thousand and twenty-five hundred Cooper Countians on his lovely Ravenswood estate some miles southwest of Boonville. Hundreds of automobiles from the surrounding area brought the party-goers. Area bands provided music; the fireworks display could be seen for miles. Revelers consumed ice cream and cake and gave more than $1,000 to the Red Cross. In Jefferson City an estimated ten thousand people held a picnic on the same day for the same purpose. The women of the city baked more than a thousand pies and several hundred cakes; the men barbecued tons of meat. All proceeds went to the Red Cross.

Knox County organized a Red Cross chapter in June 1917. About one hundred people signed the charter. Merchants Sandknop and Grantges, "Knox County's Exclusive Ready-to-Wear House for Women," advertised a donation sale benefit for the organization. Ten percent of the June 26 sales receipts would be contributed to the chapter. Members of the Browning Club, the P.E.O., and the Culture Club of Edina aided the Red Cross by knitting sweaters for soldiers. Citizens of Bethany and Harrison County started with a goal of enrolling thirty-three hundred members in the Red Cross, and by January 1918 they had surpassed their goal by almost one thousand. In nearby Gentry County two King City workers solicited Red Cross memberships and prepared to meet all sorts of responses. "In their whole drive, however, they did not get beyond their first question: 'Are you a member of the Red Cross? for the usual answer was 'No, but here's a dollar.'" In Nodaway County, also in northwest Missouri, more than seventy-five hundred women engaged in Red Cross work; the only paid official was a stenographer. That county's women used $1,500 worth of raw material a week in their effort for soldier's relief.

In Carroll County, the Red Cross chapter had nearly twelve hundred members and occupied an eight-room house as their knitting center.

Cooper County's Red Cross membership numbered more than three thousand, with eighty-four of them having been recruited by two black ministers. In its 1919 drive the county exceeded its quota by more than $1,500, raising $32,000 for the cause. Dunklin County farmers contributed agricultural products, which were auctioned off with the proceeds going to the Red Cross. During Red Cross Week in the spring of 1918, Missouri became the first state in the Southwest Division of the United States to meet its quota. Lafayette County went over its quota in two hours. In north central Missouri, J. B. Fleming brought fifty-two bushels of wheat to the town of Linneus, announcing that he would sell it at auction and contribute the proceeds to the Red Cross. Forty men volunteered to buy one bushel each for a dollar. After the purchase they returned the wheat to the Red Cross, and Fleming gave the organization another $52 for it and took his wheat back home, raising the sum of $92. Certainly, Fleming and the thousands of Missourians involved in supporting the Red Cross did so voluntarily and not from intimidation.

Voluntarism even spurred Missouri lawyers to action. In the spring of 1918, lawyers formed legal committees under the auspices of the Council of Defense. They voluntarily made their services available to people with questions about the selective service law, war risk insurance, soldier allotments, family allowances for servicemen and their dependents, servicemen's civil rights, and the interpretation of various war emergency laws. They drafted wills for servicemen and helped them arrange their property and business affairs when they entered service. They represented soldiers and sailors in court and served as intermediaries for service families in need of such agencies as the Red Cross.

The council established a state committee of lawyers, which named a chairman in each county, who in turn secured the services of two members of the bar in each county. One month after organization began, lawyers in one hundred counties had volunteered to participate. When the Missouri Council of Defense dissolved, the Red Cross asked the Lawyers Committee to continue to function under its auspices, because the legal advice offered had been so helpful.

To conserve resources needed in transportation, the Missouri Council of Defense organized a Committee on Commercial Economy under the chairmanship of Sigmond Baer, a St. Louisan. In cities, the committee succeeded in getting a variety of retailers and wholesalers to reduce deliveries from two or three a day to one. Baer formed a cooperative delivery system among large department stores in St. Louis so that they worked together to supply their merchandise to suburban towns, "saving gasoline, tires, etc." Every town of two thousand or more residents received letters from the committee asking it to reduce deliveries, and more than 80 percent created voluntary programs to comply. From its beginning on April 24, 1917, until the last bill came in on March 15, 1919, the Missouri Council of Defense spent only $76,085. The value of volunteers' time and individual expenditures remains immeasurable.

The spirit of voluntarism extended to creating a fighting force. Within thirty days after the United States entered the war, St. Louis's Barnes Hospital had sent Base Hospital Unit Number 21 to Europe. The unit set up a five-hundred-bed hospital. On June 25, 1917, twenty-eight students of the University of Missouri left for France as members of the American Ambulance Field Service. William K. Gardner, the governor's eighteen-year-old son, joined in the adventure. Before the end of July, the Twelfth Engineering Regiment had formed and had boarded a ship for Europe. Composed largely of St. Louis railroad and construction workers, it went to France and began working on the railroads in August. Recruitment of seamen and naval gunners superceded other demands. When Washington officials called for volunteers, twelve hundred Missourians responded, reaching the state's quota in fifteen days. Within a month another twelve hundred Missourians had volunteered for such service. Other Missourians quickly joined the army; more than thirteen hundred had joined the regular army by April 24, with additional numbers joining the National Guard. Missouri ranked thirteenth in percentage of enlistments during the first stage of war.

Everyone knew, however, that voluntarism would not create the military force necessary to win the war. The Missouri Council of Defense began preparing public opinion to accept conscription from the outset, noting that it "was one of the most important tasks assigned." It had little time to get support. Congress passed a draft law on May 18 and called for nationwide registration of all those between the ages of twenty-one and thirty-one on June 5.

Preparations for registration day across the state followed the pattern of Dunklin County. A registration board appointed by Governor Gardner assumed responsibility for the day. Gardner appointed Dunklin County Sheriff J. E. Hardin, County Clerk Charles S. Shultz, and County Coroner

E. F. Harrison as members. The board named registration officials for each voting precinct in the county.

Perhaps to stimulate patriotism, Kennett, the seat of Dunklin County, held a parade on June 5. A much larger crowd than anticipated watched as W. F. Shelton drove around the courthouse square in his Cadillac, decorated with "a large American eagle, mounted on the radiator." Shelton's four-year-old son sat on a high seat in the center of the car, dressed as Uncle Sam. Next came Lee Shelton's Studebaker Six, with Mrs. Shelton at the controls. Decorated in patriotic red, white, and blue, the car carried the women employees of Shelton's store. All of the women wore red, white, and blue except Ione Rosenwater, who had dressed in the garb of "Miss Columbia."

In northwest Missouri no parade occurred, but the *Bethany Republican* sought to stimulate patriotism by warning, "Any male resident of the United States who is eligible for registry and fails to so register, or makes any attempt to evade the registration command, places on himself an ignominious stigma that will cling to him to the day of his death." Despite such editorial support for the draft, Senator Reed predicted "that the nation's cities would be 'running red with blood'" on registration day. Instead, registration went off in Missouri without a hitch. Almost three hundred thousand Missourians registered; 18,915 black men signed up. Some 174,445 men who registered claimed exemptions from the draft: 170,753 whites and 3,742 blacks.

In Bethany, Dr. Jackson Walker volunteered to examine conscripts free of charge, but most of those claiming exemptions suffered from no physical disability. The conscription law allowed exemptions to those holding municipal, county, state, or federal elective office; ministers of religion and students of divinity; persons in military or naval service; workers in customhouses, arsenals, and navy yards; pilots and merchant marine sailors; married men with dependent wives and children; sons of dependent widows; sons of aged or infirm parents; brothers of dependent siblings under sixteen years of age; individuals declared morally deficient; members of recognized religions in existence before May 18, 1917, whose creed disallowed participation in warfare; and those employed in agricultural and factory work essential to the national interest.

With such broad categories, no wonder that more than half of those who registered in the rich agricultural county of Harrison applied for exemptions. Of the 1,603 who registered, 1,060 applied to escape the draft; more than 900 claimed support of dependent relatives. In the Bootheel county of Dunklin, 80 percent applied for exemptions, "principally [for the reason of] dependent relatives," and in Cooper County requests for exemptions went above the expected 50 percent.

So many exemptions caused General Enoch Crowder to revise the selective service policy in late November. Married men no longer received exemptions as a class, but married men with children remained in a lower classification. The revised policy divided men into five classifications with a number of subdivisions in each class. Only men in the first class would be called into service except in an extreme emergency.

To administer the draft, Missouri created 166 local draft boards and 5 district exemption boards. The idea of local boards came from Crowder and fit well into the overall philosophy of conducting the war espoused by Woodrow Wilson and Herbert Hoover: decentralization and self-sacrifice. Local boards received quotas based on population. Boards could subtract enlistees from their quotas. For example, in Lawrence County the board called only 27 men into service, although Selective Service set its quota at 118.

In all categories Missouri ranked about average in the percentage of people who registered, were drafted, and who volunteered. In 1917, Missouri ranked ninth among the states in population, ninth in total registrations, and ninth in cost of registration. The percentage of men drafted out of those who served stood at 66.19 percent; the percentage nationally stood at 66.10 percent. Surprisingly, few men resisted the draft.

Blacks made up a smaller percentage of total registrants in Missouri, and a larger percentage of blacks who registered received draft notices. Missouri blacks accounted for 7.11 percent of Missouri registrants; 9.36 percent of the nation's registrants were black; but 40 percent of Missouri blacks who registered became inductees while 34.1 percent received draft notices in the nation. Just under 27 percent of white registrants were drafted. Most of the more than nine thousand black Missourians inducted into the armed forces served behind the lines as truck drivers and laborers. The Ninety-second and Ninety-third divisions, both black infantry units, went to France, where the Ninety-second saw front-line action.

Discrimination dictated the role played by blacks in the war. Draft registration forms requested that race be identified, and the instructions told registrants to tear off the left-hand corner of the form if they were "of African descent." A corner missing on the form made it easy to separate black registrants from others. When the Woman's Committee planned to enroll two thousand Missouri women between nineteen and thirty-five years of age who had a minimum of two years of high school and who were unmarried, widowed, or wives of men in military service, "colored women" could be enrolled, but could not receive training in army hospital schools.

The *Boonville Weekly Advertiser* expressed its bigotry openly. In February 1917, it noted that thousands of blacks had come north to fill industrial jobs formerly held by European immigrants, "But up to this writing not a one has left Boonville, we regret to say." After the declaration of war, the editor commented that soon blacks would have the opportunity to fill new segregated regiments "and those who have 'nothing to do' can find a job. They may prove to be good for something after all—they may keep a bullet from striking a good man." Strangely, another news article was devoted to black inventor John Ernst Matzeliger, who patented a machine that revolutionized the production of shoes. The paper discussed his contributions and noted that in 1917 the U.S. Patent Office had granted more than eight hundred patents to blacks. Perhaps this was a piece of filler material that escaped the editor's notice.

Despite discrimination, the Missouri Council of Defense appointed an African American, James B. Coleman, to serve as State Director for Work Among Negroes. Coleman coordinated council projects to get blacks to conserve food, including attending classes given by county home economics extension agents. The chair of the Womans' Committee of the council reported at the end of the war that "the colored women in all the large towns throughout the State have worked splendidly along all lines."

The establishment of the Missouri Negro Industrial Commission represented the most important thrust of black Missourians during the war. Reacting to criticism by black leaders, Governor Gardner appointed the commission in February 1918. Gardner took this action to improve his standing with the black electorate, "and also to avoid appointing blacks to the white patronage positions in the state government." Nathaniel C. Bruce, head of black Bartlett Agricultural and Industrial School, served as the first chair of the commission. During 1918 the commissioners held more than forty meetings, sold more than

$600,000 worth of war bonds, taught black farmers better methods of cultivation, encouraged greater production and conservation of foods, and generally gave full support to the war effort. With power only to make recommendations, the commission could do little to change conditions of discrimination.

Discrimination extended to acceptance in the National Guard. Captain Harry Truman, who became the most famous Missourian to fight in the war as a National Guardsman, commanded no black troops. Truman's fame as a combatant came long after the fighting stopped. While the fighting continued, the most famous Missourian in the war had earned his nickname by commanding black troops during the Spanish-American War: General John J. "Black Jack" Pershing. Born and reared in Linn County, Pershing commanded the United States Expeditionary Forces that went to Europe.

Unlike Pershing, who graduated from West Point, Truman received no formal military training except that available as a member of the Missouri National Guard. He had not even gone to the Mexican border in 1916, when the Missouri Guard saw action there. But in August 1917, when the federal government called the Missouri Guard into service again, Harry left the family farm in Jackson County for the war. By then, the Missouri Guard had expanded from about five thousand to more than fourteen thousand members. Officials combined the Missouri and Kansas Guards into the "Brave 35th Division," with the Missouri unit forming two-thirds of the troops. It trained in Oklahoma from September until April, moved to New York, and landed in France on May 17, 1918. It saw time in the notorious trenches before participating in the St. Mihiel advance. At Argonne, the Thirty-fifth "for six days participated in the fiercest fighting of . . . the greatest and decisive battle of the war," forming "the razor edge of the advancing American wedge." The American force captured every objective, advancing "some eleven miles over a terrain mined and fortified with barbed wire and concrete as strongly as Prussian ingenuity knew how to defend it."

When the Missouri National Guard became a part of federal forces, Governor Gardner called for the creation of a Home Guard. He asked the Missouri Council of Defense to organize the force. Twelve thousand persons enlisted within three months, overwhelming the ability of officials to cope with the number of volunteers. The Home Guard endured normal military training, and at least one unit went into federal service in May 1918. When the war ended, more than seven thousand Missourians had served in the Home Guard.

Missouri's first draftees went to Camp Funston, Kansas, for training in September 1917. With men from South Dakota, Nebraska, Kansas, Colorado, Arizona, and New Mexico, they formed the "Fighting 89th Division" led by General Leonard Wood. The Eighty-ninth saw action at St. Mihiel and at the battle of the Argonne also. Called "one of the very finest fighting forces" in the war, the Eighty-ninth fought until the signing of the armistice on November 11, and then entered Germany as a part of the occupation force.

By the end of the war 156,232 Missourians had served in the armed forces. Missourians suffered 11,172 casualties, with more than 10,000 from the army and the rest from the marines and navy. Missourians killed in action numbered 1,270; those who died from wounds, disease, and accidents numbered 1,531. In 1919, 269 Missourians remained missing in action according to the army, and another 17 were missing at sea. Five Missourians received Congressional Medals of Honor, the nation's highest award for valor. All together, 280 Missourians received war honors; the United States gave 189 awards, France 72, Great Britain 9, and the rest were bestowed by Italy, Rumania, Belgium, Japan, Russia, and Montenegro. It must be noted also that 12,340 Missourians deserted from the armed forces, a percentage of desertions significantly below the national average.

Besides the cost in lives, Missourians and other citizens experienced some curtailment in their freedom of discussion and independence of action. So much energy went into channeling opinion to support the war that little tolerance existed for those who disagreed with the war effort. For example, the *Bethany Republican* in a May 1917 editorial warned, "This is no time to publicly express a thought that will in any way hamper the progress of the government." In editorials in August 1917 and January 1918, the paper expressed disdain for the Industrial Workers of the World and those "who may aspire to incite colored people to violence." The editor called the IWW "the criminal scum of Europe, the off scouring and stink of the four corners of the earth." He looked forward to the end of the war, when "the foreign element should be weeded out and sent back where they came from."

From its origins, the Missouri Council of Defense waged war against "disloyal criticism of the Government, and . . . all disloyal activities."

The Henry County Council of Defense created "a plan of suppression of disloyalty . . . which served as a model in Missouri." County chairs reported alleged disloyal activities to the state Council of Defense. State officials investigated the charges and sent the results to federal authorities in Kansas City and St. Louis, who then proceeded with appropriate actions. Although federal authorities saw a number of Missouri cases, they found that "a large number . . . [of] offenders were guilty of unpatriotic remarks or actions, but were within the law."

David March came to a similar conclusion and noted that organizations of super-patriots such as the National Security League and the National Protective Association made more irresponsible accusations and created more agitation than those in official positions. He called the super-patriots little better "than vigilante groups of witch-hunters" who caused federal district court dockets to be congested with "espionage and slacker cases, most of which were ultimately dismissed." Finally, March observed that these groups played a minor role in Missourians' lives.

A study of five weekly newspapers published in central, northeast, northwest, southeast, and southwest Missouri during the war supports March's conclusions. The authors found only seven cases of individuals accused of disloyal statements or behavior. Two of the incidents took place in the St. Louis area, one occurred in St. Joseph, and one in Columbia. The latter concerned University of Missouri physics instructor G. E. M. Jauncey, who, when accused by the U.S. Department of Justice of disloyalty, resigned his position. In their study of opposition to the war, H. C. Peterson and Gilbert C. Fite, in commenting on the Jauncey case, stated, "There were many other places where the professors were silenced or disciplined without the matter being reported in the press." Another student of the war found only one instance of an individual being accused of disloyalty in Phelps County. Authorities arrested Wilhelm Stemmel for reportedly wishing the deaths of a trainload of soldiers. Stemmel turned out to be a resident alien.

Nevertheless, an atmosphere of intolerance prevailed. From the beginning of its existence, the Council of Defense fought "to eliminate the use of the enemy tongue and enemy influences, as injurious and a deterrent to the various War Fund and Government Loan campaigns, as undermining the civilian morale of the nation, and as possessing possibilities of grave concern to the integrity of the nation at war." The council created an Americanization Committee in May 1918 that surveyed aliens in Missouri to see how many had taken out papers to become citizens. Because it had no statutory authority, the council depended on voluntary compliance with its regulations. Governor Gardner endorsed efforts to eliminate the German language in the state. State Superintendent of Schools Uel Lamkin refused to certify high schools that continued to teach German, and forbade elementary schools from teaching in the German language.

A meeting of Cape Girardeau citizens passed a resolution opposing the use of German in "churches, schools, lodges and in public meetings of every character." The town council of Brownfield passed an ordinance making it a misdemeanor to teach, talk, or sing the German language. The ordinance set a fine of $100 for violations. Citizens of Louisiana announced the burning of German textbooks. Councils of Defense in Cass and Linn Counties "prohibited the use of the German tongue over telephones." In the town of Lincoln, arsonists burned a Lutheran school, presumably because the instructor taught the classes in German.

Opposition to the use of the German language resulted in a reduction of Missouri's German-language newspapers from fifteen to ten during the war; several of them printed half of their papers in English. Others planned to go out of business or to print exclusively in English. In Charleston, the German-American Society voted to dissolve and to contribute its treasury to the Red Cross with the message, "We hope that this may help to send the Kaiser to hell."

The atmosphere of war caused individuals to worry about what others might think. For example, W. Lloyd Diehl of King City offered readers of the *Bethany Republican* a $100 reward "for information that will lead to the arrest and conviction of the party or parties who are responsible for the lie to the effect that I disrespectfully burned or destroyed an American Flag, and also for the statement that I have been arrested and in jail in Albany for this offense . . . and for the statement that I am siding with Germany." Diehl wrote he saluted the flag two times a day and believed slanderers sought to injure his business. So while incidents of individuals being prosecuted for disloyalty proved few, those who might oppose United States participation in the war for a variety of reasons undoubtedly felt constant constraints about expressing their views.

The Mt. Zion Mennonite congregation in Morgan County refused to support the war because of religious convictions. The Morgan County Council of Defense tried to get Brother Abraham Wenger to serve on it, and he refused. Mennonites rejected the purchase of Liberty Bonds or war stamps. "As the drives became harder and the quotas harder to raise the feelings became more intense. Finally a Federal officer came and Abraham Wenger, John R. Driver and Amos Gingerich were called to meet with him." They, in turn, asked other members of the congregation to join them in meeting the federal official.

The Mennonites successfully answered charges against them and agreed to contribute $1,500 over a three-month period to the Red Cross. "This was a pledge of good faith and evidence that the Mennonites were not just selfishly clinging to their money as a reason for not buying Bonds. When three months were up, they were told to give their money as they saw fit. There was no more disturbance."

Although organized labor in Missouri joined the war effort once the United States declared war on Germany, in its actions during the war, labor made it clear that it expected to uphold its interests. State labor leaders served as members of the five district draft exemption boards, on the Missouri Council of Defense (only one member out of thirty), and on the advisory board of the Fuel Administration. When women became a more important part of the workforce, organized labor offered no objection to their presence so long as they did not lower the rate of pay for the tasks performed.

As the war progressed, labor discovered a concerted effort on the part of employers to disregard wage-and-hour provisions announced by the United States Department of Labor. The employers sought to make Missouri an open-shop state. Of course, conflict occurred. Kansas City laundry workers struck the Laundry Owners' Association, which eventually led to a six-day general strike in the city. At least twenty-five thousand unionists conducted the walk-out. The Women's Committee of the Council of Defense finally moderated the strike. Unfortunately for labor, the strike ended without the Owners' Association recognizing the Laundry Workers Union. At the same time, strikes in St. Louis led to between thirty thousand and fifty thousand Missouri unionists walking out. During the first quarter of 1918, St. Louis ranked second to New York in number of strikes. For all of 1918, St. Louis ranked fourth in the nation in labor walk-outs.

Strikes, however, did not mean that organized labor lacked patriotism. At a meeting of the St. Louis Central Trades and Labor Union, Emmett A. Oburn, a delegate from the Carpenter's Union, "was severely beaten and suspended from the organization because he failed to stand at the meeting when the 'Star Spangled Banner' was played."

Besides the multitude of changes in life patterns produced by the experience of fighting World War I, Missourians and the nation saw the war create two major developments: one that would have long-lasting and increasingly important effects on society, and another that would have a short-range but profound impact. Of course, the passage of the women's suffrage amendment to the Constitution created the circumstances for a revolution in the role of women in American society. The Prohibition amendment to the Constitution had an ephemeral effect, but in the beer-brewing state of Missouri, it had a deep economic impact. The *Boonville Weekly Advertiser* captured the importance of brewing to St. Louis in the following anecdote: "Billy Sunday cancels his St. Louis engagement. Billy don't mind locking horns with the devil in a fair and open fight, but he evidently thinks the devil and the brewers of St. Louis are too many for him." The evangelist had planned his trip for the spring of 1917.

Finally, the mobilization of Missouri society on behalf of the war effort must impress any observer. Without radio, without television, and through the voluntary organization of citizens by such agencies as the Council of Defense and the Red Cross, Missourians met the challenge of producing and preserving food, buying bonds, and doing all of the other things the war emergency required. Using newspapers, pamphlets, and word of mouth, those responsible for promoting the war effort succeeded beyond any reasonable expectation.

ESSAY ON SOURCES

REPOSITORIES AND GENERAL SOURCES

Missouri has three major repositories that hold the most significant collections of manuscripts, records, and newspapers for the study of the state between 1875 and 1919. The University of Missouri's Western Historical Manuscript Collection and the State Historical Society of Missouri, in Columbia, hold many of the collections and newspapers consulted for this study. Each of the university's other campuses has Western Historical Manuscript Collections, also, and a researcher can draw on the entire collection from any one of the campuses. The State Historical Society's very important newspaper collection proved extremely useful. The Missouri State Archives, in Jefferson City, holds many of the state's records and a variety of local records necessary for writing the state's history. The Missouri Historical Society, in St. Louis, holds the essential documents and manuscripts for the study of that city's development and other collections helpful in understanding Missouri.

Both the St. Louis and Kansas City Public Libraries hold manuscripts, newspapers, and books that may be drawn upon in writing Missouri's history. St. Louis's Mercantile Library has strength in that city's and the West's early history and some material useful for the period 1875–1919. Other local historical societies often have material of significance.

Missouri's two major historical societies, the State Historical Society of Missouri and the Missouri Historical Society, publish quarterlies. The State Historical Society's journal is called the *Missouri Historical Review* and has been continuously produced since 1906. It is an invaluable source of good research and writing. The Missouri Historical Society has published two quarterlies: the *Bulletin* and *Gateway Heritage*. They have focused their publishing more on St. Louis topics, but have published articles on broader topics as well. In this essay the initials *MHR, BMHS,* and *GH* will identify these publications. A more recent publication focuses on the Ozark region and often publishes oral history. It is called *Ozarkswatch* and originates from Southwest Missouri State University.

Important multivolume histories of Missouri include Walter B. Steven's massive *Centennial History of Missouri, (The Center State), One Hundred Years in the Union, 1820–1921* (St. Louis, 1921). It is a general history of the state that contains information on political figures, organizations, and elections. Twenty-two years later, Floyd C. Shoemaker produced *Missouri and Missourians: Land of Contrasts and People of Achievements* (5 vols., Chicago, 1943). It treated similar topics as Steven's work, but reflected more recent research and interpretation.

The best general work on Missouri is David D. March's *The History of Missouri* (4 vols., New York, 1967). In the first two volumes, March combines extensive research with fine writing to provide a narrative of the state's history. The second two volumes are devoted to biographies of Missourians. March's history proved most useful in the writing of this study.

Shorter but informative treatments of the state include *Missouri, A Guide to the "Show Me" State* (New York, 1941), a work supported by the Works Progress Administration and primarily edited by Charles Van Ravenswaay; Paul Nagel, *Missouri: A Bicentennial History* (New York, 1977), a short personal interpretation of the state's history; Lawrence O. Christensen, "Missouri: The Heart of the Nation" in James Madison, ed., *Heartland: Comparative Histories of the Midwestern States* (Bloomington, Ind., 1988), another personal interpretation; Duane Meyer, *The Heritage of Missouri: A History* (St. Louis, 1982), a useful survey; and William E. Parrish, Charles T. Jones Jr., and Lawrence O. Christensen, *Missouri: The Heart of the Nation* (2d ed., Arlington Heights, Ill., 1992), the latest one-volume study of the state.

POLITICS

Publications that focus on interpretations of politics include John H. Fenton's *Politics in the Border States: A Study of the Patterns of Political Organization and Political Change Common to the Border States—Maryland, West Virginia, Kentucky, and Missouri* (New Orleans, 1957). Fenton devotes a chapter to Missouri, emphasizing geographic factors as a key to politics. J. Christopher Schnell's "Missouri as Microcosm: The Political Evolution of a Representative State, 1821–1932," *GH* 14 (1993–1994), 32–45, draws on Fenton and reflects the latest research. Like Fenton, Morran D. Harris examines Missouri politics from a political science approach in "Political Trends in Missouri 1900–1954" (master's thesis, University of Missouri, 1956). A highly interpretative view of Missouri during this period can be gained from David Thelen's *Paths of Resistance: Tradition and Dignity in Industrializing Missouri* (New York, 1986). Thelen emphasizes social, cultural, economic, and political conflict as the key to understanding the state between 1875 and 1919.

Specific primary sources of value include such daily newspapers as the *Kansas City Star*, the *St. Louis Globe Democrat*, the *St. Louis Post-Dispatch*, the *St. Louis Republic*, and the *Jefferson City Tribune*. Other newspapers that provided the important rural perspective included the *Boonville Weekly Advertiser*; the *Bethany Republican* and the *Bethany Democrat*; the *Dunklin Democrat*, published in Kennett; the *Lawrence Chieftain* and *The Fountain and Journal* both published in Mount Vernon; the *Knox County Democrat*, published in Edina; the *Moberly Monitor*, the *Charleston Enterprise*; the *Sedalia Democrat*; and the *Caruthersville, Twice-a-Week Democrat*.

Governor's papers, some of which are housed in the Missouri State Archives in Jefferson City and some of which are housed in the Western Historical Manuscript Collection in Columbia, proved quite valuable. These papers contain personal correspondence, speeches, memos, and other documents that give insight into politics. The papers of Joseph W. Folk, David R. Francis, Lon V. Stephens, Herbert Hadley, and William Joel Stone, among others, are all available. Of course, these collections vary in scope, quantity, and quality.

A supplement to these collections are the typed transcripts of speeches delivered by Missouri statesmen in the reference library of the State Historical Society. For example, addresses delivered by Senator George Graham Vest during the 1880s and 1890s are in this collection. Vest's material provides information on women's suffrage, immigration, the silver issue, and colonialism. The library has transcripts of speeches of a number of other political figures including Lon V. Stephens and Richard Bland.

Such published materials as Grace Gilmore Avery and Floyd C. Shoemaker, eds., *The Messages and Proclamations of the Governors of the State of Missouri* (Columbia, 1924) and Sarah Guitar and Floyd C. Shoemaker, eds., *The Messages and Proclamations of the Governors of the State of Missouri* (Columbia, 1926) contain speeches, reports, veto messages, and other pertinent documents for this period. Missouri's *Official Manual* (Jefferson City, 1878–1920) is a storehouse of information. The *Revised Statutes of the State of Missouri* (Jefferson City, 1875–1920); and the *Reports of Cases Argued and Determined in the Supreme Court of the State of Missouri* (Jefferson City, 1875–1920) should be consulted for more material dealing with legislation and the law. The printed *Journals of the House of Representatives and of the Senate* span this period and reveal much about the process of lawmaking. Besides a detailed record of the legislature's activities during each session, one can find transcripts of speeches, a record of votes cast, debates, lists of petitions, and a variety of comments. Those interested in the 1875 Constitution must consult Isidor Loeb and Floyd C. Shoemaker, eds., *Debates of the Missouri Constitutional Convention of 1875* (12 vols., Columbia, 1930). The *Debates* provide a full discussion of the most critical issues of this time.

BIOGRAPHICAL STUDIES

Historians have written dozens of biographies of Missouri politicians who influenced affairs between 1875 and 1919. They include such theses as Bernard M. Garfinkle, "The Political Career of Charles Martin Hay" (master's thesis, University of Missouri, 1956) and Marian E. Dawes, "The Senatorial Career of George Graham Vest" (master's thesis, University of Missouri, 1932); C. Joseph Pusateri contributed "A Businessman in Politics: David R. Francis, Missouri Democrat" (Ph.D. diss., Saint Louis University, 1965). Richard Bland has received attention in William V. Byars, *An American Commoner: The Life and Times of Richard Park Bland* (St. Louis, 1900) and in Harold A. Haswell, "The Public Life of Congressman Richard Park Bland" (Ph.D. diss., University of Missouri, 1951). On the 1896 presidential candidacy of Bland, see Cynthia Shook, "Richard Parks Bland: Almost a Candidate," *MHR* 68 (July 1974), 417–36. Two scholars wrote about William Joel Stone. Beryle A. Hamilton produced "The Early Political Career of William Joel Stone" (master's thesis, University of Missouri, 1950); and Ruth Warner Towne contributed "The Political Career of William Joel Stone" (Ph.D. diss., University of Missouri, 1953) and *Senator William J. Stone and the Politics of Compromise* (Port Washington, N.Y., 1979). Towne's work was important in understanding Democratic politics and Missouri's role in World War I. Another important biography is George F. Lemmer's

Norman J. Colman and Colman's Rural World: *A Study in Agricultural Leadership* (Columbia, 1953).

Louis G. Geiger's Ph.D. dissertation, which became *Joseph W. Folk of Missouri* (Columbia, 1953), remains a significant study of Progressivism. Earlier studies of Folk included Delphine Roberta Meyer's "Joseph Wingate Folk, Governor of Missouri" (master's thesis, Washington University, 1932), and Francis Landon's "The Joseph W. Folk Campaign for Governor in 1904 as Reflected in the Rural Press of Missouri" (master's thesis, University of Missouri, 1938). Currently, Stephen Piott is working on a new biography of Folk. He recently published "Joseph W. Folk and the 'Missouri Idea': The 1904 Governor's Race in Missouri," *MHR* 89 (July 1995), 406–26. Lloyd Edson Worner's "The Public Career of Herbert Spencer Hadley" (Ph.D. diss., University of Missouri, 1946) sheds light on that important political figure. See Hazel Tutt Long's "Attorney General Herbert S. Hadley v. the Standard Oil Trust," *MHR* 35 (January 1941), 171–87, for that key litigation. Missouri's important Speaker of the House of Representatives is the subject of Geoffrey Fahy Morrison's "A Political Biography of Champ Clark" (Ph.D. diss., Saint Louis University, 1972).

Political biographies are supplemented by a number of studies of political parties. Political activist Chauncey Ives Filley recorded his experiences in *Some Republican History of Missouri, 1856–1898* (St. Louis, 1898). Donald Eugene Wilson wrote "The Republican Party in Missouri, 1860–1881" (master's thesis, University of Missouri, 1930), and Mae Florence Donohue produced "The Democratic Party in Missouri, 1873–1880" (master's thesis, University of Missouri, 1930). C. Joseph Pusateri wrote "Rural-Urban Tensions and the Bourbon Democrat: The Missouri Case," *MHR* 69 (April 1975), 282–98. William Rufus Jackson, *Missouri Democracy: A History of the Party and Its Representative Members* (3 vols., Chicago, 1935) is full of valuable material on the state, including two volumes devoted to biographies of leading figures. For the very end of the period see Franklin D. Mitchell, *Embattled Democracy: Missouri Democratic Politics, 1919–1932* (Columbia, 1968).

Agrarian Politics

Several scholars have written about Populism, the political movement associated with farmer discontent that surfaced in the mid-1870s and continued in a crippled form through the 1890s. A neglected topic among recent students, the agrarian movement deserves more attention. For an interesting contemporary account see Phil Chew, *History of the Farmers Alliance, the Agricultural Wheel, the Farmers and Laborer Union, the Farmers Mutual Benefit Association, the Patrons of Industry, and Other Farmers Organizations* (St. Louis, 1891). Alma Beatrice Wilkinson, "The Granger Movement in Missouri" (master's thesis, University of Missouri, 1926) treats that significant organization. Still the best account is Homer Clevenger's "Agrarian Politics in Missouri, 1880–1896" (Ph.D. diss., University of Missouri, 1940). Also, see his "The Farmers Alliance in Missouri," *MHR* 39 (1944), 24–44. Leon Parker Ogilvie, "The Development of the Southeast Missouri Lowlands" (Ph.D. diss., University of Missouri, 1967) remains important. His "Populism and Socialism in the Southeast Missouri Lowlands," *MHR* 65 (1971), 159–83, is based on his dissertation research. Donald E. Konold, "The Silver Issue in Missouri Politics," (master's thesis, University of Missouri, 1950) shows the complex relationship between monetary policy and agrarian politics. Martin Gerald Towey, "The People's Party in Missouri," (Ph.D. diss., Saint Louis University, 1972) should be consulted. For a summary treatment of politics see C. H. McClure, "A Century of Missouri Politics," *MHR* 15 (January 1921), 315–36. Late-nineteenth-century vigilantism is the subject of a number of works, including Mary Hartman's and Elmo Ingenthron's *Bald Knobbers: Vigilantes on the Ozark Frontier* (1988). This book should be supplemented by two articles on the Bald Knobbers published in 1993 in the *White River Valley Historical Quarterly* by Kristen Kalen and Lynn Morrow.

Interested students should note the following newspapers in the State Historical Society of Missouri's collection that voiced agrarian views. They include the *Missouri Granger* (Macon), *The Newspaper* (California), and the *Farmers Union* (Memphis). A number of newspapers carried a column that reported on the Farmers and Labor Union party and the organizing efforts of such figures as U. S. Hall. See, for example, the *Boonville Weekly Advertiser* for 1890. Socialist newspapers such as *St. Louis Labor* (at times called the *St. Louis Socialist*), *Kennett Justice,* and the *Scott County Kicker* (Benton) have material on the farmer's movement and the Socialist movement. The *Annual Reports of the Missouri Bureau of Labor Statistics* (1879–1919) document some of labor's political struggles such as the eight-hour movement, the fight against convict labor, and the pursuit of child labor laws. For more material, see the holdings of the Western Historical Manuscript Collection and the reference library of the State Historical Society of Missouri on the University of Missouri–Columbia campus and the Missouri State Historical Society archives in St. Louis. A key manuscript collection on the movement is the Richard Dalton Papers, 1859–1922, in the Western Historical Manuscript Collection.

WOMEN AND MISSOURI POLITICS

Mary K. Dains edited two volumes of Missouri women's biographies entitled *Show Me Missouri Women* (Kirksville, 1989 and 1993). These volumes should be consulted on every topic dealing with Missouri women. An older and more general, but still valuable, survey of women's history is Mary R. Beard's *Woman as Force in History: A Study in Traditions and Realities* (New York, 1946). Sally M. Miller's *From Prairie to Prison: The Life of Social Activist Kate Richards O'Hare* (Columbia, 1993) records the life of a committed Socialist who lived in St. Louis during the early years of the twentieth century. See also Peter H. Buckingham, *Rebel against Injustice: The Life of Frank P. O'Hare* (Columbia, 1996) for material on Kate O'Hare and socialism in the state and nation. Among other studies on women's suffrage are Mary Semple Scott, ed., "History of Woman Suffrage in Missouri," *MHR* 14 (April–July 1920), 281–384; Monia Cook Morris, "The History of Woman Suffrage in Missouri, 1867–1901," *MHR* 25 (October 1930), 67–82; and Lorretta Mae Walker, "Woman Suffrage In Missouri, 1866–1880" (master's thesis, Washington University, 1963). Dina M. Young, "The Silent Search for a Voice: The St. Louis Equal Suffrage League and the Dilemma of Elite Reform, 1910–1920," *GH* 8 (spring 1988), 2–20, reveals the latest view. No doubt women's roles in politics and society will be an increasing subject of interest. See as well the studies on temperance and prohibition, both efforts that were led by activist women.

URBAN WORKING PEOPLE AND POLITICS

The two best books on Missouri's two largest cities are James Neal Primm's *Lion of the Valley, St. Louis, Missouri* (Boulder, 1981) and A. Theodore Brown's and Lyle W. Dorsett's *K.C.: A History of Kansas City* (Boulder, 1978). Both contain important material of the entire period and deal in detail with politics. The most thorough account of organized labor and its involvement in politics for this period is Gary M. Fink's *Labor's Search for Political Order: The Political Behavior of the Missouri Labor Movement, 1890–1940* (Columbia, 1973). As noted earlier, Thelen's *Paths of Resistance: Tradition and Dignity in Industrializing Missouri* treats consumers and efforts at urban reform. Edwin James Forsythe's "The St. Louis Central Trades and Labor Union, 1887–1945" (Ph.D. diss., University of Missouri, 1956) focuses on this important labor organization's role in politics. Russell J. Clemens wrote "A History of the United Brotherhood of Carpenters and Joiners in Missouri, 1881–1981" (Ph.D. diss., University of Missouri–Columbia, 1982). Harry D. Holmes's "Socio-Economic Patterns of Non-Partisan Political Behavior in the Industrial Metropolis: St. Louis, 1895–1916" (Ph.D. diss., University of Missouri–Columbia, 1973) treats this period. One should also take note of the importance of elite influences in Alexander S. McConachie's "The 'Big Cinch:' A Business Elite in the Life of a City, St. Louis, 1895–1915" (Ph.D. diss., Washington University, 1976).

Urban reform is the subject of Katherine Candee's "The Temperance Movement In Missouri, 1876–1884" (master's thesis, Washington University, 1937) and Clare Lucile Bradley's "The Prohibition Movement and Dramshop Law Enforcement, 1887–1910" (master's thesis, Washington University, 1941). See also G. K. Renner's "Prohibition Comes to Missouri, 1910–1919," *MHR* 62 (July 1968), 363–97. Primary research material on the topic includes the *Annual Reports of the Women's Christian Temperance Union of Missouri.*

PROGRESSIVISM IN MISSOURI

The Progressive era in Missouri has received a good deal of attention, including biographical treatment of major actors listed in the biography section, particularly Louis Geiger's *Folk,* and in James Neal Primm's *Lion of the Valley.* For a fascinating overview see Robert M. Crunden, *Ministers of Reform: The Progressives' Achievement in American Civilization, 1889–1920* (New York, 1982). An interesting comparative study is Nicholas Clare Burckel's "Progressive Governors in the Border States: Reform Governors of Missouri, Kentucky, West Virginia, and Maryland, 1900–1918" (Ph.D. diss., University of Wisconsin–Madison, 1971). Franklin Mitchell, "A Progressive's Progress: The Changing Liberalism of Charles M. Hay of Missouri," *MHR* 66 (January 1972), 230–45, provided insight into that very important politician's approach to the wave of reform.

An early appraisal of the movement in Missouri is William T. Miller's "The Progressive Movement in Missouri," *MHR* 22 (July 1928), 456–501. A major study is Jack David Muraskin's "Missouri Politics during the Progressive Era, 1896–1916" (Ph.D. diss., University of California–Berkeley, 1969). He addressed urban reform in two articles in the *BMHS*: "St. Louis Municipal Reform in the 1890s: A Study in Failure," 24 (October 1968) and "Municipal Reform in Two Missouri Cities," 25 (April 1969). Robert Dale Grinder's "The Anti-Smoke Crusades: Early Attempts to Reform the Urban Environment, 1893–1918" (Ph.D. diss., University of Missouri–Columbia, 1973) reveals the politics of that issue. Harold W. Eickhoff, "The Organization and Regulation of Medicine in Missouri, 1883–1901" (Ph.D. diss., University of Missouri, 1964) and George Mangold, "Social Reform in Missouri, 1829–1920," *MHR* 14 (October 1920), 191–213, deal with other aspects of reform. See also Ronald L. F. Davis and Harry D. Holmes, "Insurance and Municipal Reform in St. Louis, 1893–1904," *Midwest Review* 1 (1979), 1–18. H. Roger Grant, *Insurance Reform: Consumer Action in the Progressive Era* (Ames, Iowa, 1979) is a broader study of the topic.

Steven L. Piott's *The Anti-Monopoly Persuasion: Popular Resistance to the Rise of Big Business in the Midwest* (Westport, Conn., 1985) proved very useful and is well done. Piott's other contributions include "Modernization and the Anti-Monopoly Issue: The St. Louis Transit Strike of 1900," *BMHS* 35 (October 1978), 3–16; "Missouri and Monopoly: The 1890s as an Experiment in Law Enforcement," *MHR* 73 (October 1979), 21–49; "Missouri and the Beef Trust: Consumer Action and Investigation, 1902," *MHR* 75 (October 1981), 31–52; and "Giving Voters Voice: The Struggle for Initiative and Referendum in Missouri," *GH* 14 (spring 1994), 20–36. In addition, see Dina M. Young, "The St. Louis Streetcar Strike of 1900: Pivotal Politics at the Century's Dawn," *GH* 11 (summer 1991), 4–18. Julian S. Rammelkamp, "St. Louis Boosters and Boodlers," *BMHS* 36 (July 1978), 200–210, should not be overlooked. Elizabeth N. Schmidt, "Civic Pride and Prejudice: St. Louis Progressive Reform, 1900–1916" (master's thesis, University of Missouri–St. Louis, 1987), should also be consulted. Donald Bright Oster, "Nights of Fantasy: The St. Louis Pageant and Masque of 1914," *BMHS* 32 (April 1975),

A HISTORY OF MISSOURI

175–205, revealed a number of strands within that city's progressivism. Oster's "Community Image in the History of St. Louis and Kansas City" (Ph.D. diss., University of Missouri–Columbia, 1969), can be consulted with profit on a number of topics, cultural, social, and political.

William H. Wilson, *The City Beautiful Movement in Kansas City* (Columbia, 1964), is an excellent study of that aspect of Progressivism. See also Edward C. Rafferty, "Orderly City, Orderly Lives: The City Beautiful Movement in St. Louis," *GH* 11 (spring 1991), 40–62, and his "George Edward Kessler," *GH* 11 (spring 1991), 63–65. Larry L. Hunt, "A Missouri Newspaper Views Progressivism: The Unterrified Democrat and Missouri Reform, 1904–1908" (master's thesis, Northeast Missouri State University, 1982) shows how that Osage County weekly paper viewed the movement.

Contemporary assessments of Missouri during the period include Lincoln Steffens and Claude Wetmore, "Tweed Days in St. Louis," *McClure's Magazine,* October 1902, which was reprinted in Lincoln Steffens, *Shame of the Cities* (New York, 1904). Rolla Wells's autobiography, *Episodes of My Life* (St. Louis, 1933) offers that mayor's views of the period. See also "Crooked Politics in Missouri: The Apparitions of the Lobby," *The Search Light: A Monthly Review of Missouri Politics* 1 (March 1902); Frank Tyrrell, *Political Thuggery or Bribery, A National Issue* (St. Louis, 1904); and John D. Lawson, ed., "The Litigation and Prosecution of Businessmen and City Officials in St. Louis from 1902–1904 by Attorney Joseph Folk," *American State Trials* 9 (St. Louis, 1918).

AFRICAN AMERICANS, RACE, AND MISSOURI POLITICS

The complex role of African Americans and race in Missouri politics from 1875 to 1919 has been the subject of several valuable studies. The most important treatment is Lorenzo Greene, Gary R. Kremer, and Antonio F. Holland, *Missouri's Black Heritage* (Rev. ed., Columbia, 1993). Gary R. Kremer's *James Milton Turner and the Promise of America: The Public Life of a Post–Civil War Black Leader* (Columbia, 1991), shows why one must be careful in making broad generalizations about race relations during the period. Larry H. Grothaus, "The Negro in Missouri Politics, 1890–1941" (Ph.D. diss., University of Missouri, 1970), is the best study of race and politics. Lawrence O. Christensen, "Black St. Louis: A Study in Race Relations, 1865–1916" (Ph.D. diss., University of

Missouri, 1972) contains a good deal on the politics of race during this period. His "The Racial Views of John W. Wheeler," *MHR* 67 (July 1973), 535–47, discusses that black newspaper editor's approach to politics, among other things. See also his "J. Milton Turner: An Appraisal," *MHR* 70 (October 1975), 1–19, and "Race Relations in St. Louis 1865–1916," *MHR* 78 (January 1984), 123–36. David T. Kelleher, "St. Louis' 1916 Residential Segregation Ordinance," *BMHS* 26 (April 1970), 239–48, discusses the politics of that topic.

Other studies that shed light on the question include Howard F. Fisher, "The Negro in St. Louis Politics" (master's thesis, Washington University, 1951); Merle Fainsod, "The Influence of Racial and National Groups in St. Louis Politics, 1908–1928" (master's thesis, Washington University, 1929); and Henry Winfield Wheeler, *History of the St. Louis Branch of the NAACP* (St. Louis, 1953). See also Martha Cooper, *Life and the Pursuit of Happiness: Nodaway County Missouri, A Black History, 1840–1940* (1986); and Suzanna Maria Grenz, "The Black Community in Boone County Missouri, 1850–1900" (Ph.D. diss., University of Missouri–Columbia, 1979).

Finally, there is a wealth of information on black politics in the columns of the *St. Louis Palladium* (1903–1907), the *Kansas City Call* (1890–1920), and the *St. Louis Argus* (1915–1920). George E. Slavens's "A History of the Missouri Negro Press" (Ph.D. diss., University of Missouri–Columbia, 1969) is valuable for understanding the black press and Missouri politics in the era.

ECONOMICS

Use of the extensive United States Census records is essential in writing economic history. Compiled every ten years, the census material provides statistical analysis of a wide variety of activities, including manufacturing, agriculture, population changes, religion, education, housing, and many other aspects of life. Using the census materials becomes easier with experience, but always requires diligence. What federal officials collected in the censuses is varied. Census data for 1870, 1880, 1890, 1900, and 1910 are quite rich and extensive. Good material can be gleaned from reports of state agencies as well. The *Annual Reports of the Missouri Bureau of Labor Statistics* (1879–1919) contain a vast array of data on every aspect of workers' lives that informed this presentation.

Newspapers from the period are invaluable, and the weekly Bethany, Edina, Boonville, Kennett, and Mount Vernon papers, along with the metropolitan dailies, informed this study.

The journalist/historian Walter Williams put together a very significant work published as *The State of Missouri: An Autobiography,* which appeared in 1904. Authors included such writers as historians Jonas Viles and Isidor Loeb; geologist C. F. Marbut; agriculture dean H. J. Waters; animal husbandry professor F. B. Mumford; horticulturist L. A. Goodman; botanist B. M. Duggar; and urbanists Ripley D. Saunders and William F. Saunders on St. Louis, W. C. Winsborough on Kansas City, M. E. Mayer and John L. Bittinger on St. Joseph, Joel Livingston on Joplin, William Johnston on Springfield, Charles E. Yeater on Sedalia, S. J. Roy on Hannibal, Hugh Stephens on Jefferson City, H. L. Bright on Carthage, and H. A. Gardner on Webb City. Financed as a part of the $1 million appropriation by the Missouri General Assembly for the Louisiana Purchase Exposition, the volume is a primary source that proved quite useful in discussing the economic condition of Missouri. Of course, David March's *A History of Missouri* provided important material.

COMMUNITY STUDIES

No one interested in the economic and social life of communities should miss the outstanding book by Lewis E. Atherton, *Main Street on the Middle Border* (Bloomington, Ind., 1954). On St. Louis, James Neal Primm's *Lion of the Valley* is filled with good economic material, showing Primm's ability as an economic historian. A. Theodore Brown and Lyle W. Dorsett, *K.C.: A History of Kansas City, Missouri* is particularly strong on economic history. Other community studies that provide information appeared as a result of celebrations of the bicentennial of the Declaration of Independence in 1976. Among the most useful to us have been J. Hurley Hagood and Roberta Roland Hagood, *The Story of Hannibal: A Bicentennial History* (Hannibal, 1976) and Lois Roper Beard, *The History of Laclede County, Missouri* (1979). There have been more than one hundred such studies, most of which can be found in the State Historical Society of Missouri on the University of Missouri–Columbia campus and in the Curtis Laws Wilson Library on the campus of the University of Missouri–Rolla. A good place to find reviews and listings of community studies is in the *Missouri Historical Review*. The *Review* also annually lists master's theses and doctoral dissertations on Missouri topics and lists articles on Missouri that have appeared in newspapers and periodicals.

Among the best scholarly studies of communities are Robert L. Dyer, *Boonville, An Illustrated History* (Marceline, 1987); Michael Cassity, *Defending a Way of Life: An American Community in the Nineteenth Century* (Albany, N.Y., 1989); Alan R. Havig, *Columbia: From Southern Village to Midwestern City* (Woodland Hills, Calif., 1981); G. K. Renner, *Joplin: From Mining Town to Urban Center* (Northridge, Calif., 1985); Sheridan A. Logan, *Old St. Jo: Gateway to the West, 1799–1932* (St. Joseph, 1979); and Harris Dark and Phyllis Dark, *Springfield of the Ozarks* (Woodland Hills, Calif., 1981). Different from these studies but nevertheless quite informative about community economic life is Loren Reid's *Hurry Home Wednesday: Growing Up in a Small Missouri Town, 1905–1920* (Columbia, 1978). An informative article on an African American community is Gary R. Kremer and Lynn Morrow, "Pennytown: A Freedmen's Hamlet, 1871–1945," *Missouri Folklore Society Journal* 11 and 12 (1989–1990), 77–92. Susan Curtis Mernitz, "Church, Class, and Community: The Impact of Industrialization on Lexington, Missouri, 1870–1900" (master's thesis, University of Missouri–Columbia, 1981) provides a perspective on that community.

Geographers Milton Rafferty and Russel L. Gerlach have contributed materials on economics. Rafferty, Gerlach, and Dennis J. Hrebec published the very useful *Atlas of Missouri* (Springfield, 1970). Rafferty also wrote *Ozarks; Land and Life* (Norman, Okla., 1980). Gerlach produced *Settlement Patterns in Missouri: A Study of Population Origins, with a Wall Map* (Columbia, 1986), which provides information on economic life. One can profit from reading a couple of volumes produced by Marian M. Ohman published by the University of Missouri–Columbia Extension Division: *A History of Missouri's Counties, County Seats and Courthouse Squares* (1983) and *Twenty Towns: Their Histories, Town Plans and Architecture* (1985).

URBAN GROWTH

Primm's *Lion of the Valley* and Brown's and Dorsett's *K.C.* discuss the growth of those cities. The story of St. Louis's growth during the early part of this period is the special focus in Wyatt Winton Belcher's *The Economic Rivalry between St. Louis and Chicago, 1850–1880* (New York, 1947). J. Christopher Schnell, "Chicago Versus St. Louis: A Reassessment of the Great Rivalry," *MHR* 71 (April 1977), 245–65, looked at Belcher's argument again. Another perspective is provided by Johnathon Lurie, "The Chicago Board of Trade, The Merchants Exchange of St. Louis, and the Great Bucket Shop War, 1882–1905," *BMHS* 29 (July 1973), 243–59. St. Louis's struggle with prostitution is addressed in Duane R. Sneddeker, "Regulating Vice: Prostitution and the St. Louis Social Evil Ordinance, 1870–1874," *GH* 11 (fall 1990), 20–47. The 1877 strike is the subject of David T. Burbank's *Reign of the Rabble: The St. Louis General Strike of 1877* (New York, 1966).

RAILROADS

Charles N. Glaab documents the significance of the railroads to Kansas City's growth in *Kansas City and the Railroads: Community Policy in the Growth of a Regional Metropolis* (Madison, Wis., 1962). Useful is V. V. Masterson, *The Katy Railroad and the Last Frontier,* with a new foreword by Donovan L. Hofsommer (Columbia, 1988), originally published in 1952 by the University of Oklahoma Press. H. Craig Miner wrote *The St. Louis–San Francisco Transcontinental Railroad* (Lawrence, Kans., 1972), and "The Colonization of the St. Louis and San Francisco Railway Company, 1880–1882: A Study in Corporate Diplomacy," *MHR* 63 (April 1969), 345–63. An important work on railroads remains John W. Million's *State Aid to Railways in Missouri* (Chicago, 1896). See also Edwin L. Lopata, *Local Aid to Railroads in Missouri* (New York, 1973). A broad survey on railroad debt is provided in E. M. Violette, "The Missouri and Mississippi Railroad Debt," *MHR* 15 (April 1921), 487–518, and (July 1921), 617–47. H. Roger Grant showed the desire to attract railroads in "Courting the Great Western Railway: An Episode of Town Rivalry," *MHR* 76 (July 1982), 405–20; and John Hall Dalton Jr., "Dunklin County, Charles P. Chouteau, and the Courtship of the Iron Horse," *MHR* 82 (October 1987), 71–96, discussed the same subject. For railroad development in Mount Vernon one should consult the Farmer's Bank Papers, George A. McCanse Correspondence in the Western Historical Manuscript Collection, University of Missouri–Columbia campus. See also Edward J. White, "A Century of Transportation in Missouri," *MHR*

15 (October 1920), 126–62. David Thelen's *Paths of Resistance* offers a different view of attitudes toward railroad development.

MINING

Mining in the late nineteenth and twentieth centuries has been neglected by historians of Missouri and is an area wide open for researchers. Iron mining has been the subject of Arthur B. Cozzens, "The Iron Industry in Missouri," *MHR* 35 (July 1940), 509–38, and 36 (October 1941), 48–60, and of Jack B. Ridley, "Mining and Manufacturing in a Frontier Environment: The Iron Industry in South Central Missouri in the Nineteenth Century," *Locus* 1 (spring 1989), 13–30. A. M. Gibson, "Lead Mining in Southwest Missouri after 1865," *MHR* 53 (July 1959), 315–28, provides a brief survey of that metal. Gibson wrote a larger work on mining in southwest Missouri, *Wilderness Bonanza* (Norman, 1972). Coal mining has received attention from Sam T. Bratton, "Coal in Missouri," *MHR* 22 (January 1928), 150–56, and Stephen Emery Daniels, "Coal Mining in Northeast Missouri, 1850–1920" (master's thesis, Northeast Missouri State University, 1968); also on coal mining see Russell J. Clemens, "The Development of a Market Economy: Bates County, Missouri, 1875–1890," *BMHS* 35 (October 1978), 28–35. In 1968 the State Historical Society of Wisconsin published James D. Norris's *AZn: A History of the American Zinc Company*, which discussed that business's efforts in Missouri. G. K. Renner's earlier mentioned book on Joplin treats the subject of mining, and George Suggs Jr.'s *Union Busting in the Tri-State: The Oklahoma, Kansas and Missouri Metal Workers Strike of 1935* (Norman, 1985) provides material that is useful. Another discussion of extraction and labor difficulties is Gregg Andrews, "Immigrant Cement Workers: The Strike of 1910 in Ilasco, Missouri," *MHR* 89 (January 1995), 162–83.

CONVICT LABOR

The issue of the use of convict labor for profit, both by individual entrepreneurs and by the state of Missouri, has been the subject of several articles. Among the most useful are Bruce Reynolds, "Convict Labor, The Montserrat Experience," *MHR* 77 (October 1982), 47–63; Gary R. Kremer, "'Strangers to Domestic Virtues': Nineteenth Century Women in the Missouri Prison," *MHR* 84 (April 1990), 293–310, and Kremer,

"Politics, Punishment and Profit: Convict Labor in the Missouri State Penitentiary, 1875–1900," *GH* 13 (summer 1992), 28–40, and Kremer and Thomas E. Gage, "The Prison against the Town: Jefferson City and the Penitentiary in the Nineteenth Century," *MHR* 74 (July 1980), 414–32. These works supplement a firsthand account of convict labor by John N. Reynolds, *The Twin Hells: A Thrilling Narrative of Life in the Kansas and Missouri Penitentiaries* (Chicago, 1890).

AGRICULTURE

Frederick B. Mumford, "A Century of Missouri Agriculture," *MHR* 15 (January 1921), 277–97, and his *History of the Missouri College of Agriculture* (Columbia, 1944), are good beginning points. Carl O. Sauer, "Status and Change in the Rural Midwest—A Retrospect," *Mittelungen der Osterreichischen Geographischen Gessellschaft* Band, 105 Heft III (1963), 357–65, deals with Missouri. On the question of the commercialization of agriculture, R. Douglas Hurt, *Agriculture and Slavery in Missouri's Little Dixie* (Columbia, 1992), should be read for its analysis of the antebellum period. For a delightful read and for purposes of comparison with agriculture in South Carolina see Louis B. Wright, *Barefoot in Arcadia* (Columbia, S.C., 1974). Samuel M. Jordan contributed "Farming as It Used To Be and as It Is in Missouri," *MHR* 22 (October 1927), 13–29. Milton D. Rafferty, "Agricultural Change in the Western Ozarks," *MHR* 69 (April 1975), 299–322, treats that region, as does Lynn Morrow's "Modernity and the Current Wave in Shannon County, 1884–1896," *BMHS* 35 (January 1979), 92–98. Also on the Ozarks see Linda Myers-Phinney, "Arcadia in the Ozarks: The Beginnings of Tourism in Missouri's White River Country," *Ozarkswatch* 3 (spring 1990), 6–11. G. K. Renner contributed one piece on the Ozarks, "Strawberry Culture in Southwest Missouri," *MHR* 63 (October 1969), 18–40, and the important general study "The Mule in Missouri Agriculture," *MHR* 74 (July 1980), 433–57. On the nursery business the Lloyd C. Stark Papers in the Western Historical Manuscript Collection has material on apple production in the state. Kenneth W. Keller, "Merchandising Nature: The A. J. Weber and Sons Nursery," *MHR* 89 (April 1995), 307–26, should also be consulted. Robert Gilmore, "The Missouri State Fruit Experiment Station," *Ozarkswatch* 3 (winter 1990), 11 and that publication's issue on "The Farm," 6 (spring 1993), contains interesting information.

The livestock industry has received attention from Larry Allan McFarlane, "The Missouri Land and Live Stock Company, Limited of Scotland: Foreign Investment on the Missouri Farming Frontier, 1882–1908" (Ph.D. diss., University of Missouri, 1962). The development of the livestock industry is also treated in works on the Leonard family, including John Ashton, *Historic Ravenswood: Its Founders and Its Cattle* (Columbia, 1926); Kathryn A. Vogt, "The Missouri Shorthorn Industry: The Leonard Family Legacy," *GH* 2 (spring 1982), 16–23; and James M. Denny, "Vernacular Building Process in Missouri: Nathaniel Leonard's Activities," *MHR* 78 (October 1983), 23–50. L. M. White, "Heart of the Saddle Horse Story of Missouri," *MHR* 50 (January 1956), 121–31, sheds light on that topic. On meatpacking see G. K. Renner, "The Kansas City Meat Packing Industry Before 1900," *MHR* 55 (October 1960), 18–29; Frank S. Popplewell, "St. Joseph, Missouri, as a Center of the Cattle Trade," *MHR* 32 (July 1938), 443–57; and Arthur Charvat, "Growth and Development of the Kansas City Stock Yards—A History" (master's thesis, University of Kansas City, 1948).

MANUFACTURING

Alice Lanterman, "The Development of Kansas City as a Grain and Milling Center," *MHR* 42 (October 1947), 20–23, supplements Brown's and Dorsett's more complete treatment in *K.C.* Missouri is unique in producing corncob pipes, and Paula McNeill Quirk's "The Missouri Meerschaum Pipe," *MHR* 78 (October 1983), 14–22, is a study of that industry. The chief manufacturer of beer received attention in Ronald J. Plavchan, "A History of Anheuser Busch, 1852–1933" (Ph.D. diss., Saint Louis University, 1970). Also useful are Roland Krebs in collaboration with Percy J. Orthwein, *Making Friends Is Our Business: 100 Years of Anheuser-Busch* (St. Louis, 1953), and Peter Hernon and Terry Ganey, *Under the Influence: The Unauthorized Story of the Anheuser-Busch Dynasty* (New York, 1991). Herbert J. Vogt, "Boot and Shoe Industry of St. Louis" (master's thesis, Washington University, 1929), and Maxine F. Fendlenman, "Saint Louis Shoe Manufacturing" (master's thesis, Washington University, 1947) wrote on that important industry.

LABOR

Besides Gary M. Fink's important book and the *Annual Reports of the Missouri Bureau of Labor Statistics,* the John Samuel Papers at the State

Historical Society of Wisconsin proved helpful. Lee Meriwether headed the Bureau of Labor for some years and wrote about his life during this period in two autobiographies, *My Yesteryears: An Autobiography,* (Webster Groves, Mo., 1942), and *My First 100 Years, 1862–1962* (St. Louis, n.d.). For a brief survey see his "Labor and Industry in Missouri During the Last Century," *MHR* 15 (October 1920), 163–75.

LUMBER

Thomas E. Gage, "The Promise of Progress: Ripley County and the Lumber Industry, 1880–1910" (unpublished research paper, 1991), proved very helpful. Dissertations on this topic include Leslie G. Hill, "History of the Missouri Lumber and Mining Company, 1880–1909" (Ph.D. diss., University of Missouri, 1949); John A. Galloway, "John Barber White: Lumberman" (Ph.D. diss., University of Missouri, 1961); James Lee Murphy, "A History of the Southeastern Ozark Region of Missouri" (Ph.D. diss., Saint Louis University, 1982). The man who made the development of southeast Missouri possible wrote an autobiography: Otto Kochtitzky, *The Story of a Busy Life* (Cape Girardeau, 1957, a reprint of the 1931 edition). The Western Historical Manuscript Collection on the University of Missouri–Columbia campus has the Missouri Lumber and Mining Company Papers. See also "Story of a Great Enterprise," *The American Lumberman,* May 9, 1903. For a fine biography of a lumberman see Lenore K. Bradley, *Robert Alexander Long: A Lumberman of the Gilded Age* (Durham, N.C., 1989).

OTHER STUDIES

On banking see Breckinridge Jones, "One Hundred Years of Banking in Missouri," *MHR* 15 (January 1921), 345–92. On insurance see H. Roger Grant, "W. D. Vandiver and the 1905 Life Insurance Scandals," *BMHS* 29 (October 1972), 5–19. On taxation see Frederick N. Judson, *A Treatise on the Law and Practice of Taxation in Missouri* (Columbia, 1900).

SOCIAL, CULTURAL, AND EDUCATIONAL LIFE

While the general secondary works listed in the bibliographic essay on politics are important for an understanding of Missouri's social, cultural, and educational development during this period, one could

ESSAY ON SOURCES

find no more important body of records to consult than the newspapers published throughout the state during the period 1875–1920. We have found especially helpful the following: *Lawrence* [Mount Vernon] *Chieftain,* [Bethany] *Republican, Sedalia Weekly Democrat, St. Louis Globe-Democrat,* [Osage County] *Unterrified Democrat, Boonville Weekly Advertiser,* [Jefferson City] *State Journal,* [Kennett] *Clipper,* [Gasconade County] *Advertiser-Courier, Iron County Register,* [Jefferson City] *People's Tribune, Pike County Post, Glasgow Journal, Kirksville Journal, Knox County Democrat, St. Louis Post-Dispatch,* [St. Joseph] *Herald,* [Jefferson City] *State Times, Joplin Daily News,* [Columbia] *Herald, Sedalia Weekly Bazoo, Hartville Democrat,* and *Wright County Republican.*

EDUCATION

The annual reports of the State Department of Education provide useful information on educational developments in Missouri during the period under consideration. The reaction against the Drake Constitution and its effect on education is told by Arthur E. Lee, "The Decline of Radicalism and Its Effect on Public Education in Missouri," *MHR* 74 (October 1979), 1–20. Education in St. Louis during this period is the subject of Selwyn K. Troen, *The Public and the Schools: Shaping the St. Louis System, 1838–1920* (Columbia, 1975). Supplements to Troen's work include Richard Ives, "Compulsory Education and the St. Louis Public School System 1905–1907," *MHR* 71 (April 1977), 315–29. The development of education in Columbia and Boone County occupies a significant part of John C. Crighton's *A History of Columbia and Boone County* (Columbia, 1987). The history of education in Missouri's capital city is told in Jerena East Giffen, *The House on Hobo Hill: The History of the Jefferson City Public Schools* (Jefferson City, 1964). J. Merton England's "Hard Times Chronicler—An Ohio Teacher in Western Missouri, 1879–1881," *MHR* 83 (April 1989), 311–29, provides insight into education in rural Missouri during the late nineteenth century. Another older regional work that provides information on education is Robert Sidney Douglass, *History of Southeast Missouri* (New York and Chicago, 1912). Rural education in Missouri during the early twentieth century is the subject of Ruther Warner Towne, "Marie Turner Harvey and the Rural Life Movement," *MHR* 84 (July 1990), 384–403. Also of help is Carol Piper Heming, "*Schulhaus* to Schoolhouse: The German School

263

at Hermann, Missouri, 1839–1955," *MHR* 82 (April 1988), 280–98; *Rural and Small Town Schools in Livingston County, Missouri,* compiled by Leo Hopper (1986); and *The History of Rural Schools of Putnam County, 1843–1965,* compiled by the Putnam County Historical Society (1986). The only book-length history of Missouri's public higher institution of learning for African Americans remains W. Sherman Savage, *A History of Lincoln University* (Jefferson City, 1938). Also useful is Savage's "The Legal Provisions for Negro Schools in Missouri from 1865 to 1890," *Journal of Negro History* 26 (July 1931), 309–21 and Patrick J. Huber and Gary R. Kremer, "Nathaniel C. Bruce, Black Education and the 'Tuskegee of the Midwest,'" *MHR* (October 1991), 37–54.

The University of Missouri has received much historical attention. The latest book-length study is James and Vera Olson, *The University of Missouri: An Illustrated History* (Columbia, 1988). Earlier studies include Jonas Viles, *The University of Missouri: A Centennial History* (Columbia, 1939), and Frank J. Stephens, *A History of the University of Missouri* (Columbia, 1962). For the Rolla campus see Lawrence O. Christensen and Jack B. Ridley, *UM–Rolla: A History of UMR/MSM* (Columbia, 1983). Pamela Ann Miner, "Rise Like a Phoenix: The Creation of Francis Quadrangle," *MHR* 84 (October 1989), 42–62, discusses the university during the 1890s. That entire issue of the *Review* is devoted to various aspects of the university's history. A glimpse of life at Central Missouri State Normal School is contained in Susan Lee Pentlin, "The Study of German at the Warrensburg Normal School," *MHR* 83 (July 1989), 395–416.

There have been a number of useful histories of private colleges begun in Missouri during the period of this study: Cathryn Coe Craig and Jone Craig Naylor, *Tarkio College, 1883–1992: An Illustrated History of 'The Crown of the Hill'* (Rock Port, 1992); Leta Hodge, *Soldiers, Scholars, Gentlemen: The First One Hundred Years of the Missouri Military Academy* (Mexico, 1988). The story of Southwest Baptist College is told in Mayme Lucille Hamlett, *To Noonday Bright: The Story of Southwest Baptist University, 1878–1984* (Bolivar, 1984). Frank W. Clippinger and Lisa A. Cooper detail the history of Drury College in *The Drury Story* (Springfield, Mo., 1982). Also useful is William E. Parrish, *Westminster College; An Informal History* (Fulton, 1971).

For attitudes toward women in higher education during the period of this study, see Lucinda de Leftwich Templin, "Some Defects and Merits in the Education of Women in Missouri" (Ph.D. diss., University of Missouri, 1926). Templin's work should be supplemented by Janice Lee, "Administrative Treatment of Women Students at Missouri State University, 1868–1899," *MHR* 87 (July 1993), 372–86 and Lawrence O. Christensen, "Being Special: Women Students at the Missouri School of Mines and Metallurgy," *MHR* 83 (October 1988), 17–35. Also useful is Debbie Mauldin Cottrell, "Mount Holyoke of the Midwest: Virginia Alice Cottey, Mary Lyon, and the Founding of the Vernon Seminary for Young Ladies," *MHR* 90 (January 1996), 187–98.

The life of the founder of Missouri's School of Osteopathy is chronicled in Carol Trowbridge, *Andrew Taylor Still, 1828–1917* (Kirksville, 1991) and Charles E. Still Jr., *Frontier Doctor–Medical Pioneer: The Life and Times of A. T. Still and His Family* (Kirksville, 1991).

ARCHITECTURE

Among the important works on architecture and city planning to be produced are Lawrence Lowie, *The Architectural Heritage of St. Louis, 1803–1891: From the Louisiana Purchase to the Wainwright Building* (St. Louis, 1982), Charles C. Savage, *Architecture of the Private Places of St. Louis: The Architects and the Houses They Designed* (Columbia, 1987). The City Beautiful Movement in St. Louis is the subject of several essays, including Edward C. Rafferty, "The City Beautiful Movement in St. Louis," *GH* 11 (spring 1991), 40–62, and Renee West, "No Contradiction Here: Beauty and Utility during St. Louis's City Beautiful Era," *GH* 14 (summer 1993), 34–45. Also useful for the study of homes and their interiors are Katharine J. Corbett, "Gilded Images: St. Louis in the Industrial Age," *GH* 14 (summer 1993), 26–33, and Marsha S. Bray, "The Power of Home: St. Louis Victorian Interiors," *GH* 12 (spring 1992), 42–47. William H. Wilson's *The City Beautiful Movement in Kansas City* (Columbia, 1964) covers that important movement in Missouri's second-largest city of the period. The life and work of planner and promoter J. C. Nichols is chronicled in William S. Worley, *J. C. Nichols and the Shaping of Kansas City* (Columbia, 1990) and Robert Pearson and Brad Pearson, *The J. C. Nichols Chronicle: The Authorized Story of the Man, His Company, and His Legacy, 1880–1994* (Kansas City, 1994). Also important are Richard D. McKinzie and Sherry Lamb Schirmer, *At the River's Bend: An Illustrated History of Kansas City, Independence, and Jackson County, Missouri* (Woodland Hills, Calif., 1982) and George Ehrlich's "Partnership Practice and the Professionalization of Architecture in Kansas City, Missouri," *MHR* 74 (July 1980), 458–80 and his *Kansas City, Missouri: An Architectural History, 1826–1990,* Revised and enlarged edition, (Columbia, 1992). The career of Kansas City architect Louis Curtiss is chronicled in *Stalking Louis Curtiss* by Wilda Sandy with Larry K. Hanks (Kansas City, 1991), and that of Kansas Citian Nelle Peters in "The Architectural Career of Nelle Peters," *MHR* 83 (January 1989), 161–76.

Arguably, one of the most underused historical collections in the state is the archives of the State Historic Preservation Office of the Missouri Department of Natural Resources, Jefferson City. Cultural Resource Surveys and National Register Nominations are located there by county. We found especially helpful a national register nomination of the Burkholder-O'Keefe House [Randolph County] completed by James M. Denny and a national register nomination of the Pennytown Freewill Baptist Church [Saline County] completed by Lynn Morrow. Among the cultural resource surveys we consulted were ones done by Lynn Morrow on Saline County, Gary R. Kremer on Osage County, and Eslee Hamilton on Hannibal, Missouri.

LITERATURE

The career of Missouri poet and writer Eugene Field is the subject of Lewis O. Saum's essay, " 'Solomon Burch's Fighting Editor': An Early Poem of Eugene Field," *MHR* 89 (October 1994), 17–27, and his essay "Missouri's 'Monumental Ananias': 'Gene Field Looks Back," *MHR* 86 (January 1992), 113–26. See also Bonnie Stepenoff, "Freedom and Regret: The Dilemma of Kate Chopin," *MHR* 81 (July 1987), 447–66.

ENTERTAINMENT

The role of the railroads in advancing hunting, fishing, and recreation in Missouri is covered in Richard West Sellars, "Early Promotion and Development of Missouri's Natural Resources" (Ph.D. diss., University of Missouri, 1972). Also useful is Juanita J. Dempsey, "History of Parks and Recreation, City of St. Louis" (master's thesis, University of Missouri–Columbia, 1983). Recreation in northwest Missouri is the subject of Clyde Weeks, *Lake Contrary: Days of Glory, 1880–1964* (St. Joseph, 1992). The story of one of the oldest resort centers in the Midwest is told in *Noel, Missouri, 1887–1987,* compiled by the Noel Centennial Book Committee (1987). Also of great interest is Linda Myers-Phinney, "The Land of a Million Smiles: Tourism and Modernization in Taney County and Stone County, Missouri, 1900–1930" (master's thesis, Southwest Missouri State University). Rural entertainment is the subject of Robert K. Gilmore, *Ozark Baptizings, Hangings, and Other Diversions: Theatrical Folkways of Rural Missouri, 1885–1910* (Norman, Okla., 1984). The theater in Missouri is the subject of Harlan Jennings, "Grand Opera in St. Louis, 1886: A Championship Season?" *MHR* 85 (April 1991), 304–20, Miles W. Coiner Jr., "The Grand Opera House and the Golden Age of the Legitimate Theatre in Kansas City," *MHR* 67 (April 1973), 407–23 and Joe E. Smith, "Early Movies and Their Impact on Columbia," *MHR* 74 (October 1979), 72–85.

The history of the St. Louis Symphony Orchestra is chronicled in Richard E. Mueller, *A Century of the Symphony* (St. Louis, 1979) and Katherine Gladney Wells, *Symphony and Song: The Saint Louis Symphony Orchestra: The First Hundred Years 1880–1980* (Woodstock, Vt., 1980). For entertainment in Kansas City, see Alan Havig, "Mass Commercial Amusements in Kansas City before World War I," *MHR* 75 (April 1981), 316–45.

The 1904 World's Fair has been the subject of much writing, including David R. Francis, ed., *The Universal Exposition of 1904* (St. Louis, 1913), Dorothy Daniels Birk, *The World Came to St. Louis: A Visit to the 1904 World's Fair* (St. Louis, 1979), and Mark Dyreson, "The Playing Fields of Progress: American Athletic Nationalism and the 1904 Olympics," *GH* 14 (fall 1993), 4–23. Other articles include Stuart Seely Sprague, "Meet Me in St. Louis on the Ten-Million Dollar Pike," *BHMS* 32 (October 1975), 26–32; Eugene F. Provenzo Jr., "Education and the Louisiana Purchase Exposition," *BHMS* 32 (January 1976), 99–109; Jane Anne Liebenguth, "Music at the Louisiana Purchase Exposition," *BHMS* 36 (October 1979), 27–34; and Robert A. Trennert, "A Resurrection of Native Arts and Crafts: The St. Louis World Fair, 1904," *MHR* 87 (April 1993), 274–92. For the Chicago Fair of 1893 see Frank A. Cassell, "Missouri and the Columbia Exposition of 1893," *MHR* 80 (July 1986), 369–94. The emergence of the Veiled Prophet celebration is detailed in Thomas Spencer, "Power on Parade: The

Origins of the Veiled Prophet Celebration in St. Louis," *GH* 14 (fall 1993), 39–53.

The rise of professional baseball as a source of entertainment during the late nineteenth century is also the subject of a number of works, among them Rob Rains, *The St. Louis Cardinals: The 100th Anniversary History* (New York, 1992), and Jim Rygelski, "Baseball's 'Boss President': Chris von der Ahe and the Nineteenth-Century St. Louis Browns," *GH* 13 (summer 1992), 42–53.

The story of ragtime and its rise to prominence at the turn of the century is told in Rudi Blesh and Harriet Janis, *They All Played Ragtime: The True Story of an American Music* (New York: 1950). Also useful is William E. Parrish, "Blind Boone's Ragtime," *Missouri Life* (November–December 1979), 17–23 and Susan Curtis, *Dancing to a Black Man's Tune: A Life of Scott Joplin* (Columbia, 1994).

JOURNALISM

A good general work on newspapers of the era is William H. Taft, *Missouri Newspapers and the Missouri Press Association: 125 Years of Service, 1867–1992* (Marceline, 1992). It should be supplemented by Taft's "Establishing the School of Journalism," *MHR* 84 (October 1989), 63–82 and J. W. Barrett, *History and Transactions of the Editors' and Publishers' Association of Missouri, 1867–1876* (Canton, 1876). The story of the *St. Louis Post-Dispatch* is told in Julian S. Rammelkamp, *Pulitzer's Post-Dispatch, 1878–1883* (Princeton, 1967). Theodore Pease Russell penned an "Old Times" column for the *Iron County Register* from 1884 until his death in 1899. Many of those columns have been reproduced with helpful commentary by James F. Keefe and Lynn Morrow, eds., *A Connecticut Yankee in the Frontier Ozarks: The Writings of Theodore Pease Russell* (Columbia, 1988). Jim Allee Hart, *A History of the Globe-Democrat* (Columbia, 1961) tells the story of that important newspaper during this period. Loren Reid offers a memoir of growing up in a family that owned a weekly newspaper in his *Hurry Home Wednesday: Growing Up in a Small Missouri Town, 1905–1921* (Columbia, 1978). Leslie Francis Pike's *Ed Watson—Country Editor, His Life and Times* (Marceline, 1982) tells the story of a longtime editor of the *Columbia Daily Tribune*. The story of the black press during this period is told in George Everett Slavens, "The Missouri Negro Press 1875–1920," *Missouri Historical Review* 64 (July

1973), 535–47 and Lawrence O. Christensen, "The Racial Views of John W. Wheeler," *MHR* 67 (July 1973), 535–47.

CLUBS AND ORGANIZATIONS

The State Historical Society of Missouri's collection contains numerous official publications for a number of men's and women's social organizations for this period, among them the Ancient Free and Accepted Masons, the Knights of Pythias, and the Sisters of Jericho. For the story of one African American's experience with masonry, see Gary R. Kremer, "The World of Make-Believe: James Milton Turner and Black Masonry," *MHR* 74 (October 1979), 50–71. Little has been written on the women's club movement in Missouri. For a biography of a leading club woman, see Janice Brandon-Falcone, "Biography as Prism: The Life of C. F. Runcie (Ph.D. diss., Saint Louis University, 1990). Also helpful is Brandon-Falcone's essay "'It Pays Me Well and Is a Good Thing:' The Club Life of Constance Runcie," *GH* 15 (winter 1994–95), 56–65. For black women's clubs, see Gary R. Kremer and Cindy M. Mackey, "'Yours for the Race': The Life and Work of Josephine Silone Yates," *MHR* 90 (January 1996), 199–215. The lives and activities of women during this period are further revealed in diaries they kept and letters they wrote. Among the most useful compilations of such documents are the following: Adolf E. Schroeder and Carla Schulz-Geisberg, eds., *Hold Dear As Always: Jette, a German Immigrant Life in Letters* (Columbia, 1988) and Dorothy Heckman Shrader, ed., *Steamboat Legacy: The Life and Times of a Steamboat Family,* with an Introduction by John Hartford (Hermann, 1993).

The role of private organizations in helping the poor is told in Jeanette C. Lauer and Robert H. Lauer, "The St. Louis Provident Association: An Elitist War on Poverty, 1860–1899," *MHR* 77 (April 1983), 296–309.

RELIGION

Among the helpful works on religion during the period of this study are the following: Louis W. Potts, "Waves of Revivalism, 1840–1918," *MHR* 88 (April 1994), 262–278. Joseph H. Hall, *Presbyterian Conflict and Resolution on the Missouri Frontier* (Lewiston, N.Y., 1987), covers Missouri to the end of the nineteenth century. The story of the Baptists in Missouri is told in *Frontiers: The Story of the Missouri Baptist Convention* (Jefferson City, 1983), and in Jo Colay Ray, *These Little Ones: The History of the Missouri Baptist Children's Home* (Bridgeton, 1986).

WORLD WAR I

The Western Historical Manuscript Collection in the University of Missouri–Columbia holds crucial collections for the study of World War I in Missouri. The Frederick B. Mumford Papers reveal efforts to organize the state, as do the Missouri Council of Defense Papers. *The Final Report of the Missouri Council of Defense* summarizes that organization's work. The Blanche L. Howard Stephens Papers record women's support of the war effort. The Enoch H. Crowder Papers and the Harry L. Kempster Papers are also useful. Newspapers proved invaluable in measuring the way local communities responded to the war effort. In attempting to judge responses in rural Missouri the *Bethany Republican, Knox County Democrat* [Edina], *Boonville Weekly Advertiser, Lawrence Chieftain* [Mount Vernon], and *Kennett Clipper* were systematically read for the war years. Note that each paper represents a region of Missouri: Bethany in the northwest, Edina in the northeast, Boonville in the center, Mount Vernon in the southwest, and Kennett in the southeast. Other newspapers were also consulted, all of which are available in the Newspaper Collection of the State Historical Society of Missouri in Columbia.

As on any topic dealing with Missouri history, David March's *The History of Missouri* (4 vols., New York, 1967) proved most informative. Floyd C. Shoemaker wrote a series of articles on the war under the title "Missouri and the War," which appeared in *MHR* 12 (October 1917), 22–32; 12 (January 1918), 90–100; 12 (April 1918), 180–95; 12 (July 1918), 240–58; 13 (October 1918), 1–35; and 13 (July 1919), 319–60. He used the same title for an essay in the *Official Manual of Missouri, 1917–1918*, 299–313. The *Official Manual, 1919–1920* also published a piece submitted by the adjutant general's office entitled "Missouri in the War with Germany," 367–86. John C. Crighton, *Missouri and the World War, 1914–1917: A Study in Public Opinion* (Columbia, 1947) is a standard and good study of the topic. Christopher C. Gibbs, *The Great Silent Majority: Missouri's Resistance to World War I* (Columbia, 1988) offers a different interpretation of Missouri's participation in the war than is argued here. One should also see two articles by Gibbs, "Missouri

Farmers and World War One; Resistance to Mobilization," *BMHS* 35 (October 1978), 17–27, and "The Lead Belt Riot and World War One," *MHR* 72 (July 1977), 396–418. Ruth Warner Towne's *Senator William J. Stone and the Politics of Compromise* (Port Washington, N.Y., 1979) documents the struggle that influential Missourian went through as the country engaged in war. In five previously published articles Lawrence O. Christensen interpreted the war in Missouri, see: "Missouri's Responses to World War I: The Missouri Council of Defense," *The Midwest Review: A Journal of the History and Culture of the Missouri Valley*, 12 (second series 1990), 34–44; "Popular Reaction to World War I in Missouri," *MHR* 86 (July 1992), 386–95; "Prelude to World War I," *MHR* 89 (October 1994), 1–16; and "World War I in Missouri, Part 1," *MHR* 90 (April 1996), 330–54, and "World War I in Missouri, Part 2," *MHR* 90 (July 1996), 410–18. Phillip A. Grant, "Missourians In Congress, 1916–1920," *BMHS* 34 (April 1981), 151–56, sheds some light on their response to the war. See also Jerald K. Pfabe, "Missouri Congressmen and Neutrality: 1914–1917," (master's thesis, Saint Louis University, 1962) and Franziska Pawlenda Janes, "The St. Louis German Press and World War I, 1914–1917" (master's thesis, Saint Louis University, 1968).

James Neal Primm in *Lion of the Valley: St. Louis, Missouri* (Boulder, 1981) ably covers aspects of that city's reaction to the war. David W. Detjen, *The Germans in Missouri, 1900–1918: Prohibition, Neutrality, and Assimilation* (Columbia, 1985) provides the responses of large groups to the outbreak of war in Europe and to United States participation in the fighting. For Missouri's African American participation in the war see Lorenzo J. Greene, Gary R. Kremer, and Antonio F. Holland, *Missouri's Black Heritage* (Revised ed., Columbia, 1993). For the Italo-American view of the war see Gary Ross Mormino, "Over Here: St. Louis Italo-Americans and the First World War," *BMHS* 29 (October 1973), 44–53. Gary M. Fink, *Labor's Search for Political Order: The Political Behavior of the Missouri Labor Movement, 1890–1940* (Columbia, 1973) makes clear how labor leaders approached wartime conditions.

Contemporary and more specialized studies that proved useful included Frederick B. Mumford, "A Century of Missouri Agriculture," *MHR* 15 (January 1921), 277–97; C. A. Phillips, "A Century of Education in Missouri," *MHR* 15 (January 1921), 298–314; J. C. Wooley, "Agricultural Engineering" and "Animal Husbandry" (typescript) in Frederick B. Mumford Papers, WHMC, Columbia; Harvey C.

Clark, "Missourians In Service," *MHR* 14 (October 1919), 1–15; and William D. McCain, "The Papers of the Food Administration for Missouri, 1917–1919, in the National Archives," *MHR* 32 (October 1937), 56–61. For the role of the Missouri Farm Bureau, see Vera B. Schuttler, *A History of the Missouri Farm Bureau Federation* (Jefferson City, 1948).

The best general study of the reaction of the United States to the war is David M. Kennedy, *Over Here: The First World War and American Society* (New York, 1980). Ellis W. Hawley, *The Great War and the Search for a Modern Order: A History of the American People and Their Institutions, 1917–1933* (New York, 1979) is a broad interpretation, is short, and is very readable.

Three works that allow one to put Missouri's activities in clearer perspective by allowing comparisons are George Nox McCain, *War Rations for Pennsylvanians: The Story of the Operations of the Federal Food Administration in Pennsylvania* (Philadelphia, 1920); Nathaniel R. Whitney, *The Sale of War Bonds in Iowa* (Iowa City, 1923); and Ivan L. Pollock, *The Food Administration in Iowa* (Iowa City, 1923). A work that treats the entire effort of the United States Food Administration is William Clinton Mullendore, *History of the United States Food Administration, 1917–1919* (Palo Alto, Calif., 1941). A more recent volume that shows the importance of food in the war effort is C. Paul Vincent, *The Politics of Hunger: The Allied Blockade of Germany, 1915–1919* (Athens, Ohio, 1985). Herbert Hoover provided his own assessment of his work as head of the food administration in *The Memoirs of Herbert Hoover: Years of Adventure* (New York, 1951), and Craig Lloyd studied Hoover's personality in *Aggressive Introvert: A Study of Herbert Hoover and Public Relations Management, 1912–1932* (Columbus, Ohio, 1972).

Other aspects of the war effort are covered in Stephen Vaughn, *Holding Fast the Inner Lines: Democracy, Nationalism and the Committee on Public Information* (Chapel Hill, 1980), and H. C. Peterson and Gilbert C. Fite, *Opponents of War, 1917–1918* (paperback ed., Seattle, 1968). Related to some of the issues raised by Peterson and Fite but focusing on the 1920s is William G. Ross, *Forging New Freedoms: Nativism, Education, and the Constitution, 1917–1927* (Lincoln, Nebr., 1994). Some legal proceedings related to the war are covered in Lawrence H. Larsen, *Federal Justice in Western Missouri: The Judges, the Cases, the Times* (Columbia, 1994). Loren Reid in his delightful *Hurry Home Wednesday: Growing Up in a Small Missouri Town, 1905–1921* (Columbia, 1978) brought the war to Gilman City.

INDEX

Adams, Elmer B., 163
African Americans. *See* Blacks
Agrarian movement, 138, 140, 147
Agriculture: and Panic of 1873, 6;
    grasshopper plague, 9, 44; drought
    of 1881, 15; and commercial roads,
    30; railroads' effects on, 30–32,
    47–49; and economy, 31–32, 47–49,
    100–107; market production of,
    31–33; specialization of, 31, 108;
    scientific techniques for, 32, 33, 213–14;
    agricultural experiment stations, 33; and
    farm laborers' displacement, 34–35; and
    prices, 47–48; children's role in, 53,
    215–16, 221; and land prices, 104–5;
    sheriff's sales, 106–7; and blacks, 112;
    and World War I, 202, 213–22, 229,
    244; and county agents, 214, 220;
    extension service, 214, 215, 220. *See also*
    Farmers
Alcohol consumption, 130–32, 136,
    200. *See also* Prohibitionists and
    prohibitionism
Alexander, J. P., 11
Alexander, Joshua, 202
Allen, Benjamin F., 112
Allen, Henry F., 12–13
Amalgamated Association of Street Railway
    Employees of America, Local 131,
    161–63
American Ambulance Field Service, 235
Americanization Committee, 241–42
Ancient Order of United Workmen, 71
Anderson, Eli T., 107
Anheuser-Busch brewery, 43–44, 86
Antimonopoly movement, 87, 149–58,
    166, 168, 181–84
Anti-Saloon League, 131
Antitrust legislation, 149–58, 168, 181–84
Appleton City, Missouri, 49
Architecture, 74–76, 91, 134

Armour, 90, 168
August Priesmeyer Company, 51
Aurora Federal Farm Loan Association, 218
Automobiles, 123–24, 186
Ava, Missouri, 111

Baer, Sigmond, 234–35
Baldknobbers, 23–24
Bank of Joplin, 41
Banking: and railroads, 41; in urban areas,
    90, 92, 93, 105; and depression of 1890s,
    94; and agriculture, 105–6; and Folk,
    181; and Major, 194; and credit for Great
    Britain and France, 202; and World
    War I, 218
Banks, Hartley H., 231
Baptist Church, 70, 127, 129–30, 131
Bardenheir Company, 87
Barkeloo, Lemma, 60
Barnes Hospital, 235
Barnett, George I., 75
Bartholdt, Richard, 143
Bartlett Agricultural and Industrial School,
    112, 238
Bass, Tom, 104
Beard, Mary R., 165
Behrens, E. T., 192–93
Belmont, Missouri, 179
Benekie, L., 143
Benton, Thomas Hart, 177
Benton Township, 36
Berryman, Jerome, 77
Bethany, Missouri, 80–81, 83, 94, 213,
    231, 233
Bethany Democrat, 200
Bethany Republican: and entertainment, 68;
    and saddle horses, 104; and sheriff's sales,
    107; and automobile, 124; and World
    War I, 208, 211, 232, 236, 240, 242
Bethune, "Blind" Tom, 65
Bevier, Missouri, 98

273

Birch Tree, Missouri, 84
Bishop, R. R., 107
Blackburn, Missouri, 229
Blacks: and Democratic party, 25, 147–49;
    and Republican party, 25, 147–48; vote
    of, 26; and railroads, 45–47; women,
    46–47, 117, 238; education of, 55, 57,
    59, 112–13; segregation of, 55, 57,
    59, 66, 179; discrimination against,
    63–64, 237–39; and music, 63, 132;
    and entertainment, 64–65, 125; and
    sports, 66, 118; holiday festivities of, 68;
    churches of, 70, 128–29; employment
    of, 96; strikes of, 99; and agriculture,
    112; lynching of, 179; and racial tension,
    179–80; and Pendergast, 196; patriotism
    of, 212; and World War I, 236, 237–39;
    and Industrial Workers of the World,
    240
Bland, Richard P., 135, 145–46, 155
Blow, Susan Elizabeth, 56
Blue Valley Creamery, 102
Board of Pardons and Paroles, 194
Bohannon, George, 69
Bolte, August, 146
Bonnots Mill, Missouri, 36
Boone, John William "Blind," 64–65
Boonville, Missouri: Grange in, 49;
    education in, 61; entertainment in, 62,
    63, 72–73, 115, 124, 133; sports in,
    65–66; trials in, 69; churches of, 71;
    German Americans in, 71–72; utilities
    of, 76, 82–83; economy of, 80, 81; and
    Panic of 1893, 94; land offices in, 100;
    and state fair, 119; reform movement in,
    149; patriotism of, 212
Boonville Semi-Weekly Star, 106
Boonville Weekly Advertiser, 11, 62, 65,
    67–68, 69, 81, 208, 209, 210, 212, 232,
    238, 244
Bootheel region, 58, 114, 179, 193, 237
Bothwell, George, 102
Bowers Mills, Missouri, 68
Boyd, Willard W., 163
Brayshaw, Sadie, 62
Brewer's Association, 175
Brewing industry, 43–44, 86, 95, 175, 244
Briggs, A. W., 223
Brokmeyer, Henry, 74
Brookings, Robert S., 88
Brooks, John A., 18
Brown, A. Theodore, 93

Brown, Charley, 38
Brown, Luman A., 14, 23
Brown, R. W., 214
Brown Company, 87
Brown Shoe Company, 87
Brownfield, Missouri, 242
Browning Club, 116, 233
Bruce, Nathaniel C., 112, 238
Brunkhorst's Saw Mill, 38
Bryan, R. H., 229
Bryan, William Jennings, 145, 155,
    164–65, 166, 167, 180, 186, 190, 191
Buell Company, 92
Buffalo Reflex, 18, 22
Bullard, Arthur, 219
Burgess, Gavon B., 168
Burke, Steve, 128
Burkholder, Joseph, 75
Burns, Henrietta, 76
Burrows, Joseph H., 14
Bush, Mrs. B. F., 222–23, 226, 231
Business: Republican party support of,
    18, 184–85; antimonopoly movement,
    87, 149–58, 166, 168; and reform
    movement, 135; regulation of, 137, 138,
    147, 149, 187, 194; and Francis, 138;
    eastern businessmen, 139; franchise tax,
    156–57, 164; and Hadley, 184–85; and
    World War I, 208, 226, 234–35
Butler, Edward, 148, 164, 165, 168–72,
    174–76
Butler, Evaline, 46
Butler, James J., 170
Butler's Indians, 169–70

C. D. Smith Company, 92
Caldwell, Henry F., 13
California, Missouri, 72, 94
Callahan, Thomas, 54
Calumet Banner, 167
Camden Point, Missouri, 114
Camp Funston, Kansas, 240
Campbell, James, 170–71, 173–74
Canada Baker school, 62
Candy factories, 96
Cannon, Joseph, 191
Canton, Missouri, 118
Cape Girardeau, Missouri, 41, 61, 111,
    242; railways, 241–42
Carleton's, 88
Carroll, John, 157
Carthage, Missouri, 38, 86, 93, 94, 115,
    203

Caruthersville, Missouri, 114, 180
Caston, J. J., 70
Catholic Church, 58–59, 70, 127–31
Catlin Company, 87
Cavender, John H., 163
Central College, 114
Central Traction Company, 172
Central Type Foundry Company, 99
Central Wesleyan College, 114
Centralia, Missouri, 119
Centre Creek Mines, 94–95
Chadwick, Missouri, 30
Chain of Rocks Park, 132
Chamois, Missouri, 36, 68, 73
Chamois Liberalist, 36
Charleston, Missouri, 41, 242
Chicago, Burlington & Quincy Railroad, 35, 223
Chicago World's Fair of 1893, 102, 103
Children: employment of, 49–50, 95, 97, 142; and agriculture, 53, 215–16, 221; and World War I bonds, 232
Chillicothe, Missouri, 61, 94, 119, 203
Chopin, Kate, 77, 117
Chouteau, Pierre, 120–21
Christian Church (Disciples of Christ), 114
Churches, 70–71, 127–31, 224. *See also* specific denominations
Churchill, Winston, 127
City Beautiful Movement, 90–91
Civic Improvement League, 122, 132
Civil rights, 2–3, 15, 25, 147
Clarence, Missouri, 118
Clark, James Beauchamp, 190–91, 192
Clearwater, Missouri, 34
Clinton, Missouri, 72
Clum, Edward F., 70
Coal mining, 39–40, 85–86, 98
Cockefair, A. A., 215
Cockrell, Francis M., 6, 14, 17
Coghlan, Philip F., 22
Coleman, James B., 238
Colleges and universities, 58–61, 111, 112, 114. *See also* Education; and specific colleges and universities
Colman, Norman J., 6–7, 32, 33, 48, 120, 177
Colman's Rural World, 6, 32, 34–35
Columbia Exposition of 1890, 120, 121
Columbia, Missouri: education in, 59, 61, 114; entertainment in, 72, 125; and

Democratic party, 149; Butler trial and, 174–75; and World War I, 203, 241
Columbia Herald, 48
Committee on Commercial Economy, 234–35
Committee on Public Information, 219
Compromise of 1877, 25
Connet, S. S., 214
Conrath, Julius H., 67
Conscription, 235–37
Constitution of 1865, 3
Constitution of 1875, 1–4, 10, 26, 27, 59
Convict labor, 23, 50–51, 142, 194, 217
Cooper Institute, 61–62, 115
Cooperative Union of America, 140
Cordz-Fischer Lumber Company, 84
Cosgrove, John, 68
Couzins, Phoebe Wilson, 26, 60
Cowherd, William S., 185–86, 191–92
Coy, William, 35
Crittenden, Thomas T., 14–16, 18, 23, 28
Crow, Edward C., 154, 167–68, 176, 183, 199
Crow, Wayman, 88
Crowder, Enoch, 230, 237
Crunden, Robert M., 165–66, 185, 189, 199
Crystal City, Missouri, 86
Crystal City Glass Company, 98
Cudahy Company, 168
Cueny, Elizabeth, 222
Culture Club, 233
Cupples, Samuel, 88
Curley, John J., 22
Currency issues, 139–40, 142–45, 155, 156

Daily State Journal, 64
Dalton Vocational School, 112
Daughter's College, 114
Daughters of Jericho, 71
Daughters of the Queen of Heaven, 130
Davis, Ephraim, 13
Davis, Samuel C., 88
Dean, Henry Clay, 31
Decker, Perl D., 206, 209, 210
Deems, J. F., 219
Defense policy, 203–5
Democratic party: and Constitutional Convention of 1875, 1; and election of 1874, 6–7; and election of 1876, 9–11; and government's role, 10, 27, 185; Confederate faction of, 11, 17;

and election of 1878, 13; and election
of 1880, 14–15; and election of 1884,
17–18; and election of 1888, 21–22;
and Prohibitionists, 21; dominance of,
24; and blacks, 25, 147–49; political
celebrations of, 68; and Progressivism,
137, 156–57; and Stone, 137, 205; and
People's party, 138, 149; restructuring
of, 138–40; and rural areas, 138, 143,
181; Gold Democrats, 139–40, 146,
147; Silverite Democrats, 139–40, 142,
145–47, 153, 210; and third party
movements, 140–43; and election of
1892, 142–44; and election of 1894,
144; and election of 1896, 145–46;
and election of 1900, 166–67, 170;
and Butler, 169; election fraud, 171;
and Folk, 175–76, 180–81, 190; and
election of 1904, 178; and election of
1906, 180–81; and election of 1908,
185–86; and election of 1912, 192; and
Pendergast, 195; and election of 1916,
197–98; and World War I, 203; and St.
Louis, 205; and labor movements, 206;
and Wilson, 207
Dempsey, John B., 22
Depression of 1890s, 94–95, 139
Desloge Consolidated Lead Company, 85
Dickey, Walter S., 198, 206
Diehl, W. Lloyd, 242
Direct Legislation League, 158–59, 178
Direct primary, 166, 177
Dockery, Alexander M., 166–68, 177, 179,
180
Doe Run Lead Company, 85, 94–95
Doling Park, 133
Doniphan, Missouri, 84
Donover, John W., 13
Dorsett, Lyle W., 93, 195
Douglas Democrats, 10
Drake, Lyman R., 61
Drake Constitution, 1
Driver, John R., 243
Drury College, 111, 114, 126
Dry goods, 88–89, 90, 92
Duke, James B., 87
Dulle, Gerhardt, 36
Dulle Mills, 36
Duncan, Lucy Routt Bradford, 79
Dunklin County Democrat, 115, 217
Dyer, David P., 14–15
Dyer, Leonides C., 202

Eads Bridge, 43
Economy: Panic of 1873, 3, 6, 12, 41;
laissez-faire philosophy regarding,
24–25; and railroads, 28–29, 51–52,
79; and specialization in production, 28,
30–32; and localism, 29, 31; market
expansion, 30–34, 36, 41–44, 49–51,
53; and road development, 30; and
agriculture, 31–32, 47–49, 100–107;
and employment, 35–41, 89, 95–99;
towns' role in, 35, 37, 41–42, 79–84;
manufacturing, 38, 43, 49–50, 86–88,
90, 93, 99; industry, 43, 44, 49–50, 90,
95–96, 134; of St. Louis, 43, 86–89;
of Kansas City, 44–45, 89–91, 93, 95;
and land speculation, 44–45; of black
communities, 45–47; lumber industry,
80, 83–85, 90, 182, 183–85, 192;
and mineral industry, 85–86; retailing,
88–89; wholesaling, 88–89, 90, 92,
93; livestock industry, 89–92, 101–3,
185; of St. Joseph, 91–92, 93; Panic of
1893, 93–95, 144, 152; and depression
of 1890s, 94–95, 139; and farmers,
100–101, 107, 108; taxation and,
107–8; and reform movement, 135; and
Democratic party, 138; economic reform,
142; Panic of 1907, 185; and Major,
194; and World War I, 202–4, 234–35;
and progressivism, 210; and Prohibition,
244
Edens, William, 24
Edina, Missouri, 62, 63, 66, 80, 81–82, 83,
94, 103, 118, 124–25, 204, 213, 233
Edmondson, R. W., 104
Education: legislation regarding, 53,
55–56, 97, 110, 111, 113, 179; and
localism, 53–54; public education,
53–54, 113; of blacks, 55, 57, 59, 112;
and kindergarten movement, 56–57;
high schools, 57–58, 83–84; parochial
schools, 58–59, 113; of women, 60–61;
reform schools, 61; school activities as
entertainment, 61–62, 114–15; school
taxes, 107, 109; quality of, 109–13;
private education, 113–14; and World
War I, 217
Elections: of 1874, 5–7, 8; of 1876, 9–11;
of 1878, 13; of 1880, 13–15, 23; of
1884, 17–18; of 1888, 21–23; of 1870,
25; of 1892, 142–44; of 1894, 144–45;
of 1896, 145–47, 149; of 1900, 166–67,

170; of 1903, 177; of 1904, 177–78, 193; of 1908, 179, 185–86, 192–93; of 1906, 180–81; of 1912, 188–89, 191–93, 206; of 1910, 189–90; of 1916, 193, 197–98, 205–7

Eliot, Charlotte, 117

Ely and Walker, 88

Employment: and economy, 35–41, 89, 95–99; and railroads, 35–37, 39, 41; of children, 49–50, 95, 97, 142; of women, 49–50, 89, 95–97, 111–12, 222–23; and Panic of 1893, 94, 95; of blacks, 96; in urban areas, 142, 143; and conscription, 236. *See also* Labor movements

Enoch, Hunt, 70

Entertainment: school activities as, 61–62, 114–15; debating societies, 62, 114; discrimination in, 63–64; drama, 63, 72–73, 124; music, 63, 65, 72, 116, 124, 132; and railroads, 63, 72; and blacks, 64–65, 125; and holidays, 67–68, 115–16; circuses, 68–69; and political victories, 68; hangings as, 69–70; of ethnic groups, 71–72; in rural areas, 78, 114, 124–25; and parks, 91, 132–33; women's clubs, 116–17; and fairs, 118–23; moving picture shows, 124–25; and alcohol consumption, 130–32. *See also* Sports

Estes, Cornelia, 164

Estes, Frank, 164

Estill, J. R., 34

Estill, Wallace, 102

Evans, William P., 111

Exodusters, 25

Fairs, 49, 118–23

Famous-Barr department store, 89

Faris, Herman P., 146

Farmers: Democratic party support, 6–7; and Hayes administration, 12; railroads' effect on, 12, 30–31; scientific training for, 32; debts of, 33, 108; dissatisfaction of, 52; and economy, 100–101, 107, 108; and agrarian movement, 138; Francis' appeal to, 140–41; and third party movements, 140; and People's party, 141; and International Harvester, 183. *See also* Agriculture

Farmer's Alliance, 49

Farmers' and Laborers' Union of America, 140

Farmer's Club, 215

Farmer's Institutes, 220

Farmers Mill, 38

Farnsworth, Don, 224

Farr, Watson B., 75

Farris, Frank, 159

Farris Bill, 155–56

Fayette, Missouri, 114

Federated Farm Clubs, 218

Ferrel, George T., 72–73

Field, Eugene, 77

Finklenburg, Gustavus, 9–10

Finney, R. M., 67

Fite, Gilbert C., 241

Fitzpatrick, Susan, 93

Fleming, J. B., 234

Folk, Joseph W.: and Progressivism, 159, 161, 164, 177, 181, 185, 199; as governor, 161, 179–85; and St. Louis Transit Strike, 161–64; and Bryan, 164–65, 166, 180, 190; family background of, 164; and corruption, 168–76; in election of 1900, 170; and Democratic party, 175–76, 180–81, 190; in election of 1904, 177–78; and antitrust legislation, 181; in election of 1908, 185–86; in election of 1910, 189; and Major, 192

Food conservation, 223–28, 244

Ford, Nicholas, 13, 14, 17

Forest Park, 120, 132

Forsyth, Missouri, 114

Fountain and Journal, 81

Fourth Liberty Loan drive, 232

Fox, William, 180

Franchise tax, 156–57, 164

Francis, David R., 21, 23–24, 122, 136–38, 139, 140–41, 149–52, 155, 180, 185, 189, 191–92

Fraternal organizations, 71, 231

Freedmen's Aid and Southern Education Society, 113

Friends of German Democracy, 226

Fulton, Missouri, 114, 175

Furniture Workers' Union, 99

Galvin, James M., 172

Gantt, James B., 176–77

Gardner, Frederick D., 197–99, 211–12, 216, 222–23, 235–36, 238, 239–40, 242

Gardner, William K., 235

Gasconade County Advertiser-Courier, 73

Geiger, Louis G., 163, 165, 169, 174, 176–77, 189
Geisberg, Auguste, 76
General Federation of Women's Clubs (GFWC), 116
Gentry, N. H., 102–3
Gentry, North Todd, 123, 174
Gentry, William, 7–8
George, Henry, 22
George R. Smith College, 112–13
Gephart, W. P., 226
German Americans, 7, 8, 76, 96, 127, 131, 147, 196; Turn Vereins, 71–72; newspapers of, 77, 200, 242; and World War I, 200–203, 210, 212, 224, 242; and Wilson, 205–6
German language, 242
German-American Alliance, 200–203
Germany: bonds for, 202; and *Lusitania*, 203, 204; submarine use of, 204, 207, 209, 213; neutrality violations of, 206; diplomatic relations with, 207–8; and Zimmermann note, 209–10; declaration of war against, 210
Gilbert, Emma, 61
Gilbert, Harry, 109
Gilman City Guide, 228
Gingerich, Amos, 243
Glasgow Journal, 9
Gold Democrats, 139–40, 146, 147
Grady, John, 195
Grandin, E. B., 84
Grandin, Missouri, 83–84
Grange, 6, 48–49, 140, 204, 215
Green, Charles, 24
Green, Dick, 46
Greenback party, 11, 13–15, 17, 23, 140
Greene County, Missouri: zinc in, 85; and election of 1892, 142; and election of 1894, 145; and election of 1903, 177; and alcohol consumption, 200; and agricultural extension, 214, 215; and World War I, 217
Guyton and Harrington, 103

Hadley, Herbert W., 180, 182–89, 192, 193, 194, 199
Haggin, John, 46
Hall, Matthew, 179
Hall, Uriel S., 141
Halloway, Peter, 62
Hammond Company, 91, 168

Hannibal, Missouri, 12, 59, 72, 75, 76, 77, 93
Hannibal and St. Joseph Railroad, 15–16
Hardin, Charles Henry, 5–9
Hardin, J. E., 235
Harford, Helen, 131
Hargadine and McKittrick, 88
Harmon, Judson, 190, 191
Harris, John Woods, 48
Harris, Overton, 102
Harris, William Torrey, 56, 74
Harrison, E. F., 236
Harrison, Jack, 104
Harrison, John, 104
Harrison County, Missouri, 65, 107, 110–11, 216, 221, 232, 233, 236–37
Hartville, Missouri, 68
Hartville Democrat, 129
Haseltine, Ira S., 13–14
Hatch Act, 33
Haw, J. M., 180
Hawes, Harry B., 162–63, 169–71, 175, 176–77, 180, 185
Hazard, Rebeca N., 26
Head, J. W., 214
Heim family, 196
Helena, Missouri, 35
Hendricks, Thomas A., 68
Hensley, Walter L., 206, 208–9, 210
Hickman, Henry W., 141
Hill, J. H., 31
Hillis, James, 146
Hilo, Missouri, 230
Hirschland Behdheim, 42
Hirth, William, 215
Hobbs, A. B., 128
Hockaday, John A., 8
Hodges, William R., 74–75
Hoehn, Gottlieb A., 192–93
Hoffman, Clara Cleghorn, 27, 131
Hogs, John Oliver, 75–76
Holland, Thomas, 22
Holliday, Mrs. John H., 231
Holme, John T., 75
Home demonstration agents, 220, 226
Home rule, 25
Homesteading, 100
Hoose, George A., 22
Hoover Food Pledges, 223–26
Hoover, Herbert, 218–20, 224, 230, 237
Houck, Louis, 41–42
House, Edward, 219

Houston, David F., 233
Hubbard, C. M., 17–18
Hughes, A. B., 104
Hughes, Charles Evans, 198, 205–6
Humann, John F., 22
Hurst, Ezra, 13
Hutchison, Horace A., 68

Iberia Academy, 114
Igoe, William L., 210
Independence, Missouri, 45, 94
Independent, 174
Industry, 43, 44, 49–50, 90, 95–96, 134
Initiative and referendum, 136, 158–60, 166, 178–79
Insurance companies, 106, 152–55, 168, 182, 183, 185
International Harvester, 182, 183, 192
Irish Americans, 196, 200, 201, 205–6
Iron County Register, 54, 77
Iron Mountain railroad, 33, 41, 42
Ironton, Missouri, 100

Jackson, Claiborne Fox, 5, 7, 17
James gang, 16
Jauncey, G. E. M., 241
Jefferson City, Missouri: and railroads, 36; education in, 57–59, 62; entertainment in, 63–64, 67, 72; utilities of, 76; economy of, 93; libraries of, 126; World War I support of, 233
Jefferson City People's Tribune, 7, 26
Jefferson City State Times, 38
Jefferson Club, 148, 161–65, 169, 189
Jewish Relief Society, 226
Johnson, Charles P., 16, 174
Johnson, James T., 68
Johnson, Waldo P., 2
Johnston, Albert Sydney, 17
Jones, Orville D., 144, 146
Jones, R. H., 131
Joplin, Scott, 93, 132
Joplin, Missouri, 40–41, 92, 154
Joplin and Girard Railroad, 40
Joplin Daily News, 41
Joplin Railroad Company, 40
Jordan, Samuel Martin, 214, 215
Journal of Speculative Philosophy, 74
Joy, Charles F., 143
Jubilee Singers, 65
Judson, Frederick N., 3

Kahmann, George H., 42

Kansas City, Missouri: economy of, 44–45, 89–91, 93, 95; entertainment in, 72, 117, 124, 125; clay production, 86; employment in, 97; labor movements in, 99; credit in, 106; libraries of, 126; churches of, 128, 129; political machine of, 148, 194–96; and antitrust legislation, 151, 152, 153, 155; and election of 1908, 186; and election of 1912, 192; and World War I, 202–4, 225, 230, 232, 241; strikes of, 243
Kansas City Board of Fire Underwriters, 151, 153
Kansas City Concrete Pipe Company, 197
Kansas City Journal, 208
Kansas City Star, 91, 127, 150, 195, 196
Kansas City Times, 77
Katy Railroad. *See* Missouri, Kansas and Texas Railroad
Kelley, Daniel, 175–76
Kelley, Oliver Hudson, 48
Kelly, Charles, 174, 175
Kelly, Ed, 195
Kempster, Harry, 230
Kennett, Missouri, 67, 80, 81, 94, 105, 106, 114, 118, 124, 125, 128, 212, 232, 236
Kennett Clipper, 67
Kennett Commercial Club, 217
Kessler, George E., 91, 120, 132, 133
Kimball, E. E., 21–22
King, G. Tom, 104
King, W. M., 31
King City, Missouri, 233
Kinley, I. H., 168
Kinney, Nat, 24
Kirksville, Missouri, 61, 111, 118, 212–13
Kirksville Dramatic Association, 63
Kirksville Journal, 9, 11
Kissinger, J. H., 102
Knights of Labor, 19, 39
Knott, W. J., 36
Knox County Democrat, 11, 82, 204–5, 213, 231
Kobush, George J., 173
Kochtitsky, Otto, 105
Krekel, Arnold, 57
Krug Company, 91
Krum, Chester H., 174

La Grange, Missouri, 49
Labelle, Missouri, 118

Labor movements: development of, 98–100; and St. Louis Transit strike, 161–64; and Socialist party, 193; and World War I, 204, 211, 243–44; and Democratic party, 206
Labor Statistics, State Bureau of, 35
Laclede Gas Works, 95, 223
Lail, F. M., 102
Lambert, Albert Bond, 203
Lamine Township, 215
Lamkin, Uel, 211, 217, 224, 242
Lamm, Henry, 198
Land brokers, 44–45
Land offices, 100
Land prices, 104–5
Lange, John, 65
Lansing, Robert, 210
Laundry Owners' Association, 243
Lawrence Chieftain, 30, 52, 70, 203, 212, 214, 216, 217, 222–23
Lawrence County, Missouri, 8, 11, 30, 62, 85, 106, 123, 214–15; and World War I, 217, 218, 229, 232, 237
Lawyers Committee, 234
Lead production, 85, 92, 93
Lee, John Adams, 175–76
Lee, Samuel, 162
Lemmer, George S., 32
Lemp Company, 86
Leonard, Leverett, 142, 143
Leonard, Nathaniel, 101
Leonard, Nelson, 233
Lesueur, Alexander A., 150–51
Lewis, Daniel, 46
Lewis, F. E., 217
Lewis, Maud, 130–31
Lewis, Robert E., 146
Libraries, 77, 126
Liggett and Meyers, 87
Light, William, 69
Lincoln, Missouri, 242
Lincoln Institute, 59–60, 64, 111
Lindsey, Lizzie, 63–64
Linn, Missouri, 59
Linneus, Missouri, 234
Livestock industry, 48, 89–92, 101–3, 185
Long, Robert Alexander, 203
Lonmire, F. E., 217
Loomis and Snively coal mine, 98
Lorillard Company, 87
Louisiana, Missouri, 94, 128, 242
Louisiana Purchase Exposition, 132

Louisville and Nashville Railroad Company, 164
Lowe, Frank M., 22
Lumber industry, 80, 83–85, 90, 182, 183–85, 192
Lusitania, 203, 204, 205

McAdoo, William G., 231
McAuliffe, J., 168
McCall, Mrs. Louis Marion, 122
McCormick, Cyrus, 183
McCormick, Richard, 156
McCoy, Joseph G., 44
McKinley, John C., 189–90, 192
McKnight, Sumner, 75
Macon, Missouri, 118
McVeigh, J. H., 75
McWilliams, C. M., 214
Maffitt, C. C., 171
Magariel, Maurice, 230
Major, Elliot Woolfolk, 183, 191–94, 199
Malta Bend, Missouri, 212
Manning, Ahira, 13, 21
Manufacturing, 38, 43, 49–50, 86–88, 90, 93, 99
Marine Firemen's Protective Union No. 1, 99
Marmaduke, John Sappington, 16–20, 23
Marmaduke, Miles Meredith, 16
Marshall, Thomas, 190
Marshall, Missouri, 47, 114, 119
Marx and Haas Jeans Company, 88
Marxist Workingmen's party, 12–13
Maryville, Missouri, 59, 111, 179
Mason, Missouri, 49
Matzeliger, John Ernst, 238
May Company, 88–89
Mayes, Jewell, 221
Meatpacking industry, 44
Medara, Adolph, 22
Meeker, Jacob E., 202
Mennonite Church, 242–43
Merchants Bridge, 89
Merchant's Exchange, 21, 22
Meriwether, Lee, 40, 97–98
Methodist Church, 70, 127, 131, 213
Methodist Episcopal Church, 70, 71, 113
Metropolitan Street Railway Company, 195
Mexico, Missouri, 104, 119, 154
Mexico Intelligencer, 152
Meyer, A. J., 221
Midwest Paving Company, 197
Milling industry, 44

Mineral industry, 85–86
Miners' Bank, 41
Mining industry, 39–40, 84–86, 92, 94, 98–100
Minor, Virginia L., 25–27
Minor v. Happersett, 26
Missouri Alliance, 140, 141–44, 160
Missouri Bankers' Association, 100
Missouri Baptist Children's Home, 130
Missouri Baptist Hospital, 130
Missouri Bar Association, 100
Missouri Corn Growers' Association, 112
Missouri Council of Defense: mission of, 216; and voluntarism, 218, 244; and publicity, 219–20; Women's Committee of, 222–23, 238, 243; speakers bureaus of, 224, 226–27; and bonds, 231; Committee on Commercial Economy, 234–35; and conscription, 235; and blacks, 238; and Home Guard, 239; and disloyal activities, 240–43; and Americanization Committee, 241–42
Missouri Equal Rights League, 25
Missouri Farmer's Association, 215
Missouri Federation of Labor, 193
Missouri Food Administration, 222, 227
Missouri Home for Aged Baptists, 130
Missouri Horticultural Society, 31
Missouri Idea, 135, 160, 161, 176, 177
Missouri, Kansas and Texas Railroad, 29, 37, 38, 63, 75
Missouri Lumber and Mining Company, 84
Missouri Medical Association, 100
Missouri Meerschaum Company, 42
Missouri Negro Industrial Commission, 238
Missouri Pacific Railroad, 18–19, 37, 63, 157
Missouri Press Association, 73
Missouri Public Service Commission, 193
Missouri Republican, 41
Missouri Ruralist, 112, 127
Missouri School for the Blind, 64
Missouri School of Mines and Metallurgy, 60
Missouri State Fair, 119–20
Missouri State Penitentiary, 188
Missouri State Teacher's Association (MSTA), 55
Missouri Supreme Court, 151, 154, 155, 168, 173, 175, 182–84
Missouri Valley College, 114

Missouri Woman Suffrage Association, 25
Mitchell, Pearl, 123
Moberly, Missouri, 75, 119
Moffet, Eli R., 40
Moll Company, 88
Monsees, Louis M., 103
Montgomery City, Missouri, 49
Moore, J. W. E., 164
Morehouse, Albert P., 20–21, 22
Morgan County Leader, 106
Morrill Act of 1862, 32
Morris Company, 168
Morris, L. D., 104
Morrissey, Peter, 130–31
Morton, John, 159
Moser, Silas L., 158–59
Mount Vernon, Missouri, 30, 62, 68, 69, 80, 81, 94, 99
Mt. Zion, Missouri, 242–43
Mulburn Gin Company, 107
Mumford, Frederick B., 216, 218–22, 224, 227–30
Murphy, Charles F., 191

Nashville, Chattanooga, and St. Louis Railroad, 63
Nation, Carrie, 131
National Agricultural Wheel, 140
National Association of Colored Women, 60, 117
National Biscuit Company, 92
National Farmers' Alliance, 140
National Guard, 205, 235, 239
National Protective Association, 241
National Rip-Saw, 192
National Security League, 203, 205, 241
National Wheat Saver's League, 227
National Woman's Committee, 222
Navy League, 203
Nelson, William Rockhill, 91, 196
Nelson-Morris Company, 91
Neosho, Missouri, 230
Neutrality League, 201, 203, 204
New Madrid, Missouri, 114
New Nationalism, 185
Newspapers: coverage of, 76–78, 130, 154, 157; German American, 77, 200, 242; and economy, 80; and journalism school, 127; of People's party, 144; and World War I, 203, 227–28, 231, 241, 244. *See also* specific newspapers
Nicolaus, Henry, 175
Nitchy, F. A., 57–58

Nodaway Democrat, 20
Nolan, William J., 22
Norris, George, 210
Nortorni, Albert D., 192
Norvell-Shapleigh Hardware Company, 88
Novinger, Missouri, 230

Oburn, Emmett A., 243–44
O'Hanlon, John Canon, 63
O'Hare, Frank P., 192
O'Hare, Kate, 192
Olive Branch, 117
Orchard, James, 159
Orr, Sam, 69
Osterman, Alfred P., 146
Otten, Joseph, 72
Otterville, Missouri, 49
Owens, Joseph, 62
Ozark, Missouri, 30
Ozark Land and Lumber Company, 84

Pacific, Missouri, 19, 86
Pacific Railroad, 35–36, 37
Page, Inman E., 59–60
Palmer, John M., 146
Panic of 1873, 3, 6, 12, 41
Panic of 1893, 93–95, 144, 152
Panic of 1907, 185
Paris, Missouri, 49
Park College, 114
Parkville, Missouri, 114
Patrons of Husbandry, 48
Peabody and Stearns, 74, 75
Penal reform, 194, 198–99
Pendergast, James, 148, 176, 189, 194–96
Pendergast, Tom, 195–97
Penny, Joseph, 45–46
Penny, W. D., 67
Pennytown, Missouri, 45–47
People's party, 6, 7, 138, 141–46, 149
People's Record, 166
Pershing, John J., 239
Peterson, H. C., 241
Phelps, John S., 9–11, 13, 16, 50–51
Philips, John F., 14
Phillips, H. N., 67
Phoenix Mutual Life Insurance Company, 106
Piedmont, Missouri, 33–34
Pierce, S. C., 40
Pierce City, Missouri, 71
Pike County Post, 7
Pilot Grove, Missouri, 29

Pineville, Missouri, 154
Pinkerton Detective Agency, 142
Plankington and Armour Company, 44
Playground Association of America, 132
Pohlman, John H., 163
Point Lookout, Missouri, 114
Pomeroy, W. C., 69
Poplar Bluff, Missouri, 212
Populism, 135–36, 144, 145, 149, 158, 160, 166–67. *See also* People's party
Porth, Joseph P., 37
Potts, Clark, 104
Potts, J. A., 104
Powersite Dam, 133
Presbyterian Church, 70, 114, 129
Priesmeyer, August, 51
Progressivism: and Populism, 135, 166–67; and Democratic party, 137, 156–57; and reform movement, 149, 160; and antitrust legislation, 154, 168; and Folk, 159, 161, 164, 177, 181, 185, 199; definitions of, 165–66; and Republican party, 178; and Hadley, 182–88; and Clark, 191; and Major, 192–93; and economic determinism, 210; in Lawrence County, 215
Prohibitionists and prohibitionism, 17–18, 21–23, 131, 142, 146, 178, 190, 196, 200–201, 244
Provident Association, 202
Public Ownership party, 178

Rader, L. W., 110
Radical Republicans, 2, 20, 25, 147
Railey, Edward, 46
Railroads: bonds for, 4, 16, 41, 51–52, 108; regulation of, 8–9, 15, 19–20, 27, 179; and farmers, 12, 30–31; strikes of, 12–13; and Marmaduke, 18–20; rates of, 18, 20, 32; changes brought on by, 28–29; and economy, 28–29, 51–52, 79; and railroad towns, 29–30, 35; and urbanism, 29, 35; and agriculture, 30–32, 47–49; and roads, 30; and employment, 35–37, 39, 41; and manufacturing, 38; in St. Louis, 38, 89; and coal mining, 39–40; and market expansion, 42, 49, 51, 53; and Anheuser-Busch brewery, 43–44; and blacks, 45–47; and entertainment, 63, 72; as transportation means, 73, 78; and architecture, 75; railroad ties, 98; and labor movements, 99; and mules, 103;

and state fair, 119; segregation on, 179; and Hadley, 182, 184; and World War I, 209
Railway Federationist, 208
Raine, C. O., 221
Ready-Mix Concrete Company, 197
Rebstock Company, 87
Red Cross, 226, 229, 230, 233–34, 243, 244
Reed, James A., 148, 176–77, 189, 190, 191, 193, 195, 198, 205–6, 297, 211, 236
Reedy's Mirror, 127, 169
Reform movement: and Populism, 135–36, 160; and People's party, 142; and Democratic party, 144, 149; and antitrust legislation, 150–58; and women, 159
Reid, Loren, 228–29
Reno, Missouri, 30
Republican party: and Constitutional Convention of 1875, 1; and state debt, 3; in election of 1874, 7, 8; in election of 1876, 9, 11; in election of 1878, 13; in election of 1880, 14–15; in election of 1884, 17–18; and business, 18, 184–85; in election of 1888, 21–22; frustrations of, 23; and blacks, 25, 147–48; and Sherman Silver Purchase Act (1890), 139; strength of, 140; in election of 1892, 143–44; in election of 1894, 144–45; in election of 1896, 145, 146; and franchise tax, 157; in election of 1900, 170; election fraud, 171; in election of 1904, 178; and Progressivism, 178; in election of 1906, 181; in election of 1908, 186; in election of 1910, 189–90; in election of 1912, 189, 192; in election of 1916, 198, 205–6; and World War I trade disruption, 202
Rice, Theron M., 14
Rice-Stix, 88
Rich Fountain, Missouri, 58
Richardson, A. B., 180
Richardson, Henry Hobson, 74
Richmond, Missouri, 72
Ridgeway, Missouri, 67
Riley, C. V., 9
Riper, J. C., 120
Ritchey, Matthew H., 13
Roach, Cornelius, 193
Roads, 30, 32, 123, 187, 194

Robertson, Moss A., 104
Robinson, Sue, 38
Rochester Township, 35
Rock Island Railroad, 167
Roe, Samuel, 29
Rogers, Henry H., 183
Roleke, William, 213
Rolla Weekly Herald, 69
Rollins, James S., 32
Roosevelt, Theodore, 122, 176, 178, 185, 189, 192, 204, 205
Rosenwater, Ione, 236
Ross, W. A., 197
Rotterman, Francis S., 22
Rowe, Thomas J., 174
Royal Baking Company, 175–76
Runcie, Constance Fauntleroy, 116
Runcie Club, 116
Rural areas: railroads' effect on, 29; education in, 55, 109; entertainment in, 78, 114, 124–25; population trends in, 79, 200; small towns as economic link, 79; banking in, 105–6; churches of, 128; and family, 134; and Democratic party, 138, 143, 181; and Gold Democrats, 139; and Sherman Silver Purchase Act (1890), 139; and third party movements, 142; and Panic of 1893, 144; initiative and referendum vote, 179; and Major, 192; and Progressivism, 192; and Wilson, 206
Rural Free Delivery (RFD), 134
Russell, John Caro, 100
Russell, Theodore Pease, 77

S. and J. Friedman, 88
St. Charles, Missouri, 94, 118
St. Joseph, Missouri: strikes of, 12; economy of, 91–92, 93; employment in, 97; credit in, 106; entertainment in, 116; churches of, 128, 129; and World War I support, 203, 225, 229, 230, 241; women's employment in, 223
St. Joseph Herald, 17
St. Joseph Lead Company, 85
St. Louis, Missouri: strikes of, 12–13, 161–64; and election of 1888, 22; and railroads, 38, 89; economy of, 43, 86–89; manufacturing in, 43, 86–88; education in, 56–57, 59, 114; sports in, 66–67, 117–18; entertainment in, 72, 117, 124, 125, 132; philosophical movement in, 73–74; architecture of,

74–75; clay production, 86; and Panic of 1893, 95; employment in, 96, 97; labor movements in, 98–99; fairs of, 118–23; churches of, 128, 129; political machine of, 148, 164–65, 168–76; and reform movement, 149, 159; and antitrust legislation, 151, 153, 155; and initiative and referendum, 158; and segregation, 179; and election of 1908, 186; and election of 1912, 192; and Socialist party, 192; German-American Alliance in, 200; credit for Great Britain and France, 202; and World War I, 202–4, 211, 225, 231–32, 235, 241; and Democratic party, 205; women's employment in, 223; brewing industry of, 244

St. Louis and Suburban Railway Company, 171–72

St. Louis Central Trades and Labor Union, 193, 243

St. Louis Choral Society, 72

St. Louis Equal Suffrage League, 231

St. Louis Globe-Democrat, 56, 113, 201

St. Louis Labor, 193

St. Louis Philosophical Society, 74

St. Louis Post-Dispatch, 12, 113, 153, 157, 171, 173, 174, 175, 190, 201, 203

St. Louis Republican, 66, 106, 201, 203

St. Louis Sanitary Company, 174

St. Louis Star, 172, 201

St. Louis Street Car Company, 173

St. Louis Symphony Orchestra, 72

St. Louis Transit Strike, 161–64

St. Louis Woman's Committee, 231

St. Louis World's Fair of 1904, 120–23, 170

St. Louis-San Francisco Railroad, 30, 40, 93

Salt Fork Township, 46

Sanborn, Jeremiah W., 32

Sarcoxie, Missouri, 229

Sauer, Carol O., 124

Saunders, William, 224–25

Scheele, Charles, 87

Schmutz, C. W., 221

School of the Ozarks, 114

School Sisters of Notre Dame, 58–59

Schurz, Carl, 6

Schuttler, C. C., 214

Schwarzschild Company, 168

Scullin, John, 171

Sedalia, Missouri: strikes of, 12; and railroads, 37–38; economy of, 93–94; and Missouri State Fair, 119–20; library of, 126; entertainment in, 131–32; county agents in, 214; and World War I support, 230

Sedalia Weekly Bazoo, 38, 94

Sedalia Weekly Democrat, 1, 9, 26

Sergeant, John B., 40

Shackleford, Dorsey W., 206, 210

Shannon, Joseph, 189, 196

Shannon, R. D., 54

Shaw, Henry, 75, 132

Shedd, H. W., 76

Shelby, Joseph O., 17

Shelton, Lee, 236

Shelton, W. F., 236

Sheridan-Clayton Paper Company, 92, 209

Sherman Silver Purchase Act (1890), 139

Shoe industry, 49, 51, 87, 96

Shultz, Charles S., 235

Siddons, Mrs. Scott, 63–64

Silone, Josephine A., 60

Silver issue, 142–45, 155, 156

Silverite Democrats, 139–40, 142, 145–47, 153, 210

Simmons Hardware Company, 151

Simpson, J. L., 104

Sisterhood organizations, 71

Smith, C. C., 60

Smith, George, 37

Smith, Henry M., 60

Smith, O. F., 143–44

Smith-Lever Act, 214

Snowden, Henry, 35

Snyder, Robert M., 172–73

Sobieski, John, 142

Social Democratic party, 193

Social Gospel Movement, 129

Socialist party, 113, 178, 192–93, 204, 206, 210

Solomon, E. W., 221

Sons of Honor, 4

Sotham, T. F. B., 102

Southern Tenant Farmers Union, 147

Spanish-American War, 103

Special privilege, 166, 177

Sports, 65–67, 73, 117–20, 126

Springfield, Missouri, 30, 92–93, 100, 111, 114, 133, 179, 180, 223, 230

Springfield Trades and Labor Assembly, 193

Standard Oil of New Jersey, 182–83, 192

Stanford, T. D., 225

State Federation of Labor, 159, 178, 192

State government: and localism, 2, 27; deficit of, 3, 156; limitations on, 3, 4, 8–9, 10, 15, 21; and taxation, 4; role of, 15, 24–25, 27, 187–88, 199; and railroads, 20; and Francis, 137–38; and antitrust legislation, 151; and Progressivism, 181; Major and, 194
State Normal School, 217
State Normal Summer School, 110
State Times, 19, 21
Steffens, Lincoln, 174
Stemmel, Wilhelm, 241
Stephens, Lawrence "Lon" V., 119, 138, 146–47, 153, 154–56, 168, 179, 189
Stix, Mrs. Ernest, 231
Stock, Philip, 171–72
Stone, DeWitt, 51–52
Stone, William J., 137, 138, 142, 145, 150, 152, 153–54, 163, 180, 181, 185–86, 190, 202, 205–6, 207–8, 210–11, 233
Stracke and Caesar Company, 87
Styles, A. F., 104
Suburban Street Railway Company, 161–62, 170, 175
Sullivan, Mark, 185
Sulzberger Company, 168
Swain, Frederick, 22
Swift, 90, 91, 168

Taft, William Howard, 186, 188–89, 192
Taneycomo, Lake, 133
Tarkio, Missouri, 114
Tarkio College, 114
Taxation: and Constitution of 1875, 3–4; and Democratic party, 10; in St. Clair County, 12; and Crittenden, 15; for roads, 32; in St. Louis, 89; in counties, 107–8; school taxes, 107, 109; and Francis, 137–38; franchise tax, 156–57, 164; and Hadley, 188; and Major, 194; and Gardner, 198; and World War I, 230
Tays, Butler, 109
Teacher organizations, 99–100
Teacher training, 59, 61, 109–14, 179
Teasdale, Sarah, 127
Tebo and Neosho Railroad, 51
Temperance movement, 27, 131, 156. *See also* Prohibitionists and prohibitionism
Tent meetings, 70–71, 128
Texas and Pacific railroad, 19
Third Liberty Loan drive, 232
Third party movements, 6, 11–12, 23, 140–45

Thomas, A. L., 68
Tibbe, Henry, 42
Tillman, Ben, 121
Tobacco industry, 49, 87, 96
Todd, Albert, 26–27
Todhunter, Ryland, 104
Tower Grove Park, 132
Towne, K. W., 102
Towne, Ruth Warner, 208, 210
Trade, and World War I, 202–3, 208
Travel: by river, 32, 73; by railroad, 73, 78; by automobile, 124
Trenton Republican, 9–10, 14, 18
Trimble, J. McDonald, 146
Trusts, 149–58, 168, 181, 183
Turk, T. B., 62
Turley, John H., 215
Turnbo, Silas, 77
Turner, Charles H., 170–72, 175
Turner, James Milton, 25, 148
Twain, Mark, 77, 127

Underwood, Oscar W., 191
Union Labor party, 21–23
Unions. *See* Labor movements; and names of specific unions
Unitarian Church of the Messiah, 75
United Shipping Board, 202
United States Food Administration, 218, 220, 221, 224
United States Supreme Court, 16, 182, 184, 192
University of Missouri: College of Agriculture, 32, 213–14, 217, 220, 222; women's admittance to, 60; teacher training, 111; School of Journalism, 126–27
Uthoff, Frederick, 172–73
Utilities, 76, 82–83, 136, 193

Van Natta-Lynds, 91
Van Zandt, James R., 23–24
Vandeventer Place, 75
Vardeman, James, 209
Veblen, Thorstein, 123
Veiled Prophet parades, 13
Vest, George Graham, 11, 14, 17, 121, 139
Victor Mining Company, 94
Vincent, Paul, 213
Voluntarism, 218–22, 224, 230–31, 234–36, 239, 244
Voting rights, 25–27, 62, 142, 244

Wabash Railroad, 75
Walbridge, Cyrus P., 178
Walden, C. J., 209
Walker, Jackson, 236
Walker, John, 34
Walker, Missouri, 215
Waller, Alexander, 174
Walsh, Julius, 171
Warner, William, 142, 178, 190
Warrensburg, Missouri, 61, 64–65, 94, 111
Warrensburg Star-Journal, 209
Warrenton, Missouri, 114, 229
Washington University, 114, 121, 126
Weaver, James B., 142
Webster, H. C., 35
Wednesday Club, 117, 159
Wells, Rolla, 122, 170, 174–75, 180
Welsbach Company, 173–74
Wenger, Abraham, 242–43
West, John Isaac, 69–70
West, Thomas, 171
West Fork Baptist Association, 14
Westlich Post, 208
Wetmore, Claude, 174
Wetmore, Mose, 167
Whaley, John, 159
Whitaker, Edwards, 162, 171
White, J. B., 84
White City Park, 133
Whiting, Florence E., 60
Wholesaling, 88–89, 90, 92, 93
Wilder, Laura Ingalls, 127
Willard, Frances, 27
William Barr Company, 88
William Woods College, 114
Williams, O. H. P., 84
Williams, Walter, 122, 127
Williams, William M., 168
Williams, William W., 174
Wilson, William, 91
Wilson, Woodrow, 191–92, 198, 200, 202, 204, 205–8, 209, 210, 211, 217, 219, 237
Windsor, Horace, 214
Winner Investment Company, 45
Winona, Missouri, 84
Wittenmeyer, Annie, 27
Wolfe, Lloyd E., 141
Wolfe, M. L., 39
Women: voting rights for, 25–27, 62, 142, 244; and coal mining, 39; in black community, 46–47, 117, 238; employment of, 49–50, 89, 95–97, 111–12, 222–23; role of, 53, 244; education of, 60–61; reform schools for, 61; strikes by, 99, 223; as teachers, 111–12; clubs of, 116–17; of Catholic Church, 130; and divorces, 134; and People's party, 142; and reform movement, 159; and agricultural clubs, 216; as home demonstration agents, 220, 226; and Missouri Council of Defense, 222–23, 226–27, 243; food pledges of, 223–24; World War I support of, 233, 238; patriotism of, 236; and labor movements, 243
Women's Christian Temperance Union, 27, 131
Women's League, 117
Women's Suffrage Association, 26
Wood, John M., 151
Wood, Leonard, 240
Woods, Ben, 180
Woods, William Stone, 114
Woodworth, John C., 75
World War I: and German Americans, 200–203, 210, 212, 224, 242; neutrality in, 200–204, 206, 210; and agriculture, 202, 213–22, 229, 244; and economy, 202–4, 234–35; and trade, 202, 208; and newspapers, 203, 227–28, 231, 241, 244; prepared measures for, 204–5; and Zimmermann note, 209–10; declaration of war, 210–12; patriotism during, 211–13, 219–20, 224, 226–27, 230–31, 236; and education, 217; and voluntarism, 218–22, 224, 230–31, 234–36, 239, 244; and food conservation, 223–28, 244; bonds for, 230–33, 244; and conscription, 235–37; and blacks, 236, 237–39; and disloyal activities, 240–43
Wornall, T. J., 102
Wortz, C. H., 217
Wright, Harold Bell, 127
Wright County Progress, 111

Yates, Josephine Silone, 117
Yates, W. W., 60
Young, Jane, 109

Ziegenhein, Henry, 170, 173
Zimmermann note, 209–10
Zinc, 85, 93